AN IMPERIAL STATE AT WAR

AN IMPERIAL STATE AT WAR

Britain from 1689 to 1815

Edited by

Lawrence Stone

London and New York

First published 1994
by Routledge
11 New Fetter Lane, London EC4P 4EE

Simultaneously published in the USA and Canada
by Routledge
29 West 35th Street, New York, NY 10001

Editorial selection and material © 1994 Lawrence Stone
Individual chapters © 1994 the contributors

Phototypeset in Garamond by Intype, London

Printed and bound in Great Britain by
T.J. Press (Padstow) Ltd, Padstow, Cornwall

British Library Cataloguing in Publication Data
A catalogue record for this book is available from the British Library

Library of Congress Cataloging in Publication Data
applied for

ISBN 0–415–06142–3

Contents

CONTENTS

To
Shelby Cullom Davis

Notes on contributors

C. A. Bayly is Vere Harmsworth Professor of Imperial and Naval History at the University of Cambridge. He is the author of *Rulers, Townsmen and Beggars: North India in the Age of British Expansion 1770–1870* (1983).

Daniel A. Baugh is Professor of Modern British History at Cornell University. His principal works are *British Naval Administration in the Age of Walpole* (1965), and *Naval Administration, 1715–1750* (1977). He has written on government and society in England, 1660–1830, especially on relief of the poor. During the last decade his writings have focused mainly on maritime and geopolitical topics.

John Brewer is Professor of History at UCLA. Between 1987 and 1991 he was Director of the Clark Library and the Center for Seventeenth and Eighteenth-Century Studies and principal investigator on the research project 'Culture and Consumption in the Seventeenth and Eighteenth Centuries'. He is the author of *The Sinews of Power* (1989) and the editor, with Roy Porter, of *Consumption and the World of Goods* (1993).

Nicholas Canny is Professor of Modern History at University College, Galway, within the National University of Ireland. His publications include *The Elizabethan Conquest of Ireland* (1976) and *Kingdom and Colony: Ireland in the Atlantic World, 1560–1800* (1988). He is currently engaged upon editing a collection of essays on *European Overseas Migration 1500–1800* and is completing a book entitled *Ireland in the English Colonial System*, both to be published by Oxford University Press.

Linda Colley is Professor of History at Yale University and Director of the Lewis Walpole Library. As well as many articles, she has published *In Defiance of Oligarchy: The Tory Party 1714–1760* (1982), *Namier* (1988), and *Britons: Forging the Nation 1707–1837* (1993).

Thomas Ertman is an Assistant Professor in the Department of Government at Harvard University, where he teaches courses on the historical development of state institutions and on contemporary European studies. He is currently completing a book on war and state-building in medieval and early-modern Europe.

Joanna Innes is Fellow and Tutor in Modern History at Somerville College, Oxford, and editor of the journal *Past and Present*. She has published articles in various historical journals, and is working on a study of social problems and social policies in eighteenth-century Britain, to be published under the title *Inferior Politics*.

Ned C. Landsman is Associate Professor of History at the State University of New York at Stony Brook. He is the author of *Scotland and Its First American Colony, 1680–1765* (1985) and numerous articles on British provincial cultures in the eighteenth century.

John Robertson teaches Modern History at St Hugh's College, Oxford. He is author of *The Scottish Enlightenment and the Militia Issue* (1985), and has recently edited *A Union for Empire: The Union of 1707* in the *History of British Political Thought* (forthcoming), a collection of essays originating in a seminar at the Folger Institute for the History of British Political Thought, Washington.

Lawrence Stone is Professor Emeritus at Princeton University. His books include: *The Crisis of the Aristocracy* (1965); *The Causes of the English Revolution, 1529–1642* (1972; second edn, 1986); *Family, Sex and Marriage in England 1500–1800* (1977); *The Past and the Present Revisited* (1987); *Road to Divorce, England 1530–1987* (1989); *Uncertain Unions: Marriage in England 1660–1753* (1992); and *Broken Lives: Marital Separation and Divorce in England, 1660–1857* (1993).

Kathleen Wilson is the Modern British Historian at the State University of New York, Stony Brook. She has published widely on popular ideologies and domestic imperialism, and her book *The Sense of the People: Urban Political Culture in Urban England, 1715–1785* is forthcoming with Cambridge University Press in 1993. Wilson is currently at work on a study of provincial theatre, gender and power in Hanoverian England.

E. A. Wrigley is a Senior Research Fellow at All Souls College, Oxford, and was previously Professor of Population Studies at the London School of Economics. His publications include *Industrial Growth and Population Change: Population and History* (with Roger Schofield); *The Population History of England, 1541–1871* (1981); *People, Cities and Wealth* (1987); and *Continuity, Chance and Change* (1988).

1

Introduction

Lawrence Stone

One may well ask why it is only in the 1980s and early 1990s that the emergence of the modern state out of the crucible of prolonged European warfare on an unprecedented scale has become once more a growing focus of historical attention. If one looks back at the trends in historiography over the past thirty years, it is clear that the rush to social history was a mixed blessing. It certainly produced works of outstanding quality and opened up many new fields of enquiry into the past. Unfortunately, however, as Brewer points out, this asking of new questions was accompanied by a neglect – indeed, in some cases a positive denigration – of critically important older areas of historical enquiry. The most important of these was the evolution of the state as a quasi-independent agent, especially in its capacity to levy taxes and make wars.

This period of neglect is now over. Brewer has noted that the collapse of Marxism as a viable political and economic system has inevitably discredited it as an explanatory model for understanding history, thus opening the way to a new look at the state. Nor was Foucault much help in reorientating history towards the state. Although he was obsessed with power relations in history, he confined his attention to secondary institutions like the family, hospitals or prisons, or to ethical concepts, such as those governing sexual behaviour. The waning of his influence upon history has also facilitated a revival of interest in the state as a semi-independent historical variable. As a result, political scientists, historical sociologists and historians are all now more interested in the state, its definition, its composition, its method of working and its political and military power. It was in response to these rediscovered preoccupations that in November 1990 the Shelby Cullom Davis Center for Historical Studies at Princeton sponsored a colloquium on The Eighteenth-Century British State and Empire. This subject was chosen because John Brewer's recent book on *The Sinews of Power*, and the rather earlier articles of Peter Mathias and Patrick O'Brien on public finance, had drawn attention to the neglect of the formidable fiscal and military-power aspects of a state that had hitherto been regarded as weak, undertaxed, understaffed, underfunded and

1

relatively liberal. The result of their work has been to remind historians that after 1689 the British state made a dramatic return to the European stage as a major player in the game of power politics – after 250 years of virtual absence, ever since the battle of Agincourt. Admittedly, its military record continued to be patchy, with its greatest successes occurring at the beginning of the period, at Blenheim in 1705, and at the end, at Waterloo in 1815. Its naval achievements, however, which culminated at Trafalgar in 1805, were unsurpassed, and defeats at sea were few.

When one considers this phenomenon, various questions immediately arise. How was all this achieved? At what cost in money and men? Who paid for it, and how was the money extracted? Who fought, either voluntarily or because they were forced to do so? We have been reminded by Operation Desert Storm in the Persian Gulf that war is above all a matter of logistics – how to feed, equip and supply an overwhelming force on the field of battle. How did an early modern bureaucracy manage such tasks? What objectives did the leadership have in mind? What policies were adopted to gain world supremacy, first in a long and inconclusive struggle for control of the seas with the Dutch, running from about 1650 to 1680, and then in the far longer and larger second Hundred Years War with the French, running from 1689 to 1815? How much did it attract popular support? How far did it meet with resistance and scepticism at home? What were the objectives of this expansion of British power, and how did its victims, the natives, respond? What effect did almost endless war have on the society, the social structure and social values? Did it hurt or hinder the growth of the capital market, the domestic economy and overseas trade? What happened to unemployment and poor relief when so many adult male breadwinners were suddenly swept away to go and fight, or were suddenly demobilized? And, last, how did the experience of prolonged war alter ideas about matters like crime, nationalism and xenophobia? Or about mercantilism or the ethics of genocide? Was British nationalism fuelled by fear of France or hatred of popery, or were the two indistinguishable?

HISTORIOGRAPHY

Seventy years ago the history of eighteenth-century Britain seemed fairly simple. The Whig model as propounded by Macaulay and Trevelyan predominated, and all the emphasis was on the decentralized, amateurish character of the state, whose functionaries were, and acted like, gentlemen rather than professional civil servants. The main characteristics of the post-Glorious Revolution state were a parliamentary monarchy; personal liberty protected by the Bill of Rights and the common law; limited religious toleration of all Protestants; and, above all, a devotion to the protection of private property. The theorists behind this system were Locke, who spelt out the contract theory of the state, the prime purpose of which was the protection of property, and who was a persuasive advocate of religious toleration; Harrington, who saw political power as a natural product of property ownership; and Montesquieu, who believed that the English state was characterized above all by a separation of powers.

In the 1930s Sir Lewis Namier revealed that the elite who ran the state in the mid-eighteenth century were lacking any motives other than the self-interest of themselves, their relatives and their clients.[1] The political structure was exposed as riddled with corruption, nepotism and factional feuding. Clashes over ideological issues about the rights of property or the role of religion or the limits of political participation were alleged to be subordinated to these intrigues of faction, while no one really counted except that tiny minority of adult elite males who made up the political nation.

By the 1960s E. P. Thompson was busy turning this elitist picture upside-down. He felt only contempt for the great Whig families, whom he denounced as robbers and banditti; and he described the society in bipolar terms as deeply fissured between 'patricians' and 'plebeians'.[2] In retrospect it is clear that this brilliant opening-up of the social complexities of the eighteenth century revolutionized our understanding. More recently, however, it has also become clear that Thompson's bipolar model was more or less right over power relationships, but wrong over the social structure. He seriously underestimated the role of the state as a semi-autonomous entity and contrived largely to ignore the growing role in both society and politics of the 'middling sort'.

Just as this reassessment of the social structure was going on, in the 1960s, J. H. Plumb brought the state back to centre stage, and reorientated historical focus on a new problem, the causes of the shift from physical violence, political instability and rage of party which characterized English politics in the seventeenth century, to the stability and relative calm which predominated from the 1720s through to the 1780s or later.[3] He also pointed to an astonishing expansion of the electorate in the late seventeenth century, as Whigs and Tories fought fierce battles at the hustings; and an equally remarkable shrinkage once the 'rage of party' was stilled after 1720. Plumb failed, however, to offer a bridge to link his world to that of E. P. Thompson. It was left to John Brewer to point out that in the 1760s a large and vocal extra-parliamentary following among the 'middling sort' had been built up by John Wilkes, which for a while offered a serious challenge to the aristocratic political establishment.[4] The wide political involvement of the middling sort and even the poor in eighteenth-century national politics has been further demonstrated by Kathleen Wilson, while Linda Colley and others have revealed the survival within the English political system of the Tory party. Occasionally, it was even able, in alliance with rebellious 'country whigs', to defeat important government bills, the most striking example being the rejection by Parliament in 1733 of Walpole's Excise Bill.

More recently still, Peter Borsay and others have demonstrated the remarkable cultural vitality of provincial cities in the eighteenth century, whose amenities catered not only to local gentry, but also to the middling sort.[5] As a result of this reassessment of the political and social scene, the middling sort have come into their own historiographically, thereby creating a united propertied class, distinct from the plebeians. This is shown by the fact that the volume by Paul Langford in the *Oxford History of England* for this period is entitled *A Polite and Commercial People*. The balance of historical interest has thus shifted first to Macaulay's and Namier's Whig aristocracy and their clients; then to E. P. Thompson's disaffected plebeians; and now to John Brewer, Peter Borsay and Paul Langford's middling sort. The upshot of this debate seems to be that although the political and social structures were still dominated by the aristocracy, as Namier claimed, and John Cannon and others, such as myself, still claim, both the amorphous but growing middling sort and even the voiceless proletariat at times held sharply different political, religious and economic views which could occasionally influence the delicate structure of aristocratic politics. The concept of a rising tide of luxury, expressed by a passion for consumerism, has dominated recent historical writings about eighteenth-century English society and culture. In this respect the middling sort were not only makers and consumers of growing economic affluence; they also became important consumers of cultural artefacts, such as novels, assembly rooms and the theatre.

In the last few years, there have been two new shifts of historiographical focus. Both divert attention away from the old debate about the relationship of power and property inside eighteenth-century England and towards crucial political and military developments taking place elsewhere. The first is the evolution of the concept of the nation from England and Wales to Great Britain. Too little attention has been paid to the fact that Britain in the eighteenth century was little more than a somewhat precarious and recently formed federal political unit. A viable state is not necessarily coincidental with a nation, the latter being defined by a sense of community in a common culture and patriotic feeling shared by both rulers and ruled. A nation is thus the product of a state of mind, not merely of rule by a unitary state. It has been described, cynically but accurately, by Eric Hobsbawm as 'a people who share a common misconception as to their origins, and a common antipathy towards their neighbours'. This definition holds true for both England and Scotland in the eighteenth century, but Great Britain would fail to pass the test. The union of 1707 was indeed a marriage, but one merely of convenience. Wales had long been absorbed by England, and presented no special problems; but Scotland was a different matter, and it took the crisis of war on the English side and the desire to gain access to the English market on the Scottish side to drive them into reluctant union in 1707. Even so, the union still left Scotland with its own church and its own legal system, and for a long while did little to reduce mutual suspicions or create a sense of common national identity. Moreover, two serious Jacobite rebellions were launched from northern Scotland in 1715 and 1745, before the Highlands were brutally pacified once and for all by military force. As for Ireland, it continued to be a militarily occupied colony full of English troops and run by a minority of Protestant English landlords ruling over a Catholic Irish peasantry. Only rapidly growing prosperity softened the edges of this situation; but it was not enough to stop a large-scale rebellion in 1798. The savage repression which followed paved the way for a gerrymandered union in 1800, which by itself did nothing to help untangle the religious and social problems of that unhappy country, much less to create a sense of national unity with England.[6]

The second recent historiographical innovation has been to draw attention to how and why this ramshackle federal state, if not nation, plunged into continental warfare in 1689, and after 126 years managed to create a world-wide overseas commercial, and in the end territorial, empire.[7] This great military and naval effort created a paradoxical situation. On the one hand, the revolution of 1688 and its aftermath in the 1690s consolidated a uniquely decentralized political system in which local government, law enforcement, tax collecting, supervision of the militia, drafts into the armed forces and so on were largely left to the discretion and loyalty of amateur local landed gentlemen and clergy, acting in their capacities as Justices of the Peace, Collectors of Taxes, Colonels of the local Militia, and so on. This political elite was deeply suspicious of a standing army, fiscally conservative, dedicated to personal liberty (for themselves) and at the same time passionately anti-Catholic and anti-French. On the other hand, because of both Louis XIV's support for the deposed monarch, James II, and the Dutch preoccupations of the new monarch, William III, the state was drawn immediately into a major continental war with France. This turned out to be only the start of a century and a quarter of intermittent warfare from 1689 to 1815, during half of which time the two nations were actually at war. The contest was for world supremacy, and the winner only emerged at the end of an unprecedentedly massive and prolonged war with France from 1793 to 1815, with the decisive British victories of Trafalgar at sea and Waterloo on land.

To pay for these wars, Britain became the most heavily taxed state in Europe, thanks to what was, by eighteenth-century standards, a fairly efficient fiscal system, and above all to a remarkable capacity to borrow at cheap rates most of the money needed. Final victory over France, a country which in 1700 had a population four-and-a-half times that of Britain, was won not so much by military prowess, technological innovation or diplomatic skill as by overwhelming financial superiority. At bottom, victory in war was a question of money, not men, since money could always be used to hire men and Europe was full of mercenaries willing to serve a reliable paymaster.

THE BREWER PARADOX

It is only very recently that historians have begun to study this paradox of, on the one hand, the use of massive external military empire to block a rival hegemonic power and to create a maritime trading power and, on the other, the preservation of internal liberty and the rights of private property – a rare combination only paralleled by Periclean Athens and America from 1941 to the present day. Judith Schklar described eighteenth-century Britain as 'a commercial, extensive, non-military, democracy disguised as a monarchy'.[8] This is largely, but not entirely, correct. It was certainly 'non-military' in the sense that the English themselves fought as little as possible, preferring to hire mercenaries, mostly Germans or Austrians, to do the dirty work for them; and that the governing classes had a strong antipathy to a standing army and were very reluctant to have more than the bare minimum number of professional troops stationed on English soil necessary to put down the occasional public disturbance by the lower classes. In consequence, most were stationed in barracks or billets, in Ireland or the colonies. It is also true, however, that British politics and society were bound to be deeply affected by a prolonged war with France. In order to win, the ruling elite were prepared to spend immense amounts of treasure and also to run up the national debt on a scale comparable only to the activities of the Reagan–Bush administrations in the United States.

The British constitution was certainly representative, but the use of the word 'democracy' is hardly appropriate. Britain was certainly more loosely governed than the despotisms – some enlightened, some not – that prevailed on the continent. Yet, when after 1720 the 'rage of party' had spent itself, the electorate effectively shrank and the elite closed ranks again, so that political power was largely confined to nobles, gentlemen, bankers, merchants, industrialists, lawyers, higher clergy and other influential figures. In 1750 they amounted to about 20,000 adult males, out of a population of about 6 million persons. As for the monarchy, the Hanoverian kings could and did interfere with foreign policy, often in the narrow interest of Hanover, although there were strict limits to their power in the area. They could also occasionally dismiss a prime minister or force his resignation over an issue of personal principle, such as the dismissal of Pitt in 1801 over the granting of a measure of Catholic emancipation in Ireland.

Nevertheless, when all is said and done, the chapters of this book show very clearly that English society in the eighteenth century was not merely changing, as its society and economy expanded; the population still retained its 'negative liberties' against the state, as protected by law – as Wilkes triumphantly proved; and it preserved a limited toleration of worship for protestant dissenters, while quietly easing up on the penalties imposed on Roman Catholics. Moreover, from the 1760s onward the middling sort were making their own views known and at times policies had to be altered to meet their demands. The American War, in particular, nearly split the country in two. By European standards Britain before 1795 remained, as all visitors agreed, internally a strikingly open and liberal society, despite its massive war-making activities. Moreover, at sea Britain adopted a militarily aggressive naval and commercial policy, in the process acquiring more and more colonial possessions, first in the Caribbean and North America, and later in India, together with convenient naval stations and ports of call scattered around the globe, like Antigua, Gibraltar, Minorca and Cape Town.

In his intriguing chapter, Brewer defines the state as a political entity wielding public authority over a specific territory, making public rules – laws – and monopolizing as much as possible of legitimate violence. It is thus responsible for internal peace and external security. If foreign war becomes a major concern of a state, Brewer rightly argues that it is appropriate for the historian to direct attention away from the politics of domestic factions and the manoeuvring of parties in a representative institution like Parliament and towards the processes of military, naval and economic power directed by the state towards its perceived enemies. He is careful to add that such a shift of focus should not distract attention from issues such as the limits within which the state has full freedom to exercise its authority and the linkage of public to private power. Indeed, such questions directly affected the capacity of the state to wage war. Equally important were the effects of mobilization for war on internal functions and power relationships in local government.

Many historians, like Charles Tilly, are agreed that war played a central role in state-building: as he concisely put it, 'war made the state, and the state made war'.[9] The argument is that it was the mobilization of money and manpower for war during the eighteenth century that drove the machine of state to expand its role, its size, its powers and its bureaucratic efficiency; but how did Britain manage to make extensive war but at the same time to preserve its parliamentary control of finances, its decentralized government and its ideology of liberty and property?

Part of Brewer's answer is that in fact the British 'military-fiscal state' was far stronger and more like those of the continent than has hitherto been realized. Nor was this a static situation. It has been calculated that between 1665 and 1790 taxes rose sevenfold in constant money, while taxes as a share of an estimated national income rose fivefold, from 3 per cent in 1665 to 16 per cent in 1815. This means that Britain in the late eighteenth century endured a tax burden per head twice that of France and higher than that of any country in Europe, except perhaps Holland.[10] On the other hand, it was so much richer than its neighbours that it could afford to carry the burden.

To these figures about the income and expenditure of the central state, there has to be added the very substantial and growing cost of poor relief, which was paid for by local taxes raised at the parish level. In wartime, many of the recipients were the families of men drafted or pressed into the armed services, and immediately after peace was declared many were discharged soldiers and sailors who found themselves unemployed and unwanted vagrants who, if not given relief, would be almost obliged to take to robbery in order to stay alive.

The national debt incurred to pay for past wars multiplied fifteen-fold in a century, and by 1783 was larger than that of the French state on the eve of the French Revolution in 1789. To raise all this money the size of the fiscal bureaucracy had doubled. In consequence, work by P. G. M. Dickson, Patrick O'Brien, Peter Mathias and, more recently, John Brewer has destroyed the myth of the fiscal and administrative differences between lightly taxed and slackly governed Britain and the heavily taxed and tightly controlled continental powers like France, Spain, and Prussia.[11]

Britain thus seems to be the exception to the rule that there is a direct linkage between military activity involving crushing fiscal and manpower burdens, and political absolutism; but Brewer is reluctant to grant the fact of British exceptionalism. He points to strong centralizing features such as a single public fiscal system, a single powerful legislative body, and a national poor-relief system. What he omits, however, is that both Parliament and local government were in the hands of independent-minded squires and aristocrats, most of whom were deeply suspicious of armies, resented taxation and insisted on their own control of all aspects of local government, including the mobilization of manpower and the assessing and raising of taxes. Moreover, a powerful private corporation like the East India Company acted almost like a mini-state, with its own large army. Power certainly flowed from the centre, but the flow had to pass through local, independent, channels in order to reach the population at large. Brewer argues that the things which made Britain different were merely a question of the degree to which the state was autonomous, rather than any deep structural difference. He admits, however, that in Britain the size and location of the standing army was determined by Parliament; that the exclusion of many placemen from seats in Parliament limited the power of the state to control that body; and that the state was unable to tax at will. It could, indeed, be argued that the British state was used by landlords and commercial interests to pursue their own ends, rather than the other way round, and that the devolution of power was, if anything, increased as the century wore on, as more and more responsibilities were shifted by statute on to local volunteer authorities. This is an argument made by Joanna Innes in this volume.

BRITAIN AS A MILITARY-FISCAL STATE

At first sight, Brewer's phrase the 'military-fiscal state' does not seem very meaningful, since making war and raising taxes are always the two principal activities of any state, along with punishing criminals and commandeering surplus resources from which to distribute favours and gifts to the rich and powerful. It was only in the sixteenth and seventeenth centuries that some states began to add economic and trade policy and public welfare to the list, and it could be argued that it is this, rather than a propensity to tax and make war, that distinguishes the modern state from the medieval one. On the other hand, the concept of the military-fiscal state can be defended since it was only after about 1600 that the involvement of European states in warfare, and the desperate search for revenues with which to finance these wars, loomed larger and larger on the state agenda. With the introduction of guns and fire-arms in the sixteenth century, and the increase in the capacity of the state to mobilize, feed and transport increasing numbers of men, the size of both armies and navies grew to wholly unprecedented proportions. Most medieval armies do not seem to have been much larger than 14,000–15,000 men but in 1543 Henry VIII launched against France an army of 40,000. By 1700 armies of 100,000 were not unknown and by 1800 their size had doubled again, although they were hardly ever assembled in one place. The sheer scale of these enterprises thus represented a quantum leap from what it had been before, the cause being an enhanced administrative capacity (greatly aided by increased literacy and the adoption of arabic numerals), which enabled the bureaucracy to transport, arm, clothe and feed larger and larger numbers.

In wartime, no less than 60–70 per cent of the total income of the eighteenth-century British state was being spent on military activity. Perhaps more significant is that by the end of the century the proportion spent in peacetime on the military only fell to 40 per cent, since ships had constantly to be repaired, and officers on half-pay to be given their salaries. Moreover, the servicing of the debt accumulated from borrowing during previous wars swallowed up another 40 per cent, which left only 20 per cent for running the court, the bureaucracy and the domestic affairs of the state.[12]

The British government, which was dependent upon Parliament for the annual voting of supplies, was obliged to act with tact and discretion in its demands for money. It trod cautiously in remote, poor and potentially disaffected areas like Wales and Scotland, which were lightly taxed compared with the rich lowland zone in south-eastern England; it exempted from excise all the food of the poor, with the important exception of beer;

in times of peace it allowed taxes on landed property to go under-assessed; while at all times before 1798 it was administratively incapable of taxing non-landed income or personal property. The growth of its tax-base therefore depended heavily, especially in peacetime, on non-agrarian sources, especially customs and excise on imported and home-produced goods, luxury taxes, and taxes on large and highly visible production units, the most typical example being breweries.[13] The landed classes consented to pay their fair share only in the early 1700s at the beginning of the hundred-and-thirty-year period of war with France and again in the early 1800s. Both were times when the elite were deeply frightened of invasion and defeat and the installation of an autocracy, whether popish as in 1697 or revolutionary as in 1798.

The pressure of war on the British state became starkly visible during the War of American Independence. Between 1776 and 1783 the war cost £120 million, or one-and-a-half times gross national income per annum. Taxation rose by one-third, but even so, the war, as usual, was mostly financed by borrowing. As a result, by 1783 the national debt, and the service charges to sustain it, had both doubled. The government seriously feared that it had reached the extreme limit of debt burden, and that in future creditors would no longer invest in British funds.

Given this situation, it at first sight seems plausible to argue that the expansion of the British state in the eighteenth century was driven primarily by the relentless rise in the cost and duration of war, and the growth of standing armies. This is true of the great continental powers like France, Spain, the Empire, Prussia and Russia, but it hardly applies to England. Here the drain on domestic manpower remained small, at any rate up to 1800, since foreign troops were hired for the occasion either by personal recruitment overseas or on contract with some German princeling willing to rent out his army *en bloc*. Moreover, the state was barely in control of internal order. The country remained under-governed, as was shown in 1780 when the Gordon Riots raged unchallenged for three days while the authorities squabbled about who had the legal power to put them down.

Two central institutions which displayed some degree of efficiency were the tax-collecting departments of the Treasury and the Excise, and the management by the Navy Board of the dockyards, which were the largest industrial plants in Britain and perhaps the world. These were the departments upon which depended Britain's naval strength, and therefore her very existence. In the middle of the eighteenth century Fox wrote to an importunate lobbyist for office: 'Capacity is so little necessary for most employments that you seem to forget that there's one where it is absolutely so – viz. the Admiralty'.[14] It was thus recognized that in the appointment of officials in the money-raising and money-expending departments, the ancient principles of patrimony, patronage and purchase had to give way to the newer principle of competence.

Britain built the world's greatest navy, cleared the sea-lanes of the world for its commerce, established naval bases from Minorca to Antigua and hired enough foreign troops to prevent any single power developing hegemonic control over the west European continent. It is, however, noticeable that all this was done by a minute central bureaucracy, just sufficient to raise the taxes and build the ships. With two notable exceptions it was accomplished with a minimum of internal repression. The exceptions were the impressment of seamen for the navy whenever war broke out, and the suspension of Habeas Corpus and the severe repression of popular protest during the panic in the 1790s over the possibility of a popular revolution on the French model. It is, however, significant that resistance by local authorities put some curb on the excesses of the press-gang, and that when the panic ebbed, the repressive measures were repealed. British nationalism certainly developed in the period 1790–1810, but the credit must go mainly to the fears engendered by, first, the radical ideas of the French revolutionaries and then, the ambitions of Napoleon for world hegemony.

Between 1690 and 1720 the British state was weakened by friction between the landed interest and the monied interest over who were the beneficiaries and who the sufferers from a wartime economy. The heat engendered by this dichotomy was vociferously maintained by a galaxy of talented pamphleteers throughout the first twenty years of the eighteenth century and was an important element in the contemporary 'rage of party'. Between 1690 and 1720 these two interest groups had been split over war or peace, over the allegedly inequitable social distribution of the burden of taxes, over the relative benefits of a sea or a land war, over the granting of limited religious toleration to dissenters and over the succession to the throne; after about 1720, however, all these tensions at last began to ease off. The land tax, paid by the rich represented in Parliament, was reduced by shifting more of the burden of taxation on to the middling sort by raising the excise. Wars provided more jobs for the sons of the landed classes, partly as officers in the new professional army and navy, which even in peacetime kept its expanded wartime officer corps on half-pay and available for recall, and also in the expanding areas of the bureaucracy; and finally the landed classes began to join in as investors in government loans, since this provided both security and a reasonable return. By 1750, therefore, these measures had for all intents and purposes put an end to the concept of a conflict between two interest groups, those of land and money.

Despite the ending of this conflict of interests, the British state remained weak in the sense that the constitutional structure was one of checks and balances, along neo-Harringtonian and Lockean lines; that effective fiscal controls were placed on the executive, thanks to Parliament's control of the purse; that in 1688–9 effective statutory limits had been placed on the curbing of religious opinion; that censorship of the printed and spoken word was limited to the *ex post facto* use of the common-law rules governing seditious libel; that good order in the countryside was almost entirely left to amateur Justices of the Peace and parish constables; and that the one attempt by Walpole to extend a government bureaucracy throughout the country to enforce a national excise tax was defeated by an aroused citizenry and by Parliament in 1733.

The problem that faced all British governments in the eighteenth century was thus that there were limits upon what they could oblige the population to do. England was a weakly governed society, with a population always liable to riot – though rarely to kill – in defence of freedom and against authority. That was as true of the rich as of the poor. The former would not accept a reassessment of the land tax after 1697, so that the tax degenerated into a set of quotas fixed and collected by reluctant amateurs, the Justices of the Peace themselves. The government lacked the bureaucratic machinery to impose a tax on incomes. When such a tax was at last imposed in 1798, it was only a temporary measure for the duration of the war.

The weakness of the forces of law and order at the disposal of the eighteenth-century British government was publicly exposed in three areas: impressment for the navy; the control of riots; and the suppression of smuggling. Throughout the century, all three were liable to provoke violent contestations. At hangings, open battles sometimes broke out over the disposal of the body, between, on the one hand, the family and friends of the victim and, on the other, the officers of the law under orders to turn the corpse over to the doctors for lectures on dissection.[15] Minor grain riots seem to have been endemic; in the mid-century Wilkes could generate political urban riots; and in 1780 the government took several days to restore order in London during the anti-Catholic Gordon riots.

Forcible impressment of trained seamen for the navy in time of war aroused widespread physical and moral conflict. Here the government was on weak legal ground and knew it. Whether impressment of free men was lawful was at the very least a debatable point, but few doubted that it was absolutely essential in order to man the navy in an emergency.[16] The problem was that, immediately war broke out, the navy suddenly needed a huge number of extra hands, trained in the ways of the sea. Numbers are hard to come by, since many impressed men declared themselves volunteers after being captured by a press-gang, but it is generally thought that, during the middle of the century, between one-third and one-half of all naval seamen in wartime were impressed. The practice was far from edifying, since it simply encouraged 'numbers of little tyrants in all our seaports', with an open licence to capture any likely-looking passer-by. In 1727 it was said that in London 'droves of these lawless fellows, armed with great sticks, force such as they think proper into the service, and knock down any who will not submit'. For the government, impressment, lawless or not, was a harsh necessity for the salvation of the nation. In a crisis in 1729, it arbitrarily suspended Habeas Corpus, with the natural result that armed conflicts between press-gangs and enraged citizenry grew commoner than ever.[17]

As a defender of the process lamely observed: 'it is a hardship which nothing but absolute necessity can reconcile to our boasted liberty'. The harsh fact was that when war broke out, the demands of the navy and privateers for seamen exceeded the supply in the merchant marine by a factor of two to one. The navy alone expanded from 10,000 seamen before the war in 1756 to 85,000 four years later in 1760. To meet the demand it was impractical to seize all merchant seamen since this would bring overseas commerce to a standstill, thus destroying the very object for which the war was, at least in theory, being fought. It would be folly to strip the merchant fleet of Britain of all its sailors since foreign trade probably comprised a higher proportion of its gross national income per annum than that of any other country.

Even after filling the numbers for the expansion of the navy in the first year or two of war, the navy still needed a large and steady flow of new recruits to make up for the losses. These losses were due, first, to the staggeringly high desertion rate which ranged from 7 per cent *a year* in the Seven Years War to 13 per cent *a year* in the War of American Independence.[18] Desertions throughout the Seven Years War are estimated to have reached 40,000, a number so enormous that it was impossible to punish, much less court-martial and hang, the thousands who were recaptured. Desertion on this scale suggests a singular absence of patriotic enthusiasm.

The second cause of the loss was disease. Life at sea was so hard and the food and drink so poor that the death-rate was twice that of civilians ashore.[19] However, in spite of constant civilian opposition in the towns around the sea coast, frequent bloody riots and rescuers, and a constant barrage of criticism, somehow the English government did manage to cajole or coerce enough men to man the ships. So in that sense, the government achieved its objective, if only at the cost of tolerating and even encouraging a great deal of uncontrollable violence in the streets. Given the shortage of merchant sailors, landsmen had also to be pressed, while Justices of the Peace added to the numbers by compulsorily enlisting vagrants, the unemployed and other local undesirables. It was a kind of moral cleansing of the towns and the countryside.

The result was a desperate flight of potential victims of the press-gang. Thus at the opening of the Seven Years War, there were said to be 50,000 men who had obtained 'protections' – passes giving immunity from pressing – by lobbying persons in high places. In the last resort, the solution to this was adoption of the 'hot press', which for a while suspended Habeas Corpus, lifted the immunity of those with protection, and made all men of a suitably low degree liable to be seized in the street or their homes in a sea-town, or at road-blocks set up inland where refugees from the press might pass.

The navy's solution to the manpower problem in wartime was to try to increase recruits and to reduce losses by disease and desertion. That meant recruiting landsmen by offering generous bounties or by the use of the 'hot press'; and in times of sudden emergency, to 'borrow' seamen from warships in port but not ready for sea. Attempts to reduce wastage by disease meant improving the supply of fresh vegetables and meat, and the imposition of a strict hygienic regime of cleanliness and fresh air which far exceeded that of the French. The latter were alleged – implausibly – to have the deplorable habit of burying their dead in the ballast, besides being generally more casual about sanitation; and even Napoleon, on his way to St Helena, remarked on the cleanliness of British warships. Despite the insistence on hygiene, disease still took a heavy toll, especially in the Caribbean, where tropical fevers were endemic. Venereal disease was also rife in the fleet, affecting a mean of 20 per cent of all crews and about one-third of those who ventured into the Pacific in the middle- and late-eighteenth century.[20] Losses from death in battle were minimal: they removed only 1,500 sailors throughout the whole Seven Years War – as compared with 40,000 lost for desertion. Altogether the loss of manpower from disease, desertion and battle amounted to about 28 per cent a year. No wonder impressment remained an absolute necessity for national salvation in wartime.

The last areas where the eighteenth-century state was woefully inadequate to perform its task, at least in the 1780s, were in the suppression of smuggling and in the enforcement of the excise. Since customs duties on some articles like tea were as high as 100 per cent it is not surprising that smuggling was a very profitable industry. Horrifying examples of the violence employed on both sides have recently been provided.[21] The scope and seriousness of the problem was only made public in the Reports of a Committee of the House of Commons published in 1783.[22] Unfortunately for the historian, the writers of the Reports 'resolved not to enter into particulars', but their general conclusions are dramatic enough without them. The smugglers used ships of various sizes, ranging from 30 to 300 tons, and carrying from 6 to 24 guns, and crews of 12 to 100 men.

> The strength of some of them is such as to enable them to bid defiance to the revenue cruisers, some of which have recently been insulted, fired upon, and beat off, and others either been seized and carried off, or scuttled and sunk.

The number of ships employed in the smuggling trade into England alone was estimated as at least 120 large armed vessels and another 200 smaller ones.

Landings of the cargo were 'secured by large gangs of men, armed chiefly with clubs and heavy whips, generally inflamed with liquor, and assembled in such numbers as to reduce the Revenue Officers to be quiet spectators of the proceedings'. The cargo was then shipped inland in wagons or on horseback, or sent to London either 'under the open guard and protection of armed troops of men' or transported openly by the use of forged permits, which were easily obtainable. The cargo was insured for the voyage and land travel, and it was delivered directly to retail traders or private houses at two-thirds the cost of identical items that paid customs. As described by the *Report*, the whole business was highly organized, with careful planning, and made use of a large force of agents, look-outs and spies. In short, 'they are strong enough to bid defiance to the Revenue officers, whether on sea or ashore'.

Similar large-scale organization of the smugglers using overpowering armed forces was also reported from Scotland. Groups like regular trading companies ran the operations, using cutters 'mounting 40 carriage guns' to import brandy, gin, rum and wine. The cargo was then shipped into Edinburgh either illegally, 'escorted by armed parties of men and horses', or else by use of forged permits.

As for the customs officials, they 'justly observe that their Inland Establishment is utterly unfit to suppress these proceedings', being designed to detect fraud rather than to 'resist violence', while its control over the coastal waters was minimal. After pointing out that an estimated 20 million pounds of tea and 13 million gallons of brandy had been smuggled in during the last three years, and that this involved a loss to the excise of £2 million, the commissioners went on to remark that 'enormities of such violence and extent amount to a partial state of anarchy and rebellion'.[23]

The second problem, after direct smuggling by the use of intimidation and fraud, was that of corrupt collusion between revenue officers and smugglers and merchants. The *Report* went on to claim that at least part of the reason why the amount of smuggled goods that was seized was so small 'arises from collusion between the smugglers and the Revenue'. It declared that

> smuggling is managed with little risk, through the collusion and corrupt practices of the lower class of Revenue officers ... This abuse is so lucrative that neither a sense of duty nor a fear of punishment have been sufficient to restrain it.

The *Report* gloomily concludes that 'the established practice of fees' taken by the revenue officers from their clients, the complexity of the system of duties, the low salaries paid and the great temptation of quick and easy profits 'have combined to produce an intimacy and connections between the inferior officers and the merchants which is very prejudicial to the public'; but they took a philosophical view of the situation, observing only that 'from the infirmity of human nature, it is impossible to suppose that such collusion can be totally prevented'. They recommended that a shift from payment by fees, gratuities and rewards to payment by fixed and adequate salaries would certainly help.[24]

If the commissioners were telling the truth – and there is no reason to suspect they are not – then the much-vaunted efficiency of the customs service was, at least by 1783, a mirage. Moreover, things got worse after the peace with America, since small fishermen, no longer afraid of impressment into the navy as a punishment if caught smuggling, now began bringing in large quantities of spirits and tea from continental Europe, and tea, soap and salt from Ireland.[25] Further evidence that the deterioration of the customs service was recent and largely a product of the American war is that in 1784 it was officially acknowledged that 'many of the sailors employed against the enemies of this country during the late war are now engaged in these pernicious practices.[26] The losses to the revenue from the smuggling of tea alone were reckoned at £1 million a year. The *Reports* undoubtedly raise questions about the efficiency of the customs service in the earlier decades of the eighteenth century, although it is clear that many of the abuses had got much worse in recent years. Even so, it is hard to believe that the service was as competent, professional, zealous and incorruptible as has been thought, even in the earlier decades of the century.

If the customs administration was a shambles, overwhelmed by the superior armed force of the smugglers, the corrupt collusion of junior officers and a flood of forged permits, the success of the excise in levying taxes on home-produced goods was only a little better. The *Reports* listed the frauds perpetrated in the breweries and distilleries, despite constant inspections, several times a day, and noted large-scale illegal imports from Scotland: 'the quantity of spirits annually imported from Scotland, exceeds the whole quantity which has paid duty'.[27] Illicit candle manufacture was carried out on a large scale, at night, a time when the excise officers did not have the right to enter a building, unless accompanied by a constable or a Justice of the Peace. Illegal manufacture of candles for coal-mines in Wales was said to be particularly large: 'The manufacture of wax candles has fallen so much into the hands of clandestine manufacturers as to endanger the loss of the whole duty'. Similar frauds existed in the manufacture of soap, so that 'soap is sold, to a great amount, that never paid duty'.[28] The *Reports* list similar failure of the excise efficiently to tax salt, coaches, servants and licences to sell spirits.

The *Reports* pointed out that a lot of the trouble arose from 'a popular prejudice which prevails against informers in matters of revenue', some of whom were beaten up or even killed by angry mobs. As a result,

the illicit practices used in defrauding the Revenue have increased in

16

a most alarming degree; that those practices are carried on . . . with a violence and with outrages which not only threaten the destruction of the Revenue, but are . . . an interruption of all good government; that the more secret illicit practices in the internal Excise of this Kingdom have also greatly increased.

The *Report* concluded that the public revenue was being defrauded to an extent of not less than £2 million a year at a time when total net income from customs and excise was only a little over £9 million. 'The system of taxation created by public necessities has opened a large field for the exercise of interested ingenuity', the authors of the *Reports* delicately pointed out. All they could suggest was to ease the legal restrictions on the customs and excise officials, and drastically to reduce the rate of duties so as to make smuggling and fraud unprofitable. This last they described as 'the great and infallible remedy towards the prevention of frauds against the revenue'. This is exactly what Pitt proceeded to do, with very gratifying results.[29] If the *Reports* were at all accurate, neither the customs office nor to a lesser degree the excise were functioning at all efficiently in the early 1780s. In this respect, the British state was not all that different from its European rivals. If this holds true throughout the century, it means that the one way in which Brewer claimed that the British state was indeed very different from those of Europe, namely the efficiency of its tax-collecting bureaucracy, was not so striking after all. Even so, the weight of evidence points to the fact that Britain could only exercise its overwhelming financial, naval and military power, when Crown, bureaucracy and the great vested interests of commerce and the land represented in Parliament were all united behind the policy.

Even then, local administration remained in amateur local hands, the tax burden was more or less equitably distributed, and the society, even down to the small peasant, was much richer, as every British or foreign traveller in the century testified. In many important ways, the British state remained different, even if Brewer has made a good case that it was far more like its continental rivals than anyone has hitherto been willing to admit. To test his theory he calls for more comparative studies.

A TYPOLOGY OF STATE FORMATION

This challenge has been taken up by Thomas Ertman in his chapter. He more or less accepts the idea of British exceptionalism, and then proceeds to ask the question why. He points out that it is not only the geographic model of explanation of Britain's exceptionalism, hinging on the fact that Britain was defended from invasion by 20 miles of water, that is undermined by Brewer's claim for similarity; so also is the hypothesis that war is the decisive cause for state absolutism. According to this theory, military expenditure and a large army lead to a large bureaucracy, oppressive taxation by a swarm of state fiscal agents and an absolutist state to drive it. The size of this state machine depends on the size of the standing army and the prosperity or poverty of the economy. This last factor was especially important since it determined the level of commercialization. There is no doubt that today it is far easier to extract indirect taxes on goods than it is to levy direct taxes on wealth; but this may not have been true for the eighteenth century, especially since before 1798 the only wealth that was taxable was landed property. Brewer argues that while the British land tax was assessed and levied by amateur Justices of the Peace, it took a small army of skilled professional staff to run the excise office. On the other hand, it must be said that the British government found that, because of the overwhelming interest of the landed classes represented in Parliament, it was politically much less troublesome, especially in time of peace, to shift the burden from the land on to excise and customs. Even after the landed elite were frightened by a threat of invasion from France into agreeing to an income tax in 1798, they found that they could easily afford to shoulder the burden it imposed. Contemporaries believed, perhaps rightly, that it pressed far more heavily on the middle classes.

Ertman argues that there were different kinds of absolutist states in Europe in the eighteenth century and that it is a serious mistake to lump them together. Thus France and other continental powers sold hereditary public offices, as a result of which their financial administration became largely privatized, and the patrimony of family cliques. As such, it was inefficient, expensive and incapable of modernization. Moreover, France, which lacked a central bank or secure lines of credit, was forced to borrow on short-term loans at high interest rates from a class of wealthy financiers, who were themselves tax-farmers. Prussia, on the other hand, did not sell offices and was not dependent on financiers for loans. In other words, there is no uniformity in the typology of the military absolutist state of Europe in the eighteenth century.

Ertman pins his explanation of this phenomenon of a variety of state systems not on geography, or the degree of commercialization of the society, or the pressure of war, but on the timing of their emergence as fully-fledged state systems. The early developers – Italian city states like Milan and Venice, as well as large monarchies like Spain and France – emerged in the late middle ages, a time when public office was regarded as a form of private property, tax-collection was farmed out to private entrepreneurs, and when hereditary state offices were sold to raise money. The result was that during this early period the state apparatus became colonized from within by families of financiers and office-holders, who then pursued their own agenda, which did not necessarily coincide with the best interests of the state which they nominally served.

When in the sixteenth and seventeenth centuries the pressures of war intensified across Europe, these older state systems were incapable of change because of this early privatization of state offices. As a result, during every war they were obliged to resort to more and more sales of offices in order to raise money, and to extract more and more direct taxes from the peasantry, who consequently remained mired in stagnation and poverty. War thus merely increased the absolutist claims and powers of the monarch over his subjects, while at the same time crippling his long-term financial and administrative capacity to rule, and ruining his tax-base, the peasantry. It was only late developers who escaped this trap.

The British state fits perfectly into the Ertman model. For two-and-a-half centuries after 1415 it had the good fortune to be too poor to be able to intervene effectively in continental wars. Henry VIII had tried in the 1510s and again in the 1540s, but failed. So greatly did the costs of the latter venture exceed his means that, in order to pay for it, Henry was obliged to sell off much of the vast church property he had only recently seized. Charles I tried again to play a military role on the European scene in the late 1620s, this time financing his wars by forced loans and other forms of extra-parliamentary taxation. Not only were the English troops repeatedly defeated with ignominy, but these attempts to levy taxes with which to pay them without the consent of Parliament led to a major constitutional crisis. Charles's two attempts to impose religious uniformity by force upon the Scots led again to defeat, and in 1640 to the total collapse of his regime, politically, financially and militarily.

This string of military failures was caused primarily by financial weakness, which was the result of legal blockage of the sale of offices, and political obstruction by Parliament to voting taxes. The English state never got itself into the position of being able routinely to sell hereditary offices, as happened on an ever-larger scale in France, Spain, Milan and the Empire. Therefore when the major military crisis came between 1689 and 1714, as England became involved in a massive naval and continental war with Louis XIV in order to preserve its independence, the state was not burdened with a massive load of debt, and its central bureaucracy, especially the Treasury and the Navy Board, although very small, was still under state control. Britain could therefore enter the era of the military revolution with a fairly clean slate.

This does not mean that the geographical argument is without merit. Britain is an island, and there were serious technical obstacles of wind, tides and the location of ports which, in the days of sail, made very risky the launching by an enemy of a cross-Channel invasion. In consequence the English elite never saw any need for keeping a large standing army on British soil, and its cost and size were therefore both kept manageable. The third factor, apart from late development and geographical isolation, was the product of politics, the Glorious Revolution of 1688, which was itself a piece of luck, achieved by an unusually favourable wind, some treacherous defections from James II's army (especially by John Churchill) and the cowardly flight of James himself. The constitutional change of the Glorious Revolution after 1688, which at last gave Parliament control of the purse, forced co-operation of King and Parliament; but this co-operation was now willingly given, thanks to the well-justified fear of the forcible imposition of a French-inspired Catholic despotism under James II. The propertied classes were afraid of 'Popery and Slavery', which drove the landed and commercial elites to support a high level of taxation to pay for a long continental war. The result was the imposition of a land tax on the landed rich, as well as heavy excise and customs dues which bore hard on middle-class and poor consumers. Fortunately, Britain was relatively rich and could easily carry a burden of taxation higher than those of its neighbours.

The metamorphosis of Britain between 1689 and 1815 – a mere 126 years – from a marginal player in the continental power-game into the major European and world imperial power was at least as remarkable and important a phenomenon as her later Industrial Revolution. She had more options since she was not already locked into privatized office-holding and tax-farming. Her government was free to innovate administratively and to develop a more efficient centralized fiscal and military bureaucracy under government control. Above all, if she needed to borrow, as she always did in wartime, she could turn to the international money-market, where her credit was always good because every loan was backed by a specific parliamentary grant. To exploit this option, in the 1690s Britain created a modern credit system, borrowed from the Dutch. It was managed by a central bank, and its loans were guaranteed by Parliament and secured by statutes on specific taxes. Thus the parliamentary system, which had been a handicap to the Stuarts, now became the critical element in creating Britain's fiscal capacity, as compared with the authoritarian regime of Louis XIV's. Moreover, the British practice of relying heavily on borrowing to pay for war made it possible to spread taxes rather more evenly over periods of war and peace. This passed on the cost of current wars to future generations, since the peacetime cost of servicing the debt severely reduced the available revenues of the state and there was consequently little peace dividend. As Paul Langford has remarked, 'Warfare on the British model was a triumph for an enterprising and acquisitive society, not an authoritarian one'.[30]

On the other hand, in the external deployment of power, Britain was unquestionably the greatest state in Europe. Its financial superiority allowed it to build and maintain the greatest navy in the world, and to hire German or Austrian mercenaries to fight for her on the mainland of Europe. In that sense, but that sense only, it was indeed the greatest 'military-fiscal state' in Europe. Yet this military power did not lead to absolutism because this power derived from the very strength of Parliament, both ideologically and in practice, after the change of dynasty to the Hanoverians in 1714.

This paradoxical state, so decentralized and weak internally, but so strong abroad, even survived its greatest test, the war with France from 1793 to 1815. In terms of money, manpower and duration, this was a war on a wholly unprecedented scale, many times larger and longer than any previous wars, while at the same time radical ideas were spreading from France, so that internal security for a while seemed precarious. Yet the state structure survived. It did so partially due to popular revulsion against the atrocities of the Terror, and later to popular fear of invasion and conquest by Napoleon. Partly also the state survived the charge that government was largely a system of outdoor relief for the rich and titled. This criticism was slowly drained of content, as much of 'Old Corruption', as it was called by the radicals, was slowly eliminated from the public administration by a series of Tory governments from Pitt to Liverpool. Hard-pressed by Whig and radical critics, they slowly abolished sinecure offices and reversions to offices (on the deaths of current holders), stopped rewarding friends from the pension list and shifted from payment by fees from clients to payment by official salary. By 1832, when the necessary limited expansion of the franchise took place, the modernization of the administration was half-way to being accomplished.[31]

At the same time, care was taken to make full use of the safety-net of poor relief to aid the victims of mobilization for war and commercial losses. As perhaps one in five of all able-bodied men were drafted into the armed forces and the militia, their families were taken care of by the poor rates, paid for by the local authorities of parish and county. For some modest tax-payers, the poor rate amounted to one-half of the land tax. Thus it was during this Great War that Britain became the first of the new state systems that have dominated the twentieth century – that is, the model of the warfare-welfare state. This was the end-product of the slow evolution of both war and welfare, both of them in ways peculiar to England.

THE DOMESTIC BACKGROUND TO EMPIRE

After these very suggestive ideas about the state, put forward by Brewer and Ertman, the next two chapters shift attention to the society. Antony Wrigley assesses English resources for war and the effect of war on the economy. He points out that England had only one-quarter of the population of France in 1600 and still only two-fifths in 1815, but that this was no great handicap since mercenaries were so easy to hire. Thanks to Pitt's income tax of 1798, between 1770 and 1810 British taxation doubled as a percentage of the national product, whereas that of France remained stationary. Nor did the burden of war have much of an effect on the

English demography or economy. The population continued to rise in the second half of the century; despite higher taxation and losses by disease in the armed forces, the economic growth rate was high, and after 1800 there was a rise in the standard of living even of the poor.

A case can be made that it was economic factors that largely determined the outcome of the war. Here evidence of British exceptionalism is very clear. One of England's enormous advantages over France in 1800 was that, thanks to the remarkable efficiency of its agricultural sector, only one-third of the population was needed to supply all the food for its growing population. In France, between two-thirds and four-fifths of the population were still working on the land, since their productivity per head was only one-half that of the English. This was the critical difference, since in England rapid urbanization on a scale unique for Europe, made possible by this efficiency of the agricultural sector, released a huge labour-force available for productive work in the cities. One of the keys to agricultural productivity, along with enclosures, drainage and more use of animal fertilizer, seems to have been the social structure of the countryside, with the tripartite division between great landlords, prosperous farmers and landless labourers. Another reason why the English agricultural labour-force was so mobile was that it was protected from destitution by the provision of poor relief by the parish, which reduced the significance of family support in old age. At the same time, the population growth was slowed down to a manageable pace by late marriage and an increase in the proportion of the young who did not marry at all.

All this adds up to a powerful argument for the uniqueness of the English experience in the eighteenth century. It was distinct not only in its political system but also in its social and cultural arrangements. The success in raising agricultural productivity, easing urban migration, providing an effective poor-relief system, and controlled fertility (in which France had taken the lead) all contributed to Britain's early prosperity, both absolutely and per head, a prosperity that was visible well before the industrial revolution really took hold. It was this prosperity that provided the tax and loan basis which allowed the British state to become a great imperial power.

SOCIETY AND LOCAL GOVERNMENT

The chapter by Joanna Innes also studies what she calls 'the domestic face of the military-fiscal state'. First, she looks at how the relations of central to local government were affected by war. Both were primarily concerned with the preservation of public order, which was not an easy task in the eighteenth century. It involved making provision for the helpless poor, dealing with plague, suppressing crime and preventing dearth by controlling the supply and price of food. The government in London kept in personal contact with the local authorities via the circuit judges at the assizes twice a year. In addition, the local officials after 1757 had to raise and direct an embodied militia, as well as raising the land tax and later the income tax through local commissioners and parish constables.

A notable feature of the age was the rising tide of parliamentary commissions investigating all aspects of public administration and public finance. This desire for hard data upon which to base policy and reform abuses by legislation is perhaps the most striking new aspect of parliamentary activity of the age. The second was the new wealth available to the central government as a result of new taxes, some of which was filtered back to the localities for education, hospitals, prisons, the transportation overseas of felons, and so on.

Given this background, what was the effect of war? One was that major cities now had billeted troops, who at a pinch could be used to suppress riots. The main effect of war, however, was to drain the countryside of surplus manpower, on an ever-increasing scale: 100,000 men were under arms in the 1690s and 400,000 in the 1790s, including the militia. After wars, there took place a rapid demobilization, which inevitably caused major dislocations. The main effect was on property crime. As able-bodied young men were drafted or volunteered, the rate went down; when they were demobilized, it went sharply up. The poor law and vagrancy laws acted as a safety-net, while the government built huge hospitals at Chelsea and Greenwich for the invalids of war. However, partly as a result of war, the poor-rate grew rapidly, especially from 1793 to 1815, since most of the wives and children of breadwinners taken off to the wars inevitably became a burden on the parish. The families of those called to the militia even had a statutory right to this relief, which became increasingly burdensome to the parish and county authorities, who had to find the money.

Innes reaches two major conclusions. The first is that war aggravated social problems, but did not cause them; and, second, that England was indeed an exception, in that during this era of increasing warfare it actually decentralized its domestic administration, transferring more and more responsibility to amateur local authorities. This process was caused by the domination of Parliament by men anxious above all to protect local autonomy and keep in their own hands control over local income and expenditure.

POPULAR WAR IDEOLOGY

Kathleen Wilson's chapter examines a third aspect of the domestic scene – that is, the ideological motivations behind popular support for war and empire. Instead of looking for the familiar economic and political interests – trade seen as synonymous with power and property – she draws attention to the strong nationalist feelings generated by war and in turn providing support for it. The acquisition of colonies was seen not only as a source of trade leading to prosperity but also as a means of spreading virtue and the Protestant religion. Wilson argues that among all classes before 1776 there was a popular vision of imperial greatness which carried with it strong ethical overtones. Imperial outreach was thus seen not merely as a way to increase wealth but also as an extension of national culture against degenerate, corrupt and Popish enemies, France and Spain. Moreover, the economic theory favoured by the press was mercantilist, namely that trade was a zero-sum game and naval war was the only way for Britain to maximize its share and also to obtain a favourable balance of trade.

This package of material and moral arguments fell apart during the War of the American Revolution. Now one virtue, political liberty, seemed to be in direct conflict with another, imperial conquest. Burke observed that 'no free country can keep another in slavery'. Anti-imperialist sentiment also grew out of ideas about how wealth leads to personal luxury and political corruption. The concept of an empire of virtue visibly waned, only to revive again in response to the French revolutionary and Napoleonic challenge.

ATTITUDES TO MASS MOBILIZATION 1798–1806

Linda Colley takes up the same theme of popular culture serving as a justification of and support for war, this time during the Napoleonic Wars. She believes that the success of Britain in these wars was not only because of the ease and efficiency with which she could raise taxes and loans, but also because of the strong popular support which it engendered. It is noticeable that the only war that Britain lost, that of American Independence, was the one over which popular feeling was split right down the middle.

She also points out that in 1793 European warfare entered a quite new stage. By any standard, whether of troops involved, money spent, duration of time, territorial area involved, or serious threat to British independence as a nation, the wars of 1793–1815 were on a quite different scale and quality from anything that had gone before. By 1814 Britain had 250,000 men in the army, 140,000 in the navy and another 500,000 men in the Volunteers or the militia, making a total not far off a million men.

The records about the selection of men for the militia offer fascinating, but distressing, information about the degree of loyalty of the population. The system worked as follows: first, there was a census of able-bodied males aged 18–45 and over a minimal height (5' 5", later reduced to 5' 2"). Men were chosen for service by ballot, parish by parish, according to military quotas, but those selected could buy themselves substitutes for the price of 10 guineas. What is astonishing is the number of the upper and middle classes who negotiated their way out, either by joining a regiment of Volunteers – a kind of part-time national home guard of respectable local citizens – or by buying a substitute. By 1808 nearly half a million men had signed up in the militia, but in England about one-third of them took steps to avoid being drafted, if the country was invaded. This figure does not suggest that any great wave of patriotic enthusiasm was sweeping the country, at a time when Napoleon was threatening invasion. Wales was even worse, with only rather more than one-quarter agreeing to serve, and only Scotland showed appropriate sentiments by producing nearly one-half of those balloted who were willing to serve. The result was an army abroad composed mainly of the labouring poor, since so few of the middling sort were interested in becoming soldiers.

Patriotism seems to have been more intense in urban areas, rather than in the country, where one would expect deference and loyalty to the regime to have played a more powerful role. This levee *en masse* of volunteers and militia was England's response to a similar call in France. It was a gamble by the propertied classes that arms could safely be put in the hands of the labouring classes, who they hoped could be trusted to use them to halt foreign invaders. The hesitant expectation was that the newly armed masses would neither turn their weapons on their betters, nor use them as blackmail to demand constitutional reform and political participation in parliamentary elections. As it turned out, both the volunteers and the militia were entirely loyal, but the large numbers of middle-class men who bought themselves out of the latter provides striking evidence of widespread lack of nationalist zeal among the middling sort, despite a barrage of nationalist fervour displayed in the press and in Parliament. The cynical interpretation of this paradox is that fanatical jingoists are always drawn from groups least threatened by personal involvement in the hazards of war.[32]

THE ATLANTIC MARITIME EMPIRE

Daniel Baugh shifts attention away from the domestic background of war and imperial expansion and towards the motives for seeking an empire in the first place. What was the plan in the seventeenth century and how much attention did British statesmen pay to it? Baugh does not believe that there was a coherent naval policy before the 1650s, when the battle fleet was first built, the first Navigation Act was passed and the first Dutch war was fought. His argument is that thereafter, with one lamentable exception in the mid-eighteenth century, the central objective was not territorial colonization or domination, but trade. The argument was summed up by Sir Walter Ralegh in about 1600, and was hardly to change for 200 years: 'Whosoever commands the sea, commands the trade of the world; whosoever commands the trade of the world, commands the riches of the world, and consequently the world itself'.[33] One snag, however, was that navies were not cheap. Wooden ships rotted fast, and their life-span was only a decade or two, so that constant maintenance work in huge shipyards was necessary, even in peacetime. Moreover, skilled seamen were always in short supply, and large numbers had to be forced to serve by impressment. Furthermore, British statesmen were always torn between competing objectives: one was this expansive 'blue-water policy'; another was the over-riding necessity to protect Britain from military invasion across the channel and the North Sea; and a third was the desire to prevent any single power – especially France – from establishing a hegemony over most of western Europe. Baugh believes that it was Ralegh's policy for empire, but stressing trade rather than territorial occupation, that dominated strategic thinking.

As policy was formed in the 1660s onwards, the government's objectives were domestic wealth from trade, which could be used as a source of taxes and loans in time of war, and a strong navy to wrest control of the seas from the Dutch – and later the French and Spanish. Territorial colonies as such were of very little interest, except as naval bases – as proved by the readiness at peace treaties to return odd islands captured during war. The merchants, both American and British, wanted naval protection from privateers and pirates, and freedom of access to new markets. American colonial merchants in particular depended not only on trade with Britain across the Atlantic, but also on triangular trade with Africa and shuttle trade along the east coast of America, as far down as the Caribbean.

Up to the 1750s this policy worked pretty well, and all parties were reasonably satisfied. The victories of the Seven Years War, however, turned the heads of the London statesmen. At the end of the war, they chose to keep Canada rather than Guadeloupe, which meant a huge expanse of territory acquired in order to remove French bases of influence from north America. This acquisition made the American colonies more secure, since they now only had the Indians to worry about. This also meant that they were less dependent on British help for defence. As an opponent observed, ''tis needless to erect forts to keep the trees in subjection'. This was not, however, how British politicians saw it: they were determined to establish a relatively huge army of 10,000 men on American territory, to be paid for by taxing the colonists, while (to make matters worse) they at the same time imposed strict control on colonial merchant shipping.

This policy revolution – a shift from a focus on commerce to a focus on control of territory and its inhabitants – turned out to be a disaster, and after 1783 London reverted to its pre–1763 objective of an Atlantic maritime empire based on trade.

UNION WITH SCOTLAND

John Robertson is concerned not with Britain as an imperial power but with the coherence of the various states of which it was composed. A unified state under direction from London was nominally created by the negotiated Act of Union between England and Wales and Scotland in 1707. It was an act which left Scotland with its own church, its own legal system, its own administrative autonomy and its own national identity; but its destiny was henceforward decided in London, not Edinburgh.

Robertson takes a close look at the creation of this union of 1707, seen not from the centre in London, but from the periphery in Edinburgh, and placed in the pan-European context of the War of the Spanish Succession. He points out that the other great states of Europe – Spain, France, Sweden, Austria – were all composites, put together by royal inheritance or marriage, treaty or conquest, with force an essential ingredient to glue all of them together. All indulged in a rhetoric of absolute monarchy and in a practice of the widest variation of relationships between the core – the capital city and the court – and the periphery – the provinces, run by more or less powerful local elites.

Seventeenth-century Europe had been characterized by thrusts to forcible consolidation of central power; for example, by Richelieu in France and Olivarez in Spain; pressure to enforce a monopolistic territorial religion, for example by Louis XIV in France; and everywhere by rising taxation to pay for more and more expensive intra-European wars. The results were a series of provincial revolts against the centre, only two of which – those of the United Provinces and Portugal – succeeded in gaining national freedom.

By 1700 the Scottish kingdom was in a precarious situation. As an underdeveloped country, its manpower was being drained off to fight in foreign wars, the aristocracy was being lured south by the fleshpots of London and its commercial situation was desperate after the failure of the Scottish African Society in Darien. To make matters worse, in 1701, the English Parliament by the Act of Settlement transferred the crown to the Hanoverian line without consulting the Scots. By 1706 the Scots were therefore faced with two options: independence with a Jacobite monarchy, propped up by French troops, or a new federal union with England, which created a single sovereignty and Parliament in London, but preserved the Scottish church, law and local administration.

Robertson rightly points out that this did nothing to create a psychological nation, since xenophobia was still rife on both sides of the border. He sees this bullied union of Scotland and England into Britain as a forerunner to the similar attempt to bring the American colonies to heel after 1760, which failed. In view of these events and the subsequent conquests of much of India, he argues – unlike Baugh – that Britain was always concerned with territorial sovereignty as much as with trade. He compares the Scottish opponents of union in 1707 to the American colonists after 1783 and the Irish rebels in 1798, all hostile to British sovereignty. He concludes by pointing out that so far the British state has survived the disintegration of its empire in the twentieth century; but he now sees rising Scottish national-ism and the drive for European unity as possibly opening the way for a newly negotiated federal arrangement between England and Scotland.

SCOTTISH AND AMERICAN PROVINCIALISM

It is Ned Landsman's persuasive argument that although the union took place in 1707, psychological assimilation of the Scots with London took a very long time, during which direct connections were opened up across the Atlantic from Scotland to the American colonies. Scotland and America have long been identified by historians as two cultural provinces of the British empire. Direct ties were created from one to the other by com-merce, exporting tobacco and sugar from Charleston to Glasgow; by politics, with Scottish governors of American states like New York, New Jersey and Virginia; by education and moral philosophy, in the person of John Witherspoon of Princeton; by medicine, since so many doctors working in colonial America had been bred and trained in Scotland; and by large-scale emigration from Scotland to America.

Thus there were links not only between the metropolis and the provinces but also between one province and another in the Atlantic world. These ties helped to stimulate both Scottish involvement in the empire and the American lunge for independence. Both were products of an ideology, not of cultural cringe but of moral superiority over the stagnant and corrupt politics of London. Intra-provincial ties were forged in a common language, that of nationalism, freedom, dissenting Protestant piety; as were concepts about civic virtue, moral philosophy, natural law and political economy, all preached by the Scots philosophers. It is the ideas of the Scottish Enlightenment which are reflected in the Declaration of Independence.

NATIVE RESPONSE TO IMPERIAL CONQUEST

The last two chapters in this book deal with the reactions by indigenous populations to imperial rule and assimilation, reactions which turn out to have some remarkable similarities. Three times the Irish rebelled between 1600 and 1800: the first time in 1641, a rebellion which helped to trigger off the English Civil War; the second in 1689, in an attempt to restore the Catholic James II to his throne: and the third in 1798, at a moment when England faced a grave internal menace because of the spread of radical values, as well as an external threat of invasion from revolutionary France.

Various explanations have been advanced for this evidence of colonial restlessness under British Protestant occupation. Recently, there has been a reaction against Irish nationalist myths about a repressed and fundamentally unhappy people of a different race, different culture, different standard of living and different religion from their English and Scots occupiers and masters. Nicholas Canny argues that Ireland was no more unstable than Scotland, with its two rebellions of 1715 and 1745, or even England. The latter was inhabited by what was admitted to be an 'ungovernable people', always prone to local rioting – usually minor but occasionally major.[34] Second, Canny argues that the poverty gap between English and Irish has been grossly exaggerated, and that Ireland in the eighteenth century was relatively prosperous, thanks to flourishing agriculture and trade within the British empire. Dublin, after all, was the second largest city in the whole empire in 1800. In the mid-seventeeth century the old Catholic English settlers were seeking no more than a guarantee of their property rights and access by Catholics to government offices. The 1641 rebellion was conservative, loyal to the Stuart monarchy, hostile only to the Dublin administration and fearful of the English Puritans in Parliament. The revolt failed, however, and the result was a massive expropriation of Catholic landlords. In 1641 Catholics had owned about 60 per cent of the land, but by 1660 the proportion was down to about 20 per cent, sliding to 14 per cent after further confiscations in the 1690s.

As for the Irish rebellion of 1688–9, it marked a polarization between Catholics and Protestants, as two outside armies, one of James II backed by the French and one of William III aided by the Dutch, fought it out on Irish soil. The first results of defeat were not too draconian, since William III wished to make a quick peace so as to shift his army as soon as possible back to the continent of Europe. However, the Irish Protestants vented their fear and rage upon the Catholics, excluding them from all positions of influence and denying them any self-respect. Ireland in the eighteenth century was held down by an English army of occupation, and run in their own interests by a Protestant, largely urban, minority.

Canny admits all this, but points out that the Irish Catholic peasantry were totally passive for at least seventy years, from 1690 to 1760. Life for the peasants was tolerable, since they were little affected by the penal laws denying them offices, while the merchants were free to make money, even if deprived of political power. In addition, there was massive economic growth not only in towns but even in the countryside. Old tensions only revived with the French Revolution and the spread of Jacobin ideas. Ireland exploded in 1798 when a French military force landed, and a full-scale rebellion broke out, only to be crushed with extreme brutality.

Canny concludes that Ireland was not an unusually disturbed area of the empire, and that its inhabitants were generally not hostile to the state itself. They only wanted security of property and some access to political office. It was returning exiles and foreign troops who stirred up trouble.

Moreover, the marked prosperity of the country during the eighteenth century was shared by most of the population. As a result, for most of the time, the majority of the Irish were content to seek improvement of their condition by political reform inside the system, rather than by outright rebellion.

Christopher Bayly's account of the Indian response to the spreading territorial empire of Britain is not dissimilar. He disagrees with the standard historiography, seeing the imperialism of the East India Company as something more than Mughal imperialism with a white face. Resistance was not part of the Mughal political inheritance but was an outgrowth of British tactics. The explanation of British territorial expansionism has to be found, he believes, in the complex involvement of local Indian rulers and bureaucrats, all competing to grab portions of the crumbling Mughal empire.

It was British, not Indian, theories of absolute sovereignty and the rule of law that provided the justification for the British to impose their own very heavy taxation in order to support a large native army, officered by the British. It was British accounting procedures and the use of the native army as enforcers that made such heavy taxation so effective. In this respect, it was like any other military-fiscal state.

Bayly denies that there was any ideology of expansionism, but rather a willingness to rule via pliant native kings, who were turned into 'a dignified territorial aristocracy'. This situation was generally accepted in India and trouble only broke out in response to a tightening-up or altering of this traditional policy, as in 1857. There was thus no tradition of native resistance during the eighteenth and nineteenth centuries, but merely occasional violent spasms of resistance to novel, harsh and intrusive measures against landlords and peasants. The picture Bayly gives of the Indian response to empire is thus curiously similar to that which Canny offers for Ireland – or, for that matter, which Baugh offers for America. Rebellion was never endemic, but was triggered off by a previous tightening-up of imperial policy in London. On the other hand, it is impossible to ignore the role of brute force in maintaining peace, especially when it is realized that the army of the East India Company grew from 90,000 in 1793 to no fewer than 230,000 in 1820. This expansion of raw power had to be paid for by taxation on the natives.

CONCLUSION

The book covers most of, but not all, the issues raised by the 'Brewer Paradox' and by the imperial stretch of Britain in the eighteenth century. What it leaves out, however, is the question whether on balance Britain gained or lost by the whole enterprise. This is a complex and contested subject, which can only be touched on here. On the one hand, the empire and its maintenance was a major cause of war and taxes, both at home and abroad. On the other hand, Britain was more dependent than any other European power on foreign trade, which boomed through both peace and war. It is a striking fact that despite the inroads of French privateers and the struggle with the navy for manpower, the merchant marine emerged from every war larger and stronger than when it began. Whether or not the mounting national debt caused by war slowed British economic growth by crowding out the private capital market is still a hotly contested issue, where the truth depends on juggling a set of very unreliable figures. Far more work needs to be done in the areas of local government, poor relief and crime, as they were affected by the demands of war for men and money.

What is already certain, however, is that war and empire mattered enormously to Britain in the eighteenth century. The object of this volume is to open discussion rather than close it off, by providing a set of often differing explanations. It will have achieved its purpose if never again can a history of eighteenth-century Britain be written which does not give great emphasis to the problems raised by an imperial state at war, and especially by the unprecedented scale of warfare with France between 1793 and 1815. Not for nothing was the latter known before 1914 as 'The Great War'.

NOTES

1 L. B. Namier, *The Structure of Politics at the Accession of George III* (London, 1929).
2 E. P. Thompson, *Whigs and Hunters: The Origin of the Black Act* (New York, 1975); *Customs in Common: Studies in Traditional Popular Culture* (New York, 1991).
3 J. H. Plumb, *The Origins of Political Stability in England 1675–1725* (New York, 1967).
4 J. Brewer, *Party Ideology and Popular Politics at the Accession of George III* (London, 1976); 'Commercialization and Politics', in N. McKendrick, J. Brewer and J. H. Plumb (eds), *The Birth of a Consumer Society: The Commercialization of Eighteenth Century England* (Bloomington, Ind., 1982).
5 P. Borsay, *The English Urban Renaissance: Culture and Society in the Provincial Town 1660–1770* (Oxford, 1989).
6 For a brilliant analysis of British Nationalism, see Linda Colley, *Britons: Forging the Nation 1707–1837* (London and New Haven, 1993).
7 J. Brewer, *The Sinews of Power: War, Money and the English State 1688–1783* (London, 1989).
8 See G. Bock, Q. Skinner and M. Virolli (eds), *Machiavelli and Republicanism* (Cambridge, 1990), 269.
9 C. Tilly (ed.), *The Formation of the Nation States in Western Europe* (Princeton, 1975), 42.
10 *The Sinews of Power*, 166–7.
11 P. G. M. Dickson, *The Financial Revolution in England 1688–1756* (New York, 1967); P. Mathias, *The Transformation of England* (London, 1979); P. Mathias and P. O'Brien, 'Taxation in England and France, 1715–1810', *Journal of*

European Economic History, 5 (1976); P. O'Brien, 'The Political Economy of British Taxation, 1660–1815', *Economic History Review*, 41 (1988); Brewer, *The Sinews of Power*.

12 P. K. O'Brien, 'Public Finance in the Wars with France 1793–1815', in H. T. Dickinson (ed.), *Britain and the French Revolution 1789–1815* (Basingstoke, 1990), 165.

13 ibid., 167–9.

14 Quoted in N. A. M. Rodger, *The Wooden World: An Anatomy of the Georgian Navy* (London, 1986), 31.

15 P. Linebaugh, 'The Tyburn Riot against the Surgeons', in D. Hay, P. Linebaugh, and E. P. Thompson (eds), *Albion's Fatal Tree* (London, 1975).

16 Rodger, *The Wooden World;* N. Rogers, 'Liberty Road: Opposition to Impressment in Britain during the American War of Independence', in C. Howell and R. Twomey (eds), *Jack Tar in History: Essays in the History of Maritime Life and Labour* (Frederickton, New Brunswick, 1991).

17 Rodger, *The Wooden World*, 72–3

18 ibid, 72.

19 C. Lloyd and J. L. S. Coulter, *Medicine and the Navy, 1200–1900* (Edinburgh, 1961), vol. III, 182.

20 Rodger, *The Wooden World*, 78, 100–106, 145–83, 196–203, 367; G. Dening, *Mr Bligh's Bad Language* (Cambridge, 1992), 27.

21 C. Winslow, 'Sussex Smugglers', in Hay, Linebaugh and Thompson, *Albion's Fatal Tree*.

22 *First, Second, and Third Reports from the Committee appointed to Enquire into the Illicit Practices used in Defrauding the Revenue*, in *House of Commons Sessional Papers of the Eighteenth Century*, ed. S. Lambert (London, 1975), vol. XXXVIII.

23 *First Report*, 25; *Second Report*, 281–2, 284, 287.

24 *First Report*, 11; *Second Report*, 215–21, 224–6; *Third Report*, 345–7.

25 *Second Report*, 223.

26 *First Report*, 11.

27 *Second Report*, 229–31.

28 *Third Report*, 332–3.

29 *Second Report*, 239; *Third Report*, 293, 335–43, 349; I owe the information about Pitt's policy to Professor Vivien Dietz.

30 P. Langford, *A Polite and Commercial People; England 1727–1783* (Oxford, 1989), 697.

31 I owe this idea to Professor Philip Harling.

32 I owe this suggestion to Dr Dror Wahrman.

33 Quoted by D. A. Baugh, 'Great Britain's "Blue-Water" Policy 1689–1815', *International History Review*, 10 (1988), 33.

34 See Hay, Linebaugh and Thompson, *Albion's Fatal Tree, passim*; J. Brewer and J. Styles (eds), *An Ungovernable People: The English and the Law in the Seventeenth and Eighteenth Centuries* (New Brunswick, 1980).

2

The Sinews of Power and European State-Building Theory

Thomas Ertman

Many chapters in this book, as well as numerous reviews, have emphasized the importance of John Brewer's *The Sinews of Power* for the historiography of eighteenth-century Britain.[1] Yet this is not the only field to which Brewer's book speaks. Its findings are, if anything, of even greater significance for those political scientists and historical sociologists who are currently engaged in attempts to construct a comprehensive theory of European state-building. This is so because the revisionist picture that Brewer paints of the British war machine after 1688 undermines basic assumptions found in existing models of war and state development in early-modern Europe. This brief chapter will first examine the implications of *The Sinews of Power* for the state-building literature, and then go on to outline a new perspective on European political development that can better accommodate both Brewer's results and those of other authors working in the oft-neglected subfields of administrative, financial and military history.

THEORIES OF STATE-BUILDING

The past two decades have witnessed a notable revival of interest in the problem of European state-building on the part of political scientists and historical sociologists. The origins of this revival date back to the late 1960s, when the Committee on Comparative Politics of the US Social Science Research Council (SSRC), having devoted nearly fifteen years of study to political development in Africa, Asia and Latin America, decided to focus its attention on Europe. The result was a series of conferences on 'the formation of nation states in western Europe', which brought together both social scientists and historians, the proceedings of which were first published in 1975.[2] It was at about this time that Perry Anderson's two volumes, *Passages from Antiquity to Feudalism* and *Lineages of the Absolutist State*, also made their appearance. In the mid-1980s, Theda Skocpol provided further encouragement for this line of research when she launched her call both to 'bring the state back in[to]' the social sciences and to take historical cases and historical data seriously.[3]

This call has not gone unheeded. During the past five years alone, numerous political scientists and historical sociologists of widely divergent theoretical bents (structuralist, neo-Marxists, rational choice) have produced a rapidly expanding body of new work on state-building in the west.[4] Despite its theoretical and methodological diversity, there is one point on which nearly all the recent state-building literature agrees – the central causal role played by war in driving forward the development of the European state. In the words of Charles Tilly, in his introduction to the SSRC volume, 'Preparation for war has been the great state-building activity.'[5]

This nearly universal focus in the recent state-building literature on geopolitics in general, and on war more specifically, can be traced back to the influence of an earlier generation of state theorists, the group of German scholars working at the turn of the century best represented by Otto Hintze and Max Weber.[6] In an article which first appeared in 1902 on 'state formation and constitutional development', Hintze outlined an alternative to the Marxist approach to state-building which stressed the impact of geographical position and international conflict, as opposed to class struggle, on the internal structure of states.[7] In one of his last published pieces, Hintze summed up in a few sentences his analysis of European state development during the early modern period based on nearly forty years of primary research:[8]

War became the great flywheel for the whole political enterprise of the modern state. This is how the standing armies with all their consequences, the battle fleets, the war industries, the new tax-systems (the backbone of which were war taxes), the new bureaucratic administration of finances, the amassing of a war chest and the system of state debt came into being. It was precisely the constant rivalry among the [great] powers . . . which produced an unheard-of exertion of energy, especially military and financial energy.

A similar stress on war as a causal factor in the state-building process can also be found in the works of both Hintze's teacher, Gustav Schmoller, and his young contemporary Joseph Schumpeter.[9] The best-known restatement of Hintze's position occurs, however, in Max Weber's *Economy and Society*:

[I]t was most often needs arising from the creation of standing armies called forth by power politics, and the development of financial systems connected with them, that more than anything else has furthered the trend towards bureaucratization.[10]

Yet in itself the simple insight that war was central to European state-building does not take us very far: for if war is truly the powerful causal factor that so many authorities, both classical and contemporary, claim it is, then it should also be able to explain variation in institutional development across the early-modern west, that is, why, for example, certain states in the eighteenth-century possessed relatively modern administrative and financial systems and others did not. In fact, the literature contains two contrasting, fully articulated models capable of accounting for differences in state structure with the help of war, one found in the work of Hintze and the other in that of Charles Tilly. As we shall see in a moment, the significance of Brewer's *Sinews of Power* lies in the fact that it undermines key assumptions found in each model, thereby casting doubt on their general validity.

In the essays brought together in *Staat und Verfassung*, Otto Hintze returns again and again to what he perceives to be a basic contrast in both the political and administrative histories of the continental European states and England. His most extensive discussion of this contrast occurs in an essay on power politics and government organization:

> The different systems of government and administration found among the large European states can be traced back in the main to two types, one of which can be called the English and the other the continental . . . [The principal difference between them] consists in the fact that on the continent military absolutism with a bureaucratic administration develops, while in England . . . the older line of development continues . . . and leads to what we usually term 'parliamentarism' and 'self-government'.[11]

Having thus established what he believes to be the fundamental variation in the European state-building process, Hintze goes on to explore its roots:

> What then is the cause of this pronounced institutional differentiation? . . . It was, above all, geographical position which had its effects . . . [I]n order to pursue its goals, England required no large land-force, only a navy . . . and a force that swims [*sic!*] out on the ocean is less suited to influencing and changing the inner structure of a state than a great army . . . [The situation was] completely different on the continent, where at that time the great standing armies and with them the absolutist, bureaucratic state arose . . . Great historical necessity led to this [outcome], and this [historical necessity] was the constant state of war that reigned on the continent, where no nation and no state was protected by a powerful border of the kind England possessed in the sea which surrounded it.[12]

As will be apparent from this extended quotation, Hintze's model represents a kind of formalization and universalization of some of the basic assumptions that underlay the old Whig historiography: geography is destiny, and it was the protection from military pressures afforded by England's island status that permitted that country to avoid absolutism, the common fate of its continental neighbours. Moreover, in this view there exists a simple one-to-one correspondence between forms of government and the organization of the state apparatus: absolutist states are administered through bureaucracies, whereas 'constitutional' states like England have preserved 'self-government', which in this case means administration through amateurs, namely the Justices of the Peace. In summary, Hintze's model can be reduced to the following proposition: the greater the threat of land warfare (itself a function of geography) to which a country is exposed, the greater is the likelihood that that country's rulers will successfully undermine representative institutions and create a standing army and centralized bureaucracy in order to meet the external threat.

Brewer's findings confound the predictions derived from such a model in three ways. First, he shows that the view of eighteenth-century Britain as somehow less 'militarized' than its continental neighbours, a supposed consequence of its geographical isolation, is entirely false. Whether measured by military expenditure as a percentage of total government spending, military expenditure as a percentage of national income, or military effectives as a percentage of total population, post-revolutionary Britain was one of the most highly militarized states in Europe.[13]

Second, Brewer undermines the widely held belief that a navy somehow requires less in the way of administrative or financial resources – in a word, bureaucratic infrastructure – than a land army. Echoing the findings of specialist studies like those of Daniel Baugh, Michael Duffy, John Ehrman and Donald Coleman, not to mention the Pepys diaries, he emphasizes that behind Britain's naval supremacy stood a vast array of support services employing thousands, co-ordinated and directed from above using bureaucratic methods.[14] In fact, compared to the task of building and maintaining a first-class navy, the mobilization of a large land army was, organizationally speaking, relatively simple, as the very small size of the Secretary-at-War's office attests.

Finally, if this last point concerning the navy were not enough to lay to rest the myth of an 'under-administered' Britain, then Brewer's research on the excise would certainly do so. This service numbered between 3,294 and 3,745 full-time employees during the 1740s and 1750s, thus rendering it larger than the entire bureaucracy of Frederician Prussia.[15] As Brewer further demonstrates, the excise was not simply large, it was also 'modern'. It was only thanks to a highly effective administrative structure that the service was able to perform its given task – the regular policing of something like 100,000 commercial establishments on a regular basis. Brewer's conclusions concerning this key government office are worth quoting in full:

Dependent upon a complex system of measurement and bookkeeping, organized as a rigid hierarchy based on experience and ability, and subject to strict discipline from its central office, the English Excise more closely approximated . . . Max Weber's idea of bureaucracy than any other government agency in eighteenth-century Europe.[16]

The Sinews of Power does more, however, than simply correct certain stubborn misconceptions about eighteenth-century Britain. By finally 'destroy[ing] the old Whig myth of a weak [British] state'[17] largely administered through 'self-government', Brewer has also rendered untenable the view that the creation of a modern state apparatus was pioneered exclusively by the absolutist states of continental Europe, and that the institutional complex comprised of 'standing armies, new tax systems . . . new bureaucratic financial administration . . . and the new system of state debt' brought forth by that 'great flywheel', war, was somehow exclusively linked to absolutism and militarism. Clearly such organizational innovations were also possible under non-absolutist conditions, a point that will be explored at greater length below.

The alternative model to that of Hintze, the one proposed by Charles Tilly, fares little better in light of Brewer's results, for it shares a number of common assumptions with its rival. In his well-known article 'War Making and State Making as Organized Crime', Tilly attempts to account, among other things, for variations in the 'bulk' of early modern states, that is, the size and extensiveness of the state apparatus. His general hypothesis contains a number of distinct claims:

> To the extent . . . that a given government invested in large standing armies – a very costly, if effective means of war making – the bureaucracy created to service the army was likely to become bulky. Furthermore, a government building a standing army while controlling a small population was likely to incur greater costs. . . . In the case of extraction, the smaller the pool of resources and the less commercialized the economy, other things being equal, the more difficult was the work of extracting resources to sustain war and other government activities; hence the more extensive was the fiscal apparatus. . . . On the whole, taxes on land were expensive to collect as compared with taxes on trade, especially large flows of trade past easily controlled checkpoints.[18]

No model is valuable unless it can explain concrete outcomes, and Tilly goes on to apply his propositions to the cases of Prussia and England:

> Brandenburg-Prussia was the classic case of high cost for available resources. The Prussian effort to build an army matching those of its larger Continental neighbors created an immense structure. . . . England illustrated the corollary of that proposition [concerning the

ease of resource extraction], with a relatively large and commercialized pool of resources drawn on by a relatively small fiscal apparatus.[19]

The picture painted by Tilly, then, is one of an early-modern Europe where the size of a given state apparatus, which is broadly equated with its degree of bureaucratization, varies directly with the size of a state's standing army and inversely with the degree of commercialization of its domestic economy. Thus land powers like Prussia and France with largely agrarian economies should possess very substantial bureaucracies, whereas the fiscal and administrative machinery of an economically advanced sea power like England should remain relatively modest in size.

There is no need to belabour the point that Tilly's assumptions about the organizational requirements of standing armies and about the relative size and character of the English and Prussian states, both of which he shares with Hintze, are no longer tenable in the light of Brewer's findings. Tilly does make one claim, however, that clearly distinguishes his model from that of Hintze. This is the hypothesis, derived from Gabriel Ardant, that 'the choice of fiscal strategy probably made an additional difference',[20] that is, states that were willing and able to tax commerce did not require the large fiscal apparatus required by states that were forced to tax mainly land.

We have here, then, an alternative to Hintze's geography-based model that seeks to explain fundamental variations in state structures across Europe at least in part by the level of commercialization that a given state's economy has reached. Indeed, Michael Mann has taken this idea a step further and suggested the existence of separate 'fiscal' and 'mobilized' alternatives in the state-building process, which he then identifies respectively with 'constitutionalism' and 'absolutism'.[21]

Yet Brewer's excise research also confounds the logic underlying such hypotheses, for it demonstrates that trade was not relatively easy to tax compared to land. On the contrary, the accurate measuring and monitoring of commercial flows in Britain required a vast, highly trained staff, whereas it was the collection of the land tax that could be left largely to amateurs. That this finding does not merely reflect English peculiarities is illustrated by the fact that the total number of Prussian officials concerned primarily with land-tax collection could not have numbered more than 500–600, thus rendering that part of the Prussian bureaucracy less than one-fifth the size of the English excise and one-third the size of the British customs service. From a purely technical standpoint, it was commercial taxes rather than taxes on land that posed the greatest organizational challenge to developing states.

In *The Sinews of Power* John Brewer thus presents important new evidence on the inner workings of the eighteenth-century British state which undermines two established models of European state-building. The first of these models, that of Hintze, holds that the geographical position of a given state within Europe, and hence the degree of direct military pressure to which it was subjected, largely determined the path of institutional development followed before 1789, while in Tilly's alternative schema the relative level of commercialization achieved by a given country has come to replace geopolitical location as the key independent variable. Brewer's book has rendered both these theories untenable because it demonstrates that fundamental claims made by each about the character of the eighteenth-century British state are empirically inaccurate.

It should be emphasized here that John Brewer's is not the only historical work to call into question central tenets of the existing state-building literature. Another basic assumption that both the Hintze and the Tilly models share is that France and Prussia were, institutionally speaking, quite similar kinds of states – both centralized, bureaucratized absolute monarchies. Yet while it is certainly true that the political systems of these two countries had much in common, the same cannot be said of their respective administrative and financial infrastructures. Recent studies of *ancien régime* France paint a vivid picture of a state apparatus dominated by venal office-holding and dependent for its short-term credit needs on clans of financiers who had effectively appropriated large portions of the country's tax-base.[22] In eighteenth-century Prussia, by contrast, officials possessed no proprietary claims whatsoever over their positions,[23] and the country's rulers employed a variety of unorthodox expedients, from the *Kantonverfassung* recruitment system to the running of regular budget surpluses and the ruthless taxation of enemy territory, precisely in order to avoid the clutches of the financiers.[24]

TIMING

If the available theories of European state-building are incompatible with our current understanding of central cases like those of early-modern Britain and France, clearly a new explanatory framework must be found, one more in keeping with the revisionist picture of early-modern states that the historical literature is currently painting. Yet where should one begin with such a daunting task? I suggest that we look for inspiration to the neighbouring field of economic history. In that field, the concept of timing has proved to be of great explanatory value. It has become a commonplace that the moment at which a country begins to industrialize relative to all other countries has a very great influence on both the trajectory of its industrialization process and the overall character of the developed economy that emerges at the end of that process.[25] Thus many of the structural features that today distinguish Britain's economy from that of Germany can be traced back to the fact that the former was the first industrial nation, whereas the latter was a later industrializer. I believe that a similar focus on the role of timing in the process of state, as opposed to economic, development can yield equally fruitful results.

As mentioned earlier, a broad consensus exists in the state-building literature of the 1970s and 1980s that the division of Europe into competing, and often warring, political units stimulated the creation of ever-more-sophisticated state institutions across the continent. In its most general form, this geopolitical argument claims that the existence of hostile neighbours forced every European polity to raise armed forces to protect itself, and that as these forces became larger and more permanent, so too did the fiscal and administrative infrastructure created to support them. Furthermore, once this infrastructure was in place, the ever-present threat of war provided a ruler with a powerful incentive to introduce rationalizing reforms so as to gain a military advantage over his or her rivals. A competitive geopolitical setting is thus supposed to have led to a generalized process of state growth and modernization to which only special circumstances (Hintze: geographical isolation; Tilly: commercial sophistication) could furnish exceptions.

Yet what this 'consensus' theory overlooks is that while geopolitical pressure may indeed have been the single most important factor pushing forward state development in medieval and early-modern Europe, such pressure was 'non-simultaneous', that is, it did not act in a temporally uniform way across the continent. The economically and culturally more advanced regions located within the former borders of the old Roman Empire became engulfed in sustained, large-scale warfare and the requirements generated thereby relatively early. As a result, polities in those regions pioneered the construction of sophisticated administrative, financial and military systems which, though highly effective when first introduced, became increasingly dysfunctional as conditions on the continent changed. More significantly still, they proved nearly impervious to fundamental reform thanks to the determined resistance of those groups tied materially and ideologically to long-standing institutions and practices.

By contrast, the polities located in the poorer, less accessible regions to the east and north of the former Roman heartland were not exposed to similar kinds of military threats until much later, and hence could put off for several centuries the task of building large, centrally directed state apparatuses manned by permanent officials.[26] This delayed start to the process of intensive state-building brought latecomers many advantages compared to the pioneers, most notably their ready access to the most up-to-date 'technologies' of governance, much as was the case with Europe's late industrializers in the nineteenth century.

It was in the southern and western areas of Europe – Italy, the Iberian peninsula, France, England and the Netherlands – that, parallel to the revival of the money economy, paid troops first began to replace feudal levies from about the 1100s onwards.[27] As drawn-out conflicts like the Hundred Years War, the Spanish *reconquista* and the interminable rivalries among the Italian states rendered contract armies quasi-permanent, rulers saw themselves obliged to create more durable administrative structures to finance and oversee such forces. What were those structures to look like? Luckily, the secular rulers of this period possessed a model to which they could turn for inspiration and guidance – the church, the west's most sophisticated organization during the 1100s and 1200s and for a long time thereafter. The latter furnished pioneer state-builders with both trained personnel (clerics) and an emerging body of administrative law, the canon law of benefices, which would prove invaluable in the construction of state bureaucracies.

The fact that it was the canonical conception of the benefice that provided the legal framework for secular offices in western and southern Europe had far-reaching consequences for the future institutional development of those regions. This was so because canon law and church custom granted extensive, proprietary rights to office-holders such as life tenure and the opportunity, with papal approval, to resign and name one's own successor (*resignatio in favorem tertii*). Such rights were formalized and extended further in the 1300s and 1400s, when non-clerics came to replace churchmen in the nascent bureaucracies of Europe's state-building pioneers. Driven by a desire to secure the future status and economic well-being of their extended families, secular administrators exploited the legal possibilities inherent in the canon law, together with their position as valued experts vital to the national war effort, to strengthen the proprietary interpretation of office.[28] As a result, by the late 1400s, France, England, Castile, Portugal and the Netherlands, as well as the papacy and several Italian states, all possessed sophisticated administrative infrastructures, but ones in which office-holders had, albeit in varying degrees, turned their positions into private property.[29]

Even more central to the military capacity of Europe's most advanced states than trained personnel was cash, for only with cash could an army be paid on a regular basis. Where were large quantities of ready money to be found? Increasingly during the 1300s and 1400s, desperate governments turned to tax-farming as a way to generate much-needed coin in advance of tax receipts. Alternatively, key posts within the expanding fiscal bureaucracy such as tax receiverships or paymasterships of military forces could be granted or sold to moneylenders ('office-holder-financiers'), who would then be required to borrow money on their own personal credit in order to meet the state's cash needs.[30] No matter what method was chosen, the result was a growing colonization and appropriation of the state apparatus by businessmen whose motives and goals were far different from those of their nominal political masters.

The French invasion of Italy in 1494 ushered in over a century and a half of almost uninterrupted large-scale warfare that affected most areas of western and southern Europe until the Peace of the Pyrenees between France and Spain in 1659. Yet this extreme dose of geopolitical pressure did not foster a wave of institutional rationalization among the pioneer state-builders we have just examined; rather, it induced a broadening and deepening of the kinds of problematic administrative and financial practices adopted during the earlier, formative stages of state development. In the face of the financial demands of war, the traffic in offices among private owners was supplemented by the direct sale of new offices by the state itself in France, Spain, Portugal, the southern Netherlands, the papal curia, Venice, Naples, Sicily, Piedmont and Milan, an expedient which served to strengthen the proprietary character of the office-holding system more generally.[31] In England, while Cavendish's Case of 1587 shut the door on the creation and sale of new offices, it did so in the name of existing office-holders, who argued successfully that their positions were their own freehold property and hence that any multiplication of offices would undermine the value of that property.[32] Meanwhile, the intrusion of financial interests into the sphere of administration continued, either in the form of an extension of tax-farming (Spain, Portugal, Naples, England) or through an intensive use of both farming and credit advanced by office-financiers (France, Piedmont).[33]

Thus we have seen that those areas of Europe where the process of intensive state development commenced during the middle ages shared a common state-building trajectory which is striking when one considers the great divergence among them in the sphere of politics more narrowly defined (absolutism in France, the papacy, Naples and later Castile; limited monarchy in England and Aragon). This was so because the similar choices which these states made in the areas of administration and finance during the first phase of state-building laid down the path they would follow for centuries to come by narrowing the range of options available to them in the future. Proprietary office-holding, tax-farming and 'inside' finance provided by office-holder-financiers created well-entrenched, politically powerful interest groups which stood to lose from any major break with existing administrative and financial practices and which proved quite capable of protecting their corporate privileges against the assaults of 'modernizing' reformers.

Those states in northern, central and eastern Europe that developed later followed a very different trajectory. The principal reason for this was that these 'newcomers' did not begin to construct specialized, professionally staffed administrative, fiscal and judicial organs – a task already completed in France or England by the late middle ages – until after 1500.[34] By this time, the world around them had changed in significant ways when compared to the 1100s and 1200s. Whereas the rulers of Angevin England or Capetian France were acquainted with only a very limited range of administrative paradigms and financial techniques, the intervening centuries had witnessed great progress in both these areas, partly, of course, as a result of the stimulus provided by that first cohort of state-builders. In addition to canon law, Roman law had been revived, and customary and feudal law systematized and extended. Hence alternative conceptions of office to that provided by the church now existed, and an abundant supply of trained secular jurists stood ready, thanks to the new universities, to put them into practice. At the same time, the growth of the European financial community in both size and sophistication, thanks to the independent dynamics of commercial expansion, opened up a whole range of possibilities for both short- and long-term borrowing on either local or international markets.

Furthermore, the later state-builders could benefit from the experiences, both positive and negative, of the pioneers. The methods and forms of organizations which the more 'advanced' states employed could be studied and imitated, often with the help of experts with some real or pretended first-hand knowledge of foreign conditions. At the same time, a conscious effort could be made to avoid those institutions or practices that appeared to be dysfunctional, especially if they undermined military effectiveness.

If one examines in greater detail the new administrative and financial institutions that Europe's late state-builders – the German territorial states, the Habsburg Monarchy, Sweden, Denmark and Russia – called into being during the sixteenth, seventeenth and eighteenth centuries, one is immediately struck by two things. First, in none of these countries did proprietary office-holding take root. All built up substantial, relatively professional centralized bureaucracies during this period in which officials could be hired and fired at will and possessed no legal rights over their positions or the income derived from them, a far cry from the situation among the state-building pioneers.[35] Certainly, the bureaucracies of these states left much to be desired as far as quality of personnel, methods of recruitment and levels of personal honesty were concerned. Moreover, in the absolutist states among this group a continuous struggle took place between the bureaucratic imperatives of order and regularity and the desire on the part of unfettered rulers to intervene in the administrative process.[36] Nevertheless, the thoroughly non-proprietary character of their bureaucracies clearly distinguishes these latecomers from the western and southern European states discussed earlier.

Second, all these countries avoided the extensive appropriation of public rights and resources by financiers characteristic of states further to the west. Official or unofficial national banks were founded in Sweden, Denmark, Austria, Prussia and Russia between the 1660s and the 1760s, and all but Prussia used fiduciary money as their principal source of short-term credit, while at the same time borrowing long-term on international capital markets such as that of Amsterdam.[37] As mentioned above, Prussia avoided even these practices until the end of the eighteenth century in order to remain entirely free from dependence on any form of credit. Again, the contrast with the situation in a country like France, where office-holder-financiers (there called *comptables*) provided the state with most of its working cash right up until the revolution, is striking.[38]

How can we account for the similarities shared by these latecomers of northern, central and eastern Europe, similarities which set them apart so sharply from their western neighbours? Clearly absolutism is not the common thread here, as the older state-building literature would have us believe. Many of the leading German territorial states, including Saxony, Württemberg and Hanover, were never absolutist. Moreover, Sweden can only be defined as such for the period 1693–1718, and the application of that label to the Habsburg Monarchy is problematic for much of the seventeenth and eighteenth centuries.

As intimated above, the answer lies in timing. When the German and Scandinavian rulers of the 1500s and 1600s set out to reshape and expand their domestic institutions so as to meet the administrative and financial challenges posed by large-scale warfare, as well as by socio-economic change and religious upheaval, they could draw on the lessons of over five centuries of western state-building. Thanks to the benefits of hindsight, they were forewarned of the negative long-term consequences of proprietary office-holding and were free to build their bureaucracies around a newer conception of the official as a servant of the crown. In the financial sphere, the Bank of England and the Exchequer bills it managed soon provided a tangible alternative to methods of tax-farming or 'inside' finance.

The flow of lessons and innovations carried by pamphleteers and cosmopolitan experts did not, however, only occur between the western states and the eastern and northern newcomers, for timing played an important role even within the group of late state-builders. Thus the new administrative system introduced by Gustavus Adolphus, itself inspired by German precedents, provided one of the models for the reforms of the Great Elector, and Peter the Great conducted a thorough study of Danish, Prussian and especially Swedish institutions before unleashing his own revolution in government upon Russia.[39] Likewise, the successive defeats of the Austrians at the hands of Frederick the Great led that country to introduce Prussian-inspired innovations into both its administrative and its military systems.[40] In all these cases, modernizing rulers benefited from another advantage of the latecomer: because the process of state-building in their respective countries had not advanced very far by the time of their initiatives, they faced less resistance to innovation and reform from powerful entrenched interests than was the case in many western countries.

This pattern of institutional development found among the late state-builders between 1500 and the French Revolution stands in sharp contrast to the fate of the pioneers during this time. As we have seen, the latter responded to the intense geopolitical pressures of the period 1494 to 1659 not by carrying out modernizing reforms that would have substantially raised their military effectiveness, but rather by making more extensive use of established practices like proprietary office-holding, tax-farming and 'inside' finance. This remained equally true after 1660, as the case of *ancien régime* France illustrates most vividly. From 1688 onwards France found her hegemonic ambitions challenged by an ever-more-powerful coalition of opponents. The shortcomings of her financial and administrative arrangements, as well as their deleterious consequences for battlefield performance, were widely recognized, and alternative methods almost guaranteed to enhance her military performance were readily available.

Yet, contrary to the predictions of the simple geopolitical model of state development, French leaders were never able successfully to respond to this strong external stimulus with radical, permanent, modernizing reforms, although this was not for want of trying. Despite the innovation represented by the *intendants*, the character of the *ancien régime*'s bureaucracy remained fundamentally proprietary to the last, and a national bank was not created until 1800. In the end, the political power of venal office-holders, *comptables*, tax-farmers and their allies proved too great to overcome within the confines of the existing political system.[41] A similar situation obtained, though in less extreme form, on the Iberian and Italian peninsulas and in the Netherlands.

THE BRITISH CASE

This brief comparative discussion of state-building in early modern Europe allows us to see the case of Stuart and Hanoverian Britain in a new light. For, unlike other early state-builders, Britain *did* make a decisive break with the past, as the evidence provided by Brewer's book clearly shows. Though Aylmer's three 'P's – patrimony, patronage, purchase – had by no means been completely eliminated, those functions most central to the country's military effectiveness were now performed by a distinctly non-proprietary bureaucracy closer to that of Sweden than France. In the financial sphere, the country had soon equipped itself with the most modern public-credit system on the entire continent, one that never ceased to provoke awe and wonder among foreign observers.

How then were reformers in Britain able to overcome the institutional legacies of early state-building, when their counterparts in France, Spain, Italy or the Netherlands were not? *The Sinews of Power* provides two answers. First, England's relatively infrequent involvement in costly foreign wars between 1453 and 1688, combined with the restrictions on the creation of new offices imposed by Cavendish's Case, meant that that country found itself burdened in the late seventeenth century with far fewer proprietary office-holders than most of its neighbours.[42] Second, and more importantly, the presence of a strong Parliament possessed of a 'suspicious and sceptical attitude towards the conduct of government' allowed Britain to react to the heightened military threat posed by Louis XIV by constructing a *public* fiscal-military apparatus, remarkably untainted by private interests'.[43] As a result, '[b]etween 1688 and 1714, the British state underwent a radical transformation, acquiring all of the main features of a powerful fiscal-military state'.[44]

Though one might argue with Brewer's contention that the 'radical transformation' of the British state to which he refers began in 1688, as opposed to 1642 or 1660,[45] his focus on the crucial role played by Parliament in bringing about this transformation is highly suggestive. It will be recalled that the prime impediment to radical administrative and financial reform among the pioneers was not an absence of either external pressure or good ideas, both of which were in abundant supply after 1500, but rather the determined resistance of well-connected office-holders and financiers with a strong material and ideal interest in the status quo. This was as true in early-Stuart England as it was in seventeenth-century Spain or eighteenth-century France.[46] Given this fact, one can readily see why the metamorphosis of Parliament from an occasional into a standing body, dominated as it was by men hostile towards many features of the old administrative system, would make such a difference: it provided reformers with the weighty political ally they needed in order to overcome the opposition of deeply entrenched vested interests.

The broader implications of the British case as presented by Brewer seem clear. The institutional legacies of early state-building, while stubborn and long-lasting, could be overcome through political change of a kind that decisively strengthened the hand of reformers. Yet such change could take a variety of different forms, as the experience of other western and southern European polities after 1789 indicates. In France, as in Britain a century earlier, the drive against venality and 'inside' finance was spearheaded by a national legislative assembly catapulted to power by a revolution, although the character of that revolution was rather different from its English counterpart. In Spain, the Netherlands and Italy, however, it was not so much the formal activities of legislative assemblies as the force of French arms that finally enabled local reformers to sweep away institutions and practices rooted in the world of the middle ages.

John Brewer's *The Sinews of Power* has proved to be an enormously fruitful book for those of us in political science and historical sociology interested in theories of state development. By presenting uncomfortable new evidence based on pioneering empirical research, Brewer has helped to undermine the established models of European state-building, thereby forcing us to reconceptualize that enormously complex process. It is a task that will occupy us all for a long time to come.

NOTES

I would like to thank John Brewer, Samuel Cohn, Peter Hall, Joanna Innes, Paul Lucas, Peter Paret, Theodore Rabb, Bo Rothstein, Theda Skocpol, Lawrence Stone and the members of the 'State and Capitalism' study group at the Center for European Studies, Harvard University, for their helpful suggestions and criticisms of various versions of this chapter. My greatest debt, however, is to Susan Pedersen, without whose encouragement and support this piece could not have been written.

1 For example, in his review in *The New York Review of Books* (15 March, 1990), Lawrence Stone has written (p. 52): 'Brewer has thus twice changed the direction of British historiography: once, in 1976, when he destroyed the Namierite mythology of a rule by a narrow self-centered elite; and with this book now, when he destroys the old Whig myth of a weak state.'

2 Charles Tilly (ed.), *The Formation of National States in Western Europe* (Princeton: Princeton University Press, 1975). The account of the genesis of this volume was derived from ibid., ix, xiii.

3 Theda Skocpol, 'Bringing the State Back In: Strategies of Analysis in Current Research', in Peter Evans, Dietrich Rueschemeyer and Theda Skocpol (eds), *Bringing the State Back In* (Cambridge: Cambridge University Press, 1985), 3–37.

4 The most notable examples include Charles Tilly, 'War Making and State Making as Organized Crime', in Evans, Rueschemeyer and Skocpol, *Bringing the State Back In*, 169–91; Anthony Giddens, *The Nation-State and Violence* (Berkeley: University of California Press, 1985); Michael Mann, *The Sources of Social Power*, volume I, *A History of Power from the Beginning to A.D. 1760* (Cambridge: Cambridge University Press, 1986); Margaret Levi, *Of Rule and Revenue* (Berkeley: University of California Press, 1988); Brian Downing, 'Constitutionalism, Warfare, and Political Change in Early Modern Europe', *Theory and Society*, 17/1 (January 1988), 7–56.

5 Tilly. 'Reflections on the History of European State-Making', in Tilly, *The Formation of Nation States*, 3–83, 74. See also Tilly, 'War Making and State Making', 170: 'War makes states, I shall claim.' Despite many differences in detail, the importance of war (and geopolitical competition more generally) as a force for institutional change is also stressed by Gianfranco Poggi, *The Development of the Modern State* (Stanford: Stanford University Press, 1978), 60, 66, 71; Michael Mann, *Sources*, 430, 433, 440, 453 ff., 483 ff., 511–12; Levi, *Of Rule and Revenue*, 99, 105–8; Giddens, *Nation-State*, 102, 113 ff. Though Anderson, in his *Lineages of the Absolutist State* (New Left Books, 1974), is reluctant to integrate war fully into his explicit theoretical framework, it crops up again and again as a causal variable in his individual country chapters.

War and/or geopolitical competition is *the* primary causal variable in the following articles: Richard Bean, 'War and the Birth of the Nation State', *Journal of Economic History*, 23/1 (March 1973), 202–21; Ronald Batchfelder and Herman Freudenberger, 'On the Rational Origins of the Modern Centralized State', *Explorations in Economic History*, 20 (1983), 1–13; Aristide Zolberg, 'Strategic Interaction and the Formation of Modern States: France and England', in Ali Kazancigil (ed.), *The State in Global Perspective* (London: Gower, 1986), 72–106; and Downing, 'Constitutionalism, Warfare, and Political Change'.

6 Theda Skocpol has remarked upon the great influence of Hintze and Weber on current discussions of state development in her 'Bringing the State Back In', 7–9.

7 Otto Hintze, 'Staatenbildung und Verfassungsentwicklung', in his *Staat und*

Verfassung, ed. Gerhard Oestreich (Göttingen: Vandenhoeck & Ruprecht, 1970), 34–51, esp. 34–7.

8 Otto Hintze, 'Wesen und Wandlung des modernen Staats', in *Staat und Verfassung*, 470–96, here at 480.

9 See, for example, Schmoller's article 'Historische Betrachtungen über Staatenbildung und Finanzentwicklung', *Jahrbuch für Gesetzgebung, Verwaltung und Volkswirtschaft im Deutschen Reich ['Schmollers Jahrbuch']*, 33/1 (1909), 1–64; and Joseph Schumpeter, 'Die Krise des Steuerstaates', in his *Aufsätze zur Soziologie* (Tübingen: J. C. B. Mohr, 1953), 1–71.

10 Max Weber, *Wirtschaft und Gesellschaft* (fifth edn, Tübingen: J. C. B. Mohr, 1976), 560.

11 *Staat und Verfassung*, 424–56, here at 427.

12 'Machtpolitik und Regierungsverfassung', in ibid., 427–8. I have chosen to quote from this crucial essay at some length because it is not currently available in English translation.

13 John Brewer, *The Sinews of Power: War, Money and the English State 1688–1783* (London: Unwin Hyman, 1989), 37–42.

14 ibid., 34–7.

15 ibid., 66. Hubert Johnson, in his *Frederick the Great and His Officials* (New Haven: Yale University Press, 1975), has calculated that Prussian central administration employed 641 officials in 1754 (British figure: 971 in 1755), and that the entire bureaucracy, including local officials like *Landräte*, numbered between 2,100 and 3,100 (283–8). At the time, the field administrations of the British revenue boards alone were over twice as large (all British figures from Brewer, *Sinews*, 66).

16 Brewer, *Sinews*, 68.

17 To use the characterization of Lawrence Stone in his *New York Review of Books* article (see note 1).

18 Tilly, 'War Making', 181–2.

19 ibid., 182.

20 ibid.

21 Mann, *Sources*, 456. See also his earlier article, 'State and Society, 1130–1815: An Analysis of English State Finances', *Political Power and Social Theory*, I (1980) 165–208, where he states (196) 'At the other extreme, a rich trading country like England could maintain great power status without reaching a high level of tax extraction and, therefore, without a standing army.' Mann explicitly acknowledges his theoretical debt to Tilly in *Sources*, 433.

22 See, among other works, Daniel Dessert, *Argent, pouvoir et société au grand siècle* (Paris: Fayard, 1984); Françoise Bayard, *Le Monde des financiers au XVIIᵉ Siècle* (Paris: Flammarion, 1988); André Corvisier, *Louvois* (Paris: Fayard, 1983); Clive Church, *Revolution and Red Tape: The French Ministerial Bureaucracy 1770–1850* (Oxford: Clarendon Press, 1981); James Pritchard, *Louis XV's Navy 1748–1762* (Kingston: McGill-Queen's University Press, 1987); Roger Mettam, *Power and Faction in Louis XIV's France* (Oxford: Basil Blackwell, 1988), as well as the unpublished D. Phil. thesis of D. A. Parrott, 'The Administration of the French Army during the Ministry of Cardinal Richelieu' (Oxford University 1985). This recent wave of specialized studies in the area of French administrative and financial history confirms and deepens the picture of the *ancien régime* state first presented by older studies such as Martin Göhring, *Die Aemterkäuflichkeit im Ancien Régime* (Berlin: Verlag Dr. Emil Ebering, 1938); Roland Mousnier, *La Vénalité des offices sous Henri IV*

et Louis XIII (second edn, Paris: P.U.F., 1971); and J. F. Bosher, *French Finances 1770–1795* (Cambridge: Cambridge University Press, 1970).

23 Otto Hintze, 'Einleitende Darstellung der Behördenorganisation und allgemeinen Verwaltung in Preussen beim Regierungsantritt Friedrichs II.', *'Acta Borussica*, 6/1 (Berlin: Paul Parey, 1901), 277–9. On the relative importance of venality in the eighteenth-century Prussian bureaucracy see also Horst Möller, 'Aemterkäuflichkeit in Brandenburg-Preussen im 17. und 18. Jahrhundert', in Klaus Malettke (ed.), *Aemterkäuflichkeit: Aspekte Sozialer Mobilität im Europäischen Vergleich (17. und 18. Jahrhundert)* (Berlin: Colloquium Verlag, 1980), 156–76, esp. 156, 159.

24 Ernst Klein, *Geschichte der Oeffentlichen Finanzen in Deutschland (1500–1870)* (Wiesbaden: Franz Steiner Verlag, 1974), 48–60; on the *Kantonverfassung*, see Curt Jany, 'Die Kantonverfassung des alten preussischen Heeres', in Otto Büsch and Wolfgang Neugebauer (eds), *Moderne Preussische Geschichte 1648–1947* (Berlin: Walter de Gruyter, 1981), 767–809.

25 The classic statement of this view is Alexander Gerschenkron, 'Economic Backwardness in Historical Perspective', in *Economic Backwardness in Historical Perspective* (Cambridge, Mass.: Harvard University Press, 1962), 5–30, esp. 7–11.

26 In his essay on bureaucracy, Hintze remarks: 'The development of administration in Germany lay about 200 years behind that in France.' Yet he never explores in a systematic way the theoretical implications of this fact. See Otto Hintze, 'Der Beamtenstand', in his *Soziologie und Geschichte*, ed. Gerhard Oestreich (Göttingen: Vandenhoeck & Ruprecht, 1982), 66–125, here at 82.

27 Ferdinand Lot, *L'Art militaire et les armées au moyen age* (2 vols, Paris: Payot, 1946), vol. II, 423–5; John Beeler, *Warfare in Feudal Europe 730–1200* (Ithaca: Cornell University Press, 1971), 58–9; Philippe Contamine, *La Guerre au moyen age* (Paris: P.U.F., 1980), 192 ff.

28 This process of appropriation was analysed by Weber in a little-noticed passage in *Wirtschaft und Gesellschaft*, 598–604. On the influence of the canon law of benefices on secular conceptions of office-holding, see Brigide Schwarz, 'Aemterkäuflichkeit, eine Institution des Absolutismus und ihre mittelalterlichen Wurzeln', in *Staat und Gesellschaft in Mittelalter und früher Neuzeit: Gedenkschrift für Joachim Leuschner* (Göttingen: Vandenhoeck & Ruprecht, 1983), 176–96; José María García Marín, *El oficio público en Castilla durante la baja edad media* (Seville: University of Seville, 1974), 22–7; Wolfgang Reinhard, 'Staatsmacht als Kreditproblem. Zur Struktur und Funktion des frühneuzeitlichen Aemterhandels', in Enst Hindrichs (ed.), *Absolutismus* (Frankfurt: Suhrkamp, 1986), 214–48, here at 216–20. On the somewhat more complex English case, see W. S. Holdsworth, *A History of English Law* (seventh edn, 16 vols, London: Methuen, 1956), vol. III, 98, 139–42; Frederick Pollock and F. W. Maitland, *The History of English Law before the Time of Edward I* (second edn, 2 vols, Cambridge: Cambridge University Press, 1968), vol. II, 135.

29 France: François Olivier-Martin, 'La nomination aux offices royaux et d'après les practiques de la chancellerie', in *Mélanges Paul Fournier* (Paris: Recueil Sirey, 1929), 487–501; Kuno Böse, 'Die Aemterkäuflichkeit in Frankreich vom 14. bis 16. Jahrhundert', in Ilja Mieck (ed.), *Aemterhandel im Spätmittelalter und im 16. Jahrhundert* (Berlin: Colloquium Verlag, 1984), 83–111, here at 91–3; England: J. C. Sainty, 'The Tenure of Office in the Exchequer', *English Historical Review*, 80/316 (July 1965), 449–75, here at 451–3; Robin Storey, 'England: Aemterhandel im 15. und 16. Jahrhundert' (in English), in Mieck, *Aemterhandel*, 196–204; Castile: Francisco Tomás y Valiente, 'Origen

bajomedieval de la patrimonialización y la enajenación de oficios públicos en Castilla', *Actos del I Symposium de Historia de la Administración* (Madrid: Instituto de Estudios Administrativos, 1970), 125–59; Portugal: António Hespanha, *História das instituições* (Coimbra: Livraria Almedina, 1982), 389–93; Netherlands: Michael Erbe, 'Aspekte des Aemterhandels in den Niederlanden im späten Mittelalter und in der Frühen Neuzeit', in Mieck, *Aemterhandel*, 112–31; papacy: Bernhard Schimmelpfennig, 'Der Aemterhandel an der römischen Kurie von Pius II. bis zum Sacco di Roma (1458–1527)', ibid., 4–41; Naples: Roberto Mantelli, *Burocrazia e finanze pubbliche nel regno di Napoli a meta del cinquecento* (Naples: Lucio Pironti Editore, 1981), 91–2; Milan: Alessandro Visconti, *La pubblica amministrazione nello stato Milanese durante il predominio straniero (1541–1796)* (Rome: Athenaeum, 1913), 245; Federico Chabod, 'Usi e abusi nell'amministrazione dello Stato di Milano a mezzo il cinquecento', in *Carlo V e il suo impero* (Turin: Einaudi, 1983), 451–521, here at 458.

30 E. B. Fryde and M. M. Fryde, 'Public Credit with Special Reference to North-Western Europe', in M. M. Postin, E. E. Rich and Edward Miller (eds), *Cambridge Economic History of Europe*, vol. III (Cambridge: Cambridge University Press, 1963), 430–553, here at 454–69, 478–84; Miguel Angel Ladero Quesada, 'Los judios Castellanos del siglo XV en el arrendamiento de impuestos reales', in *El siglo XV en Castilla* (Barcelona: Editorial Ariel, 1982), 143–67; *La hacienda real de Castilla en el siglo XV* (Tenerife: Universidad de La Laguna, 1973), 22–30; Winifred Küchler, 'Aemterkäuflichkeit in den Ländern der Krone Aragons', in Johannes Vincke (ed.), *Gesammelte Aufsätze zur Kulturgeschichte Spaniens*, vol. 27 (Münster: Aschendorffsche Verlagsbuchhandlung, 1973), 1–26, here at 23–6.

31 For a general overview of this development, see K. W. Swart, *Sale of Offices in the 17th Century* (The Hague: Martinus Nijhoff, 1949). For the case of Milan, see Chabod, 'Usi e abusi', 458 ff.

32 Holdsworth, *A History*, vol. I, 257, 260–1. According to G. E. Aylmer, three principles structured the civil service of Charles I – patrimony, patronage and purchase: G. E. Aylmer, *The King's Servants* (second edn, London: Routledge & Kegan Paul, 1974), 89. The case of Portugal provides interesting parallels to that of England. There existing proprietary office-holders largely succeeded in suppressing the public sale of offices following independence from Spain in 1640 in order to strengthen their own grip over the administrative system: Hespanha, *História*, 391–2.

33 Antonio Domínguez Ortiz, *Politica y hacienda de Felipe IV* (Madrid: Ediciones Pegaso, 1983), 92–101, 103–110, 174 ff.; António Hespanha, *Vísperas del Leviatán: Instituciones y poder politico (Portugal, siglo XVII)* (Madrid: Taurus, 1989), 114; Mantelli, *Burocrazia*, 229 ff; Robert Ashton, 'Revenue Farming under the Early Stuarts', *Economic History Review*, second series, 8/3 (April 1956), 310–22; Robert Ashton, *The Crown and the Money Markets 1603–1640* (Oxford: Clarendon Press, 1960); Bayard, *Le Monde des financiers*; Enrico Stumpo, *Finanza e stato moderno nel Piemonte del seicento* (Rome: Istituto Storico Italiano, 1979), 109, 187 ff.

34 Georg von Below, 'Die Neuorganisation der Verwaltung in den deutschen Territorien des 16. Jahrhunderts', in his *Territorium und Staat* (Munich: R. Oldenbourg, 1900), 283–98; Gustav Schmoller, 'Der deutsche Beamtenstaat vom 16. bis 18. Jahrhundert', in *Umrisse und Untersuchunungen zur Verfassungs-, Verwaltungs- und Wirtschaftsgeschichte besonders des Preussischen Staates im 17. und 18. Jahrhundert* (Hildesheim: Georg Olms Verlag, 1974), 289–313;

Kurt Jeserich, Hans Pohl and Georg-Christoph Unruh (eds), *Deutsche Verwaltungsgeshichte* (6 vols, Stuttgart: Deutsche Verlags-Anstalt, 1983), vol. I, 289, 300 ff.; Michael Roberts, *The Early Vasas* (Cambridge: Cambridge University Press, 1968), 43–5, 187–90 and *passim*; E. Ladewig Petersen, 'From Domain State to Tax State,' *Scandinavian Economic History Journal*, 23/5 (1975), 116–48.

35 Swart, *Sale of Offices*, 94–6; Michael Roberts, *The Swedish Imperial Experience 1560–1718* (Cambridge: Cambridge University Press, 1979), 60; Birgit Bjerre Jensen, *Udnaevnelseretten i enevaeldens magtpolitiske system 1660–1730* (Copenhagen: G. E. C. Gads Forlag, 1987), 318–29; Otto Hintze, 'Einleitende Darstellung', 276–8; Jeserich, Pohl and Unruh, *Deutsche Verwaltungsgeschichte*, vol. I, 494; Brenda Meehan-Waters, *Autocracy and Aristocracy* (New Brunswick: Rutgers University Press, 1982), 18–22, 62–4.

36 Meehan-Water, *Autocracy*, 64; Jensen, *Udnaevnelsesretten*, 328–9.

37 James Riley, *International Government Finance and the Amsterdam Capital Market 1740–1815* (Cambridge: Cambridge University Press, 1980), 126–59.

38 Bosher, *French Finances*, 67 ff., 92 ff.

39 Paul Dukes, *The Making of Russian Absolutism 1613–1801* (second edn, London: Longman, 1990), 90–1; Claes Peterson, *Peter the Great's Administrative and Judicial Reforms: Swedish Antecedents and the Process of Reception* (Stockholm: Nordiska Bokhandeln, 1979); Erik Amburger, *Geschichte der Behördenorganisation Russlands von Peter dem Grossen bis 1917* (Leiden: E. J. Brill, 1966), 9–13.

40 Militärgeschichtliches Forschungsamt (ed.), *Deutsche Militärgeschichte in Sechs Bänden 1648–1939* (Herrsching: Manfred Pawlak, 1983), 72 ff., 112.

41 Bosher, *French Finances*, 16–17, 165; Church, *Revolution and Red Tape*, 8, 21–2.

42 Brewer, *Sinews*, 14–21.

43 ibid., 158, 139. See also p. 70, where Brewer states 'the presence after 1688 of a standing House of Commons, eager to root out malfeasance and reluctant to disburse moneys without good reason, created a degree of public accountability that acted as a powerful constraint on administrative malpractice'.

44 ibid., 137.

45 For an analysis of English state development in the seventeenth century which emphasizes to a greater degree than does Brewer the significance of administrative and financial reforms introduced during the Interregnum and Restoration, see chapter 3 of my doctoral dissertation 'War and Statebuilding in Early Modern Europe' (Ph.D. thesis, Department of Sociology, Harvard University, 1990).

46 On the English case, see especially the two articles by G. E. Aylmer: 'Attempts at Administrative Reform, 1625–1640', *English Historical Review*, 72/283 (April 1957), 229–59; and 'Charles I's Commission on Fees, 1627–1640', *Bulletin of the Institute for Historical Research*, 31/83 (May 1958), 58–67.

3

The Eighteenth-Century British State
Contexts and issues
John Brewer

To speak of 'the state' is to talk of something that at once seems remarkably allusive and abstract – it is, after all, a construction or conception rather than a thing – but which can also, in certain contexts, seem terrifyingly concrete. Scholars may find the state hard to identify and its functions or actions difficult to define, but there are certain situations – when the taxman calls for tribute, the executioner wields his axe, and armed forces kill, rape and pillage – in which subjects or citizens are made acutely aware of the institutions that wield public power and authority over them.

In recent years political and social scientists have 'talked up' the state as the key site at which we can understand the larger processes of both political and social change. This shift – away from society and towards the state, back from the social and towards politics – reflects a general dissatisfaction with explanations of change, whether Marxist or liberal, that omit or avoid consideration of political power or treat the political sphere as epiphenomenal, reducible to a congeries of economic and social forces. The resulting scholarship, though it has its problems, has had two salutary effects: it has focused attention on the importance of the mechanisms and processes by which the state works; and it has led political and social scientists to an interest – one that presumably alludes back to Max Weber – in the historical evolution of public authority and political power.[1]

A parallel development has occurred in history. Although the social history that became fashionable in the 1970s always contained within itself the seeds of a political critique,[2] they have only recently begun to bear fruit. Not all their progeny are relevant to a discussion of the state; but two rather different and sometimes antagonistic siblings have affected historical investigation of the subject. One, derived predominantly from the writings of Michel Foucault, addresses the issue of power and knowledge, focusing on the often concealed functions of language, ideology or discourse in sustaining and developing technologies and means of exercising power. This approach, it has to be said, has had little impact on the writing of eighteenth-century history on the British state and politics, though it has informed the study of such eighteenth-century institutions as the

52

family, hospital, asylum and prison. The second is concerned to analyse the institutions and processes through which state power is exercised and to examine how their workings affect, mediate and reflect conflict in society at large. Here the most important work has been concerned with the enactment, use and enforcement of the law, particularly those laws affecting crime.[3] Its inspiration is not French post-structuralism but Anglophone sociology, including those post-Marxist analyses which have 'brought the state back in'.[4]

Neither of these approaches has, however, made the state the centre of its analysis. Foucault's notion of power is both too specific – focused on sites of knowledge rather than the institutions conventionally taken to be the locus of state power – and too diffuse (indeed, some might say, ubiquitous).[5] When he wrote about the state his remarks were characteristically penetrating,[6] but the state itself was not central to his explication of power. On the other hand, scholars of crime and the law, though they have brought theories of the state to bear on their work, have rarely attempted to go beyond this to provide a general characterization of the English/British state and its workings. The two notable exceptions are Douglas Hay and Edward Thompson.[7]

Perhaps this neglect is salutary. It can be argued that, if historians in general use the notion of 'the state', they walk into a methodological minefield and, if British historians in particular deploy the concept, they expose themselves to the criticism that they are using a term which is both inappropriate and anachronistic.

These objections are not without substance, but they are also not compelling. Their limits will become apparent if we explore how we might define the state and what the heuristic value of the concept might be, and then turn to the question of its applicability to eighteenth-century England/ Britain.

DEFINITIONS OF THE STATE

In *The Sinews of Power* I defined the state as

> a territorially and jurisdictionally defined political entity in which public authority is distinguished from (though not unconnected to) private power, and which is manned by officials whose primary (though not sole) allegiance is to a set of political institutions under a single, i.e. sovereign and final, authority.[8]

This definition follows quite closely that of the sociological canon, though it omits one usual component, the assertion that the state has a monopoly of authoritative rule-making, backed by a monopoly of physical violence. This absence is partly explained by my attempt to define the state as an entity, rather than by what it does, but it also reflects disquiet about the definition itself. The notion that the state has a monopoly of physical violence seems extremely problematic, unless it is qualified by some indication of the character of that violence. What distinguishes state violence is precisely that it claims a legitimacy based on the claims of political authority. The important issue about rule-making is not a question of monopoly – any highly elaborated polity, including eighteenth-century England/Britain, will have a complex of both public and private rule-making bodies – but of the state governing the rules of last resort.

The definition that I offer does not include a description of the state's functions. States, it has often been remarked, are Janus-faced: they look in to civil society, and out towards other states. Their functions, therefore, are best understood as internal and external, the former concerned with the administration of justice, public order and social and economic regulation, the latter with war, diplomacy and foreign policy.

Both the definition of the state and the characterization of its functions are valuable for the questions that they encourage us to raise. What is the relationship between territorial reach and jurisdictional control? How exactly is public authority connected to private power? What is it that defines, explains or limits the sorts of allegiance that obtain both within and towards a state? Where, if anywhere, does a final source of authority lie? In what ways do such external workings of the state as the waging of war affect its internal functions and, conversely, how do such internal concerns as the maintenance of public order affect such external matters as foreign policy? All these are important historical questions.

Above all, thinking about the state encourages us to take a broader view: to look at the relations between different areas of state policy and activity; to link political bodies and administrative institutions. In the English/British case this has the salutary effect of moving our discussion beyond a long-standing national obsession with Parliament and party and towards an understanding of the larger processes of government. In general, it invites us to think about governance as a whole. This, in turn, raises basic questions about the relations between political authority and social and economic power, and about the nature of authority and allegiance. The difficulties in defining what we mean by 'the state' are a sure indication that in pursuing some definition and understanding we are asking interesting and important questions. As long as any definition is treated as a useful category rather than a paradigmatic prison it will be of value.

Yet is the term 'state' aptly applied to the political arrangements of eighteenth-century England/Britain? Implicit in this (often hostile) question are several assumptions: crudely defined, they are that there was no British state to speak of in the eighteenth century, nor was there in Britain, as there certainly was on the continent, a theory of 'the state' or 'states', although there were, appropriately enough, a number of rather sophisticated theories of society. The eighteenth-century British state, according to this view, eludes definition because there was no separately defined state interest and no body of persons attached or loyal to 'the state'; rather, British government comprised a series of attenuated institutions heavily dependent for their staffing and activation upon groups whose social identity lay outside the corridors of power; state employment was primarily a matter of providing outdoor relief for the genteel classes; power itself was not concentrated but extremely dispersed; the state and any theory about it were largely conspicuous by their absence.

These criticisms are not without merit. There was no cameralist science of government in eighteenth-century Britain, and certainly no university teaching of *polizeiwissenschaft*, unless political economy can be construed as such. Power and authority, at least by the standards of eighteenth-century France and Prussia, were indeed dispersed rather than concentrated. The political gravy-train was capable of making some men very rich. Many tasks which in Europe were performed by state functionaries were, in England at least, carried out by officers who were amateur and locally appointed. The discourse of politics was dominated by the language of party, the law and constitutionalism rather than the rhetoric of the state.

There are also serious problems with this analysis, however. First of all, it overstates the case about ideology. Though it is true that discussion of the state or states was much more limited than debate about general constitutional matters, by the second half of the eighteenth century talk of the state in a variety of contexts was a matter of common usage.

The extent to which a notion of 'the state' had become common usage can be seen in the writings of Edmund Burke. Not only did he discuss the question of the relations between church and state – a topic in which 'the state' was most frequently mentioned in the first half of the eighteenth century; he also addressed the much broader issues of international state competition and of state and society. Thus Burke was conscious of a political entity greater than the monarchy, court or Parliament. He spoke of 'the power of the state nearly melted down into this house [of Commons]', and in his early political career complained of a deliberate 'weakening the State in order to strengthen the Court'.[9] He saw the British polity as one among several states which made up a system of international powers,[10] a state which embodied what he maintained to be the most desirable features of any government: 'States may, and they will best, exist with a partition of the civil powers', he argued.[11] This assumption underpinned his account of the British Revolution of 1688 and the French Revolution of 1789: 'With us we got rid of the man, and preserved the constituent parts of the state. There they get rid of the constituent parts of the state, and keep the man.'[12] Burke was fully aware that, as the *Political Register* put it in 1772, 'private considerations cede to those of the state'.[13] Indeed, he made clear in his speech of 1780 on economical reform that 'the reigning principle of my plan' was 'the total collected exigencies of the state'.[14]

These may seem odd utterances from the proponent of prescription and the defender of private-property rights, but they demonstrate the widespread recognition in eighteenth-century Britain that there was a political authority that could override private interests, even to the extent of depriving some members of society of their property, provided such action could be justified as for the public good. The dispute was not about whether or not such a power existed; it was about the circumstances in which it could and should be invoked, and about who should wield it. In short, it was a question of when reason of state could be legitimately employed and of where sovereignty lay.

British politicians in the second half of the eighteenth century understood that the British state was both more than its domestic political arrangements and part of an international states system. In recognizing this they had a broader vision than many modern commentators. As I have remarked elsewhere,[15] the modern liberal view of the English state – typically, supporters of this position have paid little attention to the problem of Britain and even less to the eighteenth-century empire – is primarily concerned with only one of several possible functions of the state and only one of several arenas of state power. Specifically, it focuses on domestic regulation, what in the eighteenth century was known as 'police': the administration of justice, the maintenance of public order and the regulation of the economy for the benefit of some notional *salus populi*. This is undoubtedly a very important part of the business of government – perhaps its most important part – as well as a potentially vast area of state power, but it is not the only one.

The comparative absence of studies of the external functions of the eighteenth-century state can partly be explained by an understandable reluctance to draw on the most important literature on the role of the state as a military and diplomatic machine, namely those German writings which not only analysed but sometimes praised a bureaucratic, military apparatus as the exemplum of state power. Such writings, and the practices they discuss, readily lend themselves to a characterization of being not only illiberal but unBritish. Yet the best of this work, notably that of Otto Hintze, has important insights to offer. Hintze, above all, was concerned to emphasize both the internal and external functions of the state and the ways in which they affected each other.[16] In short, he offered one important line of approach which might have enabled British historians to see that the most important developments in the eighteenth-century British state were precisely those that linked the state's external workings with its domestic functions.

THE FISCAL-MILITARY STATE IN ENGLAND

The most important innovations in the workings of eighteenth-century government occurred, in the first instance, in its relations with other states – in the spheres of war, finance and diplomacy.[17] (This is not to argue that there were no important developments on the domestic side – there undoubtedly were, not least in the emergence of statute law as the dominant mechanism of regulation.) The most spectacular changes occurred, however, because of England/Britain's involvement in the second Hundred Years War: a sharp increase in the commitment of resources to military activities, a radical increase in taxation, the growth of the national debt, and the development of a sizeable civilian administration devoted to organizing the fiscal and administrative activities of the state. These developments, though they were propelled by external factors, had a considerable effect upon the domestic polity and its relations to the state.

It is worth looking at these developments in some detail. Between 1680 and 1780 the British army and navy trebled in size. Britain's pattern of military effort was, of course, somewhat different in character from the other great European powers: much more was spent on the navy and on foreign subsidies. Yet it is important to emphasize that overall effort was on a similar scale to other major states. Between 75 and 85 per cent of annual expenditure went on current spending on the army, navy and ordnance or to service debts incurred during earlier wars, roughly the same proportion of public spending as went on military matters in Prussia; and the proportion of national income devoted to military expenditure was roughly comparable to that spent in Austria in the third quarter of the century. At the height of a major war the ratio of taxpayers to military effectives was approximately 40:1, a ratio that matched that of other European belligerents.

Such commitment marked a radical departure from the previous two hundred years. Not since the end of the Hundred Years War had England been such an important international military power. With the possible exception of the 1540s, 1590s and 1650s, no period saw a comparable mobilization of resources for war. Sporadic conflict was now replaced by almost continuous hostilities, punctuated by periods of peace devoted to preparation for the next war.

The high levels of expenditure that inevitably accompanied these wars were only possible because the state was able to raise vast sums of money. After the Glorious Revolution the fiscal-military state plunged into debt and jacked up taxes. In less than a century the unredeemed debt increased fifteen-fold in current prices. For most of the century it consumed more than 30 per cent of state income, exceeding 50 per cent for some sixteen years and peaking at 66 per cent at the end of the American War. As

Michel Morineau has pointed out, this was a greater burden of debt than that which provoked the financial crisis of 1788–9 in France.[18]

Taxes also increased rapidly, though they could not match the breakneck pace at which expenditure increased. Nevertheless, between the reign of Charles II and the American War aggregate net tax revenue grew sixfold. Tax rates and fiscal incidence also increased. As Mathias and O'Brien and Morineau have all demonstrated, tax incidence in Britain was almost twice that in France, making it one of the most highly taxed nations in Europe.[19]

The effectiveness with which the British state taxed its subjects was in large part a direct consequence of a major transformation in the fiscal system that occurred gradually between the Restoration and the mid-eighteenth century. England moved from a fiscal system marked by hetero-geneity and amateurism to a tax administration characterized by the orderly collection of monies by a predominantly professional body of state officials. The end of revenue farming, the rise of the Treasury as the body controlling both income and expenditure, and the switch from direct taxes collected by locally appointed amateurs to indirect taxes gathered by a growing number of centrally appointed government officials all helped create a centralized, public administration of considerable efficiency.

Both Plumb and Holmes have drawn our attention to the growth in civil administration in the late Stuart and Hanoverian era. Holmes estimates that by 1714 114 commissioners sat on eighteen different government boards, and that by the 1720s approximately 12,000 permanent employees were in government service.[20] The majority of these functionaries worked in the revenue departments, and of these most worked for the excise. By the 1720s more men worked in the excise than for all the other revenue departments taken together. By the end of the American War the excise establishment was almost twice as large as the entire fiscal administration employed at the time of the Glorious Revolution.

The boards and departments that were either newly established or revamped in the late-seventeenth century were almost all marked by a number of features that we would describe as 'bureaucratic'. They rewarded full-time employees with salaries rather than fees and offered a career-ladder of graded appointments with progressively higher remuneration which culminated in retirement and a government pension. They also expected administrative loyalty and sought to encourage an ethos of public duty and private probity. Standards were set either by the examination of entrants into government service or by schemes of training analogous to apprenticeship. They were maintained by internal monitoring and by systems of punishment and reward. Departments developed their own systems of record-keeping, defined office procedures and routines, and attracted an increasingly inbred and institutionally loyal administrator.

This 'new' administration did not replace but was added to existing institutions. Its rules and practices were not accompanied by wholesale reform of older departments, many of which contained sinecurists, pluralists and officers whose chief source of income was fees. Administrative innovation in England, as elsewhere in Europe, either worked around existing office-holders and their interests or reached an accommodation with them by combining the old and new to their mutual satisfaction. Nor was administration free from politics; but political connection and patronage were only the necessary condition of office in the new and reformed departments; they were not sufficient to secure tenure in those offices, like the Treasury, the navy and the excise, where competence was necessary for the nation's fortunes to flourish.

Of all departments of government, the largest, the excise, best exemplifies new patterns of administrative practice. Organized as two chains of command – one for the provinces, another for the metropolis – the excise employed a complex system of bookkeeping and measuring both to tax such commodities as beer, hops, malt, spirits, tea, coffee, leather, salt, soap, candles and wire and to ensure the probity of its employees. Trained in calculus and the use of the slide-rule, and required to keep three different sorts of record in conformity, excise officers or gaugers were policed by supervisors (one for every ten officers), and their books carefully scrutinized by a central body of examiners (fifty in 1770). By the last quarter of the eighteenth century the excise was policing over 100,000 different premises: 33,000 brewers and victuallers, 36,000 publicans licensed to sell spirits, 35,500 coffee- and tea-dealers, as well as several thousand maltsters, chandlers, calico printers and paper makers. Some of these premises, like the London brewery, were policed continuously by shifts of revenue officers; others were visited much less frequently. Some sense of the scope of the excise operations can be gained when we recall that in 1970 in England and Wales there were 108,000 licensed premises. Eighteenth-century excise men covered almost as many shops, hostelries and breweries.

The English fiscal system embodied a number of features that made it unique in eighteenth-century Europe. To an unusual degree tax collection was concentrated in the hands of centrally appointed government officials. In France, Holland and even late-eighteenth-century Prussia consortia of private financiers and tax-farmers collected a sizeable proportion of state revenues.

The number of centrally appointed fiscal officials (over 8,000 by the 1780s) was large by contemporary European standards. The Prussian bureaucracy as a whole numbered little more than 3,000 in mid-century, perhaps 250 of whom worked in central administration. The United Provinces, though the most heavily taxed state in Europe, had a tiny fiscal bureaucracy (about 300–350 salaried officials at the end of the century). Though the number of fiscal officials was greater in France both absolutely and as a percentage of the population, most of them (about 23,000 in 1784) worked for the farmers and very few had the technical accomplishments and bookkeeping skills of the English. Only approximately 6,800 officials performed the tasks of assessment and collection carried out in Britain by customs and excise men.

If tax collecting in England focused to an unusual degree on the routines of quantification, it was also exceptionally well controlled by the book-keepers in Whitehall. The triumph of the Treasury in the late seventeenth century produced a remarkably centralized fiscal system in which all departments – those of both receipt and disbursement – were accountable to a single body, the Treasury Board. This enabled Britain to become the first major European state to keep full accounts of total government revenue and expenditure.

Again, this centralization was not to be found elsewhere. The federated United Provinces retained considerable regional fiscal autonomy. There was no central body of receipt. In France, as late as 1788, the French Royal Treasury was receiving only one-half of the state's total revenues.[21] Prussian monarchs concealed their assets in several different *Kassen*, thereby preventing any adequate system of centralized accounting.[22]

Finally, English finance was public finance. Not only was its functioning in the hands of public officials rather than private financial consortia, but its workings were also perspicuous and visible. Parliamentary scrutiny and systematic government record-keeping combined to ensure the visibility of the state's actions. Paradoxically, then, in a nation that is usually seen as comparatively state-less, the British fiscal apparatus was more 'state-like' than that of any other in eighteenth-century Europe.

The fiscal-military state had a considerable impact on civil society. Its institutions and policies affected patterns of employment, fluctuations in the economy, prices and wages: it created new opportunities for invest-ment, reshaped the social structure (creating a new financial interest), changed the practices of producers, shopkeepers and traders, and stimulated the growth of lobbies and special interest groups. Throughout the eight-eenth century the fiscal-military state was the largest employer, purchaser and borrower in the domestic economy. It was a major economic and social as well as military and financial force.

Of course, the fiscal-military state presented a different face to civil society, especially English civil society, than it did to the world at large. On the frontiers of the empire, in Europe and on the high seas it relied on the coercive brute force deployed by all the main military powers; but at home state power worked more subtly and less obtrusively. Its key technology was not derived from the arts of war but from the counting-house – slips of paper rather than shot and cannon, slide-rules rather than the blades of swords. Its ethos was that of bookkeeping, penmanship and political arithmetic, its ambiance entirely compatible with commercial society. Yet its unobtrusiveness did not preclude remarkable powers of surveillance: basic measuring skills, aided by calculus, the measuring rod and the slide-rule, together with exacting standards of bookkeeping, enabled the state and its functionaries to observe and record an astonishing amount of activity.

How we explain the absence of resistance to this scrutiny – at least in England – is a complex question that can be explained by the status of public authority in general; but it also, at a grass-roots level, has to do with the status of the tasks that state functionaries were performing. Revenue officers were often referred to as 'artists', They performed with some virtuosity the very tasks – measuring, calculating and accounting – that the producers, traders and shopkeepers they assessed valued as the keys to successful and profitable trading.

THE COMPARATIVE APPROACH

It is clear from this compressed account of the workings of the fiscal-military state that any interpretation of eighteenth-century British governance that emphasizes the absence of officialdom and the paucity of state activity does so because it looks in the wrong place and therefore fails to see where the action is. This is not to claim that we should simply invert the old cliché about the weak English/British state, converting it into an equally unilluminating platitude about British strength; rather, it is important to identify those areas in which the state was most active and those that it left free from intervention – to understand how the state and its powers, domestic and judicial, international and military, were configured and deployed.

Unquestionably, one of the best ways in which the specific form and workings of the English/British state can be identified is by means of comparison with other eighteenth-century European states.[23] Such an enterprise may seem to fly in the face of the long-standing belief, well enshrined in the eighteenth as well as the twentieth century, in English/British exceptionalism; but the object of comparison is to identify differences as well as similarities – indeed, to give sharpness to our analysis by alerting us to what is distinctive.

If we compare the English/British state, as opposed to society, against its continental counterparts, then several features stand out. The first is one that I have already discussed – a uniquely public system of government finance. The second was a uniquely powerful single legislature. Intermediate rights and privileges – those between Parliament and the rights of individual subjects – were comparatively weak: there were no regional assemblies of any account in England before 1707 and in Britain after the Anglo-Scottish Union. (The situation alters, of course, once one includes Ireland and the empire.) Similarly, corporate privilege in general was weak in England. Only that tiny group of the elite who were peers enjoyed significant legal privileges; other corporate rights – of towns, regions or categories of persons – dwindle into insignificance when compared with their continental counterparts. Finally, England alone among the European powers had a nationally legislated system of poor relief.

The call for a comparative approach to the study of the English/British state seems all the more attractive in view of current trends in the historiography of continental Europe. On the one hand, recent work on European states, notably France and Prussia, has played down those features usually associated with absolutism, emphasizing the limits on centralized, autocratic state power, the regional rather than central loyalties of officials, and the diversity rather than uniformity of administration. In short, it has made the state apparatus and its functionaries look a little more like the traditional view of eighteenth-century England. At the same time, it has stressed the inability of centralized authority to override local powers and has, in part, attributed this difficulty to the absence of a national representative body capable of mediating between state and nation and of legitimating royal policy. Hence, it is argued, the sharp contrast between the powers that the absolutist monarch or state claimed and those they were capable of exercising.[24]

The recasting of both the British and the continental states makes clear that we need a new comparative account, one that will enable us to reformulate our notion of 'the peculiarities of the English'. In making explicit comparisons between England/Britain and the continental powers we should, however, be sure that we are comparing like with like. This requires not only a comparison of functions but that we observe a distinction between what Michael Mann has called 'despotic' and 'infrastructural' power. The former alludes to the formal and legal entitlements that a regime may have over subjects' rights and liberties; the latter characterizes the ability that a state has to put such powers into effect.[25]

The comparative investigation of European states should, moreover, be taken as an opportunity to address the question of the relative autonomy of different states. Marxist and post-Marxist theorists of the state have all struggled with the question of how to avoid a highly reductionist account of the state in which it is treated as merely the reflection of social forces in civil society. The methodological objections to this strategy of collapsing the state into society, the political into the social, are extremely persuasive.[26] More positively, attributing a degree of autonomy to the state enables us to see the state as subject rather than object, acting on society and other states, rather than being treated as a passive receptacle for other forces. Such an approach also enables us to focus on the institutional aspects of the state, to examine the processes by which political and administrative institutions worked.

Yet the assertion that the state has autonomous power does not mean that it was immaculately conceived nor that it can ever be treated as if it could insulate or isolate itself from society. There is something of a danger that in 'bringing the state back in', we will also be 'taking society back out'. It is clear that European states had not only their own distinctive institutional configuration and ideological underpinnings but also distinctive relations with civil society which changed over time. It therefore seems far more useful to assess the changing degree of autonomy of different states – to see variations in autonomy as one of the features of states – rather than to adduce a general rule about the relative autonomy of the absolutist or eighteenth-century state – to make into a question something that is too often assumed to be an answer.

The history of the British eighteenth-century state provides a good example of the changing relations between the state, civil society and social classes. In the period when the fiscal-military state underwent its greatest expansion (c. 1680–1720) it seems to have acquired an unprecedented degree of autonomy. State policy and administrative expansion acquired a momentum all of their own. Certainly, it is hard to argue that the changes that occurred served the interests of a ruling class or classes (although they were consonant with a particular political outlook). On the contrary, the expansion of state power was bitterly opposed and strongly resented, not least by powerful members of the aristocracy and gentry. As Edward Thompson puts it: 'the State was less an effective organ of any class than a parasitism upon the backs of that very class (the gentry) who had gained the day in 1688'.[27]

Shouldering the bulk of the tax burden, squeezed by high prices and tight credit, and eclipsed by the new monied fortunes derived from public finance, the landed classes acquired an unprecedented (and aggrieved) sense of identity. Their opposition to the fiscal-military state had only limited success during the wars with Louis XIV. They did, however, manage to restrict the scope of the state: to limit the powers of the standing army in England (much less so in Britain); to secure a degree of financial accountability; to limit the political impact of more office-holders; and to define quite closely the duties of fiscal functionaries so that they could not be used (as both James II and Walpole in their different ways hoped) as a domestic police.[28]

This process of holding the state at bay was accompanied by the countervailing trend of learning to use the new political forms to advantage. Taxation was shifted away from the landed classes, gentlemen quickly learnt how to enjoy the spoils of war, empire and office, and landed proprietors, despite the fright of the South Sea Bubble, diversified their investments to include government stock and securities. Unlike commercial and industrial groups, the landed classes developed no specialized lobbies to affect state policy or legislation. This is not to say that they did not take advantage of parliamentary statute to shore up or enhance their local power; on the contrary, landed gentry and their allies were responsible for bills and acts, designed to effect all kinds of 'improvement'.

The landed classes, in other words, quickly learnt that the parliamentary state – for that is essentially what it was in north and south Britain – might have begun as a foe but could be a turned into a friend. A similar conclusion was drawn by commercial and, to a lesser extent, industrial interests, although they would never have accepted Adam Smith's view that they held the state hostage. Although, therefore, it would be a mistake to argue that the state lost its autonomy in the course of the eighteenth century, it can, I think, be plausibly argued that its autonomy was reduced.

Edward Thompson has characterized political (he might have said 'state') power in eighteenth-century England 'not as a direct organ of any class or interest, but as a secondary political formation, a purchasing-point from which other kinds of economic and social power were gained or enhanced'.[29] This seems quite apt, as long as political institutions are also recognized to have an autonomous life of their own. Thompson goes on to add that

> in its primary functions it was costly, grossly inefficient, and it survived the century only because it did not seriously inhibit the actions of those with *de facto* economic or (local) political power. Its greatest source of strength lay precisely in the weakness of the State itself; in the desuetude of its paternal, bureaucratic and protectionist powers; in the licence which it afforded to agrarian, mercantile and manufacturing capitalism.[30]

Here, it seems to me, the case is weaker. British government, by the standards of the time, was not grossly expensive or inefficient. As both a proportion of revenue and in terms of total expenditure the costs of the British government in the second half of the eighteenth century were one-quarter of the comparable French figures. Revenue gathering was exceptionally efficient by European standards. The administrative costs of domestic rule and local government must have been low because of the central role played by amateurs.

Moreover, the state was more than a passive partner in economic development. In England, it is true, there was little direct intervention in economic enterprise (in Scotland and Ireland, however, intervention was more marked) on the scale of the great state enterprises in France. Policy was also more usually initiated by interested parties and active Members of Parliament than by government officials.[31] However, the power that was being invoked was that of central government and the effect of that invocation was often to change (at least in law) the nature of local power. This, as Thompson himself has so eloquently shown, could entail the loss of common-law rights (such as trial by jury) and the destruction of local custom. The most perfunctory examination of local improvement legislation, both rural and urban, reveals an astonishing array of legal powers for local commissioners who, more often than not, turn out to be magistrates who desired additional powers. In short, we should see state power as rather more significant not only in its fiscal-military but also in its domestic context.

STATE AND EMPIRE

Up to this point I have avoided the question of how to define the English/British state territorially and have also neglected the question of how we would characterize the state's relations with the first British empire. The nettle must now be grasped.

Michael Mann, drawing on Max Weber and other social scientists, has emphasized the territorial character of state power as one of its most important and distinctive features. States consist of centralized institutions exercising sovereignty – acting as the final source of authority – over territorially demarked areas. His remarks are worth quoting in full:

> The definition of the state concentrates upon its institutional, territorial, centralized nature. This is the . . . most important precondition of state power . . . the state does not possess a distinctive means of power independent of, and analogous to, economic, military and ideological power. The means used by states are only a combination of these, which are also the means of power used in all social relationships. However, the power of the state is irreducible in quite a different socio-spatial and organizational sense. Only the state is inherently centralized over a delimited territory over which it has authoritative power. Unlike economic, ideological or military groups in civil society, the state elite's resources radiate authoritatively outwards from a centre but stop at defined territorial boundaries. The state is, indeed, a place – both a central place and a unified territorial reach.[32]

The question, of course, in the British case is what territory are we talking about? This question is made all the more complex by the changing relations within and between the political entities that made up the British Isles and the first British empire. First, there was considerable territorial expansion – by 1750 there were twenty-three separate colonies on the western rim of the Atlantic; nine more were added before the American Revolution. By the outbreak of the American Revolution there were more subjects of the British state outside England than within it. Second, relations between England, Ireland and Scotland, through processes of legislative union and independence, were transformed in this period. Then, of course, there are those peculiar territories, like the Channel Isles, Hanover and, during the French revolutionary era, Corsica, which claimed the English monarch as their proprietor or head of state. Where are we to place India in all of this? A part of Britain's informal empire, no doubt, but hardly, by Mann's definition, part of the British state.

For all this confusion, we can, I think, make a number of reasonably confident assertions about state and empire. After 1707 Britain meant north and south Britain, that is, Scotland and England and Wales. There was general agreement that Hanover was not part of the British state but the private estate of Georg Kurfurst von Hanover who also happened to be the British monarch.[33] Ireland was a source not just of dispute but confusion. It was sometimes viewed as a colony, sometimes as an independent kingdom and, by the younger Pitt at least, as part of Great Britain: 'one country in effect, though for local concern under different legislatures'.[34] The territories on the west Atlantic coast were colonies, although what colonial status entailed and particularly whether they had been acquired through settlement or conquest were matters of considerable controversy. In short, there was not a great deal of disagreement about the territories referred to when contemporaries spoke of Britain, its empire or dominions, but there was persistent controversy about the relations between them.

Much has been said, since John Pocock's seminal article, on the need to produce British histories that are neither 'Anglocentric' nor 'Anglophobic'.[35] This ecumenical and even-handed appeal is superficially attractive and often invoked; but it is difficult to imagine of what such histories would consist. Historians should not treat 'British' as a synonym for 'English', but I find it hard to imagine an account of the British state that was not written from the point of view of the metropolitan or of one or several of the putative subordinate powers. The only way to begin to transcend these partialities is to recognize that the very different versions propagated in the eighteenth century of relations between the constituent parts of empire or between the political entities in the British Isles were themselves politically contentious.

The gradual evolution of the British state and the heterogeneity of its possessions contributed to the somewhat indeterminate character of relations between the constituent parts of the polity. One of the most important features of all the crises and conflicts between England, its colonies and other dependencies of the Crown was the way in which they raised not only questions about relations between the parts of the state or empire but also questions about the nature of power at the centre: about sovereignty; relations between Crown and Parliament, prerogative and common law, privy council and legislature; and even, on occasion, between spiritual and temporal authority.

The Jacobite Parliament in Ireland in 1689, the Irish Whig, William Molyneux, in his *Case of Ireland's Being Bound by Acts of Parliament in England, Stated* (1698), a great many Scots, including those who went on to support imperial union in 1707, the Jacobite rebels in Scotland in 1745, the American colonists in the 1770s and the Irish reformers of the 1780s

– all denied the jurisdictional power of the English Parliament outside England. Their view of the British state and empire was almost federal, what the colonist Benjamin Prescott described as 'a great and glorious King, with a Number of distinct Governments, alike subjected to his royal Scepter, and each governed by its own Laws'.[36] (In the Scottish and Irish cases this took the form of the claim that historically there were three crowns, not one.[37])

The Jacobite denial of parliamentary power accorded well with the desire to assert the powers of the monarch over Parliament and to deny parliamentary sovereignty. It was a statement about the desirability of a certain type of monarchical politics in England. However, the American colonists and reformers like Grattan in Ireland also rested their claims on a version of British politics, one based on the political liberties that they believed to inhere in British constitutionalism. As Grattan put it:

> This nation is connected with England not by allegiance only but by liberty, the crown is one great point of union but Magna Carta is greater; . . . we could get a king anywhere but England is the only country from which we could get a constitution.[38]

Grattan's remarks point to the paradoxical position taken by many subjects of the British state. On the one hand, there was the desire for regional autonomy, preferably institutionalized in the form of a local representative assembly, and occasionally pushed into demands for separation; but these centrifugal and fissiparous tendencies were counterbalanced by the demand for the enjoyment to the full of the rights of Englishmen, a privilege which sometimes led to the advocacy of parliamentary union. As Jack Greene has put it, colonists

> worried over how their relationship with Britain affected their rights as Englishmen and whether those rights and the corporate and individual interests those rights had been devised to protect could be secured to English people living in dependent and distant polities.[39]

During the revolutionary crisis both British and American commentators flirted with the idea of an imperial parliament, a notion that attracted even the hard-headed Adam Smith. Similar sentiments were to be found in Ireland. William Molyneux claimed Ireland as a separate kingdom but also flirted with the idea of parliamentary union. Irish and Quebec Catholics, West Indian whites and North American colonists all laid claim to the rights of freeborn Englishmen.

Resistance to an integrated British state, in which all subjects enjoyed similar rights, was strongest in England itself. There was a general reluctance to confer English rights to those outside her borders. This was largely attributable to a self-interest embodied in the assumption that colonies were indeed all about advantage to the mother country. Conversely, demands from Scotland, Ireland and the colonies were intent on not only securing political rights but enjoying the advantages and privileges of a vast commercial empire. Concessions or changes occurred only when the commercial and strategic interests of the mother country were threatened. This reluctance to confer full economic and political rights to British subjects did not sit well with the often-repeated view that dependencies were best governed by securing the loyalty of local elites through a judicious mixture of cultural assimilation, commercial advantage and political favour. Cementing ties and making bonds was especially difficult when inequality was so apparent.

The debate about Englishmen's rights underlines the central importance in any history of the British state and empire of the means by which passive compliance and active allegiance to government was secured. (Much more could be made of the distinction between compliance and allegiance; the circumstances that affect the former may differ strongly from those that affect the latter.) In part, these questions can be resolved by examining the development of national identity, the creation, by a variety of means, of the sort of consciousness that prompted seventeenth-century white Barbadians to think of themselves as English and eighteenth-century Scots as Britons. However, nationalism was not enough. The British state was able to secure the loyalty of those who emphatically saw themselves as other than English – Irish, Welsh or American – just as it was not able to retain the allegiance of those, notably in North America, who were increasingly Anglicized. A sense of belonging was important – just as a sense of exclusion, notably on the grounds of religion, was of great consequence – but allegiance (as opposed to compliance) was conditional; it required a *quid pro quo*. It depended not just on the ideological construction of a cultural identity but upon the political gravy-train and upon the distribution of economic spoils.

FUTURE DIRECTIONS

The study of the English/British state is still in its infancy. The work that has been completed poses as many questions as it answers; it also indicates the considerable lacunae in our knowledge. Future investigation of the eighteenth-century English/British state would benefit enormously from a collaborative research project devoted to European states of the period, which brought together scholars each with a different national expertise. Only such a project can lend precision to claims about the peculiarities of the English or, for that matter, about any European nation's *Sonderweg*.

Much more work is needed, to complement existing American colonial studies, on the issues of compliance and allegiance – about the mechanisms by which the state secured or lost the attachment of its subjects. Similarly, more needs to be known about the formation of identities and the ways in which national, regional, linguistic, ethnic and religious allegiances came to clash or converge. Finally, we still know remarkably little about the effects of imperial acquisition on the English/British state. Imperial studies have traditionally been concerned with the effect of the core on the periphery, and less with the effect of the empire on the metropole. The presence of an extended research agenda, some of which is addressed in the chapters in this present volume, is presumptive evidence in favour of the claim that one extremely valuable way in which we can investigate the British polity and empire in the eighteenth century is by emphatically 'bringing the state back in'.

NOTES

1 For a useful summary of these developments see John A. Hall, 'Introduction', in John A. Hall (ed.), *States in History* (Oxford: Blackwell, 1986), 1–21.

2 See, notably, Elizabeth Fox-Genovese and Eugene Genovese, 'The Political Crisis of Social History', *Journal of Social History*, 10/2 (1976–7), 205–20.

3 For a useful summary of the literature see Joanna Innes and John Styles, 'The Crime Wave: Recent Writing on Crime and Criminal Justice in 18th Century England', *Journal of British Studies*, 25 (October, 1986), 380–405.

4 Theda Skocpol, 'Bringing the State Back In: Strategies of Analysis in Current Research', in Peter Evans, Dietrich Rueschemeyer and Theda Skocpol (eds), *Bringing the State Back In* (Cambridge: Cambridge University Press, 1985), 3–37.

5 For two interesting discussions on this topic see David Couzens Hoy, 'Power, Repression, Progress: Foucault, Lukes, and the Frankfurt School', and Edward W. Said, 'Foucault and the Imagination of Power', in David Couzens Hoy (ed.), *Foucault: A Critical Reader* (Oxford: Blackwell, 1986), 123–47, 149–55.

6 See especially 'The Subject and Power', in *Michel Foucault: Beyond Structuralism and Hermeneutics*, ed. Hubert Dreyfus and Paul Rabinow (Chicago: University of Chicago Press, 1982), esp. p. 208; 'On Governmentality', *Ideology and Consciousness*, 6 (1979), 8–11.

7 Douglas Hay, 'Property, Authority and the Criminal Law', in D. Hay, P. Linebaugh and E. P. Thompson (eds), *Albion's Fatal Tree: Crime and Society in Eighteenth-Century England* (London: Allen Lane, 1975), 17–63; Edward Thompson, 'Eighteenth-Century English Society: Class Struggle without Class?', *Social History*, 3/2 (May 1978), 133–65.

8 John Brewer, *The Sinews of Power: War, Money and the English State 1688–1783* (London: Unwin Hyman, 1989), 252.

9 *The Writings and Speeches of Edmund Burke*, vol. II, *Party, Parliament, and the American Crisis 1766–1774*, ed. Paul Langford (Oxford, 1987), 234, 270.

10 See for example, Edmund Burke, 'Heads for Consideration of the Present State of Affairs written in November 1792' in *The Works of Edmund Burke* (8 vols; London: George Bell & Sons, 1894–1900), vol. III, 394–409.

11 Burke, 'Substance of the Speech in the Debate on the Army Estimates . . . 9 February 1790', in *The Works of Edmund Burke*, vol. III, 269–81, esp. 277.

12 ibid., 279.

13 *Political Register*, 4 (1772), 163.

14 Burke, 'Speech on Economic Reform, 11 February 1780', in *The Works of Edmund Burke*, vol. II, 55–126, esp. 91.

15 *The Sinews of Power*, xvii-xviii.

16 See, in particular, 'Military Organization and the Organization of the State' and 'Economics and Politics in the Age of Modern Capitalism', in *The Historical Essays of Otto Hintze*, ed. Felix Gilbert (Oxford: Oxford University Press, 1975), 178–215, 422–52.

17 Here I rehearse the main arguments from *The Sinews of Power*, where references and detail to substantiate the following discussion will be found.

18 Michel Morineau, 'Les budgets d'état et gestion des finances royale en France aux dix-huitième siècle', *Revue Historique*, 536 (October-December 1980), 259–336, esp. 326.

19 Peter Mathias and Patrick O'Brien, 'Taxation in England and France, 1715–1810: A Comparison of the Social and Economic Incidence of Taxes Collected for the Central Governments', *Journal of European Economic History*, 5/3 (1976), 601–50; Morineau, 'Les budgets d'état'.

20 J. H. Plumb, *The Growth of Political Stability in England: 1675–1725* (London: Macmillan, 1967), 11–14, 98–128; Geoffrey Holmes, *Augustan England: Professions, State and Society, 1680–1730* (London: George Allen & Unwin, 1982), 244, 255.

21 J. F. Bosher, 'French Administration and Public Finance in Their European Setting', in *New Cambridge Modern History*, vol. VIII, *The American and French Revolutions*, ed. A. Goodwin (Cambridge: Cambridge University Press, 1965), 565–97.

22 C. B. A. Behrens, *Society, Government and Enlightenment: The Experiences of Eighteenth-Century France and Prussia* (London: Thames & Hudson, 1985), 80–1; Hubert C. Johnson, *Frederick the Great and His Officials* (New Haven and London: Yale University Press, 1975), 41.

23 For an eloquent plea for such comparisons see Charles Tilly, *Big Structures, Large Processes, Huge Comparisons* (New York: Russell Sage Foundation, 1984), 85.

24 See, for example, David Parker, *The Making of French Absolutism* (London: Edward Arnold, 1983); Johnson, *Frederick the Great and His Officials*.

25 Michael Mann, 'The Autonomous Power of the State: Its Origins, Mechanisms and Results', in Hall, *States in History*, 114.

26 They are usefully synthesized in Theda Skocpol, *States and Social Revolutions: A Comparative Analysis of France, Russia and China* (Cambridge: Cambridge University Press, 1979), 24–33.

27 Thompson, 'Eighteenth-Century English Society', 139.

28 Brewer, *Sinews of Power*, 137–61.

29 Thomspon, 'Eighteenth-Century English Society', 141.

30 ibid.

31 David Hayton, 'Moral Reform and Country Politics in the Late Seventeenth-Century House of Commons', *Past and Present*, 128 (August 1990), 48–91.

32 Mann, 'The Autonomous Power of the State', 122–3.

33 T. C. W. Blanning, ' "That Horrid Electorate" or "Ma Patrie Germanique"? George III, Hanover, and the *Furstenbund* of 1785', *Historical Journal*, 20/2 (June 1977), 311–44.

34 Quoted in T. W. Moody and W. E. Vaughan (eds), *A New History of Ireland* (6 vols t.d., Oxford: Clarendon Press, 1984), vol. IV, 282.

35 John Pocock, 'The Limits and Divisions of British History: In Search of an Unknown Subject', *American Historical Review*, 87 (1982), 311–36, esp. 314.

36 Quoted in Jack P. Greene, *Peripheries and Center: Constitutional Development*

in the Extended Polities of the British Empire and the United States, 1607–1788 (Athens: University of Georgia, 1986), 118.

37 William Ferguson, 'Imperial Crowns: A Neglected Facet of the Background to the Treaty of Union of 1707', *Scottish Historical Review*, 53/1: no. 155 (1974), 22–44.

38 Quoted in *A New History of Ireland*, vol. IV, 234.

39 Greene, *Peripheries and Center*, 18.

4

Society and the Economy in the Eighteenth Century

E. A. Wrigley

If the acid test of the strength of an economy is its ability to mobilize sufficient resources to conduct warfare successfully, then the British state in the eighteenth century was clearly underpinned by a very powerful economy. In a series of wars with leading European states in the course of the 'long' eighteenth century Britain was normally successful. The struggle with France, her principal rival, culminated in warfare lasting for a generation during the revolutionary and Napoleonic period in which Britain proved able to sustain her own war effort and to underwrite that of her allies long enough to wear down France, in spite of the French control of the bulk of the continent. It might seem tempting to indulge in an aphorism and assert that the industrial revolution proved stronger than the French revolution.

What serves to determine success in war extends well beyond economic muscle, but as the ability to invest liberally in military hardware grew in importance, and the number of men to be sustained in the field or in warships came to be numbered in hundreds of thousands, and campaigns came to be measured in years rather than weeks and months, so economic strength grew in importance relative to other factors influencing military success. Increasing the level of taxation dramatically in order to support a large increase in military effort can only succeed in the long run if economic growth takes place on a large enough scale to sustain the increased burden without inducing progressive exhaustion. A century earlier the Dutch Republic had shown how far economic strength might go in offsetting a small population and a tiny land surface. Eighteenth-century Britain, too, was in need of something to counterbalance a modest population compared with the major continental powers. If the 'long' eighteenth century is taken as starting in 1680 and ending in 1820, the English population was less than one-quarter that of France at the beginning of the century, and, in spite of a far more rapid rate of growth, still under two-fifths of the French total at its end: the comparable figures in relation to Spain were a little under three-fifths and a little over four-fifths.[1]

It might be argued, of course, that to consider England on its own is to overstate the contrast. If the populations of Wales and Scotland are added to that of England in making such calculations, the imbalance is, of course, reduced – still more so if Ireland is also counted as part of 'Britain'. In 1821, for example, when the population of France was 30.462 millions, the populations of England, Wales, Scotland and Ireland were respectively (in millions) 11.261, 0.717, 2.093 and 6.802, a combined total of 20.873 (this total excludes the population of the islands in British seas). The accuracy of the census is not above reproach but it is unlikely that the totals are seriously misleading. On the basis of these data, the populations of Wales, Scotland and Ireland (with England taken as 100) were 6.3, 18.6 and 60.4 respectively, a grand total, including England, of 185.3 (or, to put the same point differently, the population of England was only 54 per cent of the total for the British Isles as a whole).[2] Clearly, however, manpower could not provide the basis for triumph in the power struggles of the period (although it is important to note that the use of mercenary troops was so common that economy was often as important as demography in deciding the size of a country's forces[3]).

Success in war depended as much on the proportion of national income and wealth that could be mobilized effectively as on the absolute scale of available resources. A large population living close to subsistence level and dependent on peasant agriculture might experience much greater difficulty in sustaining long campaigns and in equipping an army and navy with the latest implements of war than a smaller population less tied to the land, accustomed to relying on the market for the necessities of life no less than for comforts and luxuries, and enjoying a standard of living some way removed from bare subsistence. The economic strength of such a population can be marshalled through appropriate taxation measures far more readily than the more immobile resources of a country peopled largely by peasants.[4]

Viewed in this light, British success is not hard to account for. At the end of the eighteenth century the proportion of the labour force engaged in agriculture in England was only about one-third, whereas in France at the same time the proportion was twice as large, and it is debatable whether 'peasants' were still to be found in the English countryside. Again, the proportion of the English population living in towns in 1800 was about 27 per cent, compared with 11 per cent in France; and a much larger percentage of the English rural population was employed outside agriculture in handicraft industry, manufacturing and service employment. Moreover, these indicators changed substantially in England in the course of the 'long' eighteenth century, but very little in France over the same period.[5] Real income per head is difficult to measure with any precision but there can be little doubt that it was significantly higher in England than in most of the continent. For example, de Vries estimated that, whereas in the late seventeenth century, at the time when Dutch prosperity was at its height and real wages in Holland were clearly the highest in Europe, there was a wide difference between Holland and England, by the end of the eighteenth century the gap had been closed completely. Bairoch's estimates of the level of real wages in European countries suggest that in the early nineteenth century England enjoyed a substantial advantage over most continental countries. In 1830, for example, the gross national product per head for the United Kingdom as a whole, by his calculation, was $346 (US 1960 dollars). This figure was equalled by the Netherlands, but his estimate for France was $264, and for Germany $245. The figure for England alone would have been considerably higher than that for the UK since this included both Britain and Ireland.[6]

Both the beginning and the end of the last paragraph underline, once again, the complexity of such comparisons. It is difficult to avoid alternating between reference to 'Britain' or 'the British state' as a political entity on the one hand and 'England' on the other when discussing social and economic history. This happens partly because there are many data series available for England but not for the larger whole, but also because England was in most respects more advanced than the rest of Britain, and also more uniform geographically than, for example, Scotland, where the Highland line divided two very different societies and economies. It would, therefore, take up much more space to attempt to deal fully with Britain as a whole, and any gain in comprehensiveness would be at the expense of clarity. Nevertheless, it is important to bear in mind that much of this chapter falls short of what one might wish because of a failure to treat adequately either the whole island of Britain or, still more, the British Isles as a whole.

In their important and imaginative article on taxation levels in Britain and France, Mathias and O'Brien showed that, on reasonable assumptions to cover areas of ignorance and uncertainty, the level of taxation per head was about twice as high in Britain as in France during most of the eighteenth century, rising to three times as high at the height of the Napoleonic wars. They argue that such differences cannot be attributed to differences in income per head.[7] They contrast British experience over the period between about 1770 and about 1810, when the government more than doubled the share of national product taken in taxes, with the absence of any comparable rise in France in spite of Napoleon's best efforts 'with all the administrative and institutional modernisation which was promoted under his rule'.[8] They note that Adam Smith pointed out that the French government revenue was 'not the half of what might have been expected, had the people contributed in the same proportion to their numbers as the people of Great Britain',[9] and claim his support for the view that 'the political consequences of taxation in France must be judged principally according to the political and administrative hostilities aroused by taxes, not so much by the economic burden they imposed on the economy'.[10]

Adam Smith in the same passage, however, went on to discuss the lessons to be learnt from the impact of the tax burden on the economy of the Netherlands. He claimed that, although the Dutch government had not behaved imprudently, it had been obliged by force of circumstances to impose taxes upon 'the necessaries of life' on a scale that had 'ruined . . . their principal manufactures'.[11] Adam Smith clearly believed both that high taxation could have this effect and that Britain was sustaining its contemporary tax burden without embarrassment. It is therefore important to stress a different aspect of British experience from that dwelt on by Mathias and O'Brien. Levels of taxation much higher than those experienced in France, and generally regressive in their impact, nevertheless did not cause stagnation and decline as in the Netherlands. The source of the sustained strength of home demand in Britain in the late eighteenth and early nineteenth centuries remains an issue clouded with obscurities, but it is a testimony to the strength of her economy that Britain entered the nineteenth century with living standards as high as anywhere in Europe and with a comparatively high rate of growth in gross national product in spite of having to provide for exceptionally rapid population growth and while carrying the burden of a relatively high incidence of taxation.

O'Brien has elsewhere stressed the extent to which indirect taxation, and particularly the excise, was the source of the bulk of the *increase* in revenue secured by the British state. He resists the view that this increased taxation was regressive in its incidence, remarking that 'Informed and politically important opinion concurred in the view that British citizens should contribute to the needs of the state in proportion to their incomes', and goes on to calculate that

> During the 22 years from 1793 to 1815 something like 63 per cent of the *extra* taxation required to combat France emanated from taxes falling (at least in the perceptions of the day) upon the incomes and consumption patterns of the rich. 'The war for the defence of property' seems to have been financed in large measure by taxes on those possessed of property.[12]

Describing, and where possible quantifying and explaining, British economic strength in the eighteenth century must be fundamental to any understanding of the political and military power of the British state, but it is too simple, if not indeed actively misleading, to refer to the advent of the industrial revolution as a sufficient explanation of the phenomenon. With a suitable exegesis of the processes involved, the assertion may not be beyond justification, but the industrial revolution is too loose and problematic a concept to be of value in this connection. Labelling the economic growth of the late eighteenth and early nineteenth century in this way brings no additional insight. Even the distinctiveness of growth-rates in the period in question has been called increasingly in question in recent years, as the reworking of national accounts has tended to suggest that overall rates of economic growth did not change markedly until after the end of the 'long' eighteenth century.

Crafts, for example, building upon and substantially improving the pathbreaking estimates of Deane and Cole, concluded that the annual percentage rates of growth of national product between 1700 and 1831 were as follows (Deane and Cole's estimates in brackets): 1700–60 0.69 (0.66); 1760–80 0.70 (0.65); 1780–1801 1.32 (2.06); 1801–31 1.97 (3.06). These revised figures suggest a much more modest acceleration than was once supposed, but much of the acceleration that remains was associated with the increasing rate of population growth. If rates of growth in national product per head are considered – a more telling series in this connection – the absence of any brisk acceleration until after 1831 becomes much clearer. The comparable pairs of annual percentage growth rates are 1700–60 0.31 (0.45); 1760–80 0.01 (−0.04); 1780–1801 0.35 (1.08); 1801–31 0.52 (1.61).[13] Yet the British economy diverged markedly from the prevailing European pattern in the course of the 'long' eighteenth century; indeed, the divergence began still earlier. This was especially true of England, and, when one considers the contrasts between her economy and the economies of her continental neighbours, it is possible not only to identify the sources of her superior economic performance, but also to open the way to a discussion of the relationship between the constitution of society and success in engendering economic development.

CHANGING ECONOMIC AND DEMOGRAPHIC STRUCTURES

Unquestionably the most striking and important structural contrast between the English economy and those of neighbouring continental countries lay in the proportion of the labour-force engaged in agriculture. In Britain as a whole Deane and Cole estimated that the proportion of the total occupied population engaged in agriculture, forestry and fishing in 1801 was 35.9 per cent. In England alone in 1811 the proportion of the adult male labour-force (men of 20 years or age and over) engaged in agriculture was 39.3 per cent of the male population aged 20–64.[14] The fact that England was virtually self-sufficient in basic foodstuffs though only one man in three worked on the land implied a massive difference in productivity per head in agriculture compared with the continent where the comparable figure was very seldom less than two in three and ranged as high as four in five.[15] Nutritional levels were probably higher in England than elsewhere. Fogel, for example, presents estimates of achieved final heights of adult males in Britain, Norway, Sweden, France, Denmark and Hungary from the third quarter of the eighteenth century until the third quarter of the twentieth century. *Ceteris paribus*, achieved final height reflects relative levels of nutrition in infancy and childhood fairly accurately

76

(though it can be an unreliable guide where other things are not equal, as for example in different disease environments). Fogel's evidence suggests that heights were greater in Britain than elsewhere during the later eighteenth and early nineteenth centuries, often by a considerable margin.[16] If the agricultural labour-force was proportionately only one-half as large in England as elsewhere and nutritional levels were somewhat higher, it follows that manpower productivity in agriculture must have been at least twice as high.

One man working on the land in England produced enough to feed himself and his family and to sustain two other families working outside agriculture, or three families in all, whereas in France one peasant met only the needs of his own family plus half those of another, or one-and-a-half families in all. Those not working on the land were free to make a living from manufacture, commerce, transport or service employment, without putting their food needs in jeopardy. They were relatively far more numerous in England than elsewhere. The non-agricultural sectors of the English economy were therefore as large, in terms of employment, as the equivalent sectors of a typical continental country with a population two or three times greater than that of England.

The achievement of English agriculture was perhaps even more remarkable than might appear at first sight from such calculations. High levels of output per head in farming were to be found in the colonies of settlement in North America, but across the Atlantic good land was abundant and land could be substituted for labour and capital, thereby facilitating high manpower productivity. In England all the better land had long been settled; moreover, agricultural output had to keep pace with a population rising considerably faster than on the continent. In the main, the increases in output were secured from land already in cultivation. Gross cereal yields, for example, appear to have doubled between Elizabethan times and the Regency period, in the case of wheat from 10 bushels per acre or less to 20 bushels per acre or more.[17] Net yields, of course, increased substantially more sharply, by perhaps 135 per cent rather than 100 per cent (net yield measures the quantity available for consumption; gross yield the quantity harvested: the former is therefore the relevant statistic in this context).[18]

That output per head should have risen roughly in parallel with output per acre in the seventeenth and eighteenth centuries is the more remarkable in that on Ricardian principles the pressures generated by the problem of declining returns at both the intensive and extensive margins of cultivation should have caused output per head on the land to fall, *ceteris paribus*. High yields per acre had been achieved at times in medieval England but probably at the expense of labour productivity.[19] The rise in yields that took place in early-modern England has attracted much attention, especially as over the two centuries in which it occurred there was little or no parallel increase in most continental countries. Yet, though the rise in yields deserves to be studied, the aspect of change that should occupy the centre of the stage is the increase in output per head that occurred at the same time. Greater output with unchanged productivity per head could not have sustained the rapid growth that took place in the proportion of the work-force making a living outside agriculture. The shift in employment structure was the change that mattered and that depended on the ability of those employed in eighteenth-century agriculture to produce much more each year than their great grandfathers had done, a feat which the latter in turn had achieved in relation to *their* great grandfathers.

A second respect in which events in England diverged from the continental norm was in the pattern and scale of urban growth. In the sixteenth century there was nothing in the character of urban England to set it apart from neighbouring countries. London had long been the largest city in England but it was not a giant by the standards of the rest of Europe.[20] The proportion of the population living in towns was lower than the average in western Europe, and no town other than London was a considerable urban centre judged by the standards of Italy or the Netherlands. However, the seventeenth century was London's century. Before its end London had become the largest city in Europe and faster-growing than any of its major continental rivals. It remained dominant in England, dwarfing the rest. One-tenth or more of the population of the whole country lived in the Great Wen.

In the eighteenth century London continued to grow, but now little faster than the population as a whole. Urban growth became much more widespread but highly selective. Ancient county-towns slid gently down the rank-order of English towns, while places like Liverpool, Birmingham and Manchester that had been insignificant settlements in Tudor times grew very swiftly and raced up the rankings. In 1801 these three were the largest towns in the kingdom after London, and, of the traditional major provincial centres, only Bristol, Norwich and Newcastle featured among the ten largest towns (the other three towns making up the top ten were Leeds, Sheffield and Plymouth, all comparative newcomers as major centres). Many English towns maintained rates of growth that were meteoric by the standards of contemporary Europe: there, growth was much slower and major changes in the rank ordering of towns were rare. Figure 4.1, for example, shows the contrast between England and France in this regard. Since the vertical scale is logarithmic, the slope of the lines indicates the rate of growth. The English national population, though far smaller than the French, was rising more rapidly, and the extent of the contrast became more marked as the century progressed, but the contrast in urban growth-rates was far more dramatic. In particular, there was an astonishing burst of urban growth in provincial England. Towns in this category in England were growing at an average rate of 1.7 per cent per annum between 1700

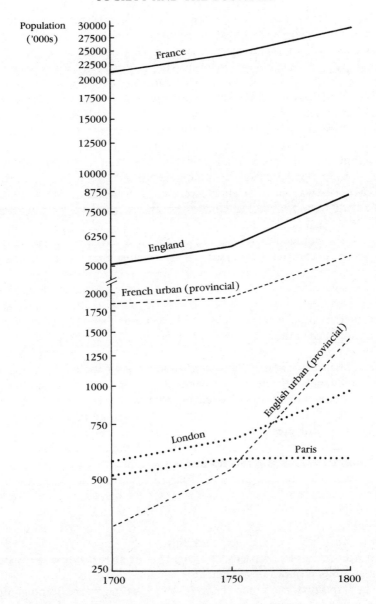

Note The urban provincial populations of England and France represent the total populations of all towns and cities with 5,000 or more inhabitants except for the capital cities of the two countries.

Sources The data used in the figure were taken from Wrigley, *People, Cities and Wealth*, tabs 7.3, 7.4, and 7.9, 166, 170 and 184–5, except for the population of Paris, taken from de Vries, *European Urbanization*, app. 1, p. 275.

Figure 4.1 The national and urban populations of England and France.

and 1800, when the comparable rate in France was 0.4 per cent. So marked was the contrast between England and the continent in general that during the second half of the eighteenth century 70 per cent of the rise in the overall proportion of the population living in towns in Europe as a whole was due to the growth of towns in England alone.[21]

The urban history of England, therefore, stands in sharp contrast with that of continental Europe. De Vries's work shows that between the end of the sixteenth century and the later decades of the eighteenth century (the phasing varying somewhat in different regions) there was little overall change in the degree of urbanization in Europe, some shrinkage in the smaller towns being offset by moderate growth in the largest towns.[22] Nowhere else was there the effervescent surge of urban growth to be found in England. The only other country to exceed the level of urbanization reached in England by 1800 was the Netherlands where more than one-third of the population was urban by the later seventeenth century, but the urban proportion decreased in the Netherlands in the eighteenth century while overall population totals stagnated.[23]

Success in raising output per head in agriculture and rapid urban growth were closely related to each other. This is obviously true in the mechanical sense that with an increase in agricultural output without much increase in the number working on the land, a steadily rising surplus of food was made available after meeting the nutritional needs of the farming work-force. Townsmen did not have to go hungry even though their numbers rose rapidly, nor were they yet dependent upon imports of food. However, the two developments were linked in other ways. The growth of towns, and above all the growth of London, afforded great opportunities to farmers who had produce to sell. In an economy without any significant urban sector, where the great majority of families were dependent on agriculture, a perennial difficulty facing the substantial farmer was that in good years when he had plenty to spare for sale off the farm, few of his potential customers had any reason to enter the market as buyers because they could cover their own needs. A large and expanding market in which demand tended to rise in the long term and did not fluctuate greatly from year to year was an immense stimulus to the larger farmer, justifying investment to increase capacity and encouraging specialization. Subsistence farming inhibited both developments.

Other aspects of economic change in the 'long' eighteenth century invite comment. For example, the progressive transformation of occupational structure, though implicit in the changes already described, would merit explicit examination. The combination of a rapidly expanding population with a largely stationary agricultural work-force meant that employment in both the secondary and the tertiary sectors grew very rapidly. It can be shown that the rise in employment in manufacturing, handicrafts, services and the professions was not solely, or even predominantly, an urban phenomenon. The urban population in England (living in towns with 5,000 or more inhabitants) rose from about 0.34 million to 2.38 million between 1600 and 1800; the rural population (living in the countryside or in towns with fewer than 5,000 inhabitants) which did not make its living from agriculture rose from about 0.9 million to 3.14 million over the same period.[24] Across the whole range of settlement sizes from tiny villages up through the urban hierarchy there was an increasing diversity of employment. Most secondary and tertiary workers continued to supply the needs of local markets for goods and services rather than responding to national or international demand,[25] but, in step with the changing structure of employment, there was a parallel change in the relative importance of different industries, and both changes took place, of course, in response to and in harmony with changes in the structure of demand.

Since all such changes were so closely linked to rising agricultural productivity and to urban growth, it seems unnecessary to treat them at length before turning to consider the ways in which the distinctive English economic experience was linked to wider features of English society. It should be noted, however, that whereas change in these interrelated features of the economy continued steadily in England in the 'long' eighteenth century, comparable changes on the continent took place much more slowly, if at all, so that the differences between England and the continent grew more marked and the relative advantages that England enjoyed advanced in step. In contrast, during the nineteenth century, often regarded as the classic century of the industrial revolution, any margin of advantage possessed by England was rapidly eroded. Before the end of the century it was readily visible that in economic matters the pace was being set by Germany and the United States. The coming of the industrial revolution quickly extinguished the relative advantage established over the two preceding centuries. In part this was probably due to the fact that advantages conferred by superior material technology are apt to be ephemeral because such technology is easily transferred whereas those due to different social characteristics are much less easily acquired. They are also, unfortunately, difficult to identify with confidence, but in the remainder of this chapter I shall suggest why some of them merit attention because of their close links with the economic changes then in train.

THE UNDERPINNINGS OF GROWTH

If the rise in output per head in agriculture was the most remarkable single aspect of English economic growth, it makes sense to begin with rural society. Several of the explanations of what used once to be termed the 'agricultural revolution' command little respect today. The chronology of parliamentary enclosure, for example, does not fit the chronology of agricultural change which now seems most plausible. The chronology of

81

enclosure of all types presents less difficulty, since there was a very large volume of non-parliamentary enclosure in the seventeenth century,[26] but there are difficulties with any argument based on enclosure as a sufficient explanation for improvement, such as the progress made in areas that had always been enclosed.

Other problems obtrude. There are good grounds for thinking, for example, that enclosure was frequently the final act in a lengthy series of prior changes in the agriculture of a local community rather than in itself the instigator of change.[27] Again, re-analysis of the material that Arthur Young collected and believed to demonstrate the superiority of agriculture in enclosed parishes suggests that there may have been far less difference between the enclosed and the unenclosed than he supposed.[28] Nor is it readily convincing to argue that the key to increased productivity lay either in changes in the material technology of production, such as the seed drill and the scythe, or in different crop combinations or rotations. There were too many instances of substantial increases in output occurring without such changes for them to appear a sufficient explanation. A more persuasive possible explanation may lie in the changing pattern of labour usage over the farming year. Reducing seasonal labour-slacks in ways that enhanced crop yields might in principle contribute both to raising output per head and output per acre.[29]

No single or simple explanation is likely to prove adequate, but the structure of English rural society was sufficiently unusual to suggest that it should receive close attention. The Brenner thesis, which might be summarized baldly as the view that only in England did those at the base of rural society gain a complete command of their own labour while those at the top gained absolute control of their property in land, is not beyond dispute, and the threefold division of rural society into landlord, substantial tenant farmer and landless labourer, is much too crude to do justice to a complex reality;[30] but the extent and importance of the contrasts between England and the near continent are readily visible. It is clear evidence of the profound nature of the change that occurred in England that the descriptive vocabulary of rural life was altered. By the mid-eighteenth century 'yeoman' and 'husbandman' had all but disappeared from usage, to be replaced by 'farmer' and 'labourer'.

Sweet Auburn has exercised a lasting influence on writing about rural society, or at least echoes a sentiment widely shared. The passing of Goldsmith's bold peasantry still evokes regret. Take, for example, the question of the emigration of young men and women from the countryside. That many left is clear beyond dispute. It does not follow, however, that the number remaining behind fell. There is no warrant for the supposition that the numbers engaged in agriculture fell until well into the nineteenth century, still less that the numbers living in the countryside declined. The number of adult males engaged in English agriculture rose continuously,

if slowly, between 1811 and 1851 from 910,000 to 1,010,000, but employment in a wide range of rural crafts and services rose much more rapidly.[31]
The alternative needs explicit consideration. If many had not left the land,
the consequences in all probability would have been dire. At issue, among
other things, is the difference between capitalist and peasant agricultural
systems.

Malthus raised this question long ago in the later editions of the *Essay
on Population*. In a brief aside in the chapter 'Of Systems of Agriculture
and Commerce Combined', he remarked that in capitalist agriculture 'upon
the principle of private property' it could never be in the interest of a
farmer to retain in his employment any man who did not produce the
equivalent of a wage sufficient to support himself and a family of average
size at whatever was the prevailing conventional minimum standard of life
for a labourer.[32] The product of the marginal man could never be less than
this minimum level and by implication the average product must exceed it
significantly. Malthus contrasted this situation with that obtaining in other
production systems where deeper poverty resulted. He did not discuss
peasant agriculture specifically in this context, but his argument can be
extended in this way, and indeed it is a commonplace to do so in the
literature of development economics. If the values of a peasant society are
such that a family will not readily countenance the departure of a son
from the family holding unless the *average*, as opposed to the *marginal*,
product has dropped to the level of subsistence, rural society will suffer
from over-population, living standards will be severely depressed and the
mobility of labour seriously inhibited.[33]

It may be difficult to establish conclusively whether the peasant agricultural systems of continental Europe were associated with attitudes on the
part of peasant families that would have tended to induce poverty in the
manner just adumbrated, when numbers were rising. Nor does it follow,
of course, that a willingness to dismiss workers who are unable to produce
as much as they cost in wages will always have benign effects on the
prevailing standard of living. Yet the release of labour from the agricultural
sector was such a prominent and unusual feature of early-modern England,
and the rise in agricultural productivity was such a crucial aspect of her
economic development, that the demise of the virgater/husbandman and
the rise of the capitalist farmer should be seen not only as a probable
source of increased efficiency of production but as a plausible reason both
for a much-increased output per head and for the avoidance of the deeper
rural poverty that might otherwise have accompanied such a rapid increase
in population.

The clutch of characteristics associated with market-orientated production on capitalist lines are the stock in trade of modernization theories:
the replacement of custom by contract, of ascription by achievement; the
attainment of a high degree of individual autonomy; the development of a

particular form of rationality closely linked to self-interest. Such features are supposed to be closely related to one another and jointly to generate a higher level of efficiency in the economy, for example by specialization of function, the process immortalized by Adam Smith when he told the parable of the pinmakers.[34]

The extent to which the nature of English society was conducive to the development of these characteristics may most conveniently be judged in the first instance by considering the question of individual autonomy. The supposition that individual autonomy is possible – a belief in the ability of the individual to pursue his rational self-interest (involving a calculus in which the unit is the individual and the accounting scale is pecuniary gain) – is plainly mistaken for all people some of the time, and perhaps for some people all of the time, for reasons that transcend the structural characteristics and behavioural patterns of particular societies. Consider the life-cycle. Everyone while growing to maturity must necessarily be incapable of autonomy in infancy and to a lesser degree during childhood. Most people then experience interludes of similar dependency because of illness, even in adult years, and those who survive into old age will relive the experience of childhood as increasing feebleness of body and mind renders them unable to maintain their independence. In some circumstances widowhood may involve similar difficulties, as may also unemployment, the inability to find a way of earning a livelihood.

All societies must develop behavioural norms and an institutional framework to enable individuals to cope with life-cycle problems of this type, but not all societies adopt the same solutions. The dominant mechanism in almost all past societies for coping with such problems was the family. For different purposes the family might be defined to extend to more or less remote kin, and such definitions varied substantially in different cultural areas, but a suitably defined family group was usually the most important and sometimes the sole source of succour. The high priority of claims upon family and kin to overcome or ameliorate the helplessness brought about by life-cycle problems was widely recognized in most societies. Since the imperative need to make such a claim might arise for any person at any time even temporary divorce from kin involved danger and permanent divorce was hazardous. Norms of behaviour were internalized to reflect the recognition of these constraints. Atomistic individualism would then appear both repugnant and unwise. Safety depended on close physical proximity to those who would recognize a claim, since claims could usually only be made in person.

Sen's analysis of exchange entitlement in conditions that might result in famine is applicable much more widely.[35] Just as he showed how individuals or groups might die from starvation even though the physical harvest was at a normal level, so failure to be able to claim an entitlement associated, say, with widowhood might jeopardize living standards, health and even life itself, whatever the degree of general prosperity in the community as a whole. At intervals during the life-cycle every individual had to face the possibility that he or she could expect to continue to survive only if able to call upon resources made available by others at their discretion, whether in the form of material aid or personal services. Where the source of such aid was the family or a wider kin-group it was dangerous to lose contact with them. Individual autonomy was a largely meaningless concept where norms of this type prevailed.

In Elizabethan England there began to develop an institutional frame-work for coping with life-cycle crises, later modified and extended, which greatly reduced the extent of dependence upon kin and thereby enlarged *pari passu* the opportunity for individual autonomy, for the establishment of atomistic individualism as a normal mode of behaviour, for the trans-action of economic affairs in a capitalist manner. The development of the poor law and its associated institutions meant that while the family *might* continue to meet the exigencies of the life-cycle affecting its members it only *had* to provide help, care and guidance for the infant and child.

The other junctures at which dependence upon others was unavoidable were dealt with by establishing a flow of resources from the local com-munity as a whole, brought into being by a local tax, on which anyone might make a claim provided that he or she could prove eligibility by having a local settlement (claim on the parish) and that the case fell into one of the categories defined as justifying a transfer payment. Thus a widow in virtue of her state and inability to fend for herself could make a claim of right upon the parish even though she might have, say, a son living in the community. In the eyes of someone from a different culture, accustomed to acknowledge the absolute claim of a parent on the resources of his or her offspring, the failure of a son to aid his mother might seem aberrant if not abhorrent, but a widow in early-modern England was not placed in jeopardy by the failure of kin to respond. An exchange entitle-ment existed irrespective of the attitude of kin. The poor-law system was the welfare state writ small.[36] The scale of such transfer payments was substantial. Stone's remodelling of Gregory King's national accounts for 1688 suggests that poor relief accounted for almost one-quarter of the total sum raised in local and national taxes combined.[37]

Changes in assumptions about what is due to whom and from whom, in related patterns of behaviour, in personal and institutional responses to need – in short, in social norms – do not take place overnight, so that it would be naïve to expect to find that the enactment of the Elizabethan poor law led to instant changes in behaviour, just as it would be mistaken to suppose that its enactment reflected a wholly new approach to the problem of coping with crises of dependency.[38] Our ignorance about any changes in attitude and practice associated with the new system remains profound, but there were features of English life which were markedly different from those to be found on the continent and which *prima facie* it is reasonable to suppose related to the comparative unimportance of close contact with family or kin to individuals in early-modern England.

An especially interesting example is the propensity to migrate. The proportion of men and women who lived out their lives in the parish of their birth was remarkably low in England. Family reconstitution studies have repeatedly shown that the percentage of children born in a given parish and surviving childhood who subsequently married and/or died there was very small, at once an irritation in that much work may yield relatively little usable demographic information and an impressive testimony to the absence of barriers, social, economic or familial to movement out of one's place of birth.[39] Similar studies undertaken in France, Germany and Italy routinely show a far higher proportion of 'stay-at-homes'.

Even in the sixteenth century immigrants came to London from all over England, and their origins show that the remote counties of the north and west were often over-represented relative to what would be expected from standard models of migration behaviour.[40] The umbilical link between the individual and his family and community was cut early in life. The several ways in which settlement in a 'foreign' parish could be secured were well understood and widely exploited. A year spent in service was one such way.[41] For a very large fraction of each rising generation, both male and female, the period spent in service, beginning in the mid-teens and lasting for most of the next decade, broke or greatly lessened family ties, at least in the sense that young men and women sensed and exercised a wide measure of independence in the decisions about marriage and future residence that would determine whether their adult life was spent in the same community in which their childhood had been passed.

Service might also provide the wherewithal to marry and set up a farming household or a craft workshop. Kussmaul has shown, for example, how, on Arthur Young's estimates of the cost of stocking and equipping a small farm, a young man and a young woman in service might reasonably hope to launch themselves into marriage after about ten years in service, provided that they were prepared to save the bulk of their money earnings (the bulk of their earnings came to them, of course, in kind).[42] Service was a pervasive experience among adolescents and young adults in early-modern England. The limited evidence available suggests that between 30 and 40 per cent of all young men and young women in the age group 20–24 were in service at any one point in time,[43] and a substantially higher proportion of all young people spent a period in service at some time between their fifteenth and twenty-fifth birthdays.

If, to the farmer, land is an asset like any other, valued chiefly as it affords a return on capital invested, and leasehold is regarded as offering as promising a base for enterprise as freehold, and the population is highly mobile, neither the economic nor the psychological prerequisites of a peasant culture are present. Agriculture is well placed to respond to opportunities presented by urban growth. Labour will find little difficulty in abandoning the countryside in favour of the town, or agriculture in favour of a handicraft or service employment, if higher wages or the prospect of fuller employment elsewhere suggest that there is an advantage to be had from making the move.

At one extreme, one might place the system of peasant agriculture in Austria described by Berkner;[44] at the other, the kind of rural community that had become commonplace in England by the eighteenth century. Austrian peasant land-holdings were indivisible and inalienable. Marriage required access to a farm or entitlement to succession to it. Those who were unlucky in this regard could assure themselves of maintenance on their native holding but at the price of permanent celibacy and a subordinate position. Any other life-strategy entailed much hazard and uncertainty. In England, too, marriage was an assertion of economic independence but it could be achieved in many different ways even within a rural community and migration might open many more. There was no fallback of right upon an ancestral holding but the parish underwrote insurance against the chief hazards of life, and the parish that afforded this support might as well be 10 or even 100 miles from a man's or woman's native heath as be the parish of birth. This same phenomenon of comparative rootlessness may well have something to do with the relatively high percentage of transatlantic emigrants who came from British shores until the early nineteenth century. The journey on from London to Boston involved far more miles of travel than an initial move from, say, Gamlingay to London but to the individual concerned the decision to make the further move may often have seemed an extension of the original decision.[45] The extremes of reluctance to settle permanently in the New World evinced by many French migrants to Quebec when compared to the reactions of English migrants in similar circumstances is partly attributable to the difference in attitude to contact with kin and native community that characterized rural society in England and France.[46]

The institution of marriage, like the propensity to migrate (the two were, of course, closely linked phenomena), forms part of the social context within which economic growth occurred in early modern England, and, again like migration, it helps to explain the form and scale of that growth. It would be as unsatisfactory to try to understand English economic history between the reigns of Elizabeth and Victoria without paying attention to such elements within the social context of the country as it would be to explain the astonishing achievements of the Japanese economy since the Second World War without reference to the distinctive attitudes and social norms that drive so many Japanese to such fierce endeavour.

It is a simple matter to show that if women marry comparatively late in life and a significant proportion remain unmarried, and if there exists a

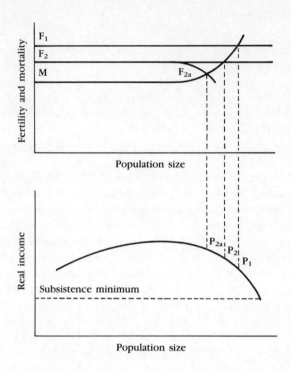

Figure 4.2 Fertility, mortality, population size and living standards

ceiling to the population growth-rate set by the productive capacity of the economy, the lower level of fertility brought about by a modest level of nuptiality will produce a higher average standard of living than could be attained if marriage were more universal and fertility higher.[47] Figure 4.2 illustrates this point. The line representing mortality in the upper part of the Figure (M) is taken as a constant until population reaches a critical size, and then rises with any further increase in population because of the pressure on resources that such a rise is assumed to entail. When marriage is early and universal, fertility is high (F_1) and population growth will continue until population pressure is intense and real incomes are in consequence little above the level of bare subsistence (P_1 in the lower half of the Figure, which shows the relationship between population size and the standard of living). Where marriage takes place later in life and celibacy is common, fertility will necessarily be lower, *ceteris paribus* (F_2); and if fertility is both lower *and* sensitive to economic circumstances (F_{2a}), real incomes will benefit (P_2, P_{2a}). An example of the latter case would be a peasant community in which holdings were not divisible and marriage was contingent upon access to a holding. In such circumstances once the land is fully settled, marriage age will rise and celibacy become more widespread until the movement of young men into marriage does no more than balance the exit of their fathers through death. The logic of this argument is strong even though the scale of the effect in a particular case may be hard to measure.

Nuptiality was low and variable in early modern England. Secular changes in real wages were closely paralleled by a lagged sympathetic change in nuptiality. When the economic horizon darkened people responded by marrying later and less; when it lightened, by embarking upon marriage earlier and more universally. Moreover, the swings in nuptiality were wide enough to dominate growth-rates: in general, through their impact on fertility, they were substantially more important than secular changes in mortality in this regard.[48] This characteristic of marriage in England probably helped to protect standards of living. If the threat to real wages posed by over-rapid population growth, a real enough threat in any pre-industrial society, was rendered largely impotent by compensatory movements in nuptiality, an important danger to economic growth and improved living standards was counteracted.

CONCLUSION

The eighteenth-century British economy was still essentially a pre-industrial economy and subject to the severe limitations inherent in all such economies. Its remarkable success should not be regarded as a foretaste of what happened later. In most respects it was doing with exceptional success what other pre-industrial economies had normally done less well rather than benefiting from some wholly new stimulus to growth. It remained an economy grounded in agriculture, a situation reflected perhaps in the very high proportion of the yield of the excise, by far the most efficient and dynamic element in the eighteenth-century tax system, which came from agricultural products in their processed forms. The excises on beer, malt and hops constituted three-quarters of the yield of all excises; soap, candles and leather much of the balance.[49] It was not until late in the century, and then only in limited areas of the economy, that the material technology employed began to differ significantly from that widely available in the more advanced pre-industrial economies. The growth-rate of the economy as a whole remained modest either by the standards of industrialized countries in the twentieth century or those of the third world today: 1 per cent per annum remained an exceptional growth-rate in the eighteenth century; in the nineteenth and much more widely in the twentieth century a rate in the range between 2 and 5 per cent per annum has been common. Given that population was growing at much the same rate as output during most of the eighteenth century, and perhaps slightly faster than output towards its end,[50] it need occasion no surprise that the question of the trend in real incomes over the period remains a matter for debate.

Although the final resolution of the uncertainty about whether the rate of growth of production would finally outstrip population growth by a decisive margin did not take place until well after the end of the eighteenth century, the scale and the radical nature of other changes in the economy stand out clearly, and represent a notable contrast with the history of the continental economies of the period. The keynote feature might be termed lopsided growth. An increase in the aggregate size of the economy and therefore in the scale of output need not necessarily imply any change of consequence in individual well-being or in the scale of government resources secured by taxation if these are measured per head (it may be like blowing up a balloon, where everything becomes larger, but the relative proportion of each part remains unchanged). Much growth in pre-industrial economies was of this type, but, in the absence of structural change, even where such growth was on a large scale it simply meant more of the same and did not increase the likelihood that the economy would become transformed nor that an acceleration into sustained growth of the type made familiar by recent history would occur. More often than not, indeed, such growth probably diminished the chance of radical change by increasing the difficulty of avoiding an unfavourable shift in the ratio of resources to population.

Lopsided growth, on the other hand, implied a greater possibility of subsequent change, of breaking free from the negative feedback patterns inhibiting secular growth which were such a striking feature of the functioning of pre-industrial economies.[51] The huge decline in the proportion of the labour force employed on the land and the sweeping changes in employment structure elsewhere in the economy; the striking rise in the scale of urban populations and the re-ordering of the rank order of cities – such changes were far more portentous than the relatively modest overall growth-rate and represented a far more clear-cut contrast with continental economies than those identified by the techniques of national income accounting. Lopsided growth did not, of course, guarantee that the industrial revolution would take place; its advent required other stimuli in addition.[52] The Dutch Republic a century earlier had experienced a broadly similar evolution for a time but there the momentum of growth died away and in the eighteenth century there was regression. It is especially in the context of lopsided growth that it is important to stress the degree to which what was distinctive about the English economy was linked to what was distinctive about English society.

Adam Smith wrote of the range of possibilities for growth open to societies that were able and willing to make the most of their opportunities. He did not envisage such growth as unlimited. Growth was always subject to strong constraints and was normally attended by increasing difficulties as it progressed, as a necessary consequence of the very process of growth.[53] Whether or not opportunities were seized depended upon the socio-political constitution of the society: whether, for example, the parable of the pinmakers could become more than an abstract possibility turned on whether a market economy prevailed, and that in turn on the nature of the legal system and the strength and nature of status divisions.[54] English society during the 'long' eighteenth century was well suited to growth of the kind he had in mind. It was so not least because of the pattern of related institutions, conventions and assumptions that went with the existence of a distinctive set of tenurial and social structures on the land, the statutory provision of a poor law system of support for those in need, the institution of service, the frequency of migration over both short and long distances and the set of conventions that governed decisions to marry. The list could be extended and the interrelations between the several elements should be more deeply explored. However, the underlying point is simple. English economic success long predated the conventional chronology of the industrial revolution and gradually set England apart from the continent, most notably in the course of the 'long' eighteenth century. Economic growth had some autonomous features but it was also bound up with the wider constitution of society, so that explanations of its nature that are confined to economic categories are foredoomed to remain unsatisfactory.

The wheel turns full circle. The rise in the power of the British state in the course of the eighteenth century was largely a reflection of the exceptional success of the British economy and its unusual nature; but that success stemmed in part from the structure of British society and the functioning of the political system. The writings of the classical economists down to the time of Ricardo reflect their understanding of this point.[55] Adam Smith and Malthus frequently sought an explanation of economic success or failure in the institutional framework in which material production took place. Arbitrary taxation, insecurity of personal property, the superiority of custom over contract or the privileges attaching to inherited status could blight the fairest prospects. Ricardo secured a more rigorous analytic framework by largely excluding such questions from his analyses, although he was aware of their potential importance and occasionally referred to them directly.[55] The subsequent splintering of academic disciplines has tended to make what was clear to Smith and Malthus less readily apparent to us. Here perhaps is a case where specialization of function has not enhanced the quality of the product.

NOTES

1 E. A. Wrigley, 'The Growth of Population in Eighteenth-Century England: A Conundrum Resolved', *Past and Present*, 98 (1983), tab. 1, 122.
2 The totals for England, Wales and Scotland were taken from the 1821 census of England, Wales and Scotland: *Parliamentary Papers* (1822), vol. XV: for Ireland from *Irish Historical Statistics: Population, 1821–1971*, ed. W. E. Vaughan and A. J. Fitzpatrick (Dublin, 1978), tab. 3, 3. The French total was

taken from B. R. Mitchell, *European Historical Statistics 1750–1975*, second rev. edn (London, 1980), tab. 31, 30.

3 There is a useful compilation of the comparative size of the armies of the major European powers at intervals during the eighteenth century in J. Childs, *Armies and Warfare in Europe 1648–1789* (Manchester, 1982), tab. 1, 42. It was common for more than one-half of the troops forming British armies to be foreigners (as, for example, during the War of the Spanish Succession: D. W. Jones, *War and Economy in the Age of William III and Marlborough* (Oxford, 1988), 9–11, but it was also common for a substantial proportion of the troops of other countries to consist of mercenaries. In wartime up to one-quarter of the French army was non-French, and in times of exceptional stress as much as one-half of Prussia's troops were hired from abroad (Childs, *Armies and Warfare*, 46–50).

4 Brewer stresses the same point: J. Brewer, *The Sinews of Power: War, Money and the English State 1688–1783* (London, 1989), 182.

5 Evidence to support these estimates of occupational structure and urban growth may be found in E. A. Wrigley, 'Urban Growth and Agricultural Change: England and the Continent in the Early Modern Period', *Journal of Interdisciplinary History*, 15 (1985), 683–728.

6 J. de Vries, 'The Population and Economy of the Preindustrial Netherlands', *Journal of Interdisciplinary History*, 15 (1985), 671–4: P. Bairoch, 'Europe's Gross National Product: 1800–1975', *Journal of European Economic History*, 5 (1976), tab. 6, 286.

7 P. Mathias and P. O'Brien, 'Taxation in Britain and France, 1715–1810. A Comparison of the Social and Economic Incidence of Taxes Collected for the Central Governments', *Journal of European Economic History*, 5 (1976), 639.

8 ibid., 635.

9 A. Smith, *An Inquiry into the Nature and Causes of the Wealth of Nations*, ed. E. Cannan (fifth edn, 2 vols; London, 1961), vol. II, 438.

10 Mathias and O'Brien, 'Taxation in Britain and France', 635.

11 Smith, *Wealth of Nations*, vol. II, 438.

12 P. K. O'Brien, 'The Political Economy of British Taxation, 1660–1815', *Economic History Review*, second series, 41 (1988), 12 and 13: see esp. also in this connection tables 4 and 6 (9 and 15).

13 N. F. R. Crafts, *British Economic Growth during the Industrial Revolution* (Oxford, 1985), tab. 2.11, 45.

14 P. Deane and W. A. Cole, *British Economic Growth 1688–1959: Trends and Structure* (Cambridge, 1962), tab. 30, 142; E. A. Wrigley, 'Men on the Land and Men in the Countryside: Employment in Agriculture in Early Nineteenth-Century England', in L. Bonfield, R. M. Smith and K. Wrightson (eds), *The World We Have Gained: Histories of Population and Social Structure* (Oxford, 1986), tab. 11.12, 332.

15 Data for a number of European countries suggest a figure in the range 60–80 per cent about 1800; see Wrigley, 'Urban Growth and Agricultural Change', 723, n. 32. On the question of the degree of agricultural self-sufficiency in England *c.* 1800 (probably in the range 90–95 per cent), see Wrigley, 'Urban Growth and Agricultural Change', 696, n. 10.

16 R. W. Fogel, *Second Thoughts on the European Escape from Hunger: Famines, Price Elasticities, Entitlements, Chronic Malnutrition, and Mortality Rates* (Cambridge, Mass., 1989), tab. 9, 50.

17 This topic has given rise to a very large literature. Among the more important recent contributions are: M. Turner, 'Agricultural Productivity in England in

the Eighteenth Century: Evidence from Crop Yields', *Economic History Review*, second series, 35 (1982), 489–510; and M. Overton, 'Estimating Crop Yields from Probate Inventories: An Example from East Anglia, 1585–1735', *Journal of Economic History*, 39 (1979), 363–78. There is a useful summary of existing estimates in D. Grigg, *English Agriculture: An Historical Perspective* (Oxford, 1989), fig. 6.1, 65.

18 Approximately 2.5 bushels of wheat per acre was needed for seed, and this figure did not rise as yields rose. When, therefore, gross yields rose from 10 to 20 bushels, net yields rose from 7.5 to 17.5 bushels, or by about 135 per cent. The significance of the distinction between gross and net yields to the understanding of the success of English agriculture in the early modern period is explored in E. A. Wrigley, 'Some Reflections on Corn Yields and Prices in Pre-Industrial Economies', in E. A. Wrigley, *People, Cities and Wealth: The Transformation of Traditional Society* (Oxford, 1987), 92–130.

19 High yields per acre, intensive cultivation and the virtual elimination of fallowing were all to be found in parts of eastern Norfolk before the sharp fall in population in the wake of the Black Death, but they were achieved only by very large labour inputs per acre: B. M. S. Campbell, 'Agricultural Progress in Medieval England: Some Evidence from Eastern Norfolk', *Economic History Review*, second series, 36 (1983), 26–46.

20 De Vries's data suggest that London was the sixth largest city in Europe in 1550. The five larger cities in descending order of magnitude were Naples, Venice, Paris, Lisbon and Antwerp: J. de Vries, *European Urbanization 1500–1800* (Cambridge, Mass., 1984), app. 1.

21 Wrigley, 'Urban Growth and Agricultural Change', tab. 7, 709.

22 De Vries's estimates suggest that the urban percentage (defined as towns containing 10,000 or more inhabitants) for Europe excluding the British Isles rose from 7.9 per cent in 1600 to 9.1 per cent in 1750 and to 9.2 per cent in 1800. These percentages were obtained by combining information from two tables: de Vries, *European Urbanization*, tab. 3.6, 36–7, and tab. 3.7, 39.

23 De Vries, *European Urbanization*, tab. 3.7, 39, suggests that the urban percentage in the Netherlands fell from 33.6 to 28.8 between 1700 and 1800. The population of the Netherlands is thought to have risen very slightly over the same period from 1.85–1.95 million in 1700 to 2.078 million in 1795: J. A. Faber, H. K. Roessingh, B. H. Slicher van Bath, A. M. van der Woude and H. J. van Xanten, 'Population Changes and Economic Developments in the Netherlands: A Historical Survey', *A. A. G. Bijdragen*, 12 (1965), 110.

24 Wrigley, 'Urban Growth and Agricultural Change', tab. 4, 700–1.

25 Wrigley, 'Men on the Land', 296–304.

26 J. R. Wordie, 'The Chronology of English Enclosure, 1500–1914', *Economic History Review*, second series, 36 (1983), 483–505.

27 See, for example, B. J. Taylor, 'The Economic and Demographic Context of Enclosure: A Case Study from Oxfordshire, *circa* 1550–1850' (Ph.D. thesis, University of Cambridge, 1988), esp. ch. 5.

28 R. C. Allen and C. Ó Gráda, 'On the Road Again with Arthur Young: English, Irish, and French Agriculture during the Industrial Revolution', *Journal of Economic History*, 48 (1988), 93–116.

29 An example of this kind of development may be found in E. A. Wrigley, *Continuity, Chance and Change: The Character of the Industrial Revolution in England* (Cambridge, 1988), 43–4.

30 R. Brenner, 'Agrarian Class Structure and Economic Development in Pre-Industrial Europe', *Past and Present*, 70 (1976), 30–75. See also T. H. Aston

and C. H. E. Philpin (eds), *The Brenner Debate: Agrarian Class Structure and Economic Development in Pre-Industrial Europe* (Cambridge, 1985).

31 Wrigley, 'Men on the Land', tab. 11.2, 300–1, and tab. 11.12, 332.

32 T. R. Malthus, *An Essay on the Principle of Population* (sixth edn, 1826), in E. A. Wrigley and D. Souden (eds), *The Works of Thomas Robert Malthus* (8 vols; London, 1986), vol. III, 405.

33 Malthus first dealt with the limits to growth in a commercial and capitalist country. If one disregards for simplicity of analysis the effects of trade, and assumes the land to be fully occupied, the limit is reached when 'the employment of another labourer on it [the land] will not, on an average, raise an additional quantity of food sufficient to support a family of such a size as will admit of an increase of population'. However, 'even this limit is very far short of what the earth is capable of producing, if all were employed upon it who were not employed in the production of other necessaries; that is, if soldiers, sailors, menial servants, and all the artificers of luxuries, were made to labour on the land. They would not, indeed, produce the support of a family, and ultimately not even of themselves; but, till the earth absolutely refused to yield any more, they would continue to add something to the common stock; and, by increasing the means of subsistence, would afford the means of supporting an increasing population. But this state of things could only be effected by the forced direction of national industry into one channel by public authority. Upon the principle of private property, which it may fairly be presumed will always prevail in society, it could never happen' (Malthus, *Essay on Population*, 405).

34 E. A. Wrigley, 'The Process of Modernization and the Industrial Revolution in England', *Journal of Interdisciplinary History*, 3 (1972), 225–59.

35 A. Sen, *Poverty and Famines: An Essay on Entitlement and Deprivation* (Oxford, 1981).

36 P. Laslett, 'Family, Kinship and Collectivity as Systems of Support in Pre-Industrial Europe: A Consideration of the "Nuclear Hardship" Hypothesis', *Continuity and Change*, 3 (1988), 153–75. The working of the poor law system has become the subject of a number of detailed studies recently: see, for example, T. Wales, 'Poverty, Poor Relief and the Life-Cycle: Some Evidence from Seventeenth-Century Norfolk', in R. M. Smith (ed.), *Land, Kinship and Life-Cycle* (Cambridge, 1984), 351–404; and W. Newman Brown, 'The Receipt of Poor Relief and Family Situation: Aldenham, Hertfordshire 1630–90', in Smith, *Land, Kinship and Life-Cycle*, 405–22.

37 R. Stone, *Some British Empiricists in the Social Sciences* (Cambridge, forthcoming), tab. 3.10.

38 M. K. McIntosh, 'Local Responses to the Poor in Late Medieval and Tudor England', *Continuity and Change*, 3 (1988), 209–45.

39 P. Clark and D. Souden (eds), *Migration and Society in Early Modern England* (London, 1987), contains a number of essays illustrating various aspects of both internal and external migration. Some aspects of internal migration are more fully explored in D. Souden, 'Pre-Industrial English Local Migration Fields' (Ph.D. thesis, University of Cambridge, 1981).

40 V. B. Brodsky, 'Mobility and Marriage in Pre-Industrial England' (Ph.D. thesis, University of Cambridge, 1978), pt II, chs 1 and 2. See also S. Rappaport, *Worlds within Worlds: Structures of Life in Sixteenth-Century London* (Cambridge, 1989), 76–86.

41 A. Kussmaul, *Servants in Husbandry in Early Modern England* (Cambridge, 1981), app. 3, 148–9.

42 ibid., 81–2.
43 P. Laslett, *Family Life and Illicit Love in Earlier Generations* (Cambridge, 1977), tab. 1.7, 34.
44 L. Berkner, 'The Stem Family and the Developmental Cycle of the Peasant Household: An Eighteenth-Century Austrian Example', *American Historical Review*, 77 (1972), 398–418. More generally, see M. Mitterauer and R. Sieder, *The European Family: Patriarchy and Partnership from the Middle Ages to the Present* (Oxford, 1982).
45 D. Souden, ' "Rogues, Whores and Vagabonds"? Indentured Servant Emigration to North America and the Case of Mid Seventeenth-Century Bristol', in Clark and Souden, *Migration and Society*, 150–71.
46 P. N. Moogk, 'Reluctant Exiles: Emigrants from France in Canada before 1760', *William and Mary Quarterly*, third series, 46 (1989), 463–505.
47 E. A. Wrigley and R. S. Schofield, *The Population History of England 1541–1871: A Reconstruction* (London, 1981), 457–66.
48 ibid., 236–48. See also D. Weir, 'Rather Never than Late: Celibacy and Age at Marriage in English Cohort Fertility, 1541–1871', *Journal of Family History*, 9 (1984), 340–54; R. Schofield, 'English Marriage Patterns Revisited', *Journal of Family History*, 10 (1985), 2–20; J. A. Goldstone, 'The Demographic Revolution in England: A Re-Examination', *Population Studies*, 40 (1986), 5–33; Wrigley, 'The Growth of Population in Eighteenth-Century England'.
49 Brewer, *Sinews of Power*, 189. See also O'Brien, 'The Political Economy of British Taxation', esp. tab. 5, 11.
50 See p. 76 above.
51 For a fuller discussion of the nature and prevalence of negative feedback in pre-industrial economies, see E. A. Wrigley, 'Why Poverty was Inevitable in Pre-Industrial Societies', in J. A. Hall and I. C. Jarvie (eds), *Power, Wealth and Belief* (Cambridge, 1992), 91–110.
52 I have set out my understanding of this issue in Wrigley, *Continuity, Chance and Change*, chs 2 and 3, which describe the contrast between an advanced organic economy (i.e. the most developed form of a pre-industrial economy) and a mineral-based energy economy (the type of economy needed to break free from the constraints found in all pre-industrial economies).
53 Adam Smith's views on this subject are described in E. A. Wrigley, 'The Classical Economists and the Industrial Revolution' in *People, Cities and Wealth*, 21–45.
54 See, for example, Smith, *Wealth of Nations*, vol. II, book III, chs II, III and IV, in which Smith conducts a memorable exploration of these issues.
55 For example, he acknowledged that the minimum 'subsistence' wage was determined by custom as much as by physical or biological necessity: 'It is not to be understood that the natural price of labour, estimated even in food and necessaries, is absolutely fixed and constant. It varies at different times in the same country, and very materially differs in different countries. It essentially depends on the habits and customs of the people' (D. Ricardo, *On the Principles of Political Economy and Taxation* in *The Works and Correspondence of David Ricardo*, ed. P. Sraffa with the collaboration of M. H. Dobb (11 vols; Cambridge, 1951–73), vol. I (1951), 96–7. Comparable digressions from a more abstract form of analysis were, however, rare.

5

The Domestic Face of the Military-Fiscal State
Government and society in eighteenth-century Britain

Joanna Innes

How did the eighteenth-century British state's increasing orientation towards interstate rivalry, war and empire affect the ways in which the central institutions of government addressed themselves to the task of ordering and governing British society, when something other than the mobilization of armed force and associated revenues was in question? And was Britain's recurrent involvement in major wars itself a source of social problems? This chapter supplies some tentative answers to both these questions.

The chapter falls into four parts. It can be argued that the reconfiguration of central government institutions associated with what John Brewer has termed the development of a 'military-fiscal' state played a part in disengaging central bodies from the traditional machinery of local government and from a range of domestic governmental activities which had previously preoccupied men at the centre as well as those in the localities. The first section of the chapter develops this case. However – as the second section of the chapter shows – the case must not be overstated. New forms of central–local interaction developed in the new institutional context. What we might loosely term 'social issues', which always bulked large among local authorities' concerns, did not disappear from the central government's agenda.

The repeated mobilization and demobilization of large armed forces during the eighteenth century did have some effect on the ways in which traditionally acknowledged social problems presented themselves – as the third section of the chapter suggests. The mobilization of armed forces created new categories of relief claimant. Crime, traditionally conceived of as an endemic problem, in this period also acquired an epidemic aspect: massive crime-waves followed the end of every war, as contemporaries both observed and came to expect. The ends of wars were also associated with upsurges in vagrancy. Finally, there was concern to ease the reinteg-

96

ration of disbanded soldiers and sailors into the productive labour-force both so that society might benefit from their labours and so that it should not suffer from their 'idleness'. Government responses to these various challenges illustrate some of the forms of state action developed in this period.

The final section of the chapter sets British experience in a European context. By comparison with what took place in numerous other European states, British developments appear modest and undramatic. The chapter concludes with some suggestions as to why they were so.

DISENGAGEMENT?

Any account of the disengagement of central governmental bodies from aspects of the work of domestic government during the late-seventeenth and eighteenth centuries must emphasize changes in the role and activities of the Privy Council. Once *the* organ of central government, intimately involved in all manner of domestic issues, the Privy Council was increasingly marginalized during the late seventeenth and early eighteenth centuries – and no other central body or bodies took on all the responsibilities once vested in it.

During the early seventeenth century, and to some extent between the Restoration and the Glorious Revolution, the Privy Council served as a central administrative clearing-house. All aspects of the work of government came under its purview, including many miscellaneous domestic and local matters. At times of crisis – harvest failure, plague, commercial crisis – the Privy Council might bombard local authorities with instruction and exhortation, and demand from them full accounts of their proceedings. Communications between the centre and the localities were sometimes channelled through the circuit judges, who spent most of the year attached to the high courts in London, but twice a year travelled around the country on circuit. Though they were most extensively exploited in times of crisis, the circuit judges might at any time be asked to bring pressure to bear on local authorities in furtherance of some central programme. In exceptional cases, errant local officers might be summoned before the Council to explain their conduct. Until its abolition during the civil wars, the Star Chamber provided a forum in which Privy Councillors might explore and deliver rulings on troublesome local matters.[1]

The objectives central authorities had in view when they put pressure on local authorities were various. Many of their efforts were designed to promote public order, both in the sense that they were intended to avert serious disorder and in the sense that they aimed to foster the proper ordering of society. Some efforts to control local government were associated with the central government's military and associated fiscal needs, however. During the first half of the seventeenth century – and to some extent during the second half as well – the central state depended upon traditional local authorities to supply it with the men and money it needed to wage war. The militia, the core military force, was levied and trained in counties and towns under the direction of local gentlemen serving as Lord Lieutenants and Deputy Lieutenants. Extraordinary taxes raised to finance wars chiefly took the form of subsidies levied by parish constables under the direction of local gentry serving as subsidy commissioners. Although it was by no means only in these connections that central authorities strove to exert their power in the localities, central dependence on local authorities in these respects provided one reason for keeping them firmly in subjection.[2]

The effective power central authorities enjoyed by virtue of these arrangements should certainly not be overestimated. Seventeenth-century historians have amply illustrated the limits on the central government's power in practice. Men at the centre acted on the basis of patchy and imperfect information. They might lack a sound grasp of realities and practicalities on the ground. Their orders were not always readily complied with. Local authorities were, moreover, entirely capable of taking initiatives of their own; men at the centre might do little more than take up and diffuse what they judged to be good local practice. These are important points to bear in mind. That men at the centre strove to direct and control local authorities is not, however, in question.

During the late seventeenth and early eighteenth centuries, the configuration of institutions at the centre of English – subsequently British – government changed significantly. In formal institutional terms, central government became increasingly polyarchic – multi-centred. Power was distributed among a number of institutions, which were co-ordinated by more or less informal co-operation between leading statesmen. Although the Privy Council remained formally the body from which certain sorts of orders and directions had to issue, decision-making and practical administrative responsibility were increasingly located elsewhere. Certain aspects of imperial administration were the most important matters remaining substantively with the Privy Council. In most other respects, power shifted towards specialized departments: notably, the Treasury, the Admiralty and the offices of the two (sometimes three) Secretaries of State. Parliament became, in practice, a more important part of the machinery of government than it had been theretofore, and absorbed much of the time and energy of leading statesmen. After 1688, Parliament met every year, and for substantial parts of each year (commonly between four and seven months). Every session, a heavy programme of fiscal measures had to gain parliamentary assent: in this connection, much information about the state of the armed forces had to be provided; Parliament might also need to be persuaded of the merits of the government's foreign policy. Leading ministers met regularly as a 'cabinet' to co-ordinate both general governmental and parliamentary activity. Only a small – if crucial – part of the business of government came up at these meetings, chiefly diplomatic and military matters. There was no longer any one central clearing-house in which any matter might be raised and through which most kinds of business might be expected to pass.[3]

Had all the miscellaneous domestic business Privy Councils had previously dealt with been parcelled out among the new specialized departments, it is not obvious where much of it would have found a home. The Secretaries of State inherited a substantial part of it, but not the whole. They took on chiefly those matters which in some way related to other of their concerns. Their prime concerns were diplomatic and military: they co-ordinated the activity of the expanding diplomatic service; they transmitted orders to the army and navy, and were consequently well placed to have a say in military strategy and tactics; they also ran what there was in the way of an intelligence service. Perhaps because of their responsibilities in relation to the movement of troops, it was to the Secretaries of State that magistrates customarily addressed reports of serious disorders. Reports and rumours of sedition were also commonly directed to them. Among their miscellaneous paper-handling tasks, the Secretaries of State – that is to say, the clerks in their office – kept records of and correspondence relating to the pardoning process, a responsibility no doubt originating in their secretarial relationship to the Crown, the fount of mercy. In consequence, the Secretaries were drawn into some aspects of penal practice, assuming some administrative role in relation to transportation and, from the 1770s, forms of imprisonment developed in lieu of transportation.[4]

Until 1782 the Secretaries of State shared responsibility for home affairs. In that year the business of the office was reallocated, one secretary taking over all the 'home' business. The Secretaries' traditional home concerns – disorder, sedition and punishment – formed a reasonably coherent package of issues. During the 1780s and 1790s, Home Secretaries (as they were subsequently to be known) further developed their responsibilities in this general area, accepting responsibility, for example, for piloting relevant legislation through Parliament. However, home affairs represented only a part of the relevant Secretary's brief: he was also charged with all colonial business.[5]

According to its original brief, the Board of Trade, an investigative and advisory body first established in 1696 in succession to several Privy Council committees on 'trade and plantations', should have numbered the condition of the poor among its concerns. It did consider the state of the poor in its earliest years, inter alia launching an enquiry into parochial poor-relief expenditure through the Church of England's visitation machinery (returns were obtained from perhaps one-half the English and Welsh counties). Parliament amended the poor laws in several respects in the

1690s, and then and in the following decade considered amending them more drastically. The board contributed to these discussions. Thereafter, however, it left such matters for others to pursue. Like its precursors, it focused its energies on 'trade and plantations'.[6]

Reconfiguration at the centre was associated with other changes affecting the character of central–local relations. An expansion in the numbers of men directly and fairly effectively controlled from the centre – most notably, in the revenue services and the army – made central government less dependent than previously on the co-operation of local authorities in certain crucial respects. In the 1670s and 1680s, the Treasury assumed direct control over customs and excise collection, previously farmed out to contractors. The collection of land taxes remained in the hands of parish constables, and land-tax commissioners appointed from among local gentlemen. However, between the late seventeenth and the late eighteenth centuries the trend (sometimes temporarily reversed in wartime) was for customs and excise to contribute an ever-greater, and land tax an ever-smaller, proportion of national revenue. The Restoration monarchs had begun to build up a 'standing army' independent of local control. On this basis, they felt able to dispense with the services of the militia. Not until the mid-eighteenth century was the militia revived – and then only to complement professional military forces. In this context, although the political reliability of local authorities continued to be a matter of concern, at least until the waning of party strife in the mid-eighteenth century, their efficiency in discharging routine business was not at most times a matter of pressing concern for central government.[7]

Other factors were undoubtedly also in play, and had been in play for a long period, shaping the tone and content of central–local relations, modifying and reworking early-seventeenth-century patterns. Historians have suggested that the Privy Council became somewhat less *dirigiste* in style even before the Civil War. The limited success of, and degree of hostility aroused by the policy of 'Thorough' may have prompted caution. The abolition of Star Chamber somewhat curtailed the post-Restoration Privy Council's coercive powers. Restoration monarchs experimented with new ways of bullying local authorities – chiefly to further their religious policies – but the most lasting effect of their efforts was to discredit such expedients. The circuit judges continued throughout the eighteenth century occasionally to be asked to communicate the central government's concerns; but their services in this line seem to have been less frequently called upon than before, perhaps in part because, after the Glorious Revolution, increasing rhetorical stress was laid upon the independence of the judiciary. At the turn of the seventeenth and eighteenth centuries, the Privy Council still sometimes summoned local officials before it, but increasingly it relied on correspondence for all communications. In the following decades, as business increasingly gravitated outwards from the Privy Council towards departments, this continued to be their normal mode of operation. Written communications were predominantly informal in character; progressively less use was made of formal instruments of government.[8]

The pattern of Scottish developments, though different in substance from the English, was arguably similar in at least some of its implications. The union of 1707 entailed the abolition of both the Scottish Privy Council and the Scottish Parliament. Scotland, or 'North Britain' as it was thenceforth commonly termed, became subject to the British Privy Council and British Parliament. New bodies were established to safeguard domestic prosperity and good order: initially, in 1711, a 'Commission of Trade and Chamberlainrie', subsequently (1714), a 'Commission of Police'. However, the Lords Commissioners treated their posts as sinecures, and did not emerge as an important force in Scottish life. The Convention of Royal Burghs, the Court of Session, the General Assembly of the Church of Scotland and a succession of voluntary societies established to promote economic development survived as foci for regional concerns, but of course none of these bodies exercised comprehensive governmental powers. During parts of the early eighteenth century, the metropolitan government assigned Scottish affairs to the care of a special third Secretary of State; but Scottish affairs only exceptionally figured more than marginally among the preoccupations of the British Privy Council, cabinet or Parliament.[9]

Extensive Scottish participation in the rebellion of 1745 served briefly to fix the attention of leading British statesmen upon the northern part of the island. Attention focused upon, among other things, the important part played by hereditary office-holders in Scottish local government – in marked contrast to the contemporary English pattern. Post-rebellion legislation abolished the 'heretable jurisdictions', in which important judicial and regulatory powers had been vested in substantial parts of the Highlands and scattered tracts in the lowlands. Hereditary sheriffs also lost their powers, being replaced by 'sheriffs depute' appointed from London – initially, local gentry, subsequently, commonly professional legal men.[10]

If it is possible to attribute greater vitality to Scottish local government in the later than in the earlier eighteenth century, however, the roots of this vitality appear to have been local rather than metropolitan, being associated with a growing fashion for county meetings to consider practical issues of domestic government, and with vigorous efforts by various voluntary societies to foster and direct the course of social and economic change.[11]

RECONFIGURATION

A persuasive case can be made for British central government having in some respects disengaged from various parts of the work of domestic government during the eighteenth century, as interstate rivalry, war and empire, and the mobilization of resources necessary to maintain Britain's international position increasingly absorbed the imagination and energies of leading statesmen. Both initiative and practical administrative responsibility may be said to have devolved on to local authorities, who – with much experience behind them and with a well-developed and increasingly ambitious and reflective culture of public service to sustain them – were at least reasonably well equipped to respond to this challenge. However, the case is easily overstated.

The reconfiguration of government, and particularly the disappearance of any central administrative clearing-house, makes eighteenth-century patterns of governmental activity at times all but impossible to reconstruct. Putting bits and pieces of information from different institutional contexts together, we can sometimes establish that some sort of agreed strategy must have existed in relation to certain domestic issues. However, rarely can we establish how, by whom or in what institutional or extra-institutional context such strategies were developed.

Clues to the existence of some sort of governmental strategy may be provided by speeches made by the monarch at the opening of the parliamentary session, bills subsequently brought before Parliament and Privy Council proclamations – most especially when these cluster in some obviously patterned way. The King's speech was drafted by members of the cabinet and approved in cabinet. In some years, a section – usually the closing section – of this speech addressed domestic issues. These might immediately be referred to a parliamentary committee or some related bill be brought in, sometimes by an office-holder, sometimes by an ordinary Member of Parliament with strong ministerial connections. Parliament sometimes specifically requested the King to issue an associated proclamation: sometimes the timing simply irresistibly suggests a co-ordinated plan. Matters for which there is this sort of evidence of a central government strategy include the relief and discipline of the poor, at the very end of the seventeenth century; the threat of plague, in the early 1720s; crime and general immorality, seen as a root cause of crime, in the early 1750s; and the threat of dearth, at various periods.[12]

The list that can be compiled in this way certainly does not exhaust even the roster of issues attracting the more ambitious, multi-partite forms of central governmental effort. Other matters were more particularly the concern of single departments or other central bodies. Most of the major bodies in the reconfigured governmental system can, in fact, be shown to have engaged – sometimes in rather unexpected ways – with aspects of domestic government.[13]

The Privy Council, as we have noted, does not appear to have been much involved with substantive domestic policy in the eighteenth century – though it sometimes became involved as a matter of form, as the proper body to issue certain sorts of orders. However, it did at this time acquire responsibility for co-ordinating quarantine policy, primarily involving the regulation of shipping. When disease was considered to pose a serious problem within the country, the Privy Council characteristically dealt with this too. When, in 1721, it was feared that plague might be imported from abroad, new legislation empowered the Privy Council to isolate affected areas. In the event, there was no need for it to act. It did, however, act vigorously against 'cattle plague' during several serious outbreaks: directing the destruction of infected animals, restricting the movement of others and receiving reports from local officials in the counties affected.[14]

The cabinet – in origin, a committee of the Privy Council – developed its form and identity in the late seventeenth and early eighteenth centuries. At an early stage it assumed – somewhat incongruously amidst its diplomatic and military concerns – a special role in relation to the administration of criminal justice. In the seventeenth and eighteenth centuries, many crimes carried the death penalty, but a significant proportion of those sentenced to death were pardoned. Until the Revolution, decisions as to whom to pardon seem to have been made by the King, usually on the advice of the circuit judges, who presided over trials for most serious crime. In the eighteenth century, this continued to be the way in which decisions about provincial pardons were made. However, the cases of those sentenced to death in the metropolis – always a disproportionately large fraction of the total – were handled differently. From the 1690s the Recorder of London began to attend upon the cabinet to discuss these cases. Commonly about one-half of those sentenced to death were pardoned, in the metropolis as elsewhere, usually on condition that they submitted to some lesser punishment, such as transportation. In this context, the cabinet's role in the pardoning process provided ministers with a real opportunity to shape the character of criminal justice, by altering the balance between different forms of punishment, according to their sense of the needs of the times. Playing this role kept them aware of trends in metropolitan crime; it also encouraged them to reflect on the relative merits of different forms of punishment. The cabinet's involvement with such matters must have helped secure for criminal justice the important place it was occasionally accorded on the governmental agenda.[15]

The Treasury was the most sprawling of eighteenth-century departments, with a large number of boards and offices associated with different branches of the revenue grouped under it. The Treasury, assisted by the Board of Trade (and its successor, the Privy Council's Committee on Trade and Plantations), clearly played a crucial part in shaping what there was in the way of an economic policy. It was upon such varied stimuli as the Treasury could supply to the national economy – by manipulating customs and excise duties, providing bounties to stimulate particular forms of production or trade, redistributing or (when possible) absolutely reducing tax burdens – that eighteenth-century governments chiefly relied to achieve and distribute the benefits of prosperity, and in general promote domestic contentment.[16]

In the generally well-developed English economy, such measures were expected to suffice. In Scotland (as in Ireland) it could be argued the case was different: more in the way of social engineering, and managed economic development was called for. Extensive Scots participation in the rebellions of 1715 and 1745 disposed ministers to look kindly on schemes to civilize the Scottish people. Special bodies set up to address this task could conveniently be linked, by more or less loose ties, to the Treasury. The year 1727 saw the establishment of a Board of Trustees for Fisheries and Manufactures, charged with promoting Scottish fishing and the linen industry. Its members were appointed by royal patent; its powers determined by two acts of Parliament; its funds supplied from a variety of central sources. The Trustees, who concentrated their efforts on education and training, quality control and the provision of financial incentives, enjoyed very substantial independence, but were required to seek Treasury approval for their plans at three-year intervals. More closely constrained by the need to gain Treasury support for its ventures was a somewhat later body, the Commissioners of the Annexed Estates, established in 1755 to administer certain estates confiscated from Jacobite rebels after the '45, with a view to the social and economic development of the Highlands. The commissioners attempted to reshape tenurial relations after the English model, to improve farming methods and to supply technical and religious education.[17]

The Treasury's capacious umbrella likewise provided shelter for a modest agency, the Inspectorate of Corn Prices, established by act of Parliament in 1770, in the context of public and parliamentary concern about the economic and social effects of adverse trends in grain prices. A team of clerks collated and publicized information collected by inspectors appointed by local magistrates in market-towns throughout Britain, in order to provide a better informational basis for regulating grain imports and exports.[18]

Some of the domestic business that had come the way of seventeenth-century central bodies came as a result of initiatives from without. In the eighteenth century, representations undoubtedly continued to be made on the basis of local experience. They were directed in various ways, and thence might travel by various routes. No doubt ministers and their staff often dealt with such business informally. Applications of this kind, when they survive, can often be found in private, rather than official, papers.[19]

In the eighteenth century, Parliament probably attracted some business that in the seventeenth century might have found its way to the Privy Council. Convened frequently, and always for several months at a time, primarily so that they could work their way through the annual programme of fiscal measures, eighteenth-century Parliaments were, by unintended consequence, more consistently accessible, and consequently more useful, than their seventeenth-century predecessors had been to men confronting problems of government in the localities. Sometimes, especially in the later part of the eighteenth century, Members of Parliament representing local interests sought to address local problems by sponsoring bills that were purely local in scope; but every session also saw a handful of measures addressing the sorts of issues that concerned local authorities by means of generally applicable regulations. It was relatively uncommon, though by no means unknown, for ministers or other leading public office-holders to introduce such bills; but they were consulted about them and might sit on parliamentary committees considering them. Parliament cannot properly be left out of any account of the workings of 'central government' in eighteenth-century Britain. It had become the main forum in which issues of domestic government were addressed. Ministers and other office-holders' attendance on Parliament meant that they could not but be kept aware of these concerns.[20]

Eighteenth-century Parliaments were more than just machines for producing legislation. They might also function as investigative bodies. Both Privy Council and Parliament at various times during this period enquired into such matters as the workings of the grain trade (in response to the threat of dearth) or issues in contention in industrial disputes.[21] Parliamentary resources could also be harnessed to the task of conducting general surveys and, in the second half of the eighteenth century, were repeatedly exploited to this end. In the early 1750s, and at intervals thereafter, the House of Commons launched inquiries into parochial poor-relief expenditure and related aspects of local practice (securing rather more comprehensive returns than those obtained in the 1690s by the Board of Trade). They also sponsored inquiries into imprisonment for debt, vagrancy and charitable endowments. When the Home Office began to collect criminal statistics in the closing decade of the century, it developed a form of inquiry first inaugurated under parliamentary auspices.[22]

Some of these latter inquiries embodied an approach to the tasks facing government that had been developing only since the late seventeenth century. Early-seventeenth-century requests for information from local authorities were usually, in effect, attempts to establish whether local authorities were effectively exerting themselves – or, indeed, were designed to goad them into action. No attempt was made to build up any kind of systematic picture from the returns obtained. In the later eighteenth century the conscientiousness or otherwise of the authorities was not the main concern; the object was rather to take the measure of a problem.

Post-revolutionary fiscal policies mobilized very substantial sums of money. During the eighteenth-century, grants from central funds were made to support a variety of domestic projects. Some monies were pumped into operations under the control of existing governmental agencies, others to voluntary bodies constituted by royal charter. Some examples must suffice to illustrate the variety of ends to which such monies were devoted. On the recommendation of Royal Commissioners appointed to survey the state of education in the Highlands after the '15, £20,000 was set aside to erect and maintain schools. From 1717 the Treasury began to subsidize certain forms of punishment. Public spending in this sector escalated steeply towards the end of the century: some £86,000 went to subsidize transportation to America from 1717 until the subsidy was ended in 1772; from 1776 government grants paid for the maintenance of prison hulks on the Thames; during the following quarter-century, over £700,000 was spent in this way; transportation to Australia from 1787 to 1797 cost something over a million pounds. In the 1730s and 1750s £7,700 was devoted to buying out financial interests which were complicating the management of the great debtors' prisons attached to the high courts; further – larger – sums were subsequently devoted to rebuilding these prisons. From 1756 until 1771 grants of the order of £30,000 a year were paid to the Foundling Hospital, on condition that it maintain an open admissions policy. The closing decades of the century saw a number of miscellaneous relief grants paid: £15,000 odd for the distribution of military stores in the Highlands to relieve distress following the poor harvest of 1783; in 1786–7 some £20,000 for the relief of 'distressed black persons', and for transporting some of them to establish a new settlement in Sierra Leone; in 1800 £20,000 (repayable) to parishes in the East End of London and the industrial north overwhelmed by the burden of relief payments in another bad harvest year.[23]

The significance of these items lies on the whole not in their absolute size: local authorities at this time were raising hundreds of thousands, ultimately millions, of pounds a year for the relief of the poor; central funding for domestic projects of all kinds was trivial by comparison. Such significance as they had derived rather from their strategic character. Injections of cash from central funds made possible certain initiatives that might otherwise not have been attempted. By no means all such monies were put to effective use. It is unclear what became of the money set aside for Highland schools. Though the Foundling Hospital did run an open admissions policy, this was associated with such high death-rates that Parliament ultimately withdrew its backing for the scheme. By contrast, in two of the cases cited – the granting of subsidies for transportation and the buying-out of vested interests in debtors' prisons – the release of relatively small sums from public funds helped to solve problems that had plagued responsible authorities for decades. Similarly, relief to the Highlands and to overburdened parishes provided a safety-net when the ordinary relief system could not cope.[24]

Clearly the notion that, in the eighteenth century, British central governmental institutions disengaged from many aspects of the work of domestic government, substantially abandoning that field to local authorities, needs qualification. Yet undeniably, governmental structures and patterns of activity had changed. Pulling together some of the themes that have emerged from our account, we might particularly emphasize four aspects of change.

First, eighteenth-century central governmental institutions, having been adapted so as to enable them to sustain more substantial military and naval forces than had their seventeenth-century counterparts, had certain novel resources at their disposal which, to the extent they were not required for other ends, could be tapped for domestic purposes. Local authorities could see many advantages in exploiting these resources. At this as at other periods, when central government presented itself as a store of resources, rather than as a source of unwelcome obligations, or as an inquisitor, we should not be surprised to find local authorities positively welcoming its activity. As we shall see further in the next section, the opportunity to off-load on to central funds burdens previously borne on local rates was commonly welcomed when offered; landed gentlemen especially could see attractions in transferring to a largely indirect-tax-base burdens that, when locally funded, fell upon land. The standing army, likewise, might well be regarded as a valuable resource by local authorities. Eighteenth-century Secretaries of State not infrequently resisted applications from magistrates for troops to help suppress disorders and for the retention of troops to keep the peace for extended periods in the aftermath of riots. It was important, the Secretaries were wont to argue, that magistrates should not depend too much on the army: the 'civil power' should be as self-reliant as possible.[25]

Second, more frequent and longer sessions of Parliament empowered men not holding central office: they gave them a forum in which they could strive to work out their concerns without the need for anything more than acquiescence on the part of ministers or other high public officers. Parliament cannot be classified in terms of any simple central/local dichotomy. It was an arena in which representatives of different levels of government met and collaborated.

Third, the contexts in which central government can be found playing a leading role do not differ greatly between the seventeenth and the eighteenth centuries: as we have noted, dearth, disease, poverty and crime all, on occasion at least, elicited high-level responses during the eighteenth century. However, the forms of central government action did change. We find legislation, proclamations, perhaps circular letters urging authorities to act, responsiveness to suggestions from elsewhere, perhaps willingness to expend central funds – but rather little in the way of close monitoring of local activity (though the case of cattle plague suggests that this was by no means beyond the system's capacity). Furthermore, although central government sometimes took the lead, it by no means always did: there is more evidence of widespread innovative activity by local authorities, in counties as well as in towns, in this period than in the seventeenth century.[26]

Finally, although we have mainly been concerned with structures of government, we should also note that ideas about how government should properly or might profitably act were changing, and affecting attitudes and expectations at all levels. The notion that, on the whole, government should interfere as little as possible in the workings of the domestic economy, for example, encouraged eighteenth-century central government to be highly selective in the forms of economic intervention it sponsored, but equally had a dampening effect on the activities of local authorities.[27]

WAR AND SOCIAL PROBLEMS

War and the fiscal pressures associated with war had many complex effects on British society; but the most immediately evident social effects of war were those associated with the repeated mobilization and demobilization of large armed forces. A necessarily sketchy survey of responses to these problems will illustrate aspects of the domestic operation of eighteenth-century government.

Fewer men mobilized to fight the War of the Austrian Succession in the 1740s than to fight the War of the Spanish Succession at the beginning of the century. With this exception, each successive major conflict saw greater numbers of men in arms. In the 1690s over 100,000 men served in the army and navy; at the end of the century, over 400,000, in the army, navy and militia. Forces were characteristically reduced by one-half or more at the conclusion of wars.[28] Sailors might expect to find immediate employment elsewhere, in the merchant ships of Britain or other nations; the tens, ultimately hundreds, of thousands of soldiers discharged faced a somewhat more problematic transition into the very different patterns of civilian life. Both the mobilization and the demobilization of forces had broader social repercussions.

The sixteenth, seventeenth and eighteenth centuries saw the development of the notion that all but the 'undeserving' among the poor had some claim to public support. In this context, one consequence of the growth of these fluctuating – and dangerous – forms of employment was the posing of a set of challenges to existing relief systems. Acceptable means had to be found to support those disabled, or simply grown aged, in military or naval service. What of the families of soldiers and sailors? Could they be left to the care of the parish? Or, if only to ease the recruitment of the armed forces, should their dependents be offered superior provision?

Demobilization at the end of wars apparently provoked an upsurge in crime: the end of every eighteenth-century war saw a sharp upturn in numbers of property offences prosecuted. In the early seventeenth century, the pattern had been different. Crime had apparently increased during wartime – an intelligible effect in a period when military campaigns were seasonal, and soldiers at home apparently not subject to effective military discipline. To cope with the disorderly-soldier problem, late-sixteenth and early-seventeenth-century local authorities had established provost marshals, charged with arresting and seeing to the punishment of vagrants and soldiers. During the eighteenth century, perhaps from the time of King William's War of 1689–97, war brought a reduction in prosecuted crime-rates; peace and demobilization, a sharp hike. Contemporaries became very familiar with this pattern. The first attempt to register it quantitatively was made in 1772, when Stephen Theodore Janssen tabulated numbers executed each year from the Old Bailey, grouping the figures into blocks of war-years and peace-years.[29]

These patterns very probably do in part reflect the socially dislocating effects of demobilization – the effects of turning tens of thousands of men loose to find their way home and find work. They also reflect the simple fact that the endings of wars released large numbers of young men – the group most commonly the objects of criminal prosecutions – most of whom had been absent from the country for the duration of the war. During wartime, moreover, some young men who committed crimes were offered immunity from prosecution if they would enlist; in peacetime, the task of coping with disorderly young men fell more squarely upon the criminal justice system. Secretary of State Townshend acknowledged this in 1783, when he brought two bills into Parliament designed to combat crime in the metropolis. Had the war continued, he observed, he might have addressed the problem by sending the press-gangs out. Contemporary expectation that the ends of wars would be associated with an increase in crime may also have introduced an element of self-fulfilling 'moral panic'.[30]

That soldiers travelling through the countryside effectively swelled the numbers of 'vagrants' had officially been recognized from at least the sixteenth century – when, on the one hand, soldiers making their way home were officially exempted from the penalties to which rogues and vagabonds were subject; on the other hand, those counterfeiting soldiers' passes were made liable to execution, and provost marshals were appointed to discipline disorderly soldiers and vagrants.[31] The cost of returning vagrants to their home parishes was laid upon counties in 1700. County expenditure totals suggest that expenditure commonly rose in the aftermath of wars. In the period following the end of the American War especially, a supposed increase in vagrancy became a focus for public and official concern.[32]

Finally, concern was expressed about how disbanded soldiers – and even sailors – were to be reintegrated into productive social roles.[33] A matter of concern in part because unemployed servicemen might be expected to swell the ranks of the poor, vagrant or criminal, this issue also attracted attention inasmuch as it was supposed that these men constituted a valuable social resource – perhaps one especially well fitted for particular purposes. It could also be argued that it was dishonourable for the nation not to make proper provision for those who had served it – and perhaps impolitic, when the next war would infallibly see the recruiting sergeants out on the streets again.

It is not suggested that these problems typified the wider range of social problems facing eighteenth-century British government. The more categorically they concerned soldiers, sailors and their dependents, the more easily they could be seen as constituting a special case, demanding – in the context of general eighteenth-century arrangements – the immediate involvement of central government. In practice, however, as we shall see, a variety of forms of central/local interaction were involved, nor were even policies narrowly targeted on the armed forces without implications for the treatment of other social groups.

Let us consider first the question of relief – pensions or other support – for soldiers and sailors and their dependants. Certain forms of special provision had been developed during the sixteenth and seventeenth centuries.[34] From the late sixteenth century, disabled sailors, or their widows, had been able to apply – by no means necessarily successfully – for payments from the 'Chatham Chest', itself financed by deductions from sailors' wages. The Chatham Chest continued to operate throughout our period.[35] Early-seventeenth-century legislation, furthermore, provided for the payment of pensions to maimed soldiers or sailors out of county rates. Such payments continued to be made in some counties down to the early years of the eighteenth century, but appear then to have been phased out. The general establishment and increasing generosity of ordinary poor relief may well have helped to make special provision seem less necessary. Certainly, it seems to have been considered that the poor and vagrancy laws between them provided a basic safety-net for soldiers' and sailors' dependants: in the 1790s Sir Jeremiah Fitzpatrick considered what might be done for Irish soldiers' dependants, given the lack of an Irish relief system comparable to the English.[36]

At the same time that county-funded gave way to parish-funded relief, however, new forms of central provision also came into play. Military hospitals and arrangements for the care of sick and wounded sailors established during the Commonwealth had been abandoned at the Restoration. Yet within a few decades, interest in such schemes revived. Charles II inaugurated plans for the construction of a 'hospital' for former soldiers; Chelsea Hospital was some years in the building, opening its doors only in 1690. Greenwich Hospital, originally conceived in 1691 as a hospital for sick and wounded sailors only, was in 1695 reconceptualized as a 'hospital' in the broader early-modern sense – an asylum both for the sick and for disabled and aged seamen. As such, King William believed that it would serve as a memorial to the charitable impulses of his recently deceased Queen. Finances for both came from a number of sources – Greenwich in particular was endowed with substantial lands, augmented after 1715 by the gift of the forfeited Derwentwater estate; but both depended in part on compulsory stoppages from wages (an arrangement probably in part to be viewed as a device for tying public subsidies to the size of the forces).[37]

The number of men maintained on the funds of the two hospitals was considerable, and grew in the face of rising demand in the course of the century. Chelsea Hospital had from its foundation house room for some 472 pensioners. The expansion of the army in the 1690s ensured that demand for these places would almost immediately exceed supply. Further provision was made in the form of 'out-pensions'. The number of out-pensioners escalated with every subsequent war: in the 1690s out-pensioners numbered in the hundreds: in 1713, some 4,000: in 1750, over 8,000: in the 1760s, 14,000: and by the end of the American War, over 20,000 – all supported at the rate of 5d. a day. By this time, the number of out-pensioners was greater than the mainland peacetime establishment! The much larger Greenwich Hospital – which was extended during the first half of the eighteenth century – housed some 1,000 men by the 1740s, over 2,000 by 1780. The attachment of out-pensioners to Greenwich was first authorized by act of Parliament after the Seven Years War; by the first decade of the nineteenth century they numbered over 3,000. In the second half of the century it was provided that both forms of out-pension should be payable on presentation of the appropriate warrant at any local excise office.[38]

The militia, revived on a new basis in the 1750s, with the backing on the one hand of William Pitt and a small core of militia enthusiasts, on the other hand of certain country gentlemen, depended to a very much greater degree than the regular army on collaboration between central and local authorities. Militiamen were selected by parochially administered ballots. Although those chosen were allowed to find substitutes to serve in their place, the element of coercion aroused popular hostility, especially in the militia's early days. It appears to have been largely because of the need to allay popular hostility that special provision was made for allowances to militiamen's families. These were to be paid by ordinary poor-law officers, but were claimable as of right, and their amount determined by fixed rules, relating on the one hand to locally prevailing wage-rates, on the other hand to the size of the militiaman's family. Payments were reclaimable from county funds. This arrangement was unwelcome to many landed gentlemen, who would have preferred the cost to fall on central funds – an arrangement Pitt would have been prepared to make, but which failed to win general support within the ministry or in the Commons.[39]

New responsibilities, imposed on local authorities by government-sponsored legislation, may ultimately have helped to shape practice in relation to the poor more generally. As is well known, in the mid-1790s magistrates in many counties began to fix scales for relief payments, often taking family size into account – although they had no legal warrant to act in this way. Given that at the same time they were involved in organizing support for militiamen's families, on fixed scales, is it not probable that this should have influenced their thinking?[40]

Crime-waves which erupted at the end of eighteenth-century wars evoked responses from all levels of government. Crime had not, in the seventeenth century, been a focus for very much innovative effort on the part of central authorities. Though the 1660s and 1670s saw a rash of innovative bills brought into Parliament, it is not evident that these enjoyed ministerial backing, and all failed. In the eighteenth century, by contrast, central government was more conspicuously active. This was in part perhaps because more markedly fluctuating crime-waves provided a recurrent spur to action, in part because the cabinet's involvement in the pardoning process increased its sensitivity to the problem. There were also pressures from without, increasing in the later part of the century, when how crime might best be policed and punished became a favourite talking-point among the literati and governing classes.

The subject is too large – and has been too thoroughly dealt with by other historians – for any comprehensive treatment to be thinkable. We might, however, briefly note some aspects of central government involvement, first in the policing of the metropolis, and second in the punishment of crime. In each case, the century saw increasing central government involvement, change apparently being driven by the impact of post-war crime-waves.

Responsibility for overseeing the policing of the metropolis was divided between three groups of magistrates: those of the City, Westminster and the county of Middlesex. Already in the seventeenth century, it is said that ministers were in the habit of maintaining especially close links with, and perhaps paying some sort of salary to, one member of the Westminster bench, Westminster being the home of both court and Parliament, as well as the district in which the aristocracy and gentry were most likely to live. At the end of the War of Austrian Succession, Henry Fielding, who was then 'Court Justice', was given a Treasury grant to combat crime, which he used to maintain a set of 'runners' attached to his Bow Street 'office'; a few years later, his half-brother and successor Sir John Fielding succeeded in converting this one-off payment into a regular grant of £400 a year. At the end of the Seven Years War further money was granted for one year for the establishment of a highway patrol; after the American War, for the same purpose, but on a regular basis.[41]

Also after the Seven Years War, other Westminster and metropolitan magistrates followed the Fieldings' example, and established 'offices', staffed, during office hours, by magistrates sitting in rotation. Following the American War, it was proposed that this system should be formalized and extended by the establishment of a set of salaried or 'stipendiary' magistrates to do duty throughout the metropolitan area. The Metropolitan Police bill of 1785, brought into Parliament by the Solicitor General, was defeated, in part, it seems, because of opposition from the City of London. A modified version of the bill, excluding the City, was introduced and passed in 1792. The act set up seven police offices, staffed by stipendiary magistrates appointed by the Home Secretary, each with a team of runners attached to it. The customary fall in prosecuted crime following the outbreak of war in 1793 ensured that the new system had a relatively easy ride in its early years.[42]

Sheriffs were traditionally entitled to claim from the Exchequer in their annual 'cravings' an allowance for the maintenance of convicts in gaol, and for the costs of executions. When, in the seventeenth century, transportation was introduced as an alternative to execution for those given the appropriate form of conditional pardon, the new system seems to have been expected to pay for itself, since the merchants who transported the prisoners had the right to sell them as indentured servants. In practice, transportation functioned in only a limited and erratic way on this foundation. When, following the conclusion of the War of the Spanish Succession, Whig ministers decided significantly to enhance the role of transportation within the penal system, they ensured that the practice was given better public support. New legislation, authorizing the courts to sentence convicts to transportation, also provided that counties must levy rates to cover the costs of conveying prisoners to ships; a Treasury subsidy was in addition supplied at the rate of £5 per head for all convicts transported from the metropolis and Home Counties. (Warwickshire magistrates petitioned in 1730 for the subsidy to be extended to the country as a whole, but were refused).[43]

By mid-century it was argued by some that transportation to the American colonies was too mild a punishment: following the War of the Austrian Succession, again apparently at government instigation, a bill was brought in authorizing punishment by hard labour in the dockyards, but this failed to win parliamentary approval. In the 1770s colonial rebellion itself put an end to transportation. The end of the war made the development of an alternative a matter of urgency. In practice, a greater proportion of convicts than before were thenceforth sentenced to imprisonment in local 'houses of correction', but a further substantial proportion were transported, at vast expense, to a new penal colony at Botany Bay.[44]

Turning from crime to vagrancy, we find very different patterns of interaction between central and local authorities. That soldiers and sailors formed an important constituent part of the stream of potentially problematic poor travellers was acknowledged in legislation from the six-teenth century – and military authorities did take care, in disbanding soldiers, to try to minimize the trouble they might cause as they dispersed. Vagrancy was in general a problem left for local authorities to grapple with, however. This they did in part through community and county-level initiatives, but also through applications to Parliament for successive modifications to the law.

In the sixteenth and early-seventeenth centuries, special provision had been made, in various pieces of legislation, to facilitate – although at the same time to regulate – the movement of poor soldiers and sailors about the country. Soldiers and sailors equipped with a pass from their command-ing officer or captain (later acts were to say 'from a magistrate'), specifying a route and a time within which they were to travel, were granted immunity from arrest as rogues and vagabonds. They were also empowered to ask relief from constables along the route, constables being entitled to reclaim such outlay from the county maimed-soldiers' fund. It may be that these laws simply authorized, in respect of soldiers and sailors, practices already common in relation to poor travellers in general; alternatively, it may be that they provided a model that was later to be generalized. Whichever was the case, by the eighteenth century we find many poor travellers equipped with passes issued by magistrates, although magistrates had no legal authority to grant such passes to ordinary travellers. Furthermore, we find many poor travellers, and not soldiers and sailors alone, presenting themselves to constables asking for relief, although such payments could no longer in any case be referred to non-existent maimed-soldiers' funds, but were apparently instead borne on parochial constables' rates.[45]

Military authorities tried to minimize the difficulties that might be expected to arise when tens of thousands of men were disbanded within a short period. Disbanded soldiers were given subsistence money to support them for a short period – for example, two weeks – and were ordered not to travel in large groups. Regiments recruited in particular regions of the country might be disbanded within those regions.[46] The endings of wars were by no means the only periods associated with marked upswings in vagrancy in the eighteenth century: bad harvests, which seem to have sent people off towards towns looking for work, had a similar effect. Neither vagrancy legislation nor circular letters from the Privy Council urging the more vigorous enforcement of vagrancy laws (what prompted these, one might wonder) clustered at the ends of wars.[47]

However, the ends of wars were associated with upturns in spending on the removal of vagrants, and sometimes with flurries of concern at the local level, perhaps most especially towards the latter end of our period. Concern about high levels of vagrancy associated with the end of the American War (and perhaps also with the wet summer and bad harvest of 1783) persisted for a decade – in fact, until the next war once more siphoned off a large portion of the male population. Peace in 1802 prompted the re-enactment of the sixteenth-century provision that counterfeiting soldiers' and sailors' travelling passes should count as felony. The end of the Napoleonic Wars saw much agitation about vagrancy as well as crime.[48]

The texts of eighteenth-century vagrancy laws furthermore reveal that travelling soldiers and sailors – or people representing themselves to be such – were a continuing focus of concern. The vagrancy act of 1740 provided that, though soldiers and sailors with passes were not to be treated as rogues and vagabonds, those pretending to be soldiers or sailors should be regarded as prime targets for discipline (such people might, under Elizabethan law, have been charged with felony, but providing for their punishment as rogues and vagabonds represented a more realistic assessment of the kind of penal response local authorities might be prepared to apply).[49] In 1790 a national convention of magistrates, summoned by the self-appointed 'Society for Enforcing His Majesty's Proclamation against Vice and Immorality' (of 1787), recommended *inter alia* that soldiers and sailors who begged should be liable to punishment as rogues and vagabonds; this provision would need to be coupled, they thought, with another entitling them to claim relief from constables. The vagrancy act of 1792 incorporated the penal but not the entitlement provision. (Members of the Society made several attempts to amend this feature of the act, but were rebuffed by the Commons.[50])

No clear consensus existed in the eighteenth century as to whether former soldiers and sailors could be expected to find new employment for themselves. Some thought soldiers in particular could be expected to face difficulties; others believed that, if they were willing to work, the market would operate to provide jobs for them.[51] Ministers did sponsor some moves to facilitate the reintegration of discharged servicemen into productive economic roles – perhaps moved by a sense of responsibility, perhaps fearing opposition criticism (ministerial lack of concern for those who risked their lives for their country was an issue the opposition were always ready to exploit); but the moves that were made were all modest and limited ones.

The only routine form of provision targeted those disbanded soldiers and sailors who had completed long terms of service. From the mid-seventeenth century, it was customary for acts to be passed at the ends of wars empowering such men to practise trades wherever they pleased, regardless of whether they had completed a proper apprenticeship. By the mid-eighteenth century, these measures were usually brought in by the Secretary at War. The first acts of this kind also guaranteed such men immunity from imprisonment for debt for three years, but such provisions were omitted in 1749 and thereafter. The act passed at the end of the Seven Years War, however, added a new form of privilege: parish officers in any parish or town to which such men might choose to migrate were prohibited from removing them back to their parish of settlement (as they would normally have been able to do under the provisions of the settlement laws), unless they applied for parish relief. This exemption was extended to militiamen in 1784, so long as they had completed a mere three years of service and been honourably discharged.[52] The settlement laws were at this time attracting criticism from some who argued that they were a clog on mobility and exposed the poor to unreasonable harassment. Though such critics were initially unsuccessful in obtaining a general reform of the law, their thinking probably influenced the forms of provision made for working men thought to merit especially generous treatment. Similar immunity was extended to members of friendly societies in 1793, and finally made general in 1795.[53]

Other provision was commonly made only when it was thought that two birds might be killed with one stone. In 1749 it was decided on the advice of the President of the Board of Trade, Lord Halifax, that 3,000 newly discharged soldiers and sailors should be recruited to form a nucleus of colonization in Nova Scotia, newly acquired from the French. Undoubtedly, such men's fighting skills made them highly attractive for this purpose. This policy was speedily implemented, and the new town of Halifax grew from nothing to modest proportions. Although they acquitted themselves well in beating off assaults on the town, the new settlers had no appetite either for clearing the wilderness or for developing the fisheries, and within a few years a majority had departed.[54] A scheme for settling Chelsea Pensioners in the Highlands, as emissaries of civilization, was floated in the same year, but came to nothing. In 1763, however, the Commissioners for Annexed Estates did try to interest former soldiers and sailors in settling on the estates, the soldiers being encouraged to become crofters, the sailors fishermen. Once again, the settlers' lack of appetite for the mode of living proposed to them proved a source of difficulty. (Whether men traditionally kept in order 'by the rod' made plausible emissaries of civilization had been questioned by sceptics from the start.[55])

When eighteenth-century observers tried to think what sectors of the economy might absorb substantial quantities of new labour, fisheries and the development of wastelands tended to come to their minds. Legislation to promote the development of the fisheries followed most eighteenth-century wars. It was suggested that fisheries would serve as 'nurseries of seamen' for future wars, but the need to employ the recently discharged was also cited in parliamentary debate.[56] Planning for the next war usually began immediately on the establishment of peace. In this context, concern might be expressed about the state of stocks of oaken timber, needed for the construction of warships. In the closing years of the American War it was suggested that disbanded soldiers and sailors might appropriately be employed in the woods and forests. When concern, both about the effective management of national resources, and about the state of naval timber

116

supplies, combined in 1787 to prompt the appointment of Royal Commissioners to inquire into the management of royal forests and wastes, the hope that their inquiries might result in the creation of new jobs was again voiced. The Commissioners themselves appear to have been relatively little concerned with the employment of labour. To the extent that they attended to the matter, their view (also that of many they questioned) was apparently that, if the object were to promote 'produce and population', the best course would be to convert forests to farmland.[57]

At the conclusions of eighteenth-century wars, statements that the time had now come to focus on the domestic scene, to take up the task of reformation at home, were often made officially – in, for example, the King's Speech – or unofficially, in newspapers or pamphlets. The timing of such statements was partly determined by the fact that the ends of wars were apparently associated, and were expected to be associated, with the intensification of a range of social problems, partly by the fact that wars themselves posed various obstacles in the way of ambitious domestic programmes. They did so partly through their economic effects: wars were associated with high taxation, and high rates of interest, both of which made it difficult to raise money for domestic projects; also with high wages, which served to discourage building projects in particular. Wars also discouraged ambitious governmental projects on the domestic front because of the demands they placed on the time and energy of ministers, and on parliamentary time (fewer acts dealing with domestic issues passed in years of war than in years of peace). The waging of wars stretched the resources of eighteenth-century British government to the limits; but in years of peace, machinery that had come into being largely to serve the needs of war could be turned to other ends.

EUROPEAN COMPARISONS

Interstate rivalry, war and empire between them did much to shape the institutional structures of the eighteenth-century British state. A case can be made for these developments having disengaged central institutions from certain aspects of domestic government. However, the case is easily overstated. If local authorities – to whom much responsibility for such tasks had long been confided – were subject to less heavy-handed supervision in the eighteenth century than in especially the earlier part of the previous century, none the less, within the new institutional framework central and local authorities continued to interact in responding to a wide range of domestic issues. Wars, especially the social dislocation associated with the end of wars, posed social problems in their own right. A survey of responses to these illustrates a variety of forms of interaction between central and local authorities.

Although the case for central government having disengaged from certain aspects of domestic government in Britain during these years is easily overstated, a comparison between British experience and the experience of certain continental states none the less suggests that emphasis on this feature is not entirely misplaced. In France, Prussia and the Habsburg lands the eighteenth century saw an intensification of central government control over local authorities that finds no real parallel in Britain. This intensification of control had its roots at least in part in military and associated fiscal pressures. New agencies, tightly linked to the centre, were created with special responsibility for levying or supervising troops or gathering in revenues. As time passed, these agencies were assigned increasingly broadly defined supervisory powers in relation to traditional institutions of local government, increasingly condemned either as insufficiently dynamic or as excessively local in orientation. In both France and the Habsburg lands administrative reforms undertaken in the late-seventeenth and early-eighteenth centuries gave way, in the closing decades of the century, to more ambitious attempts comprehensively to restructure governmental and to some extent social institutions – perestroika, eighteenth-century style. Both such ventures, of course, ultimately came more or less cataclysmically to grief.[58]

Why did the development of the British military-fiscal state not bring in its train analogous consequences? How was it that the amalgam of new military and fiscal and substantially traditional local governmental institutions forged in the late-seventeenth and early-eighteenth centuries survived with relatively little change – some tinkering on the northern periphery apart – for the next century and a half, while Britain's continental counterparts engaged in an ever-more-hectic sequence of institutional innovations? The explanation for these differences probably lies in features both of British government and of British society.

By early – and even later – eighteenth-century continental standards, British local governmental structures were, we should first note, relatively centralized, even given the winding-down of conciliar supervision and control.[59] Justices of the Peace, in whose hands much local governmental power was vested, outside (and increasingly also inside) the towns (in Scotland: Justices of the Peace, sheriffs and commissioners of supply), operated within a framework of statute law and proved relatively responsive to central direction, when it came their way. Latent command structures, linking central with local authorities, were more frequently activated in the later than in the earlier eighteenth century. Put to the test, they proved reasonably serviceable. By the end of the century, local authorities were raising substantial military forces in the form of militia regiments, to supplement the forces of the regular army; they had made preparations to levy the *posse comitatus*, the English equivalent of the *levée en masse*, should invasion make it necessary to maximize forces for home defence; they had assisted in a series of crop surveys: gauges of the nation's food-

118

producing capacity; and they were about to assist in the compilation of the first census.[60]

British central–local links held up relatively well in the face of strains imposed by the French Revolutionary Wars. It was no doubt fortunate, however, that British social and economic circumstances, both in this war and in earlier wars (which had not always attracted such broadly based support among local elites), made it possible to avoid putting the power and resilience of these links too severely to the test. The men who forged the basic structures of the British military-fiscal state in the late-seventeenth century, and their successors who developed and maintained them, took advantage of British social and economic circumstances to cast these arrangements in forms that minimized the need for potentially problematic interaction between new state agencies and traditional structures of local government. A sophisticated system of deficit finance shielded taxpayers from the immediate costs of war; when these costs were ultimately borne, they were increasingly borne by customs and excise duties. This being so, British governments were able to avoid confronting the task many continental governments had to confront, that of wringing ever more revenue from the land – a task which, in the judgement of several such governments, could not be pursued in the long term except on the basis of a comprehensive reassessment of land values. British naval and military forces were recruited in as *ad hoc* a manner as possible: royal naval crews, forcibly, from the merchant marine; the army, from volunteers, sought especially in manufacturing towns and among the Scots. In these ways, it proved possible to mobilize sizeable regular forces without resort to elaborate systems of conscription (though it should not be forgotten that, in the later eighteenth century, the British did devise a system of conscription to man the militia, and persisted in this policy, despite initial popular hostility and complaints about the extent to which costs fell on the land). Had it been necessary, as in other states, to raise money or men in other ways, more restructuring of traditional institutions might have been necessary.[61]

Never did the rulers of continental states test the limits of their domestic power more than when they attempted to use the machinery of government radically to restructure society – when they tried, as successive Habsburgs tried, to reduce the scope of serfdom; or, as successive French revolutionary governments tried, to restructure relations between landed proprietors and peasants. Eighteenth-century British governments were not unprepared to lay their hands to social engineering of this kind. They sponsored it in the Scottish Highlands. They contemplated a similar exercise in Canada – and backed down chiefly because advised by military men on the spot that the status quo was best adapted to the mobilization of effective fighting forces (a high priority, as relations with neighbouring American colonists deteriorated). In India too they were to preside over a restructuring of landed society, if in the name of obtaining a stable 'settlement'.[62] British statesmen did not believe, however, that any significant social reconstruction was called for within the British heartland. Why should they have thought so, when Britain's dynamic society and economy attracted admiration from aspiring states? Continental rulers who attempted such remodelling exposed the limits of the power even a revolutionized machinery of government had given them. Britain's eighteenth-century rulers were spared the need to confront so formidable a task.

NOTES

I am grateful to Geoff Hudson for his help with the third section, on War and Social Problems, and David Eastwood for suggestions about the fourth section, on European Comparisons.

1 E. R. Turner, *The Privy Council of England 1603–1784* (2 vols, Baltimore: Johns Hopkins University Press, 1928); P. A. Slack, 'Books of Orders: The Making of English Social Policy 1577–1631', *Transactions of the Royal Historical Society*, fifth series, 30 (1980); J. A. Cockburn, *A History of English Assizes 1558–1714* (Cambridge: Cambridge University Press, 1972), ch. 8.

2 L. Boynton, *The Elizabethan Militia 1558–1638* (London: Routledge & Kegan Paul, 1967); A. Hassell Smith, 'Militia Rates and Militia Statutes 1558–1663', in P. Clark, A. G. R. Smith and N. Tyacke (eds), *The English Commonwealth 1547–1640* (Leicester: Leicester University Press, 1979); J. Kent, *The English Village Constable 1580–1642* (Oxford: Clarendon Press, 1986), ch. 5; T. G. Barnes, *Somerset 1625–1640* (London: Oxford University Press, 1961). There has been less work on such topics in the eras of the Interregnum or Restoration, but see now A. Fletcher, *Reform in the Provinces: The Government of Stuart England* (New Haven: Yale University Press, 1986), esp. ch. 9; A. Coleby, *Central Government and the Localities: Hampshire 1649–89* (Cambridge: Cambridge University Press, 1987), and P. J. Norrey, 'The Restoration Regime in Action: The Relation between Central and Local Government in Dorset, Somerset and Wiltshire 1660–1688', *Historical Journal*, 31 (1988).

3 For an overview of late-seventeenth-century developments see H. Tomlinson, 'Financial and Administrative Developments in England 1660–1688', in J. R. Jones (ed.), *The Restored Monarchy 1660–1688* (London: Macmillan, 1979). For the Privy Council see Turner, *Privy Council*, vol. II; J. J. Carter, 'The Administrative Work of the English Privy Council 1679–1714' (Ph.D. thesis, London University, 1954); O. Dickerson, *American Colonial Government 1696–1765* (Cleveland, Ohio: Arthur H. Clark Co., 1912), esp. ch. 2. For specialized departments see H. Roseveare, *The Treasury* (London: Allen Lane, 1969); D. Baugh, *British Naval Administration in the Age of Walpole* (Princeton: Princeton University Press, 1965); M. A. Thomson, *The Secretaries of State 1681–1782* (London: Frank Cass and Co., 1968). For Parliament and the operations of executive government see P. D. G. Thomas, *The House of Commons in the Eighteenth Century* (Oxford: Clarendon Press, 1971), ch. 4; A. Guy, *Oeconomy and Discipline: Officership and Administration in the British Army 1714–63* (Manchester: Manchester University Press, 1985), 3–9; Baugh, *Naval Administration*, ch. 9; G. C. Gibbs, 'Parliament and Foreign Policy in the Age of Stanhope and Walpole', *English Historical Review*, 77 (1962). For the cabinet see E. R. Turner, *The Cabinet Council of England 1622–1784* (2 vols, Baltimore: Johns Hopkins University Press, 1930).

4 Thomson, *Secretaries of State*; T. Hayter, *The Army and the Crowd in Mid-Georgian England* (London: Macmillan, 1978).

5 R. R. Nelson, *The Home Office 1782–1800* (Durham, NC: Duke University Press, 1969).

6 I. K. Steele, *Politics of Colonial Policy: The Board of Trade in Colonial Administration 1696–1720* (Oxford: Clarendon Press, 1968); S. Macfarlane, 'Studies in Poverty and Poor Relief in London at the End of the Seventeenth Century' (D.Phil. thesis, Oxford University, 1982), 263–76, and T. Hitchcock, 'The English Workhouse: A Study in Institutional Relief in Selected Counties 1696–1750' (D.Phil. thesis, Oxford University 1985), ch. 2, discuss the board's activities in relation to the poor.

7 J. Brewer, *The Sinews of Power: War, Money and the English State 1688–1763* (London: Unwin Hyman, 1989), ch. 4; J. R. Western, *The English Militia in the Eighteenth Century* (London: Routledge & Kegan Paul, 1965), chs 1–3; N. Landau, *The Justices of the Peace 1679–1760* (Berkeley: University of California Press, 1984). See also works listed in the latter part of note 1 for the practical operation of this system during the transitional Restoration period.

8 R. B. Outhwaite, 'Dearth and Government Intervention in English Grain Markets 1590–1700', *Economic History Review*, 3 (1981) for declining *dirigisme* even before the Civil War. For Restoration initiatives see J. Miller, 'The Crown and Borough Charters in the Reign of Charles II', *English Historical Review*, 100 (1985); J. R. Jones, *The Revolution of 1688 in England* (London: Weidenfeld & Nicholson, 1972), ch. 6. For eighteenth-century examples of instructions to judges see J. M. Beattie, *Crime and the Courts in England 1660–1800* (Oxford: Clarendon Press, 1986), 553n (1754), J. M. Innes, 'Politics and Morals: The Reformation of Manners Movement in Later Eighteenth-Century England', in E. Hellmuth (ed.), *The Transformation of Political Culture: Late Eighteenth-Century England and Germany* (Oxford: Oxford University Press, 1990), 65, n. 16 (1781); for general trends see Cockburn, *English Assizes*, pp. 259–61; Landau, *Justices of the Peace*, 39, 60; see also pp. 355–9; Carter, 'English Privy Council', 94, 361.

9 P. W. J. Riley, *The English Ministers and Scotland 1707–27* (London: The Athlone Press, 1964), ch. 12; J. S. Shaw, *The Management of Scottish Society 1707–1764* (Edinburgh: John Donald, 1983).

10 A. Whetstone, *Scottish County Government in the Eighteenth and Nineteenth Centuries* (Edinburgh: John Donald, 1981), ch. 1. For heretable jurisdictions in operation, see S. J. Davies, 'The Courts and the Scottish Legal System 1600–1747: The Case of Stirlingshire', in V. A. C. Gatrell, B. Lenman and G. Parker (eds), *Crime and the Law: The Social History of Crime in Western Europe* (London: Europa, 1980).

11 Whetstone, *Scottish County Government*, 69–70; R. Mitchison, *Agricultural Sir John: The Life of Sir John Sinclair of Ulster* (London: Geoffrey Bles, 1962), chs 8, 9 and 14.

12 The King's Speech was printed in the *Commons Journal* (henceforth *CJ*) for each session; proclamations are most easily traced through *Bibliotheca Lindesiana*, vol. VIII, *Handlist of Proclamations Issued by Royal and Other Constitutional Authorities* (Wigan: 1913). For the poor, see e.g. *CJ*, vol XIII, 1, 4, 8; for general accounts of policy in this period, see above note 5. Plague: *CJ*, vol. XIX, 646; P. Slack, *The Impact of the Plague in Tudor and Stuart England* (London: Routledge, 1985), ch. 12. Crime, *CJ*, vol. XXVI, 3, 298, 345, 519, 841; Beattie, *Crime and the Courts*, 219–22, 520–31, 553n. Dearth: proclamations against forestalling and engrossing were issued in 1709, 1740, 1756 and

1766. The King's Speech did not mention the problem in all these years – in some years other matters were more immediately pressing – but did in 1740 and in 1756. Problems associated with high prices provided the chief reason for convening Parliament in 1767. Until the 1760s, after which acts recurrently empowered the Privy Council to regulate grain export, changes in ordinary practice to deal with crisis conditions were usually authorized by Act of Parliament. For a survey of changing policy, see D. G. Barnes, *A History of the English Corn Laws 1660–1846* (London: George Routledge & Sons, 1930), chs 3–5. There has been much work on grain rioting in recent years; policy tends to be incidental to these accounts. For a collection of brief pieces by some of those working in this field, see A. Charlesworth (ed.), *An Atlas of Rural Protest in Britain 1548–1900* (London: Croom Helm, 1983). R. Wells, *Wretched Faces: Famine in Wartime England 1793–1800* (Gloucester: Alan Sutton, 1988), Parts 3 and 4, provides the most thorough study available of public responses in one period of crisis.

13 I focus here only on a few major institutions, but the list could be extended. See e.g. for the Mint's activities in relation to 'clippers and coiners', and a case study of its involvement in a particular campaign, which also excited other governmental interest, J. Styles, 'Our Traitorous Money Makers', in J. Brewer and J. Styles (eds), *An Ungovernable People* (London: Hutchinson, 1980), esp. 183–6, 220–7.

14 C. F. Mullett, 'A Century of English Quarantine (1709–1825)', *Bulletin of the History of Medicine*, 23 (1949); 7 Geo 1, s. 1 c. 3; Slack, *Impact of the Plague*, for general discussion, J. Broad, 'Cattle Plague in Eighteenth-Century England', *Agricultural History Review*, 31 (1983).

15 J. M. Beattie, 'The Cabinet and the Management of Death at Tyburn after the Revolution of 1688', in L. Schwoerer (ed.), *The Revolution of 1688–9: Changing Perspectives* (Cambridge: Cambridge University Press, 1992).

16 Although the nature of the sources makes the subject a relatively difficult one to grapple with, it is none the less remarkable how little work has been done on the role of the Treasury in shaping and executing economic policy in eighteenth-century England. Roseveare's study *The Treasury* focuses narrowly on the Treasury, not including its subordinate boards, and on the issue of financial control.

17 A. Durie, *The Scottish Linen Industry in the Eighteenth Century* (Edinburgh: John Donald, 1979); Shaw, *Management of Scottish Society*, 124–32; A. M. Johnson, *Jacobite Estates of the Forty-Five* (Edinburgh: John Donald, 1982).

18 10 Geo III, c. 39, Barnes, *Corn Laws*, 41, 50.

19 J. Innes, 'Parliament and the Shaping of Eighteenth-Century English Social Policy', *Transactions of the Royal Historical Society*, 40 (1990), 77–8. See also Innes, 'Politics and Morals', for an account of a royal proclamation against vice and immorality being elicited by extra-official campaigners to serve their own ends.

20 Innes, 'Parliament and Social Policy'. Scottish interests were certainly less well represented: see Shaw, *Management of Scottish Society*, 126 – though the picture appears to have changed a little later in the century.

21 M. Beloff, *Public Order and Popular Disturbances 1660–1714* (London: Frank Cass and Co., 1963), 69; Barnes, *Corn Laws*, 35, 37, 38, 54–5, 73, 77, 84; Turner, *Privy Council*, vol. II, 491; G. Henson, *History of the Framework Knitters* (orig. 1831; Trowbridge: David & Charles, 1970), 132–5, 194–232, 383–416.

22 Innes, 'Parliament and Social Policy', 86–7.

23 M. G. Jones, *The Charity School Movement* (Cambridge: Cambridge University Press, 1938), 179; R. Ekirch, *Bound for America: The Transportation of British Convicts to the Colonies, 1718–1775* (Oxford: Clarendon Press, 1987), 70–1; H. Colvin (ed.), *The History of the King's Works* (6 vols, London: HMSO, 1963–73), vol. V, 350–7; vol. VI, 627–8; R. McClure, *Coram's Children: The London Foundling Hospital in the Eighteenth Century* (New Haven: Yale University Press, 1981), chs 7–9; C. Smout, 'Famine and Famine Relief in Scotland', in L. M. Cullen and C. Smout (eds), *Comparative Aspects of Scottish and Irish Economic History 1600–1800* (Edinburgh: John Donald, n.d.); F. Shyllon, *Black People in Britain 1555–1833* (London: Oxford University Press, 1977), Part 2; Wells, *Wretched Faces*, 313–14. Increasing confidence about spending public money for such purposes seems to be reflected in the patterns of compensation payments to farmers ordered to kill diseased cattle (Broad, 'Cattle Plague', 106, 113). Some, but not all, such payments can be traced in *Parliamentary Papers* (1868–9), vol. XXXV, Part 1, I and Appendices 2 and 3, where they are classed as expenses of 'civil government'. An even more selective overview is provided in Sir J. Sinclair, *A History of the Public Revenue of the British Empire* (third edn, London, 1803).

24 Beattie, *Crime and the Courts*, 470–83, 500–6; *CJ*, vol. XXI, 274 ff., 376 ff., 513 ff.; R. Mitchison, 'North and South: The Development of the Gulf in Poor Relief Practice', in R. A. Houston and I. D. Whyte (eds), *Scottish Society 1500–1800* (Cambridge: Cambridge University Press, 1989).

25 See e.g. Hayter, *Army and the Crowd*, 95–6.

26 See Innes, 'Politics and Morals', 64–71, for the extraordinary range of initiatives launched by local authorities in the 1780s.

27 R. K. Kelsall, 'Wage Regulation under the Statute of Artificers', in W. E. Minchinton (ed.), *Wage Regulation in Pre-Industrial England* (Newton Abbot: David & Charles, 1972), ch. 7, asks whether the gradual abandonment of regulation should be traced to 'the removal of the strong hand of the Council' and concludes not.

28 Brewer, *Sinews of Power*, 30–3; C. Emsley, *British Society and the French Wars 1793–1815* (London: Macmillan, 1979), 94.

29 P. Lawson, 'Property, Crime and Hard Times in England 1559–1624', *Law and History Review*, 4 (1986), 114–17; L. O. J. Boynton, 'The Tudor Provost Marshal', *English Historical Review*, 77 (1962); D. Hay, 'War, Dearth and Theft in the Eighteenth Century: The Record of the English Courts', *Past and Present*, 95 (1982); S. T. Janssen, *Tables of Death Sentences* (London, 1772; broadsheet, of which a copy is held by the Guildhall Library, London).

30 Hay, 'War, Dearth and Theft'; J. M. Innes and J. Styles, 'The Crime Wave: Recent Writing on Crime and Criminal Justice in Eighteenth-Century England', *Journal of British Studies*, 25 (1986), 393; W. Cobbett (ed.), *Parliamentary History* (36 vols; London, 1806–20), vol. XXIII, cols 364–5. See also R. Paley, 'Thieftakers in London in the Age of the Macdaniel Gang', in D. Hay and F. Snyder (eds), *Policing and Prosecution in Britain 1750–1850* (Oxford: Clarendon Press, 1989), 324–6, 339, on the effect of special rewards offered by royal proclamation in stimulating prosecutions.

31 39 Eliz 1, c. 4, 39 Eliz 1, c. 21; Boynton, 'Tudor Provost Marshal'. The county of Devon, which continued to appoint marshals down to the early eighteenth century, may have been the last to persist with the practice.

32 For war and vagrancy in the sixteenth and seventeenth centuries, see A. L. Beier, *Masterless Men: The Vagrancy Problem in England 1560–1640* (London: Methuen, 1985), 93–5. For the eighteenth century, see Beattie, *Crime and the*

Courts, 232, n. 60; S. Pole, 'Crime, Society and Law Enforcement in Hanoverian Somerset' (Ph.D. Thesis, Cambridge University, 1983), tab. V.7; '28th Report from the Select Committee on Finance. Police and Convict Establishments', in *Reports from Committees of the House of Commons*, vol. XIII, 398–9; *Victoria County History: Shropshire*, vol. V (Oxford: Oxford University Press, 1979), 122; Innes, 'Politics and Morals', 63, 65 and refs.

33 See e.g. *An Enquiry into the Rights of Free Subjects, in which the Cases of British Sailors and Common Soldiers are Distinctly Consider'd and Compar'd* (London, 1749), 42–3.

34 I have greatly profited from discussing these matters with Geoff Hudson, whose Oxford D.Phil. thesis is concerned with the treatment of 'maimed soldiers' in the seventeenth century.

35 I. G. Powell, 'The Chatham Chest under the Early Stuarts', *Mariner's Mirror*, 8 (1922); J. Ehrman, *The Navy in the War of William III* (Cambridge: Cambridge University Press, 1963), 130–1. Trinity House, established to support merchant seamen and their families, may also have provided relief: when sailors switched back and forth between the merchant marine and the Royal Navy, it is not clear on what basis their eligibility for one or another form of relief was determined. Trinity House Hull noted in 1699 that their poor had much increased since the war (*CJ*, vol. XIII, 167).

36 O. Macdonagh, *The Inspector General: Sir Jeremiah Fitzpatrick and Social Reform 1783–1802* (London: Croom Helm, 1981), 257–67. For pressure for pensions for soldiers' dependants in the 1690s, see J. Childs, *The British Army of William III* (Manchester: Manchester University Press, 1987), 157. For three years in the early eighteenth century, monies were paid out from land-tax receipts to parishes supplying soldiers, to defray the cost of supporting those soldiers' dependants, at the rate of £3 per soldier. That system was then abandoned, however, in favour of bounties, from the same source, paid directly to volunteers (Ann 7, c. 2; Ann 8, c. 13; Ann 9, c. 4; Ann 10, c. 12). I am informed by Alannah Tomkins that the records of Exeter Corporation of the Poor show that it received £46. 9s for the support of soldiers' families from this source in 1709, so the provision was no dead letter. The Corporation's committee for the poor was ordered 'to examine into the Case of such ffamilyes whose Relations have been lately impressed and order them Such parts of the Said money given by Act of parliam^t as they shall think fit'. During the American War public subscriptions were set on foot for the support of poor soldiers and their families – in part a reflection, no doubt, of the peculiarly ideologically fraught character of this war, but in part perhaps too of changing fashions in charity (J. Bradley, *Popular Politics and the American Revolution* [Macon, Georgia: Mercer University Press, 1986], 152–6).

37 [G. Hutt], *Papers Illustrative of the Origin and Early History of the Royal Hospital at Chelsea* (London: Eyre & Spottiswood, 1872); Ehrman, *Navy*, 441–4; C. C. Lloyd, *Greenwich: Palace, Hospital, College* (London: Royal Naval College, 1969); '34th Report of the Select Committee on Finance. Chatham Chest, Greenwich Hospital, Chelsea Hospital', *Reports from Committees of the House of Commons*, vol. XIII (London, 1803). An act of 1729 provided that seamen must contribute for the support of Greenwich wherever in the empire their wages might be paid (2 Geo II, c. 7).

38 [Hutt], *Chelsea Hospital*, 83–5, lists numbers of out-pensioners; they were also given to Parliament each year with the army estimates, and may be found in *CJ*. See also *Parliamentary History*, vol. XX, cols 475 ff., esp. col. 495; *A Description of the Royal Hospital for Seamen at Greenwich. Published by the*

Chaplains (London, 1806), 42. Chelsea Pensioners initially collected their money from agents, but Pitt, responding to accusations of abuse, changed the system in 1754: *Parliamentary History*, vol. XV, cols 374–5; 28 Geo 2, c. 1. Some soldiers' and sailors' widows were given jobs in the hospitals. In the 1760s, special provision was made for the orphans of soldiers and sailors who had died abroad and whose settlement could not be ascertained: the Secretary at War asked the Foundling Hospital, then in receipt of a parliamentary grant, to give them priority (McClure, *Coram's Children*, 137).

39 Western, *English Militia*, see index under 'Families' and esp. 142, 168–73, 269, 287–90. The revived militia was a purely English force; a Scottish militia was authorized only in 1797.

40 Magistrates' part in setting the scale is of more interest than the precise form of the scale, which in any case varied from place to place. Precedents for such magisterial action have been cited (e.g. by M. Neumann, 'Suggestion regarding the Origins of the Speenhamland Plan', *English Historical Review*, 84 [1969], but all date from the latter part of the century. Although there are other contexts in which magistrates' assumption of new powers can be set, experience in paying militiamen's family allowances is one worth taking into account.

41 Sir L. Radzinowicz, *History of English Criminal Law and its Administration from 1750* (5 vols; London: various publishers, 1948–86), vol. III, ch. 2, 135–6. For the Fieldings' expenses, see PRO T38/671, T1/387, 449, 454. An early 'patrole' had been established on the London–Chelsea road, on the petition of the inhabitants of Chelsea, after the War of the Spanish Succession, the patrol-men being a troop of specially selected Chelsea Pensioners. This patrol was still in operation in the early nineteenth century (*An Historical and Descriptive Account of the Royal Hospital and Royal Military Asylum at Chelsea* [London: T. Faulkner, 1805], 67–8). One proposal made in 1764 amounted to a generaliz-ation of this scheme: it was suggested that 300 able-bodied Chelsea Pensioners might be formed into a 'patrolling watch' (Radzinowicz, *History*, vol. III, 136, n. 13, and pp 486–7).

42 Radzinowicz, *History*, vol. III, 36–7, ch. 5; D. Philips, 'A New Engine of Power and Authority', in Gatrell, Lenman and Parker, *Crime and the Law*; R. Paley, 'The Middlesex Justices Act of 1792: Its Origins and Effects' (Ph.D. thesis, Reading University, 1983).

43 For a collection of mid-eighteenth-century cravings, see PRO T90/146; Beattie, *Crime and the Courts*, ch. 9; Ekirch, *Bound for America*, chs 1–2, 8; *Calendar of Treasury Papers 1729–30* (London: HMSO, 1897), 472. Scottish transpor-tation was systematized, and brought under the scope of national legislation, only in 1766 (Ekirch, *Bound for America*, 86).

44 Beattie, *Crime and the Courts*, ch. 10; Ekirch, *Bound for America*, ch. 8.

45 For the regulation of vagrancy in general see S. and B. Webb, *English Poor Law History*, I, *The Old Poor Law* (London: Longmans, Green & Co., 1927), ch. 6, esp. 387–91. Beier, *Masterless Men*, 142, notes that in the sixteenth and seventeenth centuries counterfeit passports usually stated that the holder was a soldier or sailor. For payments to travellers in the eighteenth century see e.g. W. E. Tate, *The Parish Chest* (Cambridge: Cambridge University Press, 1969), 183–5.

46 Childs, *The British Army of William III*, 199–200, 203; R. E. Scouller, *The Armies of Queen Anne* (Oxford: Clarendon Press, 1966), 321–5.

47 The 1713 vagrancy act (13 Ann, c. 26) – a consolidating statute – did follow the end of a war, but its timing was at least in part determined by the expiry of previous legislation. The Webbs (*Old Poor Law*, 367–9) suggest that the

central executive took an interest in vagrancy only when they wanted to mobilize vagrants into the armed forces. This would not explain why counties were circulated on the subject in 1786, for example.

48 Innes, 'Politics and Morals', 63, 65; 43 Geo 3, c. 61; L. Rose, *Rogues and Vagabonds: Vagrant Underworld in Britain 1815–1985* (London: Routledge, 1988), 18, and see also 72, 120.

49 13 Geo 2, c. 24.

50 Innes, 'Politics and Morals', 95; *Statement and Propositions from the Society for Giving Effect to His Majesty's Proclamation against Vice and Immorality* (London: George Stafford, 1790), 8–9; *Resolutions of the Magistrates Deputed from the Several Counties of England and Wales* (London: George Stafford, 1790), 13–14; *Lords Journals*, vol. XXXIX, 463, 466, 469, 484, 655, 686, 689, 693; *CJ*, vol. XLVIII, 806, 823–4, 847, 924; S. Lambert, *House of Commons Sessional Papers of the Eighteenth Century* (Wilmington, Dela.: Scholarly Resources Inc., 1975), 43–54, 483–4. An act of 1803 (43 Geo 3, c. 61) – mentioned above for its criminalizing provision – reimmunized soldiers and sailors with passes, extended this protection to wives separated from them at embarkation, and gave statutory authority to Admiralty and War Office passes (which had long been in use). Unfortunately, it is unclear whether such passes were also issued to women and children before the passage of this act. Detailed accounts kept by the constables of Stone in Staffordshire in the early nineteenth century reveal that about one in seven of the travellers or groups of travellers they relieved were travelling on War Office passes, a majority of these being women and children, (S. R. Broadbridge, 'The Old Poor Law in the Parish of Stone', *North Staffordshire Journal of Field Studies*, 13 [1973], 15–16).

51 See e.g. *Parliamentary History*, vol. XIV, cols 616, 726–8, 750.

52 10 Will 3, c. 17; 12 Ann, c. 14; 22 Geo 2, c. 44; 3 Geo 3, c. 8; 24 Geo 3, s. 2, c. 6.

53 For general criticism, see e.g. [W. Hay], *Remarks on the Laws Relating to the Poor* (London: J. Stagg [1735]); P. Langford (ed.), *Writings and Speeches of Edmund Burke*, vol. II (Oxford: Clarendon Press, 1987), 401–3; 33 Geo 3, c. 54; 35 Geo 3, c. 101.

54 W. S. McNutt, *The Atlantic Provinces: The Emergence of Colonial Society 1712–1867* (Toronto: McClelland & Steward, 1965), 37, 53–4.

55 Shaw, *Management of Scottish Society*, 185; Johnson, *Jacobite Estates*, 145–54.

56 J. Dunlop, *The British Fisheries Society* (Edinburgh: John Donald, 1978), esp. chs 2–3; *Parliamentary History*, vol. XXV, cols 137–8.

57 T. Gilbert, *Plan for the Better Relief and Employment of the Poor* (London: G Wilkie, 1781), 25–7; *An Account of the Workhouses in Britain in the Year 1732* (3rd edn; London: 1798), preface; *CJ*, vol. XLVII, 274–6.

58 C. B. A. Behrens, *Society, Government and the Enlightenment: The Experiences of Eighteenth-Century France and Prussia* (London: Thames & Hudson, 1985), provides a convenient overview. See similarly M. Bordes, *L'Administration provincial et municipale en France au XVIII$_e$ siècle* (Paris: SEDES, 1972), ch. 5. P. G. M. Dickson, *Finance and Government under Maria Theresia 1740–80* (2 vols; Oxford: Clarendon Press, 1987), is authoritative, and see also 'Joseph II's Hungarian Land Survey', *English Historical Review*, 106 (1991), for some fruits of his work in progress on the later period.

59 L. J. Hume, *Bentham and Bureaucracy* (Cambridge: Cambridge University Press, 1981), 20–54, develops this theme.

60 D. Eastwood, 'Amplifying the Province of the Legislature: The Flow of Information and the English State in the Early Nineteenth Century', *Historical*

Research, 62 (1989); 'Patriotism and the British State in the 1790s', in M. Philp (ed.), *British Popular Politics and the French Revolution* (Cambridge: Cambridge University Press, 1991).

61 Paul Langford suggests that 'Warfare on the English model was a triumph for an enterprising and acquisitive society, not an authoritarian state' (*A Polite and Commercial People: England 1727–1783* [Oxford: Clarendon Press, 1989], 697).

62 C. Bayly, *Imperial Meridian: The British Empire and the World 1780–1830* (London: Longman, 1989), 155–60; G. S. Graham, *British Policy and Canada 1774–91* (London: Longmans & Co, 1930), ch. 2; R. Guha, *A Rule of Property for Bengal: An Essay on the Idea of a Permanent Settlement* (Paris: Mouton & Co., 1963); R. Ray, *Change in Bengal Agrarian Society c.1760–1850* (New Delhi: Manohar, 1979).

6

Empire of Virtue
The imperial project and Hanoverian culture
c.1720–1785
Kathleen Wilson

I have observed those countries where trade is promoted and encouraged do not make discoveries to destroy but to improve mankind – by love and friendship to tame the fierce and polish the most savage; to teach them the advantages of honest traffic by taking from them, with their own consent, their useless superfluities, and giving them in return what, from their ignorance in manual arts, their situation, or some other accident, they stand in need of.

> Merchant-apprentice Trueman in George Lillo's
> *London Merchant* (1731), III.i.11–19

Britain will never want a Race of Men, who prefer the publick Good before any narrow or selfish Views – who choose Dangers in defence of Their Country before an inglorious safety, an honourable Death before the unmanly pleasures of a useless and effeminate life . . . it is now the Birthright of Englishmen, to carry, not only Good Manners, but the purest Light of the Gospel, where Barbarism and Ignorance totally prevailed.

> Richard Brewster, *A Sermon Preach'd . . .*
> *on the Thanksgiving Day* (Newcastle, 1759)

What could be more flattering to an Englishman, in the utmost pride of his heart . . . than to see his country, the seat of such an empire, the mistress of such a world, [and] how are all our well-founded expectations destroyed! Where are we now to seek our glorious dependencies?

> *Norfolk Chronicle* (17 January 1778)

Eighteenth-century British imperialism has been unevenly served by historians. Although the expansion of Britain in the Hanoverian decades was a central subject of historical enquiry for generations of scholars, their accounts invariably eschewed large-scale political, ideological or cultural forces in favour of great events, of battles won and lost and military and naval strategies that in the long run succeeded in wrenching some colonies from France and Spain. From this perspective, 'empire' consisted of a series of wars between Britain and her European rivals for domination in the Americas and East Indies; and, once that domination was achieved, of a series of policies (some just, some badly calculated) designed to consolidate and build upon a hard-won imperial ascendancy.[1] Certainly such an approach has enhanced our understanding of the international, strategic and diplomatic contexts of war and peace, and colonial acquisition and loss in the eighteenth century; but it is of limited usefulness to those who wish to know the meaning and significance of empire at home. How was the empire retailed and understood in Britain by those for whom it existed more in ideology and imagination than in policy? Such a question is difficult to answer, for despite all the rich and resourceful work that has appeared in recent years on popular politics, communications, class-relations and protest in eighteenth-century England, the meanings and significance of empire in public political consciousness have scarcely been investigated. Indeed, although historians have recently begun to take on the development of popular nationalisms with important results, the evidence of pro-imperial attitudes among a wider public has continued to be dismissed rather than examined, uncritically categorized as instances of chauvinistic excess, crudely visceral in motivation and unremittingly lower-class in provenance, without any effort to relate them to larger social and political contexts.[2]

This reluctance of historians to take seriously the complex connections between empire and the expanding and increasingly vociferous political nation of the Hanoverian decades is made all the more unfortunate in light of recent work on the state, the transatlantic economy and the empire-wide nature of eighteenth-century trade, credit and consumption networks. A number of writers have demonstrated the broad social basis within Britain of investment in the imperial project, from the financing of ships and investment in cargoes to money-lending to merchants and shipowners and colonial land speculation, as well as the distribution, consumption and population patterns which spread colonial and British goods across regions, oceans and nations.[3] There were strong material reasons, in other words, for ordinary English people to be avidly interested in imperial affairs. Moreover, as John Brewer has argued, if the expansion of the eighteenth-century English state was predicated upon seven decades of almost continuous warfare with her European imperial rivals and the need to finance it, then the success of that effort depended increasingly on the successful appropriation of a growing portion of income per head through indirect taxation, which affected the entire population.[4] Clearly, in several ways, even the most humble citizens were drawn into the imperial effort, however distant or immediate that effort may have seemed.

It is against the broader socio-economic and political contexts that we must examine domestic conceptions of empire in the eighteenth century; but such an undertaking requires semantic caution. 'Imperialism' – defined in this chapter as the ideologies and values which supported Britain's push for colonial acquisition and imperial consolidation – is, in all periods, a historical phenomenon, an amalgam of practices, values and attitudes that are historically embedded and multivalent, bearing different cultural and political meanings in different contexts. As such, the drive for empire in the eighteenth century had distinctive motives and rationales and generated different images and responses within the domestic culture from the imperial project of the nineteenth century. It is the specificity of eighteenth-century imperial sensibilities that needs to be uncovered: the various ways in which the empire was imagined, the forums through which it could be represented, debated and discussed, and, above all, the specific meanings that empire held for the various groups involved in or engaged by the mesmerizing spectacle of Britain's global expansion.

Empire – its existence, aggrandizement and concerns – certainly permeated Hanoverian culture at a number of levels: literature (both adult and children's), theatre, music, painting, leisure pursuits, gardening, philanthropy, fashion, religion, politics and graphic and literary propaganda.[5] Obviously, the present effort must be limited by requirements of space and coherence. In this necessarily exploratory chapter, I will examine just a few of the ways in which a popular (in the sense of socially inclusive) vision of imperial greatness was embedded in domestic culture and politics, exhibited in artefacts and activities that mirrored and expressed the interests, values and ideologies attached to empire at different periods by the audiences that most supported it at home – a conception of empire which was not necessarily oppositionist or conservative, and which could support competing notions of the state, nation and polity. To do this necessitates looking beyond official and theoretical pronouncements about the purpose of colonies to the convergence of interests, images, values and belief that gave empire its meaning and vitality to ordinary citizens who participated in it, imaginatively or materially, at home. Such a methodology has historical verisimilitude, for however much the eighteenth-century British state produced and supported mercantile imperialism, the imperial sensibilities within the broader political nation were not 'imposed' from above, the unmediated result of official policy or elite manipulation. Rather, they emanated equally from below, as successive governments were castigated for not pursuing a more aggressively expansionist foreign policy abroad or for insufficiently protecting and nurturing imperial relations. It was the domestic supporters of empire, in other words – some, but by no means all, of whom were members of the mercantile community – who most forcefully articulated and elaborated empire's rationale.

I have argued elsewhere that the cultural, political and ideological significance of empire was both greater and less straightforward than much current scholarship has led us to believe. Not only was empire intimately, if intermittently, linked with opposition patriotism and libertarian politics throughout the century, but the resounding articulations of imperialist sensibilities that emanated from all social levels make it clear that empire had an appeal that frequently transcended socio-economic and political allegiances. Further, empire was central to contemporary arguments about the nature of consent, liberty and authority in the British political system, the limitations of state power and the effectiveness and legitimacy of its counsels.[6] What I want to sketch in below are some of the ways in which a mercantilist, libertarian view of empire was disseminated in a variety of forums; its links to populist and oppositionist political ideologies; and its instrumental role in helping men and women to measure the place of Britain in the world and their own place within the polity. I will focus on three important discursive structures within Hanoverian culture, all parts of the fairly wide-ranging 'media' which helped shape and expressed public perceptions and consciousness of the imperial project – the press, theatre and politics – with a view to uncovering the ideological significance that empire had for the wider and predominantly urban, middle-class public of this period.

The examination of the press, as fountain-head of the communications revolution in the eighteenth century, is of course crucial to any effort to pin down the content of pro-imperial attitudes and the mechanisms of their dissemination. As Benedict Anderson has convincingly argued, it was the rise of 'print capitalism' that was the key to the emergence of national-isms and imperialisms in the eighteenth and nineteenth centuries, for it made possible the construction of 'imagined communities' of readers for whose benefit and in whose interest national, international and imperial news was condensed and refracted.[7] Eighteenth-century theatre, in both its justification and productions, was deeply embedded in the imperial project of the age, serving as a vibrant forum for the dissemination of images, beliefs and rhetoric about the empire and its importance, or irrel-evance, to British national standing and prosperity. Empire, in other words, provided both texts and contexts for late-Stuart and Hanoverian drama.[8] Above all, extra-parliamentary political culture concentrated and focused the expression of pro-imperial sensibilities at several different junctures (frequently using the press and theatre to do so), where they were linked to libertarian, populist or nationalistic ideologies and agendas. My dis-cussion will proceed by examining some of the imperial visions expressed in each of these three forums, and the social and political environments in which they flourished; and will conclude with a consideration of the way the eighteenth-century empire mediated contemporary notions of class, gender and nation.

THE PRESS

Belief in the desirability of empire in the eighteenth century rested upon a bedrock of nationalistic, mercantilist and libertarian beliefs that lay behind commercial thinking of the period generally, all of which were galvanized in this period by Britain's obsessive rivalry and protracted wars with the continental Catholic powers. Put simply, the British empire was imagined to consist of flourishing and commercially viable colonies, populated with free British subjects, that served as bulwarks of trade, prosperity, naval strength and political virtue for the parent state.[9] As one commentator put it, colonies were the 'sinews of our naval strength, on which avowedly the very being of the kingdom depends'; while another extravagantly claimed that all British wealth and grandeur was attributable to her colonies – 'She draws from thence . . . all that is *good* and *valuable*'.[10] Historians who insist that the British public was more interested in trade than in empire in the eighteenth century thus miss the point: the imperial project existed to maximize trade and national power, and colonies were considered crucial to the 'empire of the sea' that contemporaries believed Britain had, or should have, dominion over.

Behind this view of empire lay the tenets of an adulterated mercantilism, popularized through a plethora of pamphlets, essays, newspaper articles and parliamentary speeches that had appeared arguing about commercial issues since the early years of the century. These principles could be summarized as follows: the world was possessed of finite amounts of wealth and resources; national power and prosperity depended upon capturing the greatest proportion of these riches relative to other nations; attaining national self-sufficiency and a 'favourable balance of trade' (that is, more exports than imports) were means to this end, which depended in turn upon procuring a monopoly of international trade and colonial markets, and pursuing policies geared to increasing population and industry at home; and if trade was the best means of civilizing the world (and most agreed that it was), then colonies were the most useful way of maximizing its benefits for the mother country. Within this framework, the navy was considered to be the prime instrument of national power and the guarantor of commercial wealth; colonial interests were to be subordinated to those of the mother country; and the state was to support and pursue these goals, not only through the encouragement of the production of people and goods at home, but also through a foreign policy that concentrated on maintaining England's naval power and colonial supremacy – 'The acquisition of tracts of land and territories to enlarge dominion and power', as one writer put it, which by 1730 represented the most recent incarnation of the 'blue-water policy' advocated since Anne's reign.[11]

If contemporaries were to have given this amalgam of beliefs a slogan, it would perhaps have been 'Production at Home, Acquisition Abroad' –

a motto which may not have rivalled 'Wilkes and Liberty' in evocative pithiness but certainly states the priorities of the imperial vision. It was also one which highlights the orientation of mercantilist thinking towards counting, measuring and assessing national wealth numerically against that of other nations. The eighteenth-century press brilliantly reflected and encouraged such sentiments, for, among other things, it provided the information necessary to make endless calculations about incoming and outgoing wealth, goods and profits, production and consumption. From mid-century, the very structure and content of newspapers in London and the provinces mirrored a world-view in which trade and the accumulation of wealth appear to be of the highest national and individual good. The progress of wars in Europe, America, Africa and the East Indies and the prizes taken in battle; the comings and goings of merchant ships, with often-lengthy lists of the products of their laden bottoms; prices, stocks and bullion values; and advertisements for luxury goods from international and colonial markets – tea, coffee, chocolate and tobacco; calicoes and silks; wines, rum and spirits; fruits and seeds; furs, exotic birds and plants, and ivory – together could account for one-third of the contents of individual issues of eighteenth-century newspapers from the capital and outports, and an even higher proportion in wartime.[12] As one scholar has noted for the imaginative literature of the period, both the enumeration of goods and their seemingly endless variety encapsulated on a small scale the contemporary fascination with the movable products of imperialist accumulation.[13] They also evinced a widespread interest in the processes of colonial acquisition and possession. By the 1740s and 1750s several provincial papers and most magazines had sections on 'American Affairs' or 'British Plantations' that included not only current news on politics and trade, but also the histories and settlement patterns of individual colonies, the competing claims of European powers to them and the 'etiquette' of colonization.[14]

In conjunction with other items in the papers,[15] the format and content of newspapers mirrored contemporary conceptualizations of power and market relations, at home and abroad, and expressed the interests and priorities of those who read them, from landed elites and overseas merchants to humble middling tradesmen, shopkeepers and artisans – all individuals who had an interest, material or ideological, in commerce and colonies. Newspapers were thus central instruments in the social production of information: both representing and verifying local experience, they functioned like imaginative literature in reproducing and refracting world events into socially meaningful categories and hierarchies of importance; and the processes of imperial acquisition were clearly significant here.[16] In this way, newspapers produced an 'imagined community' of producers, distributors and consumers on both sides of the Atlantic, who shared an avid interest in the fate of the 'empire of goods' that linked them together in prosperity or adversity. They also, significantly, familiarized their readers with a discourse that diagnosed the structure, location or distribution of power in the state as the source of many imperial, political and social discontents and grievances.

Naturally, these patterns were not limited to newspapers: pamphlets, novels, travel-books and histories, and the periodical press were similarly caught up in the mechanics and fruits of imperial acquisition. John Old-mixon's two-volume *British Empire in America*, for example, provided a history of each colony which included the most salient points about its history, settlement, current state and products, the unassailable claims of the British to it, as well as beautifully produced maps with towns, plantations and settlements clearly marked. His histories of the northern mainland colonies included detailed recountings of their settlement and constitutional evolutions, while his histories of the islands also dwelt on their character as exotics, with different origins, customs and culture from the metropolis. The projection of absolute identities or differences on to colonial cultures, of course, was a salient feature of European imperialist mentalities as a whole in this period;[17] but Oldmixon's enthusiasm for 'foreign' cultures, like that of many other writers on empire, was clearly attributable to their status as potential or actual contributors to Britain's favourable balance of trade.[18]

The periodical literature of the day was similarly marked by broad and sustained interest in the imperial project and its contribution to Britain's national stature and strength. At least one-third of periodicals such as the *Gentleman's Magazine, London Magazine* and *Newcastle General Magazine* were taken up in foreign and imperial affairs in the mid-century, and articles, essays, songs and poems which concerned themselves, either directly or indirectly, with the state and health of the empire. The *Gentleman's Magazine*, for example, which prided itself on its judgement in selecting and condensing news and cultural items and representing a balance of different views for its broad and heterogeneous audience, was a prodigious chronicler of imperial affairs, particularly in the 1750s. The volume for 1756, for example, included full accounts of the loss of Minorca, public reaction to it across England, and the first months of the trial of Admiral Byng, which stretched out across several issues (and continued well into the next year). There were also pointed reminiscences about Britain's historical escapades as an intrepid and robust imperial power, from the swashbuckling performances of Ralegh and Drake to Vernon's much more recent, and vividly remembered, siege of Porto Bello in 1739. At the same time, the 'Journal of American Affairs', which had been a regular feature of each monthly issue since the magazine began, providing snippets of information on colonial curiosities, cultivation, politics and trade, was expanded to include more extended accounts of individual colonies which sought to establish the clear right of possession by the British. They also included histories of French, Spanish and Indian aggression against the brave, stalwart and virtuous English settlers, who managed to survive and triumph despite the odds against them. The columns of the *Gentleman's Magazine*, and of rival publications like it, thus exuded not only contemporary fascination with the processes of colonization, but also the importance of their recounting to germinating conceptions of the national and patriotic character.[19]

The *London Magazine*'s coverage of the Seven Years War was similarly noteworthy in the wealth of detail on imperial affairs, providing accounts of battles, strategies and engagements at sea and land, illustrated with dozens of maps and engravings. In 1759 it began publishing the *Impartial and Succinct History of the Origin and Progress of the Present War* in serial instalments, which were copied in rival publications so often that the magazine's publisher, bookseller Richard Baldwin, began printing his copyright to the history of the first page of each volume in an effort to ward off pirate editions. Indicating the continuing demand of the public for the saga of Britain's imperial ascendancy, or maybe just Baldwin's continuing paranoia, the publisher was still warning off would-be plagiarizers of the history in the *London Magazine* for 1775.[20]

Graphically expressive of imperial aspirations were the scores of maps produced from the 1730s onwards that demarcated British possessions, past, present and future. Indeed, maps of the colonies seem to have predated the proliferation of English gazetteers and trade directories that took off in the 1750s and 1760s. In the 1730s and 1740s it was, naturally, the West Indies that riveted cartographers' attention, while from the early 1750s on maps of America and Canada competed for prominence.[21] The periodical press, again, was prolific in this respect. Like the *London Magazine*, the *Gentleman's Magazine* in 1756–60 printed dozens of maps which ranged from the theatres of war in Europe, Africa, America and India, to Caribbean islands, the possession of which was or could be contested, all appropriately scaled in 'English miles' and longitude from London.[22] It is within the context of extensive cartographic mania over the colonies, providing emblematic evidence of British global aspirations and claims, that the production of tradesmen's directories must be seen. Publications like *The General Shopbook: or the Tradesman's Universal Directory. Being . . . a . . . Compendium . . . Comprehending and Explaining the Domestic and Foreign Trade of Great Britain and the Plantations . . . by Companies or Private Persons . . . [with] Commodities and Manufactures Exported and Imported*, published in 1753, must be read against a tradition of colonial 'directories', which first refined the technique of making the empire palatable and comprehensible for domestic consumption.

A wide range of printed materials, made available through commercial printing, was instrumental in supporting and extending consciousness of and attitudes about the empire in the wider public, though they are beyond our scope here. What is suggested by the brief overview above is the degree to which the newspaper and periodical press, even in its most apolitical manifestations, supported an accumulationist and mercantile view of empire – that is, that empire was at heart about trade, commerce, accumulation and consumption, and as much augmented national, as well as individual, standing, wealth and power. Such accounts, in conjunction with histories and topographies of the colonies, also fed the growing enthusiasm for the exotic and primitive, fostered an illusion of cosmopolitanism that actually strengthened English ethnocentricity, and legitimated British domination in terms comprehensible to empire's domestic consumers.[23] They were thus instrumental in disseminating a broader consciousness of the significance of Britain's imperial project among an avid public at home.

THE THEATRE

Theatre was deeply implicated in the imperial project as well as in the struggles for national definition that eighteenth-century imperialism entailed, providing a focus and a forum for debates about the empire and its relationship to Britain's international stature and prosperity.[24] Theatres, both licensed and unlicensed, flourished not only in the capital but also in provincial cities, such as Newcastle, Liverpool, Bristol, Hull, Norwich and Manchester, where audiences were comprised of the same urban classes who made up the wider political nation, from local gentry and government officials to merchants, tradesmen and artisans. They thus represented a lively and frequently volatile cross-section of social classes, a feature that did not change until the late eighteenth and early nineteenth centuries.[25]

The connections of eighteenth-century theatre with the imperial project were both implicit and explicit, and empire provided both a context for understanding the significance of theatre as a cultural arena and a text for specific plays. In the first instance, theatre was certainly a forum in which national stereotypes were constructed and perpetuated with a vengeance. French Fops, adventuring Irishmen, ridiculous Italians and bullying Spaniards – as well as rowdy, robust but essentially honourable Englishmen – were all stock characters in farce, sentimental comedy and drama in this period.[26] But the nationalist and imperialist sensibilities embedded in much English theatre were more subtle and complex than the presentation of 'others' as grotesques. For theatre both drew upon and exaggerated national cultural identities, and socialized audiences into the mores of differentiation on the basis of sex and nationality in ways that directly affected domestic conceptions of the imperial project.

For example, the legitimacy and morality of the English stage was frequently defended against its critics by protestations of its importance to national manners and character in a way that endowed theatre with particular patriotic significance. In the context of Britain's obsessive competition with France – particularly of fears that the British nation had declined into 'effeminacy' and effeteness, largely through French influence and contagion, that were fanned by a host of cultural, political and social commentators in the 1740s and 1750s[27] – theatre proponents marshalled the images and rhetoric of patriotism to make their case that English theatre was a crucial bulwark of national manners, language, morality, virtue and spirit – both an offensive weapon and a defensive battlement against 'foreign' and especially French contagion, that could also contribute to British expansion abroad.

Not only was theatre instrumental, indirectly, in spreading English culture throughout the world – the high proportion of ship-captains and seafaring men in the audience 'thereby carry abroad a Taste of Politeness and Generosity, and give the World a Better Idea of *English* Manners', as one advocate argued in the 1730s – but a flourishing theatre was also a sign of flourishing liberty, honour and national vigour, as the support given to Shakespeare by good Queen Bess had shown.[28] That the Whig government should attempt to curtail English theatre while permitting foreign acting troupes to perform and, it seemed, flourish, was seen as a doubly insidious form of betrayal, or national honour and countrymen. Not surprisingly, attacks on both licensing acts and imported actors and genres could take the form of strident xenophobic diatribes against perceived foreign contagion. As one particularly vitriolic defender of English theatre put it, 'Barbarous Thought! . . . A Freeman of *London*, a Native of England . . . shall be denied the Liberty that is allowed *French* Dancers and [Italian] Harlequins – to Effeminate Eunuchs, and Sod[omitica]l *Italians*; yet such shall be encouraged, and *Englishmen* despised!' Is it any wonder, he went on, that England is 'so debauch'd with Effeminacy and *Italian* airs . . . [that] we daily see our Male Children . . . dwindle almost into Women? Is the ancient *British* Fire, Spirit and Bravery, to be supported by such as these?' Clearly, only indigenous British theatre could inculcate the appropriately manly, civilized patriotic virtues and manners in its audience. Such nationalistic attitudes, which defined the 'other' as barbarous, ignorant, effeminate or obscene (and hence defined Englishness as their opposites – civilized, cosmopolitan, manly and virtuous) were deeply entrenched in the entire imperial effort, from the competition with other European countries for empire to the confrontation with the 'primitive' and exotic indigenous cultures of the lands being colonized.[29]

Nationalistic and protectionist defences of the stage were not confined to extremist reviewers or high-placed cultural arbiters, however; they were also shared by a wider public. Theatre riots (for which the century was notorious) were frequently precipitated by the use of 'foreign' entertainers on London and provincial stages, such as those against French and Italian comedians at the Haymarket in 1738 and 1749 and against French dancers at Drury Lane in 1755. These disturbances, where the rioters cried 'Remember the poor English players in Gaol!' and 'No French strollers' can quite plausibly be seen as crude attempts to enforce the tenets of balance of trade through the institutional imperatives of theatre, protecting its territory and labour-force from foreign domination; they were certainly interpreted by their participants as supremely patriotic activities. At the 1755 Drury Lane riots, occurring at a time when war with France was imminent, the leader of the disturbances was alleged to have faced the gallery and exclaimed, 'O Britons! O my countrymen! You will certainly not suffer these foreigner dogs to amuse us. Our destruction is at hand. These sixty dancers are come over with one desire, to undermine our Constitution!' Significantly, the rioters included many members of the francophobic Anti-Gallican Society, an association of merchants, tradesmen and craftsmen dedicated to promoting English manufactures and art in order to eliminate French imports.[30]

Indeed, the riots of 1755 were defended in print by no less a theatrical luminary than Theophilus Cibber, actor, playwright and son of the Poet Laureate, in a way that clarified what some observers saw as an evident link between the fate of theatre in Britain and the fate of Britain in the world. Cibber began his *Second Dissertation on the Theatre* with a prefatory address to the 'Anti-Gallicans, and the Trading Part of the Nation', lauding them for their superior and patriotic actions in removing the French dancers from the stage. The appearance of the French troupe 'at so critical a Juncture, when the Minds of Men were naturally inflam'd, against an insidious Enemy, who premeditated a daring Invasion of our Country' was bound to provoke a disturbance, Cibber declared. The audience's actions proved to the world that

> the Natives of this Sea-Girt Island will not readily forget our Navy's our best Bulwark, that our Traffic is the best Support of that Navy: that not only Riches, but Power, and Glory are added to this Nation, by its extended Commerce. With that, our Arts and Sciences Increase. In you, then, Gentlemen, we trust for an Amendment of our Taste, by a sensible Correction of our Public Diversions.[31]

Although Cibber had no little degree of self-interest in adopting these patriotic arguments – he wanted to diminish the popularity of his rival, David Garrick, who had hired the French troupe to perform in the Drury Lane production of *The Chinese Festival* – the francophobia and identification with the imperial project would strike resounding chords in the public, and indicate how deeply theatre was involved in the social and political debates of the day.

Cibber's arguments also underscore the close and deliberate identification of contemporary theatre with the attitudes and personnel that supported the imperial project. In the outports, for example, such as Bristol, Liverpool and Newcastle, it is clear that the commercial middle classes made up a major portion of the theatre audience, and merchants were prodigious contributors to new theatre buildings.[32] Theatrical prologues and epilogues of the period reflected this social milieu in the employment of the language and metaphors of trade and commerce to explain the significance of particular plays or the English stage generally, purposefully catering to audience sensibilities. The prologue to Colman's *English Merchant* of 1763 justifies the debt of the playwright to Voltaire (on whose *L'Ecossaise* the play was based) by likening such borrowing to English manufacturers' use of raw materials culled from the rest of the world to make their products. Just as the Spitalfields weavers make 'English silk' from materials brought from Europe and the east, Colman declared, so with 'the whole world of Letters' English playwrights can 'fairly Trade': ''Tis *English* Silk when wrought in *English* Loom'.[33] In a similar vein, Garrick's prologue written for the opening of the Theatre Royal in Bristol inverted the 'All the world's a stage' conceit by describing the commercial theatre world as a shop trafficking in 'Dramatic Ware' that allows 'from small Retailers, Merchants [to] rise'; it ends by wishing continued success to Bristol's pivotal role in Britain's imperial project:

> May honour'd Commerce with her Sails unfurl'd
> Still bring you Treasures from each distant World,
> From East to West, extend this City's Name,
> Still to her Sons, encreasing Wealth with Fame,
> And may this Merit be our Honest Boast,
> To give you Pleasure, and no Virtue lost.[34]

Clearly, the precarious existence of theatre, both as a closely-supervised political medium dependent upon magisterial tolerance and as a commercialized cultural arena requiring the sympathy and support of its audience, necessitated the adoption of the 'patriotic', commercial idiom, which vindicated the stage simultaneously as a nursery of loyalty to the state and as bolsterer of an appropriately aggressive and imperial national identity and spirit. In this regard, too, theatrical benefits held in London and the provinces for patriotic, imperial causes – such as the Anti-Gallican Society, the Marine Society, which apprenticed young paupers as seamen, or various institutionalized charities, such as foundling hospitals, which preserved the nation's youth for useful and productive employment – no doubt served to underline the stage's advanced sense of civic responsibility and its stature as a prop of patriotic sentiment.[35]

The role of eighteenth-century theatre in promoting and supporting pro-imperial sensibilities extended beyond its location in a nexus of cultural and ideological issues to the content of the plays themselves. Such a topic is too vast for justice to be done to it in a short space, so two examples must suffice. George Farquhar's comedy, *The Recruiting Officer*, first

139

performed in 1706, and George Lillo's *London Merchant*, first performed in 1731, had many successful runs at London, provincial and colonial theatres throughout the eighteenth century. Both provided, in different ways, images, rhetoric and attitudes through which the imperial project could be comprehended by those at home.[36] Farquhar's comedy is a highly topical and amusing account of the dubious recruiting practices during the War of the Spanish Succession (when Farquhar himself served as a recruiting officer in Lichfield and Shrewsbury). Its continued popularity, particularly in wartime, when it became standard fare at provincial theatres during recruitment drives, was based not only on its witty dialogue, multiple plot-lines (involving love, masquerade and social and gender inversion as well as recruiting) and splendid spectacle, but also upon public familiarity with the chicanery and bribery that were so essential a part of the processes of recruiting soldiers and seamen from the civilian population. Equally important for our purposes, it uses Britain's military and imperial efforts abroad as the standard for illustrating relations between the sexes at home, thus pointing up the ideals of manliness and masculinity for both. Indeed, the dominant trope of the play is conquest – sexual, military, imperial and recruiting; the language and images of sexual – and national – potency that suffuse the play are one and the same. The army officers, though lampooned for their vices and conceits, are nevertheless local agents of wider international processes, and are worldly, experienced and, above all, inexhaustibly virile. Captain Plume's expression of surprise at the shortage of bastards in the town for impressment is just one of the many lines which plays on the supposed libertinism and virility of England's fighting-service:

> What! No bastards! And so many recruiting officers in town. I thought 'twas a maxim among them to leave as many recruits in the country as they carried out.
>
> (I.i.218–20)

The use of the language of balance of trade neatly links sexual and national commerce with the military effort, giving an old theme of English comic drama – the equation of sex and commerce – a topicality that forcefully played on eighteenth-century sensibilities and experience.

The conceited Captain Brazen – whose slogan with regards to women is '*veni, vidi, vici*' – equally illustrates the connections between domestic and foreign, military and sexual conquest; in one scene, he brags of his amorous intrigues abroad to Melinda, whom he hopes to make his current prize:

> you must know, madam, that I have served in Flanders against the French, in Hungary against the Turks, and in Tangier against the Moors ... I have always had the good luck to prove agreeable. I have had very considerable offers, madam. I might have married a

140

German princess worth fifty thousand crowns a year ... The daughter of a Turkish bashaw fell in love with me too, when I was a prisoner among the infidels. She offered to rob her father of this treasure and make her escape with me, but I don't know how, my time was not come.

(III.ii.47–65)

And, as Brazen's self-parodic speech implies, women were a highly prized part of the booty of warfare, at home and abroad. The female characters in the play are well aware of the double significance of sexual conquest:

MELINDA: Flanders lace is as constant a present from officers to their women as something else is from their women to them. They every year bring over a cargo of lace to cheat the Queen of her duty and her subjects of their honesty.

LUCY: They only barter one sort of prohibited goods for another, madam.

(III.ii.7–12)

Indeed, it is the army officers' role as the defenders of British liberties and properties (including property in women) against foreign aggression that ultimately valorizes and excuses their libertinism. As Justice Balance points out, echoing stock arguments of the period in support of the army,

They expose their lives to so many dangers for us abroad that we may give them some grains of allowance at home ... were it not for the bravery of these officers we should have French dragoons among us that would leave us neither liberty, property, wife, nor daughter.

(V.i.3–5, 9–12)

The interchangeability of the language and images used to describe recruiting, foreign conquest, love, marriage and sex – and even relations between the localities and the state – thus both plays on and coaxes awareness of the links between Britain's glory, liberty and property, successful sexual relations and the military-imperial effort: conquest and defence were the ends, and manliness and virility the means. Indeed, *The Recruiting Officer*'s comic representation of martial virility and potency was undoubtedly reassuring at a time when fears of creeping 'effeminacy' were impinging on public perceptions of Britain's military performance. In the hands of Farquhar's amorous officers, British sexual and military power (and British masculinity) were safe from 'illegitimate' appropriations, whether from women or rival nations.[37]

An equally successful play with a different but related agenda was the 'excellent moral tragedy', *The London Merchant*, written by the former merchant Lillo. A tale of the ruin of a young merchant apprentice, George Barnwell, by a scheming vixen who has declared war on the opposite sex, it satisfied contemporary requirements for moral drama by giving vice its just deserts (Barnwell dies in the end, a broken and betrayed young man, the knowing victim of lust and greed). The whole play was also a cautionary tale about the links between national prosperity, commerce, empire and virtue that spoke to current sensibilities and concerns. Set in Queen Elizabeth's reign, it skilfully played on the growing anti-Spanish sentiment in London and the outports in the 1730s that arose from continued *guarda costa* attacks on English merchant ships and Spanish encroachments on English colonies. Hence the anachronistic setting in the England that had repelled the Armada evoked what Lillo obviously saw as a more intrepid age, when the English were successful in thwarting Spanish pretensions; it was also an effort to re-write the history of that era to give the starring role to English merchants themselves. Indeed, deliberately didactic, *The London Merchant* differs from earlier, Elizabethan attempts to write tragedies based on middle-class life, not merely by being written in prose, but also by being exceptionally militant in its pride in the middle classes, especially merchants.[38]

The hero of the piece is Barnwell's master, Merchant Thorowgood. He is prosperous, upright, principled, stern, kindly and fond of repeating mercantilist platitudes, which are worth examining for what they reveal about the marketing of empire at home. Mercantile capitalism is a 'science', Thorowgood asserts, '[which] promote[s] humanity . . . keeps up an intercourse between nations . . . and . . . promote[s] arts, industry, peace and plenty' (III.i.5–9). 'It is the industrious merchant's business to collect the various blessings of each soil and climate, and, with the product of the whole, to enrich his native country', he instructs his eager apprentice Truegood (III.i.30–3). Truegood agrees, reflecting that trade diffuses 'mutual love', allowing English merchants to 'tame the fierce and polish the most savage; to teach them the advantages of honest traffic by taking from them, with their own consent, their useless superfluities' (III.i.14–20). As these excerpts and the quotation at the beginning of the chapter illustrate, the language of science, mutuality, consent, love and duty are employed to emphasize the paternalistic, romantic and fair-minded nature of British commercial imperialism. This, in turn, is contrasted to the imperialism of the 'haughty and revengeful Spaniard[s]' (I.i.5–7) who, in their colonies in the New World, 'plundered the natives of all the wealth they had and then condemned the wretches to the mines for life to work for more' (I.iii.25–7).[39] It is, then, English merchants who stand as a buffer between their 'happy island' and the world, keeping both out of the hands of the 'revengeful Spaniards'. Needless to say, Thorowgood is the fulfilment of mercantile ideals: honest and prompt in his accounts with aristocrats and tradesmen alike, virtuous and upright in his personal life, generous in hospitality and charity, he succeeds in teaching Truegood 'how honest merchants may sometimes contribute to the safety of their country, as they do at all times to its happiness' (II.i.16–18).

Barnwell, on the other hand, is ruined by not attending to the advice and example set by his master, thus becoming victim to the wicked seductress Millwood. Significantly, Millwood herself provides the domestic counterpart to the meanness and immorality of 'foreign' imperialism; she is the domestic 'fierce savage', the woman who refuses to be tamed, and she expresses this role in her pledge to dominate the enslaving sex of men, to treat them like the Spanish treat the conquered and plundered natives of the New World (I.iii.24–7). She accordingly promises to love Barnwell and delivers instead ruin, betrayal, defeat and death. Such is the punishment for weakness and corruption, in private as in public, individual and national life. The virtuous apprentice, Truegood, on the óther hand, stands to gain all Thorowgood's wealth through marriage to his beautiful daughter: hence the principles of virtuous acquisitiveness prove victorious, at home as well as abroad. The play is clearly the ultimate mercantilist fantasy and morality tale, in which commerce, empire and their agents, the merchants, are justly admired and supported as the founts of national wealth and strength and conduits of civilization, and the colonies serve to display English paternalism to the world while aggrandizing both the nation and individual Britons at home. As such, it remained popular in the theatres and fairs of the outports throughout the middle decades of the century.

Other plays of the period are equally revealing when read against the imperial effort and sensibilities of the day, such as Southerne and Hawkesworth's version of *Oronooko* (1759), Colman's *English Merchant* (1763); Cumberland's *West Indian* (1771); Colman Jr's *Inkle and Yarico* (1787); Foote's francophobic *Englishman in Paris* (1753) or his pillorying of empire as a source of domestic corruption in *The Nabob* (1772). Clearly, in a number of ways, theatre contributed to public discourse on empire, converging with other branches of the contemporary 'media' to promote language, images and ideologies through which the empire could be comprehended and signified at home. At the same time, the imperial effort provided the context that gave theatre a particular cultural and nationalistic significance.

POLITICAL CULTURE

Political culture was perhaps most crucial in coaxing, focusing and disseminating beliefs about and support for empire in public consciousness. Here empire was linked not only to material interests but also to opposition and libertarian ideologies, to strategies of extra-parliamentary organization and resistance, and to the form and content of popular political consciousness. This can be seen at several important junctures, but I will limit my discussion here to two: the Minorca crisis in 1756 and the opening years of the American War, with a brief glance at the late-Walpolean period.

The mercantilist vision of the empire as the sole means to national greatness was first aggressively retailed to a wider public during the 1730s and early 1740s, when it became a central part of the 'patriotic' campaign against the stultifying corruption of the Walpolean state. Although commercial grievances were first spectacularly integrated into the 'patriot' opposition's case against the ministry during the excise crisis of 1733, it was during the agitation over war with Spain in 1738–41, and particularly after Admiral Edward Vernon's defeat of the Spanish at Porto Bello in 1739, that imperial acquisition became a predominant theme in popular politics and demotic political consciousness.[40] Indeed, Vernon's acclaimed victory was seen as vindicating both the opposition's prescription for an aggressive blue-water policy abroad (against Walpole's Eurocentric and timid foreign policy) and a purified body politic at home (against the myriad forms of Walpolean corruption that tainted the political system). The imperial project of the 1740s thus appeared in propaganda as the ultimate patriotic one: it diffused wealth among the entire population, protected domestic freedoms (including freedom of trade and navigation in the world) from the threats of both foreign powers and rapacious ministries, coaxed 'public-spiritedness' (exemplified by Vernon) from British subjects and extended Britons' birthrights to the colonies. Simultaneously libertarian and mercantilist, this conceptualization of empire celebrated an aggressive imperial presence and flourishing colonies as bulwarks of trade, power, liberty and virtue for Britons at home and abroad.

Similar patterns emerged at the inauguration of Britain's greatest imperial effort in the century, the Seven Years War. In this period it was French power and the colonies in North America that were the focus of public attention, and popular imperialism became attached to anti-aristocratic critiques of the state and polity. By the early 1750s imperial anxieties and widespread francophobia had become mutually reinforcing, producing many oral and printed expressions of anxiety over the security and viability of Britain's American colonies and the dangers posed to them by the strong French presence in Acadia and the upper Ohio country. A vast number of histories, pamphlets and maps of British holdings in America were published, for example, arguing for the need for better management of the colonial defence, particularly after the French defeated American and British troops in confrontations along the Ohio in 1754–5.[41] These demands were bolstered by a chorus of voices both in and out of Parliament that stressed the 'High importance of the *British* possessions and rights in *America* to the trade and well-being of these Kingdoms' and called for colonial conquest – particularly of Canada – as the most effective means of defence.[42] The clamour for a strong and aggressive defensive policy in America, along with the sheer wealth of detailed information provided in the daily and periodical press about the French naval and military build-up in the first half of the decade, made the fall of Minorca in May 1756 appear doubly damaging to the Newcastle administration, and doubly catastrophic to the political nation, for it seemed to augur both the beginning of French imperial supremacy and the hopelessly ineffectual and effete nature of the British aristocractic state.

Minorca, situated on the main trade-route to Italy and the Levant, was deemed of vital strategic importance for the protection of English commercial interests, and its fall, in conjunction with other territorial losses in America and India and the threat of French invasion, precipitated a sense of crisis that reverberated at all social levels. The unlucky commander of the British squadron sent to defend Minorca, Admiral Byng, was burned in effigy by outraged crowds across the country soon after news of the island's conquest, and a barrage of addresses and constituency instructions demanded a national inquiry into the disaster, as well as a change in ministry, greater accountability from the government, the establishment of a militia, and even parliamentary reform.[43]

The significance of the Minorca crisis and of the ultimate success of Britain in the Seven Years War must be seen, however, against a broader political and cultural context. The early 1750s were marked by a deepening sense of national malaise, stimulated by xenophobia and tinged by sharpening anti-aristocratic sensibilities. Gerald Newman has documented the cultural protest against foreign and especially French 'influence' that was so marked an aspect of much literature and propaganda in the 1750s, whereby the aristocracy (and the sycophantic *nouveau riche* who aped them) were seen as the agents of 'alien cultural influence and the associated moral disease'.[44] These fears and grievances were further aggravated by the perception that the cultural contagion from above had infiltrated political channels. A virulent strand of anti-aristocratic sentiment had entered political discourse by the mid-1750s, caused by anger at government neglect in America, the subsidizing of troops on the continent and the use of foreign mercenaries at home; and also by such self-regarding pieces of legislation as the game laws, which were presented by their critics as the ultimate in class-legislation, mean-spirited and self-serving in orientation and reflecting the genuine priorities of the nation's aristocratic leadership. The letter addressed 'To the Nobility and Gentry, Associated for the Preservation of the Game' and printed in a number of newspapers and periodicals, aptly indicated the prevailing mood when it praised the association for its 'most useful, most excellent, and most laudable purpose' before reminding them of another issue, 'however trifling it may appear to you, and how much soever hitherto neglected . . . the preservation of our country'.[45]

Equally damaging, the aristocracy's feckless pursuit of self-interest was also held responsible for the chilling spectacle of the British nation's inexorable and, some feared, irreversible slide into 'effeminacy'. According to this theory – the most recent variant of a perspective forged by both anti-Catholic and English civic-humanist discourse that condemned the iniquitous effects of luxury and wealth in society – the effeteness and selfishness of Britain's ruling classes had seeped down and corroded the polity, sapping patriotic fervour and leaving weakness, ineffectuality and supineness in its place. 'Effeminacy' denoted a degenerate moral, political and social state that opposed and subverted the vaunted 'manly' character-istics – courage, aggression, martial valour, strength – that constituted patriotic virtue. In the current circumstances, 'effeminacy' was chiefly objectionable because it had produced a weak and enervated fighting-force that was undermining Britain's position in the world by relinquishing to France her 'empire of the sea'.

The Revd John Brown of Newcastle, who in his *Estimate of the Prin-ciples and Manners of the Time* perhaps most forcefully propounded the theory of 'effeminacy' as the cause of Britain's distress, was merely system-atizing ideas that were percolating through the heated political and cultural debates of the mid-1750s (and, indeed, of the previous two decades). A variety of observers, from political propagandists and journalists to village shopkeepers, decried the nation's corrupted and 'effeminate' spirit, that had resulted in displays of national 'impotency' abroad and ignominious imperial decline, as shown by the defeats of 1755–7.[46] Prints echoed these themes: one, titled *The Imports of Great Britain from France* and dedicated to the Anti-Gallican Society, emphasized the material causes of national effeminacy and decline by showing swarms of French fops and dancers, tradesmen and goods, waiting at British ports to infiltrate the nation.

The instructions that poured into Parliament on the heels of the Minorca crisis expressed similar beliefs and fears, while placing responsibility squarely on the nation's leadership. Ipswich constituents' instructions to the esteemed Admiral Vernon blamed the 'childish timidity' of the English fleet and the abandonment of the colonies in America to the nation's 'injudicious leaders, who have fallen victim to their own inexperience and temerity'; while those from the grand jury of Chester declaimed against the 'ignorance, cowardice, or treachery' by which 'our fleets and armies had been rendered of none effect [sic]' and challenged their representatives not to remain 'tamely degenerate; for, as yet, you would imagine yourselves free'.[47] And anti-Byng demonstrators in the localities were no less reticent in identifying the Minorca disaster with ineffectual aristocratic counsels; the fact that Byng was himself the son of a peer added further credibility to the connection.[48]

Hence the aristocratic state was identified with 'French influence' and corruption at home, and timidity, effeminacy and ignominy abroad, because of which it looked as if France would triumph. As one broadside put it, not only do the people see their land and dominions in the hands of mercenary troops, they also see

Figure 6.1 *The English Lion Dismember'd* (courtesy of the Print collection, Lewis Walpole Library, Yale University, British Museum catalogue no. 3547)

your Fleets and Armies rendered useless by the ignorance or iniquity of those who direct them ... *Minorca*, that Island so essential to your Fleet and Commerce neglected or betray'd into the hands of *France* ... *America* the great fountain of your wealth, in the utmost danger of being overrun by the Arms of the *French* King ... [and] this Kingdom, this once glorious Kingdom, become the Scoff of all the Nations upon Earth.[49]

The demands for an inquiry into Minorca were, therefore, also demands for an uncorrupted and accountable government that actively protected and pursued the national – that is to say, the imperial – interest. As the *Monitor* reminded the Newcastle ministry, after reviewing the crisis in public and imperial affairs,

Remember that government is not given you for venal ends, nor power delegated for your convenience and pleasures; ... forget not that you are accountable servants of the public, and that a learned and inquisitive people are to be judges of your actions.[50]

Equally important, in the context of the public outcry against Minorca and Britain's poor initial performance in the war, empire represented the antidote to aristocratic 'cultural treason' and effeteness, the bulwark and proving-ground of the true national character, of national (and middle-class) potency, identity and virtue. As a number of writers noted, it was among the middle ranks alone that a 'spirit of liberty' and national defence still thrived, as was proved in the martial valour of colonial militias.[51] Prints of the period gave visual form to these connections, such as *The English Lion Dismember'd; Or, the Voice of the Public for an Enquiry into the Loss of Minorca* (Figure 6.1), which associated imperial decline and national disgrace with courtiers, game laws and foreign troops; the way out is shown through stout-hearted and patriotic middling Englishmen, willing to defend their country's interests.[52]

In the context of these nationalistic anxieties and concerns, the anguish at the loss of Minorca in 1756 and the subsequent euphoria over the victories of 1758–60, which removed the French from the North American colonies, take on their full significance. The Seven Years War was the fulfilment and ultimate expression of mercantilist imperial aspirations: it bolstered the Atlantic economy, especially the colonial trade in sugar, slaves, tobacco and rum; produced profits for speculators and privateers alike; and catapulted Britain to the status of a world power, correspondingly (so it was thought) plummeting France to a new low of despair and defeat. Through the fears about French influence and cultural contagion, the war also allowed British global expansion to be seen as an ultimately benevolent and patriotic act (Figure 6.2).[53] The imperialist vision, was, in other words, one of expansive wealth and liberty for British citizens on

Time, turning to a terrestrial Globe, and pointing to Louisbourgh. He shews it to HISTORY, who leans on his Shoulder, writing the Great Events that have happened. BRITANNIA appears on the other side, pleased with the LABOURS OF HISTORY. She is led by CONCORD, who points upward to the figure of VICTORY, intimating that Britannia shall be always successful.

Figure 6.2 Frontispiece to *The London Magazine*, 1758 (courtesy of the Print Collection, Lewis Walpole Library, Yale University)

both sides of the Atlantic, thereby concealing, through nationalistic competition, the exploitative relations upon which the empire was based.

Pitt's genius consisted in playing to the bellicose, patriotic imperialism of the mercantile and middling classes, by pursuing an aggressive and expansionist policy in the New World (where the monopoly companies had little sway),[54] and emphasizing the primacy of colonial over continental campaigns.[55] It was largely due to his astute grasp of the strength of libertarian and pro-imperial sentiment in the nation that his administration marked the unlikely convergence, for the eighteenth century, of a popular war and a popular ministry. The victories at Louisbourg, Quebec, Guadeloupe, Niagara, Ticonderoga, Goree and Montreal demonstrated and valorized the national character – courageous, aggressive, conquering, manly – in a way that surpassed even those spectacular historic conquests that had passed into national mythology. The recovery of British patriotism and manliness through the imperial cause was epitomized, perhaps, for those at home by the death of General James Wolfe at the Battle of Quebec, as the expressions of national pride and grief on the occasion indicated. An 'Emblematical scene' of this historic moment, for example, which ended a performance at the Manchester Theatre in 1763, depicted

> the *General* expiring in the Arms of *Minerva*, while she crowns him with a Laurel; the Figure of *Hope* with a broken Anchor, weeping over him, an Emblem of past Recovery. *Britannia*, the Genius of *England*, seated in *Commerce*, with an *Indian Prince* kneeling at her Feet, resigning up *America*: And *Fame*, triumphing over *Death*, with this Motto: *He never can be lost, who Saves His Country.*[56]

The war had demonstrated, then, that 'Britain will never want a Race of Men . . . who choose Dangers in defence of Their Country before an inglorious safety, an honourable Death before the unmanly pleasures of a useless and effeminate life' as the Revd Brewster proclaimed on Thanksgiving Day in 1759. Britain's spectacular successes clearly constituted a forceful repudiation of the anxieties of three years before, while reifying the imperial effort into both a national duty and an international blessing.

The imperialism supported and confirmed by the Seven Years War was, however, short-lived, fractured by differing perceptions of the significance and purpose of Britain's expanded empire. To many members of the public, the end of the war promised to inaugurate a new era of British imperial ascendancy and American expansion that would diffuse civilization throughout the globe.[57] To the government, newly acquired territories meant burdensome and expensive imperial responsibilities, necessitating revenue-raising schemes and restrictions on colonial settlement west of the Ohio.[58] To patriots at home, Pitt's resignation and the Peace of Paris indicated that the old disjunction between the virtuous and imperialistic public and corrupted and self-serving 'court' government had returned.

Further, within a decade, conflicts with the American colonies and apprehensions about the socially and morally corrosive force of empire raised
doubts about the viability of the libertarian, imperial dream. Brewer has
argued that the war with the colonies revealed the limits of Britain's
military power.[59] Yet the war for America also revealed the limitations
of the libertarian-imperial nexus that had suffused popular and anti-
government politics for most of the century, and underlined its central
contradictions.

Certainly once hostilities had commenced, coercive actions in America
were easily interpreted as but the latest instance of the simultaneous assault
on empire and liberties by a corrupt and tyrannical government. The
London and provincial radical press propagated such views with great
fervour, identifying the outbreak of 'civil war' across the Atlantic with
government despotism at home. In prints, pamphlets, newspapers, broad-
sides and periodicals, both the ministry and its apologists in Britain were
indicted as members of a 'Butean' conspiracy to overthrow legal authority,
crush colonial and domestic liberties and introduce popery and slavery
throughout the empire.[60] It was these perceptions that the war emanated
from the corrupt, occluded institutions of the aristocratic state which
prompted the organization of anti-war petitions and addresses in London
and dozens of provincial towns, and which ultimately led to new demands
for measures of democratic political reform.[61]

Even from the early stages, many English observers were aware that the
issues stemming from the war were ones connected not only with political
liberty and authority, but with the mercantilist vision of empire itself. In
this context, some of the most forceful anti-war arguments were those that
emphasized the commercial and imperial, as well as libertarian, reasons for
opposing the war. The City of London's 'Letter to the Electors of Great
Britain', printed in most provincial newspapers, castigated the folly of
loyalist writers who argued that government actions would preserve the
British empire and colonial commerce: 'Desolated fields, and depopulated
provinces, are little likely to contribute to our necessities', the address
stated, 'To secure our commerce, therefore, can neither be the aim, nor
the issues of this war'.[62] Other writers attacked government aggression for
its sheer impracticality and the mercantilist system itself for its short-
sightedness: 'It is a war of absurdity and madness', one opponent of the
war declared; 'We shall sooner pluck the moon from her sphere, than
conquer such a country'; while another contended that it was folly to
believe Britain could forever 'tie the hands of the inhabitants of a great
continent abounding with raw materials, . . . restrain them from using the
gifts of nature, and . . . force them to take the products of your own
labour'.[63] Although virtually all those who opposed the war did so in the
hopes of preserving the British empire in North America, the anti-war
arguments, simultaneously commercial and libertarian, clearly contradicted

certain tenets of the mercantilist imperial vision that had been articulated in previous decades. Yet they drew a substantial, and, after 1779, increasing number of citizens of all ranks into the anti-war camp, even from among the middling groups for whom empire and colonial acquisition had always had an appeal, and who were in the present crisis hardest hit by the economic dislocation of credit and currency caused by the war.

At the same time, the American crisis undermined long-held beliefs in the morality and virtue of the imperial project. British commentators had long insisted that Britain's virtue as an imperial nation lay in not seeking conquest, but having conquest thrust upon her: colonial acquisition in the Seven Years War was thus continually justified, in and out of Parliament, as a defence against French aggression.[64] Further, traditional libertarian doctrine on colonies insisted that force could have no place in their government: as 'Cato' stressed, 'liberty and encouragement' alone would allow colonies to flourish, which is why 'arbitrary countries have not been equally successful in planting colonies, with free ones'.[65] Government policies in America clearly contradicted these notions. The Quebec Act, which provided for the continuation of French civil law, government without representative bodies and the 'free exercise' of Roman Catholicism, was justified as a requirement of empire by North and his supporters, and vehemently denounced by his opponents for contradicting what were believed to be established principles of imperial government. 'No free country can keep another in slavery', Edmund Burke warned in the House of Commons. 'The price they pay for it will be their own servitude.' Chatham and his followers were even more unequivocal in their condemnation of the bill, calling it 'a most cruel, oppressive and odious measure, tearing up justice and every good principle by the roots'. Out-of-doors, opposition to the act's support for the establishment of 'popery and slavery' in the empire was strenuous and violent.[66] Hence, the establishment of 'despotic' government in certain colonies, as well as the inefficacy and immorality of forcing submission upon an unwilling population, threatened the loss of a virtuous empire, once 'as much renowned for the virtues of justice and humanity as for the splendour of its arms', as the Middlesex electors lamented in their address for reconciliation with America in 1775.[67]

As such, the colonial crisis created an opportunity and audience for the arguments of the anti-imperialists (always an articulate minority) that empire itself was the primary source of national luxury and corruption. Josiah Tucker, for example, turned the conspiracy theory of the radicals on its head, arguing that the American colonies had become dangerous to Great Britain, because they threatened the polity at home with the contagion of dissenting and republican principles; they were also unnecessary, he claimed, because the mainland colonies had become more the competitors than the supports of British manufacture and commerce.[68] Even those sympathetic to the American cause could perceive that the empire could be a corrupting and enervating force. Foote's scathing indictment of the moral corrosiveness of empire in India in *The Nabob* was paralleled by other condemnation of the Asian empire's polluting impact, which was increasingly seen as a conduit of 'luxury, effeminacy, profligacy and debility' to those at home.[69] The West Indian planters or 'Creoles' were equally seen as potent sources of parliamentary corruption and mismanagement, who, 'being bred the tyrants of their slavish blacks, may endeavour to reduce the whites to the same condition by an aristocracy'. The Beckfords of London were similarly lampooned in political ballads.[70] Further, the wave of anti-Americanism that broke out after the fighting had commenced made some observers despair of the mindlessly authoritarian attitudes that empire had produced among English subjects, who clearly saw their brethren across the Atlantic as possessions.[71] Both the war and the reaction to it at home led some observers to attack the acquisitive, machismo model of patriotism and the national character that the imperial project had crystallized. A lecturer at a philosophical society in Newcastle thus claimed that 'in every point of view, the laws of war, and the laws of thieving are exactly alike', both valorizing conquest, self-interest and force, while a local writer suggested that the safety and glory of the state may best be found in its adoption of 'feminine' values, as the alleged 'weakness of women hath not ushered in such a flood of calamities, as these fatal virtues of men'.[72] Clearly, empire benefited some English citizens more than others, and could warp as well as nourish libertarian and public-spirited sensibilities.

Hence, the American crisis had forced a recognition that the empire of virtue, founded in consent and nurtured in liberty and trade, had been irrevocably altered. As Peter Marshall has noted, it was clear by the 1770s that the British empire was comprised not just of free British subjects, but of large numbers of alien peoples, incorporated into the empire by conquest, not consent, and sustained 'not just by the Royal Navy but by the deployment of British troops across the world in a way that was to last until the 1960s'.[73] For British radicals in particular, the colonial conflict exposed the internal contradictions of the libertarian, mercantilist imperialism that had played so large a part in dissident political agitations since the 1730s. The anonymous writer in the *Norfolk Chronicle* quoted at the beginning of this chapter unwittingly illustrated this predicament when he decried the loss of empire as the loss of Britain's 'glorious dependencies', for that very notion was an oxymoron in the patriotic, oppositionist ideology that exalted independency as the highest political, moral and national good.[74] As Trenchard and Gordon noted in the 1720s, the whole idea of colonies and plantations, like that of slavery, was an abrogation of the laws of nature – 'It is not to be hoped, in the corrupt state of Human Nature, that any Nation will be subject to another, any longer than it finds its own Account in it, and cannot help itself' – and this view gained currency along with Smith's exposé of mercantilism and balance-of-trade theory in 1776.[75] Anti-war activists in the late 1770s were accordingly forced to face the essential incompatibility of mercantilist imperialism with the increasingly expansive and participatory views of English men's birth-rights, and with the new notions of the just relationship between the individual and the state that were articulated in the radical politics of the day.

For many English supporters of the empire, then, the war was both an imperial and constitutional catastrophe, but it forced a rethinking of empire's benefits, dangers and ethics. Some of the more radical members of the pro-imperial public retreated into anti-imperialist internationalism, like Richard Price; others, like Cartwright, theorized about a new imperial relationship based on the internal independence and sovereignty of the colonies and the external regulation of trade by Britain.[76] Still others – no doubt the majority – transferred imperial confidence and aspirations east-ward, to India, as the foundation of a grander, more glorious – and more authoritarian – empire. For all, imperial identities would have to be reformulated on less-tarnished bases than those of a discredited mercantil-ism and a tenacious, if embattled, libertarianism.

CONCLUSIONS

It remains to draw some conclusions about the significance and meaning of empire in eighteenth-century politics and culture. 'Imperialism' was clearly an amalgam of mercantilist, libertarian and nationalistic beliefs, given form and substance by the contexts in which they were invoked. For most of the period, the imperial project – the 'empire of the sea', consisting of colonies and markets – was clearly believed by many contem-poraries to maximize trade, liberty, prosperity and national power. As such, pro-imperial sensibilities were compatible with both oppositionist and loyalist political positions, and empire appealed to a heterogeneous range of interests, grievances and aspirations at any given moment. Never-theless, for most of the century, empire, although never straightforwardly repudiated by the government, was linked in extra-parliamentary political culture with oppositionist ideologies and a popularized mercantilism that castigated the state for not pursuing a more expansionist or nurturing imperial policy. At such junctures as the Vernon agitation, the Minorca crisis and the beginning of the American War, imperial aspirations were enmeshed with the patriotic critique of corruption and a populist, liber-tarian vision of the polity, in which accountable government, a public-spirited citizenry and imperial ascendancy all went hand in hand. Linked in this way with the development of extra-parliamentary political culture, empire entered popular political consciousness as a birthright, as much a part of the national identity as the liberties and constitutional traditions for which Britain was celebrated the world over. This outlook, embedded in a range of cultural artefacts and pursuits, justified British imperial ascendancy as a salvation to the world.

However, empire was not an end in itself in the eighteenth century; it was the means through which national power and ascendancy could be proved and demonstrated. At the heart of the imperial project, then, was the nationalistic effort to define and vindicate the nation, in opposition to other nations, whether it was Britain against Spain, Holland or France, or Britons against the native 'others' – Indians, Africans, 'savages'. In both senses, the rationale for empire coaxed the expression of nationalist as well as imperial identities, and imperial struggles were viewed at home as battles over the national character. Through Britain's rivalry with France, anti-gallicanism and imperialism became mutually reinforcing: both were reified in this period into national duties, a connection that endured through the years of the American War and beyond. It is in the context of these nationalistic struggles that eighteenth-century imperialism justified both the rights of Britons to trade freely with the world and their domination of it: they were fairer than the French, less barbarous than the Spanish, more civilized that the savages.

Moreover, and closely related to the above, empire mediated notions of class that were articulated in both social and political terms. Aristocratic 'effeminacy', foreignness and corruption seeped into the polity through social and cultural patronage and political power, corroding both national manners and political virtue. Aristocratic effeteness was proven, above all, in the inability or disinclination of the 'court' to pursue the national, imperial interest. Hence empire – its acquisition, settlement and protection – was represented in graphic and literary propaganda as a middle-class paradise, promoting wealth, strength, independence and virtue, for both individuals and the nation. The antidote to court and aristocratic corruption, empire was, in contemporary conceptualization, the means to becoming more independent and self-contained as a nation, rejecting 'foreign' influences and introducing English virtue wherever the latter dared to tread.

Finally, the significance of the stridently gendered rhetoric and images of eighteenth-century imperialism deserves the last word. Despite the persistence of an iconography that symbolizeed the British imperial presence as the female figure of Britannia, colonial conquest was described and glorified as a manly occupation, the proving-ground for national, as well as individual, potency, strength and effectiveness, and the vehicle of paternalistic largess and duty. The basic categories through which the imperial project was valorized (or, later in the century, denigrated) thus both reinforced and exaggerated dominant cultural categories of sexual difference. Empire cultivated and bolstered 'manly' characteristics – strength, fortitude, courage, aggression – or it fostered an insidious and 'effeminate' moral luxuriousness and corruption. In either case, eighteenth-century discourses of imperialism were carried out simultaneously in the language of rights and duties and in the language of sexual difference, thus eliding and suppressing the 'feminine' in their constructions of patriotism and the national character. As Brown had charged, 'What strength of thought or conscious Merit can there be in *effeminate* Minds, sufficient to elevate them to ... Public Spirit?' An 'effeminate nation' is 'a *Nation which resembles Women*', characterized by cowardice, 'irrational pity' and a 'dread of suffering' and thus clearly destined for international ignominy and derision.[77] As the antidote to national effeminacy, the imperial project was described and valorized in the images of an aggressive masculinity. It was thus the male conquerors rather than the mother country who appeared as the heroes of the imperial saga: in this way, empire became a crucial instrument in constructing exclusive definitions of the British nation and the requirements for citizenship – as nineteenth-century experience would prove.

NOTES

Versions of this essay were read at Harvard University, Lincoln College, Oxford, and the University of Newcastle upon Tyne as well as at the Shelby Cullom Davis Center at Princeton University; I would like to thank the discussants at all these forums for their lively commentary. For helpful suggestions and advice I would like to thank Jan Albers, John Brewer, Michael Dobson, Elizabeth Fowler, J. Jefferson Looney, Peter Marshall and Alex Owen. Portions of the research were funded by a grant from the National Endowment for the Humanities.

1 See, e.g., H. H. Dodwell, *The Cambridge History of India*, vol. v (Cambridge, 1929); Walter Dorn, *Competition for Empire* (New York, 1957); Richard Pares, *War and Trade in the West Indies* (Oxford, 1936); Frank W. Pitman, *The Development of the British West Indies* (New Haven, 1917); and, most recently, Kenneth Andrews, *Trade, Plunder and Settlement: Maritime Enterprise and the Genesis of the British Empire, 1480–1630* (Cambridge, 1984). Ironically, the most distinguished work on the ideological ramifications of the imperial project has focused on anti-imperial sentiment and theory in Georgian England: see J. G. A. Pocock, *The Machiavellian Moment: Florentine Political Thought and the Atlantic Republican Tradition* (Princeton, 1975), and *Virtue, Commerce and History* (Cambridge, 1985).

2 See, e.g., Gerald Hertz, *British Imperialism in the Eighteenth Century* (London, 1908); George Rudé, *Paris and London in the Eighteenth Century* (New York, 1973), 17–62, 201–318; John Stevenson, *Popular Disturbances in England, 1700–1870* (London, 1979), 35–90; Gerald Newman, *The Rise of English Nationalism* (New York, 1987), esp. 208–10; and, most recently, Paul Langford, *A Polite and Commercial People: England 1727–1783* (Oxford, 1989), 49–59, 172–5, 333–50, 617–21, who insists that the wider public in the eighteenth century had no interest in empire or colonies, except to support wholeheartedly the suppression of colonial rebellion in 1775–82. More balanced are Richard Koebner, *Empire* (Cambridge, 1961) (although his almost exclusive focus on official pronouncements about the imperial project gives rise to grave inaccurac-

ies in his account of the nature of imperial attitudes within the nation as a whole); and the fine studies of Peter Marshall on ruling-class attitudes to the colonies: see 'Empire and Authority in Later Eighteenth Century Britain', *Journal of Imperial and Commonwealth Studies*, 15 (1987), 105–22, and ' "A Free though Conquering People": Britain and Asia in the Eighteenth Century' (published lecture, Kings College, London, 1981). I would like to thank Professor Marshall for making this lecture available to me. Finally, Linda Colley's work has successfully avoided dismissive and socially reductive assessments of the content and social provenance of nationalistic sensibilities: see 'The Apotheosis of George III: Loyalty, Royalty and the British Nation, 1760–1820', *Past and Present*, 102 (1984), 94–129, and 'Whose Nation? Class and National Consciousness', *Past and Present*, 113 (1986) 97–117. Ralph Samuel (ed.), *Patriotism: The Making and Unmaking of British National Identity* (3 vols; London, 1989), also makes an important contribution but focuses largely on the post–1789 period.

3 Bernard Bailyn, *The Peopling of British North America: An Introduction* (New York, 1986), 20–85; T. H. Breen, 'Baubles of Britain: The American and Consumer Revolutions of the Eighteenth Century', *Past and Present*, 119 (1988), 73–104, and 'An Empire of Goods: The Anglicization of Colonial America, 1690–1776', *Journal of British Studies*, 25 (1986), 467–99; John Brewer, 'English Radicalism in the Age of George III', in J. G. A. Pocock (ed.), *Three British Revolutions* (Princeton, 1980), 322–67, and *The Sinews of Power: War, Money and the English State 1688–1783* (New York, 1989); Ralph Davies, *The Rise of the Atlantic Economies* (New York, 1973); Kenneth Morgan, 'Shipping Patterns and the Atlantic Trade of Bristol, 1749–70', *William and Mary Quarterly*, third series, 46 (1989), 506–38; Jacob Price, 'The Excise Affair Revisited: The Administrative and Colonial Dimensions of a Parliamentary Crisis', in Stephen B. Baxter (ed.), *England's Rise to Greatness* (Berkeley and Los Angeles, 1983), 257–321; S. P. Ville, 'Patterns of Shipping Investment in the Port of Newcastle-upon-Tyne, 1750–1850', *Northern History*, 25 (1989), 135–52; and Kathleen Wilson, 'Empire, Trade and Popular Politics in Mid-Hanoverian Britain: The Case of Admiral Vernon', *Past and Present*, 121 (1988), 74–109.

4 Brewer, *Sinews of Power*, 88–133. By the end of the American War, indirect taxes were the chief source of state income, accounting for almost 80 per cent of government tax revenues.

5 As both historians and literary critics have just begun to point out: see, e.g., G. S. Rousseau and Roy Porter (eds), *Exoticism in the Enlightenment* (London, 1989); Felicity Nussbaum and Laura Brown (eds), *The New Eighteenth Century* (London, 1987); and Terry Castle, *Masquerade and Civilization* (Stanford, 1986).

6 See my 'Empire, Trade and Popular Politics', and *The Sense of the People: Urban Political Culture in England, 1715–1785* (forthcoming). The recent work of other scholars has also drawn attention to the complex repercussions of the imperial effort: see Linda Colley, 'Radical Patriotism in Eighteenth-Century England' in Samuel, *Patriotism*, vol. I, 169–87; and Nicholas Rogers, *Whigs and Cities: Popular Politics in the Age of Walpole and Pitt* (Oxford, 1989).

7 Benedict Anderson, *Imagined Communities: Reflections on the Origin and Spread of Nationalism* (London, 1983), 50–79.

8 Such is the argument of my current work in progress on provincial theatre in the eighteenth century in *Staging the Nation*.

9 See the discussions on Koebner, *Empire*, 85–90, and Marshall, 'Empire and Authority', 106.

10 *London Magazine*, 24 (1755), 403–5; *Craftsman* (28 December, 1728).

11 Wilson, 'Empire, Trade and Popular Politics', 97. The role and benefits of free trade certainly were canvassed and debated long before Adam Smith, but few observers quarrelled with the idea that the government had the responsibility of regulating economic matters for the public and national good. For a discussion of mercantilist thinking and its impact on the state see Brewer, *Sinews of Power*, 164–78. I would like to thank Daniel Baugh for his comments on my argument in this portion of the chapter.

12 These observations are based on extensive examination of London and provincial newspapers, including *London Chronicle, London Evening Post, Public Advertiser, Farley's Bristol Journal, Bristol Gazette and Public Advertiser, Cumberland Pacquet, Newcastle Journal, Newcastle Courant, Norwich Gazette, Norwich Mercury, Liverpool General Advertiser, Manchester Mercury* and *Worcester Journal*. For rare birds and plants, see J. H. Plumb, 'The Acceptance of Modernity', in J. H. Plumb, Neil McKendrick and John Brewer, *The Birth of a Consumer Society* (London, 1982), 321–2; for ivory, *Liverpool General Advertiser* (6 July 1770). Kenneth Morgan has also noted the propensity of newpapers from the outports to track the movement of vessels and provide lists of ships' names, masters and destinations ('Shipping Patterns', 537).

13 Laura Brown, 'The Romance of Empire: *Oroonoko* and the Trade in Slaves', in Nussbaum and Brown, *The New Eighteenth Century*, 51–2.

14 See, e.g., *Newcastle Journal* (27 January; 9 June 1750); *Newcastle Magazine*, 8 (1755), 7–15, 241–4, 405–9; *Liverpool General Advertiser* (17, 24 November; 8, 15 December 1769; 15 June; 6, 27 July; 3 August 1770); *Lancashire Magazine*, 1 (1763) 11–12; *London Magazine*, 24 (1755), 307–12, and issues for July, August, September, *passim*.

15 Such as the marriages of local gentry and wealthy bourgeoisie, national politics, local philanthropic and economic initiatives, land and properties for sale or rent, and notices of the meetings of clubs and societies.

16 This becomes particularly significant by the 1740s, by which time the economic balance of power in literary and newspaper production had shifted from individual printers to associations of bookseller-publishers and the reading public: see Michael Harris, 'The Structure, Ownership and Control of the Press, 1620–1780', in George Boyce, James Curran and Pauline Wingate (eds), *Newspaper History: From the 17th Century to the Present Day* (London, 1978), 94–6.

17 John Oldmixon, *The British Empire in America* (2 vols; London, 1708; second edn, 1741); Brown, 'The Romance of Empire', 48–50; V. G. Kiernan, 'Noble and Ignoble Savages', in Rousseau and Porter, *Exoticism*, 86–116; P. J. Marshall, 'Taming the Exotic: The British and India in the Seventeenth and Eighteenth Centuries', in Rousseau and Porter, *Exoticism*, 46–65; and Roy Porter, 'The Exotic as Erotic: Captain Cook at Tahiti', in Rousseau and Porter, *Exoticism*, 117–44. See also William Robertson, *History of America* (London, 1777); Admiral Anson, *Voyage Round the World* (London, 1748); and Daniel Defoe, *A Tour through the Whole Island of Great Britain* (London, 1726), who is eager to note the wider imperial connections of individual towns.

18 See Carole Fabricant, 'The Literature of Domestic Tourism and the Public Consumption of Foreign Property', in Nussbaum and Brown, *The New Eighteenth Century*, 257.

19 *Gentlemen's Magazine*, 26 (1756), *passim*. See also *Lancashire Magazine*, 1–2 (1763–4); *London Magazine*, 24–9 (1755–60); and *Newcastle General Magazine*, 8–9 (1755–6).

20 *London Magazine*, 28 (1759), 227–30, 459–64, 529–35, 593–9; 44 (1775), facing p. 3.

21 *Carribbeana* (London, 1740); [Nathaniel Crouch], *The English Empire in America* (London, 1739); Thomas Jeffreys, *The West Indies, Exhibiting the English, French, Spanish, Dutch and Danish Settlements* [London, 1752]; Emanuel Bowen, *A Map of the British American Plantations Extending from Boston in New England to Georgia; including All the Back Settlements in their Respective Provinces, as Far as the Mississippi*, [London], 1754; John Bowles, *A New Map of North America wherein the British Dominions in the Continent of North America, and on the Islands of the West Indies, are Carefully Laid Down from All the Surveys . . . and the Most Accurate Accounts and Maps Lately Publish'd. Also the French Encroachments on the English Provinces Particularly Described* (London, 1754).

22 See, e.g., *Gentleman's Magazine*, 26–9 (1756–9), *passim*. *London Magazine*, 24–7 (1755–8), includes separate maps of North America, the French settlements in North America, Virginia, Senegal and Quebec, and the table of contents for 1758 refers the reader to twenty-seven different maps published in earlier issues.

23 Kiernan, 'Noble and Ignoble Savages', and Porter, 'The Exotic as Erotic', 86–116, 117–44; Carole Fabricant, 'The Literature of Domestic Tourism and the Public Consumption of Private Property', 256–7.

24 Of course, eighteenth-century drama was retailed not only as performance but also as literature. As such, plays should be considered equally a part of the culture of print, read by an even-wider audience than that which viewed them.

25 This assessment of theatre audiences is based upon archival research that is part of my work in progress on provincial theatre in *Staging the Nation*. Although the establishment of Theatre Royals in provincial cities from the middle decades of the century augured the beginnings of a more exclusive clientele, there remained ample opportunities for middling and humble folk to attend theatrical performances, at 'ordinary' theatres at inns, taverns and fairs, as well as at the status-conscious Theatre Royals themselves. See also Harry William Pedicord, *The Theatrical Public in the Time of Garrick* (New York, 1954), 19–43; Sybil Rosenfeld, *Strolling Players and Drama in the Provinces* (Cambridge, 1939), 32–5; and J. Jefferson Looney, 'Cultural Life in the Provinces: Leeds and York, 1720–1820', in A. L. Beier, D. Cannadine and J. Rosenheim (eds), *The First Modern Society: Essays in Honour of Lawrence Stone* (Cambridge, 1989), 483–510.

26 Certainly such representations were not monolithic: a great deal of farce, comedy and drama of the period was designed to ridicule the national vices and follies of the age and was frequently articulated in class-terms; but the discussion of the representations of class in the English theatre will have to await another occasion.

27 See, e.g., John Brown, *An Estimate of the Manners and Principles of the Times* (2 vols.; London, 1757–8); Newman, *Rise of English Nationalism*, *passim*; and the section on Political Culture below.

28 *To the H-nble Sir J— B—* [London, 1734], reprinted in Theophilus Cibber, *Two Dissertations on the Theatres* (London, 1756), Appendix, 74–5; see also 83. I am grateful to Michael Dobson for this reference.

29 *To Sir J— B—*, 74, 76, 73; for the role of nationalistic identities in the imperial effort, see Oldmixon, *The British Empire*, and Hans Sloane, *A Voyage to the Islands of Madera, Barbadoes, Nieves, S. Christophers and Jamaica* (2 vols; London, 1707), which detail the cultural, botanical and topographical marvels of these lands admiringly, yet in a way which managed to uphold the superiority

of English difference; and the essays by Kiernan, Marshall and Porter in Rousseau and Porter, *Exoticism*.

30 *London Evening Post* (10/12 October 1738); George Winchester Stone, *The London Stage: A Critical Introduction 1747–76* (Carbondale, 1968), 1x–1xi, clxxxvi–clxxxvii; quotation, ibid., clxxxvi.

31 Cibber, *Two Dissertations*, 11.

32 G. T. Watt, *Theatrical Bristol* (Bristol, 1915), 69; Liverpool Record Office, Holt-Gregson Papers, vil. xii, ff. 12–15; Newcastle City Library, List of Subscribers to the Theatre Royal, 1789.

33 George Colman, *The English Merchant* (second edn; London, 1768), iii.

34 Avon County Library, Calcott MS 22477, 25–8. See also Liverpool County and Reference Library, Holt-Gregson Papers, vol. xii, ff. 15–18, for a similar prologue written by Colman for the opening of the Liverpool Theatre in 1772, the thrust of which was that theatre is a fruit of commerce: 'Whenever Commerce spreads her swelling sail, Letters and arts attend the prosperous gale'.

35 To take one example, the Manchester theatre had benefits for the local Infirmary, the Marine Society, bounties on volunteer seamen, and freemasons: see Manchester Central Library, Playbills, Marsden Street Theatre and Theatre Royal: 27 November 1753; 30 October 1757; 11 December 1759; 26 November 1760. For foundling hospitals, see Stone, *London Stage*, cvii–cviii. The loyalist overtones of theatre became increasingly pronounced as the century progressed: during the revolutionary wars of 1792–1815, dramatic spectacles, focusing on battle-scenes and heroic deaths of British officers or explorers were sanctioned by the state and sanctified by the public, such as *The Mouth of the Nile, a New Serio-Comic Intermezzo of Pantomime, Song, Dance and Dialogue*, which portrayed Nelson's famous victory over the French in Egypt; or *War and Peace*, 'Calculated to display the united firmness of the Country in opposing the Common Enemy, and anticipating the Blessings resulting from an honourable Peace . . .': Asa Briggs, *The Age of Improvement* (London, 1959), 141n; Harvard Theater Collection, Playbills, Canterbury Theatre, 1 March 1798.

36 George Farquhar, *The Recruiting Officer*, ed. Michael Shugrue (Lincoln, Neb., 1695); George Lillo *The London Merchant*, ed. William H. McBurney (Lincoln, Neb., 1965); all citations come from these editions. *The Recruiting Officer* had eighteen runs at the Drury Lane theatre and eighteen at the Covent Garden Theatre between 1747–76, with the best runs coming in 1750–1 and 1754–5; Lillo's play had nine runs at Covent Garden and twenty-four at Drury Lane in the same period, with the best coming in 1749–50 and 1767–8: Pedicord, *Theatrical Public*, Appendix C. Both were also performed regularly in provincial theatres, such as those at Bristol, Canterbury, Liverpool, Manchester, Newcastle, Norwich and Richmond: Harvard Theatre Collection, Provincial Playbills, 1760 ff.; Bristol Central Library, MS 11204, Jacob Wells Theatre Account Book (1741–8); Playbills, 1672–1841, MS 1976–80, vols I–II; Liverpool Record Office and Local History Library, Holt-Gregson papers, MS 942 HOL/12, and Playbills, 1,767 ff.; Manchester Central Library, Playbills, 1,750 ff.; Rosenfeld, *Strolling Players*, 58, 207, 224, 286, 301. They were also popular in the New York and Philadelphia: J. N. Ireland, *Records of the New York Stage, 1750–1860* (2 vols; New York 1866–7; repr. 1968), vol. I, 22–5, 37, 58–60; T. C. Pollack, *The Philadelphia Theatre in the Eighteenth Century* (Philadelphia, 1933), 74–5, 123.

37 Contemporaries were obviously well aware of the significance of these connections in the play: *The Recruiting Officer* was a perennial object of attack in Reformation of Manners campaigns to close down the stage, for its bawdiness,

and representations of army officers as whoremongers and libertines were alleged by dour observers to undermine respect for authority. 'The Debauching of the Country Wenches is represented as a main Part of the Service', the Revd Arthur Bedford rightly charged in *The Evil and Danger of Stage Plays* (Bristol, 1706; repr. 1730), 152; and these objections to the play were repeated by George Pryce in *The Consequences of a New Theatre to the City of Bristol Considered* (Bristol, 1765), 29–30.

38 G. Nettleton, A. Case and G. W. Stone (eds), *British Dramatists from Dryden to Sheridan* (Carbondale, 1969), 595–6.

39 Cf. the remarks of Brown in *Estimate of the Manners and Principles of the Times*, vol. II, 143: 'The Spaniards, in Course of Time, will have converted one-half the vast Southern Continent [to popery], and murdered the other'. Favourable comparisons of British with continental imperialism were well established in economic and political literature by the eighteenth century.

40 See my 'Empire, Trade and Popular Politics in Mid-Hanoverian Britain', for a detailed discussion of the way in which empire was inserted into patriotic ideology, and its appeal to a wide range of interests in the extra-parliamentary political nation in the 1730s and 1740s.

41 *Newcastle General Magazine*, 8 (1755), 10–15, 241–4, 405–9; *French Policy Defeated. Being An Account of All the Hostile Proceedings of the French, Against the Inhabitants of the British Colonies in North America, For the Last Seven Years... Embellished with Two Curious MAPS, Describing All the Coasts, Bays, Lakes, Rivers, Soundings, Principal Towns and Forts* (London, 1755); *A Miscellaneous Essay Concerning the Courses Pursued by Great Britain in the Affairs of her COLONIES: with Some Observations of the Great Importance of our Settlements in America, and the Trade thereof* (London, 1755); *The State of the British and French Colonies in North America, With Respect to Number of People, Forces, Forts, Indians, Trade and Other Advantages; in which are considered, I. The Defenseless Condition of Our Plantations... II. The Pernicious Tendency of the FRENCH Encroachments and the Fittest Methods of Frustrating Them ... With a Proper Expedient Proposed for Preventing Future Disputes* (London, 1755). See also Dan E. Clark, 'News and Opinion Concerning America in English Newspapers, 1754–63', *Pacific Historical Review*, 10 (1941), 75–82.

42 *Proceedings and Debates of the British Parliaments respecting North America, 1754–83*, eds R. C. Simmons and P. D. G Thomas (5 vols; New York, 1982), vol. I, 81. See also 11–16, 65–7, 94–106, 195–6, 299–301; *Newcastle General Magazine*, 8 (1755), 15–16; *A Letter from a Merchant of the City of London* (second edn; London, 1757), 26; John Shebbeare, *A Letter to the People of England, on the Present Situation and Conduct of National Affairs* (fourth edn; London, 1756).

43 For demonstrations, see *Newcastle Journal* (24 July; 31 July 1756), *Salisbury Journal* (2 August; 16 August 1756); *Worcester Journal* (5 August; 2 September 1756); *York Courant* (14 September 1756); for addresses and instructions, see *The Voice of the People: A Collection of Addresses to His Majesty and Instructions to Members of Parliament by their Constituents* (London, 1756); most of these are reprinted in the London and provincial newspapers for August–November 1756. As the *London Evening Post* charged, all ranks, from 'Coronet to Cobler' discerned that the blue-water policy was the only way to maintain 'our *Independency* on *Shore*, and our *Empire* at Sea' (24–26 June 1756). The Newcastle administration was only too aware of the extent and seriousness of opposition that had broken out across the country, and took steps to contain

it, though with little effect (see Add. MSS 32,866–35,964). The ministry was also eager to place the blame for the disaster on Admiral Byng, even though there was ample evidence that Byng was only executing bad and belated orders from the government: see Wilson, *The Sense of the People*, ch. 3.

44 Newman, *Rise of English Nationalism*, 68–84.

45 *Gentleman's Magazine*, 26 (1756), 384; *Newcastle General Magazine*, 9 (1756), 434–6; see also John Shebbeare's *Letters to the People of England*, esp. the *Second Letter, Fourth Letter* and *Fifth Letter* (London, 1756–7).

46 Shebbeare, *Letters to the People of England*, *passim*, esp. the *First Letter, Fourth Letter* and *Fifth Letter*; *Newcastle General Magazine*, 9 (1756) 484–94; *The Diary of Thomas Turner, 1754–1765*, ed. David Vaisey (Oxford, 1984), 124–5.

47 *The Voice of the People*, 19, 53–4.

48 See the description of the anti-Byng demonstration in Darlington, in *Newcastle Courant* (11 September 1756): the effigy of Byng wore a sign with the following message: 'A curse on French gold, and great men's promises/I have never done well since I took the one,/And depended on the other: but/take heed my countrymen, *I am not alone*.' Byng was the son of Viscount Torrington.

49 *A Serious Call to the Corporation of London, to Address his Ministry to Remove from his Councils and Person forever Weak, and Wicked Ministers* (broadside, n.d. [1756]).

50 *Monitor* (30 October 1756).

51 Brown, *Estimate of the Manners and Principles of the Times*, vol. II, 30; *Monitor* (13 December, 19 December 1755), (13 March, 11 September 1756), (8 January 1757); *Gentleman's Magazine*, 27 (1757), 509–12; Shebbeare, *First Letter*, 46–8.

52 Shebbeare and Brown reinforced these themes, insisting that virtue, principle and manliness remained only among the middling ranks: Shebbeare, *First Letter*, 6–7, 47–8, 50–6; Brown, *Estimate of the Manners and Principles of the Times*, 25–6. Not surprisingly, this period witnessed the creation of extra-institutional supports for a formalized anti-gallicanism, largely through associative activities of private middle-class citizens, which sought to make England less permeable to French influence and more formidable a counter to French power and aspirations, such as the Marine Society, the Anti-Gallican Society and the Society for the Encouragement of Arts, Manufactures and Commerce: Isaac Hunt, *Some Account of the Laudable Institution of the Society of Antigallicans* (London, 1781); *Rules and Orders of the Society, Established at London For the Encouragement of Arts, Manufactures and Commerce* (London, 1758); Jonas Hanway, *A Letter from a Member of the Marine Society, Shewing the Piety, Generosity and Utility of their Design* (London, 1757).

53 Pares, *War and Trade*, 85–125; R. Davis, 'English Foreign Trade, 1700–74', *Economic History Revue*, second series, 15 (1962), 285–303; Jacob Price, 'Capital and Credit in the British Chesapeake Trade, 1750–1775', in V. B. Platt and D. C. Skags (eds), *Of Mother Country and Plantations* (Cleveland, 1971), 9–15.

54 Despite their publicity, the gains of Africa and Asia did not capture the public imagination the way the victories in America did. This is largely because the trade to India and Africa was dominated by monopoly companies, whose similarities to the corrupt, occluded organs of state – exclusionary in both membership and benefits – made them an object of vilification rather than celebration in the middling communities at home. For an attack on monopoly companies for their exclusionary practices and private ends, see *Newcastle Journal* (27 January 1750); Edward Baines, *History of Liverpool* (Manchester, 1893), 441–2; and any of the dozens of pamphlets from the 1720s–1750s that argue these points.

55 Certainly, Pitt as much as Newcastle felt the pull of 'global' aspirations in this period; but he was careful to emphasize the primary importance of removing the French threat from North America, which also allowed him to win support for military expenditures on the continent: see Add MSS 32,855 ff. 523–6; *Proceedings and Debates of the British Parliaments*, 265–7.

56 *The Death of the Late General Wolfe at the Siege of Quebec*, Manchester Central Library, Playbills, Marsden St Theatre, 17 August 1763. At the celebrations on Quebec at Kensington Palace, an illumination across six windows read: 'Praise . . . General JAMES WOLFE, who Dauntless, but Deliberate, Under numerous Difficulties, September 2, 1759, Engaged to employ his little army, For the Honour and Interest of his Country; and In a few Days after, Gloriously fulfilled his Promise, by the Conquest of Quebec, at the Expence of his Life': *Gentleman's Magazine*, 29 (1759) 495.

57 See the Address of the Protestant Dissenting Ministers of London and Westminster to the King, printed in *Gentleman's Magazine*, 33 (1763), 291.

58 Klaus Knorr, *British Colonial Theories, 1570–1850* (Toronto, 1944), 108–10.

59 Brewer, *Sinews of Power*, 176–8.

60 The evidence on this point is vast, and is documented in Chapters 4, 6 and 8 of my forthcoming book, *The Sense of the People*, as well as in several already-published monographs.

61 See, e.g., James Bradley, *Popular Politics and the American Revolution in England* (Athens, Geo., 1987); John Brewer, 'English Radicalism', Kathleen Wilson, 'Inventing Revolution: 1688 and Eighteenth Century Popular Politics', *Journal of British Studies*, 28 (1989), 349–86.

62 *London Evening Post* (3/5 October 1775); *Norfolk Chronicle* (7 October 1775).

63 *Peace with America, or RUIN to England*, printed in *Norfolk Chronicle* (7 March 1778); *Newcastle Journal* (16 December 1776). As William Alexander commented, observing the progress of the conflict from France, 'Can any Man seriously expect to Compell a Nation to trade with you whom you cannot Conquer, by taking their Ships burning their Towns and Cutting their Throats?' (Huntington Library, Pulteney MSS, Box 15, WA to Sir WP, 20 December 1777).

64 *Proceedings and Debates of the British Parliaments*, 104–9, 265–7; Jonas Hanway, *Thought on the Duty of a Good Citizen* (London, 1759) 10.

65 *Cato's Letters: Essays on Liberty, Civil and Religious, and Other Important Subjects* (4 vols; London, 1755), vol. iv, 7–8.

66 *Debates of the House of Commons in the Year 1774, on the Bill for Making More Effectual Provision for the Government of Quebec*, ed. J. Wright (London, 1839; repr. 1966), 89, iii–iv, 15–24. For demonstrations against the act see *London Evening Post* (11–14 June 1774), *Newcastle Journal* (9 July; 30 July 1774); and Jonathan Paul Thomas, 'The British Empire and the Press, 1763–74' (Oxford D.Phil. thesis, 1982), 329–68.

67 Petition of the Freeholders of the County of Middlesex to the King, PRO HO 55/13/2, reprinted in Bradley, *Popular Politics*, 230–1.

68 Tucker, *Four Tracts and Two Sermons on Political and Commercial Subjects* (Gloucester, 1774), 128–30 and *passim*; *A Letter to Edmund Burke, Esq.* (Gloucester, 1775), 18–20, 43; and *An Humble Address and Earnest Appeal to Those Respectable Personages in Great Britain and Ireland* (London, 1776; repr. in *Gentleman's Magazine*, 46 [1776]), 78–9. See also Pocock, *Virtue, Commerce and History*, 37–50, 157–92.

69 *Public Advertiser* (14 March 1774); Samuel Foote, *The Nabob* (London, 1772). Foote's protagonist, Sir Matthew Mite, was a moral grotesque, ruthlessly

exploitative of the Indians and equally so of the English at home, whom he strove to rob of their ancestral and native rights. For other expressions of distaste for the Asian empire's enervating and corrupting effects, see *Public Advertiser* (10 July 1769), (26 March 1771); *Lancashire Magazine*, 1 (1763), 60–2; 2 (1764), 515–6; and Marshall, ' "A Free though Conquering People" ', 7–10, and Thomas, 'British Empire and the Press', 232–328.

70 *Daily Gazetteer* (2 November 1767); Seymour Drescher, *Capitalism and Anti-Slavery* (London, 1986), 178–9.

71 These attitudes were displayed in anti-American demonstrations in which colonial patriots were burned in effigy, in sermons, pamphlets and addresses to the crown, and in prints, ballads and drinking-songs: see Wilson, *Sense of the People*, ch. 4. Significantly, against this type of jingoistic loyalism, English radicals ascribed to the colonists the heroic attributes of the national character: see Horne Tooke's description of his 'American fellow-subjects, who, faithful to the character of *Englishmen*, prefer death to slavery', quoted in Newman, *Rise of English Nationalism*, 199.

72 *Newcastle Weekly Magazine*: (31 July 1776) 'On the Folly of War, and Love of our Country', 4–5; (16 October 1776) 'On the Equality between the Sexes' 201–4.

73 Marshall, 'Empire and Authority', 115.

74 The justification of colonies as dependencies rested upon the family analogy: the 'mother country', in return for founding, supporting and protecting her colonies, expected them to carry on trade and commerce solely under her direction, so that their commerce could be regulated to coincide with her interests. The tensions of this theory with libertarian ideologies arise because the model of colonial development stops short of adulthood: what happens when the children grow up? See *Essays Commercial and Political, on the Real and Relative Interests of Imperial and Dependent States* (Newcastle, 1777), 15–16.

75 Cato's Letter No. 106, *London Journal* (8 December 1722); Adam Smith, *Wealth of Nations* (London, 1776), bk 4. For a discussion of the impact of Smith's work on contemporary thinking about the colonial conflict, see Pulteney MSS, Box 15, WA to Sir WP, 18 May 1778. The social contours of support for the war, and particularly the extent of merchant hostility to the colonists' claims, also forced radicals to recognize that there was no necessary connection between merchants, empire and liberty: 'Merchants and genuine patriots are *not* synonymous terms,' one observer fumed on surveying the loyalist merchant addresses to the throne (*London Evening Post*, [8–10 September 1778]; I owe this reference to Nick Rogers).

76 Richard Price, *Discourse on Love of Country* (London, 1789); John Cartwright, *American Independence the Interest and Glory of Great Britain*, (London, 1775). Price's view, in particular, found expression in the early nineteenth-century condemnations of empire as part of 'Old Corruption': Knorr, *British Colonial Theories*, 241–3.

77 Brown, *Estimate of the Manners and Principles of the Times*, vol. I, 62; vol. II, 40.

7

The Reach of the State, the Appeal of the Nation

Mass arming and political culture in the Napoleonic Wars

Linda Colley

On 26 July 1803, when panic about an imminent French invasion was at its height, James Gillray published one of his most striking, yet most ambiguous, prints. An English volunteer soldier, oak leaves flourishing from his three-cornered hat like holly out of a Christmas pudding, waves aloft a pitchfork. On top of it is the head of Napoleon Bonaparte. It is just 48 hours since the French have landed, and the man who has conquered most of continental Europe has been brought to heel and destroyed by a corps of plebeian volunteers, the Union Jack raised high in their midst. So far, so inspiring: a typically professional piece of patriotic propaganda from a master artist. Yet the closer we look at this imaginary scene, the more likely we are to feel troubled. The face of the volunteer hero is bloated and coarse, his lips are gluttonous, his eyes dull. Bumptious and trite, he celebrates his victory as if the French consul were deaf not dead: 'Plunder old England, hay? Make French slaves of us, hay? Ravish all our wives and daughters, hay? O Lord help that silly head!' Yet, for all this boasting, it is in fact the victim's severed head, and not the oafs who have decapitated him, which captures our attention. Gaunt, drained of blood, ruthlessly exposed, Napoleon Bonaparte still retains his high cheek-bones, his finely chiselled Roman nose, his hair fashionably cut *à la* Titus, his altogether classical profile. The arch-enemy, he is still in death an officer and a gentleman, and Gillray clearly cannot resist drawing him as such. Equally clearly, the artist has found it impossible to celebrate the ordinary civilian volunteer who is his fellow countryman without simultaneously demeaning him.[1]

Gillray's failure to come to terms with plebeian patriotism was far from exceptional at this time.[2] All over Europe, the scale and danger of the Napoleonic Wars had necessitated mass arming on an unprecedented scale. War, as Clausewitz put it, had become 'the business of the people'.[3] All over Europe, there was considerable anxiety and bewilderment among

165

the propertied about the likely social and political repercussions of such extraordinary mass mobilization. As far as Great Britain is concerned, however, this inability to *see* the ordinary fighting man of this period has proved remarkably persistent. Although the impact of mass arming in revolutionary and Napoleonic France has been analysed with great skill by Richard Cobb, Alan Forrest and Isser Woloch and others, and although there are many able works examining mass resistance to the French in Prussia, Russia and Spain, the hundreds of thousands of Britons who joined the ranks of the regular army and the militia and volunteer corps during these wars have been comparatively little studied.[4] Just like Gillray, we still fail to see these men as they really were.

In part, this is because Great Britain, unlike so many other European and extra-European states at this time, was not invaded. Consequently, the impression has persisted that, for the British, these were wars fought for property, dominion and the existing order, with very little voluntary popular input. More broadly, however, the failure to examine mass mobilization in this society during the Napoleonic Wars reflects assumptions that are implicit in the work of many social historians of eighteenth- and nineteenth-century Britain: namely, that the only interesting mass behaviour is obviously dissident mass behaviour, and that the opposite of popular dissidence is popular conservatism and deference. This chapter is intended as a challenge to such assumptions. I want to examine, first, how the British state was able to mobilize its male civilian population against the invasion threat posed by Napoleon's armies. Second, I want to investigate how many Britons associated themselves with this civil-defence effort and why it was that they did so. Finally, I want to suggest that plebeian patriotism at this time was a larger and more complex phenomenon than is often acknowledged.

PATTERNS OF MOBILIZATION

How many Britons could be got to fight? How were large numbers of men living on the edge of poverty to be brought to risk life and limb for a state in which active citizenship was denied them? Although eighteenth-century Britain had been pre-eminently a warlike state, its rulers had not had to address these questions seriously before 1793. With the exception of the Jacobite invasions of 1715 and 1745, it had been able to fight its battles abroad or at sea, and rely on its own regular forces and on foreign mercenaries.

All this changed with the wars against revolutionary and Napoleonic France. More than twice as long as the First and Second World Wars added together, they were almost as geographically extensive as far as British involvement was concerned, sweeping through Europe, into Asia, Africa, North America, Latin America, and even provoking sea battles off the coast of Australia. As it turned out, war did not cross the Channel into Great Britain itself, but those living between 1793 and 1815 could not know that. Napoleon's Army of England was by far the most formidable invasion force assembled against Great Britain up to that time, the threat it represented was a protracted one, and it came very close to succeeding. There was a major but abortive invasion attempt against Ireland in 1796, and a more successful French landing there two years later. In 1797 a small expeditionary force landed in Wales. From 1798 to 1805 the conquest of Britain was Napoleon's primary strategic objective. Even after the Franco-Spanish fleet had been smashed at Trafalgar, there was still the prolonged challenge of the French blockade.[5]

In the face of these dangers, Britain's armed forces had to grow at a faster rate than those of any other European power. When the Bastille was stormed in 1789 the British army was 40,000 strong. By 1814 it had expanded more than sixfold to some quarter of a million men. The Royal Navy, bedrock of defence, aggression, empire and trade, grew faster still. Before 1789 it had employed 16,000 men; by 1812 it employed over 140,000. Supplementing these regular land and sea forces was an expanding penumbra of part-time and volunteer units defending the home front itself, almost half a million men by 1804.[6] Mobilizing them presented those in power with their greatest challenge in this period. It was simply no longer enough to maintain civil order and obedience by way of professional soldiers, barracks, surveillance and sermons. Nor was it even enough to foster loyalty by means of an intensive campaign of propaganda and patriotic ceremonial.[7] In the face of economic distress, social upheaval and the lures of French revolutionary doctrines, a major effort had to be made for almost a quarter of a century to encourage large numbers of civilians to take up arms in support of the British state. In these circumstances, the question became imperative: how many Britons could be got to fight?

The only civil defence force in existence at the onset of the wars with France was the militia. This had been remodelled in 1757, when Parliament replaced the old system, whereby property-owners furnished arms and men to the king in times of need, with an order that each English and Welsh county must supply a given quota of men between the age of 18 and 45 and pay for them out of the rates. Some 32,000 men, all of them good Protestants, were to be chosen by ballot, subjected to martial law in time of active service, and dispatched during peacetime for a month's military training every year under the enthusiastic and voluntary leadership of the local gentry. This, at least, was the law.[8] In practice, the system proved only patchily effective and was profoundly unpopular. As in *ancien régime* France, the burden of militia service fell overwhelmingly on the illiterate poor, and – as far as this duty was concerned – there were not enough of them. County quotas were rarely met; and no attempt was made to adapt the quotas to the changing balance of Britain's population.

In 1796 the proportion of eligible men serving in the militia in Dorset, Bedfordshire and Montgomeryshire, all heavily agricultural counties, was found to be more than one in ten. By contrast, more industrialized counties where population growth had accelerated since mid-century were getting off lightly. Only one in thirty eligible men was serving in the militia in the West Riding of Yorkshire, only one in forty-five in Lancashire.[9]

For five years after the outbreak of war with revolutionary France in 1793, the government's response to these inadequacies was careful and limited. By the Supplementary Militia Act of 1796, it demanded a further 60,000 militiamen from England, and another 4,400 from Wales, taking care this time to ensure that quotas fell far more equally on each county. The following year, it extended the militia for the first time to Scotland, hoping thereby to raise another 6,000 men for home-defence duties. This brought the total strength of the militia throughout Great Britain to some 100,000 men.[10] In addition, the authorities encouraged 'gentlemen' to found their own private volunteer corps of infantry or cavalry. No state subsidies were given to these early volunteers. London had no say over what they wore or who the officers were, and no control over what their precise duties should be. Instead, the fact that these corps were self-funding was seen as a further guarantee of their members' social respectability and political soundness. What the government wanted at this stage of the war were landowners or substantial manufacturers enrolling as volunteer officers, with farmers, professionals, shopkeepers and men with established trades to their name serving as their rank and file. This was very largely what they got. Some 40 per cent of Edinburgh's volunteers in the mid-1790s, for example, were lawyers. Of the seventy-five heroes who volunteered to defend Ely in Cambridgeshire, sixty-nine were farmers, or attorneys, or snug tradesmen, butchers, blacksmiths, victuallers and the like; only six were labourers.[11]

As artists and cartoonists delighted in pointing out, it was their uniforms that gave these early volunteer corps away. Very often, they were gorgeous, impractical and extremely expensive. More graphically than anything else could do, they indicated that volunteering at this stage of the war was primarily, though not exclusively, a prosperous man's game.[12] In some counties, generous subscriptions were raised to clothe and equip poorer men; but many volunteers took pride in equipping themselves, and many attached themselves to volunteer corps not so much to fight for survival against the French, as to defend their shops, homes, businesses or land against the more seditious and riotous of their own countrymen.

The evidence suggests, then, that in the early years of the war the British government was as afraid of its own people as it was of the French. Labouring men might be the bedrock of the regular forces and fill the ranks of the militia, but they were neither welcome nor very much trusted in the less-structured world of the volunteers. Not an armed people, but a propertied and respectable home guard to restrain domestic disorder was what the authorities were most anxious to create at this stage of the conflict. The change came in the winter of 1797, when Napoleon's Army of England encamped along the French coastline. Desperate, and by now without European allies, the government had no choice but to make the shift from seeking quality support at home to seeking it in quantity.

The most well-known outcome of this frantic search for numbers was Great Britain's first census, ordered by Parliament in 1800, on the grounds that 'in every war, especially in a defensive war, it must be of the highest importance to enrol and discipline the greatest possible number of men.'[13] Much less well known are the detailed returns that the Defence of the Realm Act of April 1798 demanded from each county: details of the number of able-bodied men in each parish, details of what service, if any, each man was prepared to offer to the state, details of what weapons he possessed, details of the amount of livestock, carts, mills, boats, barges and grain available, details of how many elderly people there were, how many alien and infirm. Compiled by harassed constables or schoolmasters, checked by clergymen, parochial vestries and deputy-lieutenants, these returns, which were repeated in 1803, supplied the British state with the most ambitious and precise taxonomy of its people compiled since the Domesday Book. These same documents, singularly neglected by historians and demographers, allow us to get behind the administrative details of civil defence, to reach the men themselves, the 'living beings in action' as Richard Cobb called their French counterparts.[14]

Of course, these questionaires do not provide an infallible index of popular patriotism. Some have simply not survived; and others – particularly those relating to Wales and Scotland – probably still lie undiscovered in private archives. Those returns that do still exist are not always complete or reliable. Not all the participating constables and schoolmasters did an efficient job. Not all of them told the truth. In some areas they did not even try. Nevertheless, the statistics of civilian response that survive are impressive: impressive in the thoroughness and care with which they were generally garnered, but impressive too in terms of what they reveal. In 1798 the state demanded that local officials interrogate every eligible male between the ages of 15 and 60 about his willingness to take up arms in the event of an invasion; in 1803 it wanted further examinations, this time of all eligible men between 17 and 55 years of age. It would have been easy, and it must have been tempting for the men who had to scurry round implementing these directives simply to claim that their respective localities were united in a patriotic consensus. Some did just that. John Kinsey, for example, acting constable of Crickadarn parish in Brecknockshire, assured the authorities in 1803 that all its eligible men were 'ready and willing to serve for the defence of the Kingdom'.[15] We shall never know how close to the truth this statement was.

Yet the crucial point is that such blanket assurances were not what the government sought or asked for. The returns demanded in 1798 and 1803 were never printed in full and were never intended as propaganda to impress a doubting people. The information they provided was only for the eyes of the local Lords Lieutenant and members of the central government, and what these men badly wanted was accuracy not reassurance. The majority of the constables and schoolmasters seem to have done their level best to provide exactly that, reporting – often verbatim – the candid and widely varying replies they received as they trudged round asking men if they were willing to fight. That is why these returns were and are so valuable. They undermine almost every facile generalization made at the time and since about civilian responses in wartime Britain. They confront those who argue on the one hand for widespread deference throughout Great Britain at this time, and those who want to claim on the other that the mass of people were alienated from their rulers, with grittily assembled, unaccommodating facts.

The returns demonstrate conclusively that even at the height of patriotic excitement about a possible French invasion, in 1803, some Britons were averse to fighting for their country and felt able to tell the authorities so point-blank. In East Grinstead in Sussex, for example, the local constable estimated that there were 556 men between the ages of 17 and 55 eligible to volunteer. Of these, 34 had already enrolled in private volunteer corps and a further 169 declared that they were willing to serve in the event of invasion; but that still left some 350 men who were not willing to serve. Most of these, as the return makes clear, were older, married men with children, naturally disinclined to leave their families.[16] In other towns and villages, there were younger men as well who said 'no'. Jacob Phillips, a 17-year-old unmarried articled clerk in Exeter refused to join a volunteer corps that year; so, more predictably perhaps, did his fellow townsman Francis Ellis, a young weaver who stoutly refused the local constable's suggestions that he should take up arms for his country not just once but twice.[17] We do not know why these two men refused. They may have disliked the prospect of military discipline. They may have been too engrossed in their personal affairs to care. Or, like one London coachmaker who actually scribbled his reasons on the local constable's return, their refusal may have been politically based:

No law or power under the canopy of Heaven shall force me to take up arms ... I pray to God, that I may never live to see my country become a province of France, but if this war is suffered to go on I know it will be conquered, for I am positively sure that the King,

Lords and Commons . . . have long since lost the hearts, goodwill
and affection of a very great majority of the people of this nation.[18]

To judge by his own words, this man was neither actively seditious nor
irreligious. Nor was he poor. He owned a substantial house in Oxford
Street and had a good trade. Those who refused to co-operate at this time,
like those who conformed, cannot be slotted into any of the more predictable categories.

They did not, for instance, come from any particular occupational
groups. Nor do areas in England and Wales where Protestant dissent was
strong seem to have responded differently from securely Anglican regions,
though the old Puritan heartland of East Anglia *may* have been an exception. Cambridgeshire had been one of the last counties to obey the Militia
Act of 1757, refusing to ballot its men until 1778.[19] Twenty years later,
this county, together with Huntingdonshire, had the smallest proportion
of men enrolled in volunteer corps of any of the English counties. In
1803–4 Cambridgeshire, like Bedfordshire, failed to supply the state with
adequate details of its defence arrangements; while only 13 per cent of
eligible men volunteered in Huntingdonshire, and only 20 per cent did so
in Essex.[20]

Yet even here, dissent may not have been the crucial factor behind this
unevenness in war patriotism. Anyone familiar with East Anglia knows its
peculiar separateness, its distinct scenery, its bare and dismal fens, huge
skies and omnipresent water, felt in the damp air and regulated by strange
networks of sluices and dykes. Not until 1914 would state mobilization
penetrate this waterland to any significant degree; it was simply too sparsely populated, too insulated, too complacent within itself to care much
about the nation beyond its borders. Very different was the experience of
that broad swathe of counties on the western and southern coasts of
England – Gloucestershire, Somerset, Devon, Wiltshire, Hampshire, Sussex
and Kent – which had much stronger military traditions and were geographically far more vulnerable to French attack. On average, 50 per cent
of all men aged between 17 and 55 in these counties volunteered to take
up arms in 1803. In Great Britain, as in other European states at this time,
it was these kinds of peculiarities of place that more than anything else
seem to have influenced men's willingness to fight. The kind of region and
community in which they lived, rather than how they worshipped God or
what social class or occupational group they belonged to, was the factor
that mattered most.

How, then, should we see the map of war patriotism in Great Britain?
Granted that there were individual and regional discrepancies in response
to the call for volunteers, what sort of broad generalizations can be made
about the declared willingness to fight? There are three conclusions that
can be drawn from the statistics assembled at this time. First, Wales and

Scotland responded to the need for mobilization differently from England, and differently too from each other. Second, the more industrialized and urbanized a region was, the more likely it was to produce a high level of volunteers. Third, the state's call for large numbers of men to defend it after 1798 was answered, not indeed unanimously but certainly abundantly.

In May 1804 the House of Commons was informed that some 176,000 Britons were serving within Great Britain in the militia, regular army and in various private volunteer corps. A further 482,000 men had indicated their willingness to arm in the event of an invasion, and many of these were now training in state-subsidized volunteer corps. Some of these men had agreed to serve throughout the military district in which their town or village was situated (there were fourteen military districts throughout Great Britain); but the majority had been told that in an emergency they might be sent to any part of Great Britain, and had volunteered on these terms. The majority of them had also been supplied with arms.[21] All this was very gratifying, but if Members of Parliament studied the figures before them carefully, they would have noticed not only the regional differences in response that I have already discussed, but also differences between the three component parts of Great Britain. Whereas all but three of the English counties had sent in their returns, five of the Welsh counties had failed to supply the central government with adequate information, as had eleven of the Scottish counties.

Why was this? As far as Scotland is concerned, we can put aside any simple assumption that its people remained aloof from the war effort. By the end of 1803 over 60,000 Scots were serving as rank-and-file members of volunteer regiments, some 17 per cent of the total number in arms throughout Great Britain. The following year, information dispatched to London suggested that some 44 per cent of the eligible male population in Scotland was willing to serve, most of them in any part of Great Britain. This was actually a better rate of response than was to be found in England, where an average of 37 per cent of eligible men were willing to serve. The Welsh, however, were noticeably far more averse to military mobilization. The eight returns sent in by Welsh counties in 1804 suggested that on average only 28 per cent of their eligible menfolk were willing to volunteer; but no more than in Scotland were all of its people invariably unresponsive to the call to arms.

Indeed, before the British state committed itself to popularizing civil defence in 1798, the statistics it compiled revealed that a higher proportion of Welshmen and Scots joined volunteer corps than Englishmen (just under 4 per cent of the total male population in these two countries as against 2.4 per cent in England). Moreover, in this early stage of the war, Scots and men from south Wales were far more extrovert in their military commitment than their English neighbours. Almost one-half of the 84,000 volunteers known to have enrolled in England by the start of 1798 stipulated that they would only defend their own town or village. By contrast, 88 per cent of volunteers in Pembrokeshire and Glamorgan claimed to be willing to defend their military district as a whole, and over 90 per cent of the Scottish volunteer corps were willing to serve throughout all Scotland. Only in Selkirk and Lanark, prosperous lowland counties, did substantial numbers of Scots reveal an inclination to defend just their own backyard.[22]

At this early stage of the war – before 1798 – the fact that England was a much richer and better-populated country than either Wales or Scotland may actually have worked against efficient home defence in this particular part of Great Britain. Many comfortable Englishmen saw no reason to volunteer at all at the beginning of the war. Those who did were often more interested in defending their own homes and businesses against civil unrest than in protecting the nation at large from a foreign enemy. Prosperity in these circumstances fostered the most outrageous localism. By contrast, the comparative poverty and predominantly rural economies of much of Scotland and Wales initially aided militarization. Landowners and employers could exercise a much starker and more ubiquitous control here than in England.[23] Consequently, a higher proportion of Welshmen and Scots were drawn into the early volunteer corps, and on much more generous terms than their English counterparts.

Precisely because defence measures in parts of the Celtic fringe were more heavily dependent on widespread deference to local landlords than in England, the response of their inhabitants to the call to arms could become less impressive after 1798. The Defence of the Realm Act passed that year, and the mass of civil-defence legislation that followed it, showed that the initiative in home defence had now passed decisively from local magnates to Parliament. As a result, some Scottish and Welsh landlords, who had been happy enough to organize their own private volunteer corps, seem to have given these new measures less than their full backing. Without such backing, the state's directives could have only a muffled impact in areas so distant from London. Moreover, if it was to be genuinely effective, mass mobilization needed to draw on mass enthusiasm; and the potential for this was more evenly distributed in England than in either Wales or Scotland.

Englishmen and women were more widely prosperous than were their Welsh or Scottish neighbours. Their patriotism was therefore more likely to be reinforced by self-interest if they could be convinced that a French invasion was genuinely imminent. By 1803 most do seem to have been convinced of this, with predictable results: 'England never can be overrun', purred Arthur Young, '... her infantry is as numerous as her property is diffused'.[24] England was also a far more urbanized country than Wales or Scotland, with much better communications; and this too made a difference. Attachment to the British state was not, could not, be a given. It

173

had to be learnt; and men and women had to see some advantage in learning it. Those who lived far from centres of wealth, population, information and activity learned it very slowly, and some of the inhabitants of Scotland and Wales, like some of the inhabitants of the more peripheral regions of England, chose not to learn it at all. The Welsh record in civil defence after 1798 bears this out. Counties such as Brecknockshire, Carmarthenshire and Radnorshire which were isolated, mountainous, sparsely populated and heavily dependent on agriculture, responded poorly to the state's defence measures. Flintshire, by contrast, enriched by urban centres like Wrexham and by its close trading-links to Chester over the English border, responded well: 51 per cent of its eligible males were enrolled as volunteers by 1804. Over 4,400 men joined the volunteers in Glamorgan, the most anglicized, urbanized and accessible of the Welsh counties. War patriotism, it seems clear, was more likely to flourish where towns and trade did.

This was not what Britain's rulers had anticipated. As soon as war with revolutionary France broke out, William Pitt's administration had acted on the straightforward assumption that loyalty was likely to be commensurate with property. Those without some stake in society were regarded as suspect; but not all were suspect to the same degree. Rural labourers in England and Wales, Highlanders in Scotland and domestic servants everywhere, it was believed, were likely to be personally bound to their landlords and employers and therefore more tractable. Simple, traditional and picturesque folk living in the depths of the countryside, pursuing their lives in time-hallowed fashion, undisturbed by any hint of modernity, were assumed to be more deferential and therefore more loyal. Just like many social historians today, however, ministers anticipated protest and sedition from those 'accustomed to associate together' – workers in manufacturing industries, urban artisans, miners, colliers and dockers.[25] It was a cliché by 1800 – reinforced, of course, by events in Paris – that men massed together in towns or workplaces were potentially volatile. Yet as the Loyalty Returns of 1798 and 1803 demonstrated very clearly, these assumptions about the split between urban and rural responses were by no means invariably justified in fact.

Some of the most detailed information we have about civilian responses in 1798 concerns the predominantly agricultural parishes of North Hampshire.[26] This was an area running close to the boundaries with Berkshire and Surrey, stocked with small parishes like Steventon where Jane Austen's father served as vicar (and she herself wrote her early novels). A quiet and conservative area, then, virtually untouched by modernity or mobility of any kind. The census of 1800 revealed that all but six of Steventon's 150-odd inhabitants worked on the land. In nearby Cliddesden, only ten men and women earned their living in occupations other than agriculture. In Mapledurwell, only three did so; in Stratfield Turgis, only two, and in Tunworth, none at all. In this unquestionably rural backwater, there was sometimes deference to local authorities; to the siren calls of the nation state, however, most people remained stubbornly deaf. As a conscientious clergyman, the Revd Austen was able to undertake that thirty-five Steventon men would volunteer if need be. But no such promises came from Cliddesden or Mapledurwell, where the responsible constables left the relevant part of the government forms blank. Nor was active loyalty to be found in Stratfield Turgis, where the constable wrote honestly: 'No one would say he was *willing* to serve'. As for Tunworth, its scrappy and incoherent return suggests that the local constable was either incapable of understanding his instructions or simply unable to write.

What was true of rural North Hampshire seems also to have been true of other profoundly rural areas in England.[27] Many of their inhabitants – though by no means all of them – seem to have responded to national mobilization in much the same way as the villagers of Provence reacted to the ambitious centralization attempted by the new French Republic after 1789: with stolid unconcern, marked suspicion, dumb resentment and sometimes downright resistance.

In general, it was the more urbanized and industrialized regions of Great Britain that supplied the state with its most active civilian auxiliaries (just as these same regions supplied the bulk of men for the regular army and the militia). The Loyalty Returns show this very clearly. The census had revealed that in only seven English counties (Oxfordshire, Cambridgeshire, Berkshire, Essex, Herefordshire, Huntingdonshire and Lincolnshire) was the number of agricultural workers more than double the number of men and women engaged in other occupations. Of these seven predominantly rural counties, two – Cambridgeshire and Oxfordshire – failed to supply the government with volunteering statistics in 1803–4. In the other five, the proportion of men who enrolled as volunteers at that time was on average only 22 per cent. A very different pattern emerges if we look at those provincial English counties where the work-force was predominantly engaged in trade or industry. According to the census, there were eleven such. Ten of these – Cheshire, Derbyshire, Durham, Lancashire, Leicestershire, Northamptonshire, Nottinghamshire, Staffordshire, Surrey and Warwickshire – supplied the authorities with detailed returns of their volunteers in 1803–4. These show that on average 35 per cent of the eligible male population in these counties volunteered to defend the nation. Only one English county deviates conspicuously from this general rule that population density and industrialization were actually more congenial to mobilization during the invasion crisis than predominantly agricultural regions.[28] That county is Yorkshire, where only 20 per cent of the male population was willing to volunteer. It is Yorkshire, of course, which supplies much of the evidence for mass alienation during the Napoleonic Wars in Edward Thompson's marvellous classic *The Making of the English Working Class*.

We need to recognize that in terms of war patriotism, popular responses in Yorkshire may – and I stress may – have been more the exception than the rule; and we need to recognize something far more important. Historians of France have explored grass-roots responses to war in this period far more extensively than have their counterparts in Britain. As a result, they have been quicker to recognize that new economic forces, in particular the massing of men that occurs in urbanization and industrialization, often aided the militarization of society.[29] British historians, by contrast, have often written as though economic change was invariably disruptive – that the countryside naturally fostered obedience, while the towns spawned only protest. The reality, as we have seen, was rather different. In 1804 a writer in the *Edinburgh Review* complained that rural labourers had been so idealized by conservatives that the civic potential of the urban artisan had been badly ignored. Yet, he argued:

> If the bodily strength of the artisan is less than that of ploughmen, they possess in a much greater degree, that manual dexterity and skill, so necessary in the evolutions, especially of modern war . . . Modern warfare consists in reducing men to a state of mechanical activity, and combining them as parts of a great machine. For this use, which of the two is most fitted by his previous habits – he who has been all his life acting the part of a mechanical implement with a combination of movements – or he who has been constantly employed as a thinking, independent, separate, and insulated agent?[30]

The urban artisan, because he had been acculturated, because he was more easily reached by propaganda and recruiting parties and, crucially, because he was not tied to the land, could be a more useful citizen in time of war than the solitary ploughman. Far from automatically making Great Britain more susceptible to revolution, precocious industrialization and urbanization almost certainly helped to keep the forces of the French Revolution at bay.

MOTIVATION

The arithmetic of mobilization alone, of course, cannot tell us why it was that so many men undertook to defend Great Britain at this time. We can be sure, however, that for many civilian volunteers patriotism was not the only motive, and that for some of them it was no motive at all. Unemployment drove some to volunteer, particularly in the towns. Others were compelled to take up arms by more or less subtle pressure from landlords and employers, especially, though not exclusively, in parts of Wales and in the Scottish Highlands. Some must have enrolled in volunteer corps out of self-interest. Joining a volunteer corps exempted a man from being balloted for the militia and thereby coming under martial law; it could also gain him the approval of the local gentry who supplied the bulk of volunteer-corps officers; and might even earn him useful military contracts if he was a tradesman of some kind.[31]

Yet, in recognizing that some men volunteered to suit themselves, and that others did so out of deference or because they were coerced, we must be careful not to duplicate the condescension of some contemporaries. The failure of imagination and sympathy that led men like Gillray to represent the mass of volunteers as no more than gullible bumpkins, or alternatively as self-serving plebs, should not be our failure as well. The role of ordinary human courage, of endeavour, of excitement, of a natural desire to protect one's own hearth, should not be downplayed just because those who experienced these emotions happened in the main to be poor. All the evidence suggests that volunteers who were working men, like volunteers who were not, could be swayed by a variety of different motives, not just by direct incentives, but also by patriotism, by instinct, by desperation – and by youth.

By the early nineteenth century, almost 55 per cent of the British population was under 25 years old.[32] In absolute terms, more young, unmarried men were available than ever before – brash, eager, hungry for a chance to fight (particularly, perhaps, on home ground) and desperately concerned not to seem a coward in the eyes of peers and lovers. The cult of aggressive maleness, which was so prominent in patrician art and literature at this time, seems to have been just as prominent in popular ballads and songs. As in this Newcastle song, for instance, where hope for a speedy peace mingles uneasily with relish at the prospect of clobbering the French:

> Then to parade the pitmen went,
> Wi' hearts both stout and strong man,
> God smash the French we are so strang;
> We'll shoot them every one, man:
> God smash me sark if I would stick,
> To tumble them a down the pit,
> As fast as I cou'd thra a coal[33]

It seems at least probable, then, that numbers of volunteers were not so much anxious to fight for anything in particular, as simply anxious to fight – period.

Between 1798 and 1805, at least, the prime incentives to volunteer among all classes were fear and anger – fear and anger at the prospect of invasion from without. Of course, we know now that Britain, unlike Russia, Switzerland, the Netherlands, Spain, Poland or various Italian and German states, was never overrun by French armies. No patriotic war of liberation was required here of the sort that took place in Prussia after 1807, or still more in Spain after the *Dos de Mayo* in 1808. In those countries men and women were swept into the fighting to defend their homes, families and culture, because the stark alternatives to resistance were annihilation or conquest. As it happened, Britain escaped these brutal imperatives; but it is vital to remember that those living at the time could feel no assurance that this would be the case. Contemporary propaganda, whether in the form of sermons, tracts, cartoons or patriotic ballads, was designed quite deliberately to foster their insecurity.

With the bogey of Bonaparte hanging over them, poor men, more so perhaps than the prosperous, were drawn into military service not just by apprehension but by the excitement of it all, by a pleasurable sense of risk and imminent drama, by the lure of a free, brightly coloured uniform, even by the powerful seduction exerted by martial music – those drums and trumpets which working men and women normally never got a chance to hear, and which therefore had an enormous impact when deployed by recruiting parties. Suggestively, it was in terms of sound that the cartoonist George Cruikshank described the nation-wide impact of volunteering in 1806:

> Every town was . . . a sort of garrison – in one place you might hear the 'tattoo' of some youth learning to beat the drum, at another place some march or national air being practised upon the fife, and every morning at five o'clock the bugle horn was sounded through the streets, to call the volunteers to a two hours' drill . . . and then you heard the pop, pop, pop, of the single musket, or the heavy sound of the volley, or the distant thunder of the artillery.[34]

Surrounded by loud and exhilarating noises, equipped with brand-new uniforms and unfamiliar pikes and muskets, bombarded with tales of French atrocities in other lands, and constantly told that only they could prevent similar evils from befalling their own shores, their own home-town or village, some labouring men, it is clear, saw in volunteering a window on a broader and more vivid existence. To them, going to war seemed to offer a brief chance to attempt something big, some slight opportunity to escape drudgery and mundane obligations and become for a time a person who mattered. We do not know how many men thought in these terms, and it seems inherently unlikely that they did so for very long; but such men indubitably did exist at all social levels, and though their voices have been virtually ignored subsequently, they emerge loud and clear from the loyalty returns, recorded verbatim by the men who compiled them. 'Give me a sword and pistol' urges a carter from Exeter in 1803; 'Will mow down Bonny [sic]' boasts a husbandman; 'If Buoney-parte [sic] comes will do anything to make him repent', declares another; 'Will crip [sic] the wings of the French frog-eaters' says a man who digs gardens for his living; 'Fight sword in hand if the French come' promises a labourer.[35]

The theatricality of such remarks is sad and revealing. In real life, few working men ever had the chance of handling a sword, never mind of learning how to use one. Yet the nation's emergency clearly gave men like this a chance for fantasy and wishful thinking, an opportunity for drama. For a brief time, they could imagine themselves what so many folklore heroes were – doers of daring deeds, men of destiny, winners not losers; and they relished it. What one working man described as the 'universal pant for glory' – the romance of a warrior's life and the prospect of a hero's death – could prove as seductive at this social level as it was among contemporary patrician youths in public schools and Oxbridge.[36] Since men at war are rarely entirely rational, why should it not?

POLITICAL CONSEQUENCES

What of the wider political consequences of all this? According to Henry Addington, Prime Minister from 1801 to 1804, the entrusting of arms to some half a million British civilians, most of them from the working population, constituted a triumphant renewal of the contract between government and governed:

> A determination on the part of the government to put arms into the hands of a whole people, and a resolution on the part of the people to accept them . . . proved a double security, a double pledge. It was a pledge on the part of the government, that they should never attempt anything hostile to the constitution. It was a pledge on the part of the people that they valued as well as understood its excellence; that they were steadily attached to it, and determined to preserve it.[37]

This was far from being the whole story, but it was the case that by entrusting arms to men from every part of Great Britain and from all social classes, the authorities had taken a calculated gamble. They had abandoned, at least for a while, the repressive attitude towards popular participation adopted in the immediate aftermath of the French Revolution. In return, apparently, Britain's volunteers had justified their rulers' confidence. They had not attempted to use their weapons and military training to revolt. They had not even tried to employ them – as the corps of Protestant volunteers formed in Ireland during the American Revolution had done – to extort political concessions from London. That they did neither of these things, while volunteering in such abundant numbers, is the most powerful indication we have that at the end of the day, and in time of extreme danger from without, the unreformed British state rested on the active consent of substantial numbers of its inhabitants.

Consent, however, is too static and limited a term to cover the full political and social significance of mass arming. Although the volunteer corps were savagely cut back after 1808, to be replaced by a new local militia, there were still some 350,000 men involved in civil defence when the war ended in 1815. In addition, as many as 500,000 men may have been serving in the regular forces in Europe and the empire.[38] In Great Britain, as in other major European powers, it was training in arms under the auspices of the state that was the most common collective working-class experience in the early nineteenth century, not labour in a factory, or membership of a radical political organization or illegal trade union. Here, as in continental Europe, it was the pressures of war, rather than the experience of work or the example of political revolution, that had the most obvious potential to change lives, ideas and expectations.

This was so not least in that mass arming inevitably changed attitudes to the state itself. By summoning men of all classes, all political opinions and all religious denominations to its defence, as it had no choice but to do, by treating its male population indiscriminately as patriots, the British state ran an obvious risk of encouraging demands for political change in the future. It ran this risk knowingly, because the men who led it recognized they had no choice. A state where formal political power at the centre was concentrated in the hands of a few had no alternative but to look to the many to win its wars and preserve its independence. The prime opponent of revolution in Europe and revolution at home had itself to employ revolutionary methods in order to stand a chance of succeeding. 'If we employ the mass of the people for our internal defence', an army officer had written to a member of the government in 1803, 'it will only be recurring to the same expedient for the defence of our independence as a nation, which France has successfuly employed during the last ten years'.[39] This was the point precisely. To beat the French, the British were obliged to imitate many of the devices of the French revolutionary state, and the challenge this presented to its existing order was a considerable one.

Reformers recognized this quite as clearly as ministers did. It was Samuel Bamford, a Lancashire weaver and dissenter-turned-radical, who pointed out to William Cobbett that the government's lists of militiamen and volunteers would supply a marvellous guide to the number of adult males in each county who might in the near future win the right to vote. For if all adult men were worthy to fight for Great Britain, then surely they had the right to take part in its politics as well?[40] Cobbett certainly thought so. In 1816 he printed a best-selling address 'To the Journeymen and Labourers of England, Wales, Scotland and Ireland', urging them to rejoice that they belonged to 'the most powerful nation in the world', overflowing with signs of wealth and prosperity:

> Without the journeymen and the labourers none of them could exist . . . It is the same class of men, who must, by their arms, secure its safety and uphold its fame. Titles and immense sums of money have been bestowed upon numerous naval and military commanders.

Without calling the justice of these in question, we may assert that the victories were obtained by *you*.[41]

This line of argument – that popular contribution to the state, in manpower terms as in fiscal terms, must receive political acknowledgement – would become an important part of reformist arguments after 1815. It was a case, not so much of alienation from the state, as of taking advantage of the state's extraordinary demands to make demands in return.

CONCLUSIONS

What, then, can we conclude from all of this? First, and most obviously, that the unreformed British state showed itself conspicuously able and willing to mobilize large numbers of its male population against the threat posed by Napoleon's legions. The evidence suggests that it was actually aided in this achievement by the structure of Britain's economy – by the precocious extent to which it was an industrialized and urbanized land.

The scale and quality of the response to the invasion threat also underlines the importance of re-examining the degree and meanings of consent in this society. Given that Great Britain in the eighteenth century was such a conspicuously successful state in war, and so successful too in repelling invasion attempts, it seems almost perverse that such a disproportionate amount of attention should have been devoted to those Britons who violently opposed the existing order, Jacobites in the first half of the century, Jacobins in the second half. I am not for one moment suggesting that such folk did not matter, or that they should be left out of our picture of this society; but I am suggesting that what did happen is more important than what could have happened, what might have happened, or even what should have happened. Like it or not, successive British regimes between 1688 and 1815 were able to mobilize considerable popular support. It is high time that those supporters, in all their diversity, were rescued from the condescension of posterity.

This is so not least because we cannot and must not conflate mass support for British territorial integrity against successive foreign invasions with mass conservatism or mass deference: very often, it was merely a case of working men and women opting for the lesser of two evils. More positively, supporting the state in its hour of need could also be a form of self-assertion, a way of demanding something closer to active citizenship, just as banding together to bear arms in the state's defence could serve as a training in solidarity between men of similar social status. To incite mass patriotism in any society is always to open Pandora's box. What emerges from it, however convenient it may be to governments in the short term, can rarely be entirely controlled thereafter. In this last and most dangerous of wars with France, the men who governed Great Britain had no choice but to open the box.

NOTES

This chapter was delivered as a lecture at the Conference of Anglo-American Historians at the Institute of Historical Research in London in July 1991. A much-extended and fully annotated version of it is included in my book *Britons: Forging the Nation 1707–1837* (London and New Haven, 1992), 282–319.

1 'Buonaparte, 48 hours after landing', in F. G. Stephens and M. D. George, *Catalogue of Prints and Drawings in the British Museum: Political and Personal Satires* (11 vols, London, 1870–1954), vol. VIII, 167.

2 None of the many brilliant graphic artists at work in Britain at this time – Isaac Cruickshank, Thomas Rowlandson, George Woodward, Charles Williams or Gillray himself – was able to forge a convincing and uncondescending image of the plebeian patriot. The reasons for this were aesthetic as well as political: see John Barrell, *The Dark Side of the Landscape: The Rural Poor in English Painting 1730–1840* (Cambridge, 1980).

3 Geoffrey Best, *War and Society in Revolutionary Europe 1770–1870* (London, 1982), 63.

4 See, for example, Richard Cobb, *The People's Armies*, translated by Marianne Elliott (New Haven, 1987); Alan Forrest, *Conscripts and Deserters: The Army and French Society during the Revolution and Empire* (New York, 1989); and his *Soldiers of the French Revolution* (Durham, NC, 1990); Isser Woloch, *The French Veteran from the Revolution to the Restoration* (Chapel Hill, NC, 1979); Charles J. Esdaile, *The Spanish Army in the Peninsular War* (Manchester, 1988); T. C. W. Blanning, *The French Revolution in Germany: Occupation and Resistance in the Rhineland 1792–1802* (Oxford, 1983). For published work on the British volunteers, we are still heavily dependent on Sir John Fortescue's *County Lieutenancies and the Army 1803–14*, which appeared in London in 1909.

5. Paul Kennedy, *The Rise and Fall of the Great Powers* (London, 1988), 155–80.

6 Ibid.; Clive Emsley, *British Society and the French Wars 1793–1815* (London, 1979).

7 On this aspect of the war effort, see my 'Apotheosis of George III, Loyalty, Royalty and the British Nation', *Past and Present*, 102 (1984); and H. T. Dickinson, 'Popular Conservatism and Militant Loyalism 1789–1815', in *Britain and the French Revolution 1789–1815* (London, 1989).

8 J. R. Western, *The English Militia in the Eighteenth Century: The Story of a Political Issue* (London, 1965).

9 See I. F. W. Beckett, 'Buckinghamshire Militia Lists for 1759: A Social Analysis', *Records of Buckinghamshire*, 20 (1977); Return of the state of the militia, 13 August 1796, PRO, 30/8/244 fo. 92.

10 Western, *English Militia*, 219–24; and his 'Formation of the Scottish Militia in 1797', *Scottish Historical Review*, 117 (1955).

11 *A View of the Establishment of the Royal Edinburgh Volunteers* (Edinburgh, 1797); I am grateful to Professor J. E. Cookson for allowing me to consult his 'Patriotism and Social Structure: The Ely Volunteers, 1798–1808' in advance of publication.

12 See Ann Hudson, 'Volunteer Soldiers in Sussex during the Revolutionary and

Napoleonic Wars, 1793–1815', *Sussex Archaeological Collections*, 122 (1984), 179.

13 D. V. Glass, *Numbering the People: The 18th Century Population Controversy and the Development of Census and Vital Statistics in Britain* (London, 1978), 107.

14 Cobb, *The People's Armies*, 10. For a list of many of the extant returns from English and Welsh counties, see I. F. W. Beckett (ed.), *The Buckinghamshire Posse Comitatus 1798* (Aylesbury, 1985), 363–6.

15 Return for Crickadarn parish, National Library of Wales, Maybery MSS 6941–64.

16 *Sussex Militia List, Pevensey Rape 1803 Northern Division* (Eastbourne, 1988), under 'East Grinstead'.

17 W. G. Hoskins (ed.), *Exeter Militia List 1803* (Chichester, 1972), 52 and 74.

18 Quoted in J. R. Dinwiddy, 'Parliamentary Reform as an Issue in English Politics, 1800–1810' (Ph.D. dissertation, London University, 1971), 56–7.

19 Western, *English Militia*, 447–8. Professor Conrad Russell tells me that East Anglia was equally reluctant to mobilize in the sixteenth and early seventeenth centuries; only in the 1640s did it leap – comparatively – to arms.

20 Abstracts of the subdivision rolls in Great Britain, 7 May 1804, *Hansard's Parliamentary Debates*, 1st series, vol. II (London, 1804), lxii–lxiii.

21 ibid. In December 1803 the House of Commons was told that 217,196 firearms had been distributed among volunteer corps: *Hansard's Parliamentary Debates*, 1st series, 1 (London, 1803–4), 381–2.

22 The paragraph is based on information in PRO 30/8/244 fo. 237.

23 For the kind of pressure Scottish grandees were able to exert in recruitment, see Eric R. Crageen, *Argyll Estate Instructions: Mull, Morevern, Tiree 1771–1805* (Edinburgh, 1964), 195.

24 Quoted in Hudson, 'Volunteer Soldiers in Sussex', 169.

25 See, for example, the arguments of William Withering to Henry Dundas, 26 April 1798, Scottish RO, GD 51/1/931.

26 Defence of the Realm returns for Basingstoke hundred 1798, Hampshire RO, B/XVIIa/5/3.

27 See, for instance, M. Y. Ashcroft, *To Escape the Monster's Clutches: Notes and Documents Illustrating the Preparations in North Yorkshire to Repel the Invasion Threatened by the French from 1793* (North Yorkshire County RO Publications, no. 15; 1977), 75.

28 These calculations are based on a comparison of the 1804 returns cited in note 20 with the abstract of the 1801 census.

29 See Forrest, *Conscripts and Deserters*, 79–81, and *Soldiers of the French Revolution, passim*.

30 *Edinburgh Review*, 5 (1803), 10–11.

31 On unemployment and enlistment, see Clive Emsley, 'The Impact of War and Military Participation on Britain and France 1792–1815', in Clive Emsley and James Walvin (eds), *Artisans, Peasants and Proletarians 1760–1860* (London, 1985), 71–2.

32 E. A. Wrigley and R. S. Schofield, *The Population History of England, 1541–1871* (Cambridge, 1981), 529. In Scotland over 60 per cent of the population was under 30 in 1821: T. C. Smout, *A History of the Scottish People 1560–1830* (Glasgow, 1972), 262.

33 'The Pitman's Revenege [sic] against Buonaparte' in *A Collection of New Songs* (Newcastle, n.d.).

34 Quoted in Hudson, 'Volunteer Soldiers in Sussex', 180.

35 All responses recorded in Hoskins, *Exeter Militia List*, 51, 53, 54, 59.

36 William Rowbottom, an Oldham weaver, quoted in G. A. Steppler, 'The Common Soldier in the Reign of George III, 1760–1793', (D.Phil. dissertation, Oxford University, 1984), 30.

37 Reference untraced at time of going to press.

38 In 1815 the economist Patrick Colquhoun calculated that the total military and naval strength of the British empire was over one million men, an estimate that included the East India Company's armed forces: C. A. Bayly, *Imperial Meridien: The British Empire and the World 1780–1830* (London, 1989), 3.

39 Proposals from J. G. at Royal Military College, May 1803, PRO, 30/8/245, fos 21–3.

40 *The Autobiography of Samuel Bamford*, ed. W. H. Chaloner (2 vols; London, 1967), vol. II, 19.

41 G. D. H. and M. Cole, *The Opinions of William Cobbett* (London, 1944), 207.

8

Maritime Strength and Atlantic Commerce

The uses of 'a grand marine empire'

Daniel A. Baugh

Whoever goes about to reason on any part of the policy of this country with regard to America, upon the mere abstract principles of government or even upon those of our own ancient constitution, will be often misled. Those who resort for arguments to . . . authorities, ancient or modern, or rest upon the clearest maxims drawn from the experience of other states and empires, will be liable to the greatest errors imaginable. The object is wholly new in the world. It is singular; it is grown up to this magnitude and importance within the memory of man; nothing in history is parallel to it. All reasonings about it that are likely to be at all solid must be drawn from its actual circumstances.

(Edmund Burke, 1769)[1]

This chapter examines the problem of how England's oceanic empire served to sustain the state's means of defence against external enemies. As will be shown, the English state had no coherent imperial policy before 1650. It will be argued that between 1650 and 1675 the English government acted aggressively to build up a maritime-imperial system and that, during the heyday of this system (roughly 1675–1750), imperial policy was directed toward encouraging the growth of maritime and financial sinews of power, in a manner least costly to the state. Finally, it will be argued that the imperial and commercial policy instituted in 1763–4 represented a significant departure and was based on a serious misconception of the actual functioning of the maritime system of power that had been so successfully built up. The last section of the chapter will explore the nature of this misconception and the historical circumstances developing from the late 1740s onward which enabled it to take hold of policy.

The central focus, however, will be on the period from about 1650 to 1750. During the 100-year span the English state developed a uniquely successful mode of national defence, heavily dependent on financial and naval means, which I have elsewhere described under the name of 'blue-water policy'.[2] Because the states of early-modern Europe developed very much along lines laid down by the realities of warfare, this particular mode of national defence left a permanent mark on the character of English government. In the English case, overseas expansion was thoroughly inter-twined with the development of the 'fiscal-military state'.[3]

Seaborne trade was the primary provider of both the financial and maritime ingredients. On the financial side it supplied a plethora of readily taxable transactions; an augmentation of private monetary wealth that might be loaned to the government in time of war; and various means of accumulating and replenishing specie to compensate for wartime haemor-rhaging, since the optimal strategy often required England to send hard cash abroad to subsidize allies, hire mercenaries or meet operational expenses of British expeditionary forces. (Industry was important too, but industry depended heavily on commerce in the English instance.) Since the object was to sustain resources in time of war as well as peace, the need for naval protection was obvious.

The task of maintaining a strong and well-prepared navy has always entailed unusual demands upon a state. Navies are expensive and their upkeep requires cash. While there are many examples throughout history of land forces having been recruited and sustained (at home as well as in conquered territories) by non-treasury methods, naval forces have inevi-tably burdened the treasury. This is due not only to their specialized equipment but also to the need to provide many months' supply of food, drink and replacement stores at the outset of any undertaking. Further-more, during the early-modern period, which coincides with the heyday of sailing ships of war, there was the particular difficulty of obtaining skilled seamen, without which a navy was at a severe disadvantage. The difficulty was practically insurmountable for a state that had failed to build up its merchant marine. Obviously, financial, maritime and naval capabilities were thoroughly interdependent.

The 'empire' that was designed to serve these purposes is best thought of as a 'maritime-imperial system' because its value was seen to derive from maritime commerce rather than territory and dominion. From the perspective of 'blue-water policy' the positive benefits from possessing colonies were that they stimulated commerce by producing commodities for export and markets for English goods; they protected and sustained overseas naval bases; and they served to enlarge the pool of English-controlled shipping and seamen. Otherwise, from a policy standpoint colonies had to be regarded as a potential burden.

Although this way of looking at the policy of England's oceanic empire is familiar to some historians, it is not the one commonly found in textbook histories. There are many sources of confusion and misunderstanding. One is that the use of the words 'empire' or 'colonial empire' has tended to shift the focus toward territory and thus to introduce categorical mistakes.[4] Still, it would be wrong to abandon the word 'empire', since it was used by Englishmen of the time to give grandiose expression to the very system of power that this chapter describes. As Richard Koebner observed, ' "Power" . . . [was] synonymous with "Empire", but it is not the power of conquest. It means the steady exploitation of rewarding establishments beyond the seas'; the 'assumption of grandeur was clearly based on English maritime and mercantile achievements'.[5] Another source of misunderstanding is that historians have readily employed evidence drawn from the decades after 1750 to interpret the policy prevailing during the seventy-five years before that date.

The most pervasive cause of historical misunderstanding, however, has been the founding text of modern economic science, Adam Smith's *Wealth of Nations* (1776). The book's whole approach – on which its analytical purity depends – is grounded in an economic idealism that presupposes an eternally peaceful world featuring unfettered and harmonious marketing. In keeping with this, the 'Mercantile System' is presented as a purely economic conception. Smith was aware of considerations of power and national survival, most notably where he observed, 'As defence, however, is of much more importance than opulence, the act of navigation is, perhaps, the wisest of all the commercial regulations of England'. However, he did not pursue this proposition in the slightest; his observations on British war-making are distinguished by considerable ignorance; they are incoherent in the sense of offering scattered and often contradictory postulates; and they are prejudiced by a hopeful assumption that wars could be sterilized. Not only does the general analysis avoid the question of how the 'act of navigation' served national defence, but every opportunity is taken to show the folly and needless expense of systemic and strategic measures which had been taken to ensure that, globally, maritime and monetary resources would remain available to the state.[6] While Smith's prejudice against what he termed the 'Mercantile System' is well known to historians, they have not noted his extreme ignorance of the actual ways in which overseas empire facilitated English war-making. As for his interpretation of mercantile and colonial policy, it would probably have become an antiquarian curiosity had there not emerged during the nineteenth century – at least in mainstream British experience where Pax Britannica held sway – an ever-broadening extension of secure and peaceful commercial conditions. Notwithstanding two great twentieth-century wars, the historiography of the colonial Atlantic empire has continued to focus on economic concerns and to place considerations of power and national security outside the analysis of the 'mercantile system'. The historical debate carried on during the past century over whether mercantilism was essentially concerned with 'power' or with 'plenty', though now resolved in a manner acknowledging primary roles for both, is a symptom of the conceptual compartmentalization that has dominated research.

In respect to the English Atlantic empire between 1650 and 1750, however, the historical debate should never have arisen in the form it took. Everyone then responsible for public policy thought that English wealth could not be long sustained without power to defend both trade and the realm, and also thought that England's power to defend could not be long sustained without trade and wealth. The evidence is ubiquitous and consistent. (The first place to look is to the opening words of the 1651 and 1660 navigation acts.[7]) Moreover, in the decades after *The Wealth of Nations* was published practically no one shared Smith's outlook on this question. Power and prosperity could not be separated. A question remains, of course, whether one factor was dominant. The position set forth in what follows is that, whatever appeals were made in political discourse and pressure-group manoeuvring about maximizing wealth, the state's power needs were the central concern of ruling policy-makers.

In contrast with eighteenth-century debates over home defence and European relations which, in spite of sharp differences of opinion, were generally disinterested and characterized by well-directed arguments, debates over mercantile and imperial matters were often spearheaded by special interests, and were further confused by ignorant assumptions and exaggerated hopes and fears. The method to be followed below for assessing policy during the heyday of the maritime-imperial system does not rely on the confused discourse. It concentrates on what the English government fashioned, executed and adjusted in the light of experience. It construes policy from actions, especially those that entailed predictable fiscal and political costs. In short, policy is defined here as what the state was prepared to fight and pay for, politically and financially. By this method a historian may discriminate between proposals and policy, and also perceive that lack of action in the face of probable costs and difficulties may be as historically interesting as action.[8]

EMERGENCE OF THE ATLANTIC SYSTEM 1650–1675

During most of the first era of English transatlantic expansion (c.1570–1675) the motives were various. English traders and shippers ventured to distant seas, but there was no real policy and no coherent commercial system. Fishing, coastal trade in coal and other goods, the Mediterranean and the East Indies were the large spheres in which English shipping grew fastest.[9] Taken as a whole, England's maritime activity was assuredly commercial in nature, but in regard to transatlantic activity, it is hard to find much that was commercial until quite late in the period. Granted the commercial value of fishing on the Newfoundland banks was tremendous, and the Queen's great advisor Lord Burghley well understood its contribution to national income and also as a 'nursery for seamen'.[10] Yet Tudor adventurers like Hawkins, Gilbert, Drake and Ralegh employed 'martial rather than entrepreneurial skills': while not denying the import-ance of fishing, they had other things in mind. Their activities were com-mercial only to the extent that organized crime is commercial – sometimes legitimized by active war between England and Spain, sometimes not. In either case the mode was based on the use of force and aimed at aggrandiz-ing.[11] Moreover, it appears that during Elizabeth's reign indifference and apathy were the main responses of the London merchant community and English public to distant oceanic projects.[12] All in all, it would not have been obvious in the year of Elizabeth's death that both 'the Atlantic and the oriental drives had in the long term the same general purpose in view – commercial gain'.[13]

In 1604 a new dynasty made peace with Spain, and a strong emphasis on peaceful trading quickly emerged to dominate English maritime thinking; looking at English maritime enterprise as a whole, one sees at this juncture an unmistakable swing toward commercial motives which lasted until the Civil War. Even in the transatlantic sphere, where English piratical activity was always on the verge of re-eruption, the predominant conception of enterprise became an essentially peaceable one.

None of this, however, may be taken to signify the inauguration of some coherent view of maritime policy. Most Jacobean Englishmen seemed little concerned about the neglect of the kingdom's capabilities for waging war. Their blithe attitude toward this subject has baffled modern historians as much as it frustrated the party whose mistrust of Spain never softened. To cite just one instance, English negotiators more than once refused to admit the validity of the Dutch argument that trading in the East Indies needed warship protection.[14] Generally speaking, English expansion in this period was shaped by merchants and promoters. In the sphere of trans-atlantic colonizing, social, religious and other motivations were dominant, whatever might have been said in the promotional literature about com-merce.[15] It took a while for tobacco and sugar to alter the priorities, and even then the emerging commercial focus did not translate into any consen-sus on maritime policy. The upshot was an impressive maritime expansion with manifold attributes and aspects, but no coherence in terms of state or national policy.[16] With respect to the beginnings of colonies of settle-ment one must still agree with the conclusion Charles M. Andrews reached over half a century ago: 'In other words, England began her career as the greatest and most prosperous colonizing power that the world has ever known without any fixed policy, in fact, without any clear idea of what she and her people were doing.'[17]

Only in the 1650s did an English government seriously address the task of harnessing commerce and colonial empire to the needs of national defence and state administration. To conduct a blue-water defence policy the state needed more than the naval and financial resources (mariners, auxiliary vessels, imported naval stores, commercial transactions to underpin public finance and means of replenishing specie); it also needed a few reasonably efficient bureaucracies to administer revenue collection and disbursement as well as to meet the operational requirements of the armed services. In fact, the administration of the army remained relatively underdeveloped well into the nineteenth century; this is attributable partly to political phobias and partly to heavy reliance on foreign mercenaries and subsidized allies during the eighteenth century. By contrast, the treasury and naval establishments grew rapidly and were made remarkably efficient during the century after 1650. One thinks not only of the Treasury and Admiralty boards, but also the subordinate offices: Customs, Excise, Navy, Victualling, and Sick and Wounded Seamen. Most visibly, the period witnessed a huge expansion of the naval dockyards. The contrast serves to underline the naval and financial emphasis of the English state's new national security policy.

The path toward long-term administrative effectiveness lay in disengaging revenue collection from expenditures and services and adhering to methods of public finance that did least economic and administrative harm. Without a thriving commerce to facilitate taxation, borrowing and liquidity, such methods were beyond the reach of most states in the early-modern era. These features would distinguish this 'fiscal-military state' from all its rivals on the continent except the Dutch republic.

Developing these English sinews of power was mainly the work of six decades, roughly from 1650 to about 1710. Of course, the altercations of the rulers and their Parliaments occasionally interrupted the course, but looking back upon it from a historical distance one sees that the task was pursued with consistency and determination. The whole business seems to have proceeded as if the notable constitutional fractures of 1660 and 1688, and the changes in attitude and style from Oliver Cromwell to Charles II to James II to William III, made little difference to its progress. The main reason for this administrative continuity through a period of political upheaval is that this system of power was congenial not only to the Lord Protector, the later Stuart monarchs, William III and Anne, but also to Members of Parliament and the public.[18] There was no clear plan, no single directing hand in the manner of a Colbert, and progress often came in unforeseen ways; but the goals were widely understood from the outset, and men like Sir George Downing, Sir William Coventry, Samuel Pepys and William Blathwayt instinctively and effectively pursued them.

The year 1650 may be fixed upon as the moment of beginning. In that year the need of the English state for a permanent navy that could control the surrounding seas and defend trade became unmistakable. Actually, the need had begun to emerge in the 1630s, but merchants and shippers then had too many reasons for doubting whether the Crown would develop a navy useful for their purposes; Charles I's 'ship money' navy was not well adapted to the task of protecting trade. By 1650 the leaders of the revolutionary state had ample cause to remember how the parliamentary navy had deprived royalist forces of continental assistance during the Civil War, and their conception of the defence of the commonwealth involved not only securing the kingdom from invasion but also its commercial interests.

There were also in the year 1650 particular circumstances that argued for maintaining a strong navy. The navy was indispensable to the consolidation of power in Ireland and the overseas colonies, and rendered important military assistance in subduing Scotland. It could be used to intimidate ports and kingdoms that gave help to Prince Rupert, who roamed the seas harassing English shipping. It soon proved itself to be a ready and effective instrument for fending off external threats and instilling awe and caution among foreign princes and predators. English merchants and ship-owners, operating under a pariah regime, found their goods and ships to be uncommonly at risk in European waters, and they naturally pressed the government for protection and commercial leverage. The regime did not hesitate to answer the call, and the English navy quickly and unprecedentedly extended its commerce protection beyond the 'British seas' to the western Atlantic and Mediterranean.[19] Above all, the regime sensed the danger inherent in Dutch maritime prowess. With this threat in mind the momentous Navigation Act of 1651 was passed.[20]

The specific provisions of this statute reveal how purposefully it was directed toward the long-term goal of ensuring an independent foundation for English naval power.[21] As a distinguished historian of British expansion observed, 'the Navigation Act of 1651 must be taken out of the category of commercial measures and placed amongst the efforts made by the Commonwealth to equip the country with a sea power adequate to its security'.[22] Soon after, in 1652 and 1653, came the massive build-up of an English battle-fleet to defeat the Dutch navy in the First Dutch War. All this added up to the most profound change in the English navy's long history.

After the Dutch War ended, Oliver Cromwell demonstrated again and again, notwithstanding the navy's huge cost and the persistent weakness of Interregnum finances, how much he was willing to risk in order to keep it in being. Still, this 'New Model Navy' almost died in infancy because the Cromwellian state could scarcely finance its continuance. The Spanish war of 1655 was undertaken in the hope that the navy could be kept in being by capturing treasure in the West Indies, and in that respect it failed.[23] Cromwell never found a way to pay for maintaining both a strong navy and a strong army, and he would not – politically, could not – reduce the army. Parliament's fruitless struggles to reduce the expense and political position of the army had the side-effect of inhibiting votes of supply for the navy. In fact, the financial drain caused by trying to maintain both forces contributed significantly to the crisis that brought the regime down.[24]

When Charles II came to the throne, however, he reduced the army of 60,000 men to a mere 6,000 'guards'. Steady parliamentary support for a permanent navy thus became feasible, in terms of both cost and the preferences of Members of Parliament. A durable political basis now existed for developing the 'Royal Navy'. It was Charles's idea to give it that official name. He, and also his brother James as Lord High Admiral, recognized the navy's contribution to the power and prestige of the English monarchy. Thus the restored monarchy rescued the 'New Model Navy' from impending ruin and put it on a permanent and increasingly professional footing.[25] In the year of the Restoration the navigation laws were promptly re-enacted in revised form.[26] The act of 1660 and the subsequent amplifying and amending statutes, while designed in some degree to augment national wealth and induce favourable specie flows, were carefully drawn with urgent needs of the state in view – that is, to develop English maritime sinews and customs revenues. These statutes provided the backbone of policy in the Atlantic empire.[27]

The original American settlements were, of course, the product of private enterprise, and the framework of the English Atlantic trading system was first laid down in a small and informal way by New England merchants, before the Navigation acts existed and without state intervention.[28] However, in the quarter-century after 1650 the English state was aggressively active overseas. Not only were the navigation laws elaborated in this period, but in addition Jamaica was captured (1655), the predecessor of the African Company was created (in the early 1660s) and New Netherlands was taken, lost and retaken. The bid to take over most of the African slave-trade and the decisions to capture and to retain New Netherlands were compatible with the needs of an emerging maritime trading system.[29] Of course, private enrichment was a motive, but these moves succeeded not only in elbowing the then primary maritime rival out of important trading positions, but also in expanding commerce and navigation. (New Netherlands offered the positive advantages of a centrally located seaboard territory with important rivers that opened the way to the interior, but by taking it the English also diminished Dutch shippers' chances of serving English settlers and planters.[30]) Admittedly, Jamaica was an exception; its capture was not designed to extend or consolidate a trading system but rather to provide a base for further plunder. Thus it was initially a privateering base and often a pirate base. Yet, as we shall see, Jamaica's trade with Spanish America became in due course more important than privateering – indeed, became a crucial building-block in the maritime-imperial system. Surveying the situation in 1675, one notes that Pennsylvania, Georgia and Nova Scotia were still to be founded, but nevertheless by that year 'the English had declared and defended an Atlantic maritime empire' whose primary purpose from the government's viewpoint was to foster commerce and shipping.[31]

On the other hand, the patterns in which transatlantic commerce and shipping thrived were almost entirely the creations of private merchants and mariners, not of the state. The state had added and consolidated territories and given its formal blessing; there was sponsorship in high places, and concerned committees and councils were formed; regulations and restrictions were imposed; but the measure of direction, assistance and shelter given to transatlantic commerce by the English state's navy, army or treasury was very slim. Unlike the Mediterranean trades, the transatlantic trades enjoyed almost no naval protection until many years had passed. In fact, in the later seventeenth century English traders in the Caribbean received less naval assistance from home than did their French rivals.[32] Whitehall was remarkably slow to take the diplomatic and naval steps required to defend the islands and keep commercial access to Spanish America open, and even slower to offer naval assistance in North America except with regard to the fisheries. Naval protection of English transoceanic shipping followed rather than led its expansion.

Still, in view of the steps that the state did take, one must regard it as an actuating force in developing the Atlantic empire between 1650 and 1675. After that it was a shaping and containing force, and even in this role its imperial directing power was restrained by material and political considerations. Granted there were moments when Charles II and James II seemed bent on bringing the whole operation under strict rules and authority (the Dominion of New England scheme is an obvious instance). They were frustrated first by colonial obstructionism and eventually by adverse political circumstances at home, but that is not the main point here. The main point is that Kings, Councils and Parliaments well knew that the goal was to develop resources of wealth and naval power. These were recognized as obvious necessities of state in an increasingly dangerous European world. Looking to a greater royal revenue from growing commerce, and wary of injuring, or even appearing to injure, the nation's maritime strength, a penurious later Stuart monarchy not only felt the constraints but also accepted competent advice which allowed the resources to develop.

HEYDAY OF THE SYSTEM 1675–1750

The maritime-imperial system was based on a *quid pro quo*. The metropolitan government wanted customs revenues, naval resources and expanding wealth that would facilitate taxes and loans. Colonists, merchants and shippers acquiesced in trade regulation and acknowledged London's authority, in return for naval protection and participation in a large, privileged shipping and marketing arena.[33] Even when the collar of metropolitan authority was tightened, there was no serious colonial wish to escape the system. Necessity played a role here. New England, for instance, was well marked early for its independent spirit, but its maritime entrepreneurs had really no practical alternative to the emerging system because the difficulties of standing alone in the world of seventeenth-century seaborne commerce were forbidding. If the New Englanders were to link their fortunes to Bourbon France, their carrying trade would be subject to English restrictions and possibly become prey to predators commissioned against them by the English Crown. If they did not link up with France, their fishing to the northward would be exposed to French depredations.[34]

Regarding the naval aspect of the quid pro quo, it has already been hinted that the Royal Navy's presence in Caribbean and North American waters was not adequate in the second half of the seventeenth century – nothing like the degree of protection the government gave to Mediterranean shipping. Two or three cruisers were put on station in the Caribbean during the 1680s, but when the first great war with France came in 1689 the colonial shippers were badly let down. They could take some comfort in knowing that they were not the only sufferers; trade protection in all seas was sacrificed to William III's policy of employing his naval force to assist strategic campaigns in Europe.[35]

Toward the end of the 1689–97 war the government began to take a special interest in the Caribbean (Rear-Admiral John Benbow was sent out with a squadron of men of war). At the war's end, an English effort to suppress piracy, which had been launched more in form than substance in the 1680s, was revived. This effort was partly stultified because of a scandalous, quasi-public scheme which employed Captain Kidd for the purpose. The regular navy also participated in the general effort, but the return of war and legitimate privateering after only five years cut it short.[36] When peace returned in 1714, however, naval patrolling against pirates on the far side of the Atlantic took on a new dimension, and by the late 1720s it appears that most transatlantic trading ships were able to dispense with deck guns. One factor contributing to successful suppression in the post–1714 decade was French co-operation. The result was a momentous achievement:

> Indeed, the remarkable thing is . . . that they should finally have been
> put down at all. The English and French Governments contrived to
> suppress their own pirates. It was perhaps the first time in the history
> of the modern world that such a thing had happened.[37]

The British navy's determination to keep a continuous presence in the West Indies may be seen in its establishment of permanent, well-equipped bases for cleaning and refitting at Antigua and Jamaica, the first bases of this calibre outside European waters except for Spain's growing arsenal at Havana.[38] The French navy's facilities did not begin to match, so Britain enjoyed the strategic advantages of longer deployment.[39] By the 1730s the stationing of ships in American waters in peacetime became the rule rather than the exception; those based in North America were supplied and serviced locally through private contractors but usually went to Antigua and Jamaica in winter to be refitted.[40] The earliest British naval base on the North American coastline was Halifax, a project begun in 1749. All in all, the quid pro quo was approximately in balance. If colonial naval protection was minimal in the seventeenth century, so also was the enforcement of commercial regulation. When regulatory enforcement was somewhat tightened in the later 1690s, it coincided with a policy of strengthening naval protection, and that policy endured.

The efficacy of naval protection after 1714 also signalled the emergence of a viable and mature system based on trade rather than plunder. Whereas before the 1660s economic theoreticians as well as bold adventurers had tended to be transfixed by mines and precious metals – the allure of sudden riches by discovery or plunder – trade was now seen to be a superior form of venturing because it created not just wealth but sinews of power:

> Spain, indeed, has greater countries and more subjects in America, than we have, and yet does not navigate in that trade a tenth part of the shipping that we do. By a lucky kind of poverty, our dominions there have no mines of gold or silver: we must be and ought to be, contented to deal in rum, sugar, rice, tobacco, horses, beef, corn, fish, lumber and other commodities that require great stowage; the perpetual carriages of these, employ above 100,000 tons of shipping. The value of 5000*l.* in these wares loads a vessel, which in the Spanish trade would be freighted homeward with half a million of pounds sterling.

The author of this reasoning (Malachy Postlethwayt, an inexhaustible enunciator of eighteenth-century mercantilism) went on: 'Thus the Almighty placed the true riches of this earth on the surface of it'; sugar, rice, tobacco and the like, having to be shipped, create thereby 'a power to defend our possession of them' without which 'all wealth is precarious'.[41] In this view two kinds of resources were being magnified, and the second kind served to protect not only national wealth, as Postlethwayt noted, but also national security and prestige. In 1735 another writer summed up the connections succinctly: 'That our trade is the Mother and Nurse of our Seamen; Our Seamen the Life of our Fleet; And our Fleet the Security and Protection of our Trade: And that both together are the WEALTH, STRENGTH, and GLORY of GREAT BRITAIN'.[42]

Some key features of policy in respect to this mature Atlantic system may be noted. First, diplomacy was resolutely directed toward sustaining it. Great Britain negotiated the treaty of Utrecht with a view toward upholding a protected trading system that had access to the Mediterranean and the Spanish Empire. These are the most salient of innumerable instances of diplomatic concern for trade and navigation throughout the period.[43] Second, the British government's proclivity for holding down the costs of colonial defence – evinced to a fault in the seventeenth century – remained an important influence on imperial policy during the first half of the eighteenth century. The accent was meant to be as little military and as largely commercial as circumstances would allow. The responsible Secretary of State, Shrewsbury, suggested in 1695: 'I would . . . humbly offer that the Governors may have more of the breeding of merchants than soldiers, and not of a quality or humour too big for their business or salaries, or the people they must converse among, men of business and some experience'.[44] After 1682 the only permanent garrison supplied by the Crown was that in New York. By contrast, French administration in North America acquired, early on, a distinctly military character, and Crown infusions for maintaining French troops were an important source of cash for Canada.[45] Of course, there were elements of military culture in English colonial rule, but the contrast with French Canada is striking, and it is chiefly due to mercantile objectives, which created a different set of administrative needs and a different atmosphere.[46] A third point is that the government, while holding down its military costs in the colonies, gave substantial naval support to defence of trade in American waters, especially the Caribbean. The Royal Navy's establishment of permanent naval bases across the Atlantic was indicative of the firmness of its commitment; the proof of naval effectiveness is that peacetime insurance rates fell.[47]

The maturity of the maritime-imperial system is also revealed by its success. The immense growth of commerce and shipping within the English Atlantic trading system is undeniable.[48] It involved triangular oceanic trades, direct trade from America to southern Europe, shuttle trades between North America and the Caribbean, coastal trades and so on. The multilateralism reflected a specialization of commodity production and of services. There was intense competition within the imperial system as well as in the foreign markets to which it had access.[49] The destination of exports from Great Britain shifted dramatically away from traditional European markets and toward imperial markets.[50] By 1750 North America had become transformed into a tremendously important market for British manufactured goods. With regard to shipping, it has been estimated that already in 1686 38 per cent of English tonnage was engaged in transatlantic trading, and at least 50 per cent of English foreign-going ships were engaged in that region eighty years later, on the eve of the American Revolution, notwithstanding the general expansion of English shipping in the East Indies and other regions.[51] Clearly, the Atlantic maritime-imperial system was successful in terms both of prosperity through commerce and of augmentation of maritime sinews of power.

The size and security of the system contributed mightily to its success;

but success also stemmed from its multilateral complexity, responsiveness and openness, and this raises an important question about policy: was the degree of multilateral openness (which will be described more fully in what follows) the intent of the mother country's policy or contrary to it? It has been too easy for historians to suppose that one key element in this, colonial traders' access to non-British markets, was simply an unintended consequence of imperial neglect and corruption.

A preliminary step in dealing with this great question is to understand the significance of terms like 'illegal', 'illicit' or 'contraband'. Such terms may apply to trading which, though forbidden by foreign authorities, was not forbidden by the English government. For instance, although English trade with Spanish America was in most respects forbidden by Spanish laws, it was not forbidden by English commercial laws. Similarly, English peacetime trade with the French West Indies was generally forbidden by French laws, but for many decades not by English. The French government frequently protested that England was bound by treaty to prohibit such trade, but time and again during the eighteenth century, high legal authority in London set forth opinions holding that trade of this sort did not contravene British laws so long as it was carried on in British (including British-empire) vessels.[52]

These facts serve to unveil certain priorities. Maximizing profitable commerce and seeing it carried on in British ships were more important government objectives than was placing a general curb on colonial trade with foreigners. It should be noted that British trade with the French islands, while it was known to abet French sugar productivity, tended to discourage the growth of the French merchant marine. The contraband trade with Spanish America was strongly favoured by the British government, as will become clear, since a third priority was to promote an influx of bullion into the system.

It is therefore a great error to imagine that the thriving multilateralism of the British Atlantic trading system arose from unwanted leakiness, from corrupt evasions which authorities should have tried to halt, from ministerial ignorance and indifference rather than awareness, from 'salutary neglect' rather than considered priorities. The maritime-imperial system in its heyday was rigid on some matters and quite open on others. The flexibility denoted by particular or general relaxations did not arise merely or mainly because certain regulations proved to be unpopular or unenforceable, but because they were found to operate against the goals that held priority.

From this it may be inferred that the goal of a 'self-sufficient economic empire' was not in actuality given high priority during the period before 1750. The idea that self-sufficiency was the overriding objective of colonial policy – allegedly the (mercantilist) guiding principle of the 'Old Colonial System' – crops up almost everywhere in historical literature. Certainly the idea permeated many mercantilist tracts and may be found in a good many statutes. Like the 'balance of trade' it could be handily invoked by lobbyists, and in a mercantilist age it seemed logical – especially when the focus was on the issue of whether colonial products could substitute for foreign imports. To assess how English policy-makers weighed the attractions of 'self-sufficiency' against other goals and priorities, it is necessary to do what theorists and advocates of the time rarely did – that is, to consider the trading system as a whole rather than just colonial commodities.[53]

The issue of vital strategic materials provides the best litmus test. On the surface it appears that, through encouragements and restrictions, self-sufficiency in such materials – all were naval materials – was earnestly sought. Even in this vital sector, however, the measures enacted early in the eighteenth century, when hostilities curtailed Baltic supplies, were later allowed to drift into minor significance, for self-sufficiency was not a realistic goal. The government might reserve for the navy all the large masts in New England, but most small and medium-sized masts continued to come from Norway; it was wiser strategically and economically to obtain them nearby. Tar from any other source than Sweden rarely met the standard for naval rope-making. Getting Americans to produce hemp was impossible; the Russian product shipped from Riga continued to be the mainstay. So, in reality, northern Europe continued to be the main source. Naval and diplomatic power were applied throughout the eighteenth century to ensure access to the Baltic, and a chronically unfavourable balance of trade with that region was accepted. The specie deficit there was satisfied multilaterally.

The trade of the American colonies was far more multilateral than is commonly supposed. Enumerated commodities from America were channelled to Britain, but other goods could legally go straight to European ports if carried in British-flag vessels. Southern Europe was an important market for American goods. The primary markets for North Atlantic fish were Iberia and the western Mediterranean. Moreover, during the eighteenth century the navigation acts were eased and the method of customs collection revised so that some enumerated products from the mainland colonies, such as rice, could be shipped to ports 'south of Cape Finisterre'. In fact, English and North American vessels called so often at Lisbon that a recent study has declared that port to have been part of 'the English Atlantic'.[54]

All this points to a policy that favoured increased volume of trade and 'traffick' (a word that often implied multilateralism as well as carriage and volume of business) over self-sufficiency and particular trade balances, so long as English shipping was used and the best sources of customs revenue were shielded. Strict attention to particular trade balances would have tended to reduce England's trading-pattern to an array of bilateral spokes, and in reality this was not allowed to happen.

The London government's concern for the Spanish-American trade further reveals the tilt of *de facto* policy toward multilateralism and openness. Spanish and Portuguese coins were essential nutrients, without which the complex trading of the English Atlantic would have been stunted. Through this medium various trade imbalances were neutralized. Eighteenth-century Englishmen were not bullionists, but they knew that precious metals constantly flowed out to the Baltic and East Indies. Policymakers were also aware – agonizingly after 1689 – of the drain on specie caused by financing military campaigns in Europe.[55] Everyone moderately acquainted with American trade knew that hard money from the foreign Caribbean was vital enabling the more northerly American colonists to purchase British manufactured goods.[56] The money flowed northward in payment for food, lumber and other basic supplies needed in the Caribbean. By this trade, especially the trade with Spanish possessions, 'England was able to drain some of "the benefit of the Spanish gold and silver mines" without the "labour and expense" of working them.'[57] As long as the trade was carried on in English ships, English officialdom regarded it as legal. It was clandestine because it contravened Spanish law and clauses in Anglo-Spanish treaties by which the English government had promised to forbid it. Since the English government usually wished to avoid offending Madrid, for both diplomatic and commercial reasons (the trade through Cadiz also brought in hard money), it enunciated prohibitions but did not follow through. The diplomatic dance of the two countries during the eighteenth century was understandably awkward and embarrassing.[58]

The trade was based on Jamaica, but the vessels engaged in it came from all over the empire.[59] In the beginning, the sale of African slaves to the Spanish territories was the major element, and to secure this lucrative trade London allowed Spanish ships, but no other foreigners, to call at Jamaican ports. Toward the end of the seventeenth century, as the range of commodities expanded and the English Atlantic system grew, the money came to be regarded as indispensable. It was therefore in the Caribbean that London's thoughts about defence of the overseas empire were centred before 1750. During the 1690s two English regiments were stationed at Jamaica. Acute rivalries – first with the Dutch, though this was replaced in the 1680s by fears that the French would (by force or by diplomatic influence at the court of Madrid) monopolize Spanish-American trade – were the main considerations that shaped policy in the Caribbean.[60] Nevertheless, trade with the French islands (in British vessels) was still permitted during the first half of the eighteenth century. It may seem that the Molasses Act of 1733, which placed a prohibitive duty on such trading, represents a triumph for a 'mercantilist' policy of closure; but it was the British sugar interest, seeking to protect its profits by invoking arguments about the national danger posed by rising French sugar production, not the British government, that wanted the measure. In the years that followed, the government disclosed its own priorities by allowing a farcical level of enforcement to persist.[61] One other reason why the trade with French and Dutch islands was permitted – only in British ships – was that return cargoes could be more readily found, thus tending toward a more profitable and thriving shipping industry.[62] Not until 1763 did the British government decide that the benefits of cutting off commerce with a rival power even in peacetime outweighed the benefits of enlarging the imperial money supply and shipping pool.

It has been all too common, especially in the earlier historiography, to forget how seriously the question of 'navigation' was taken.[63] ('Navigation' as they used the word meant both shipping and traffic.) In time of peace the rules pertaining to shipping were tight and so was enforcement. Yet on the whole colonial shippers benefited since all parts of the empire enjoyed the privileges of this protected sphere equally. Constraints on colonial shipbuilders and owners, when proposed by shipbuilding interests in England, were turned away or soon disposed of by the government.[64] The northern colonies were in a good position to seize the opportunities; availability of timber and spars, plus a degree of immunity from naval impressment, actually gave the colonists some advantages.[65] The plantation colonies, inconvenienced at the beginning, were soon able to count on the services of a vast and competitive system.[66] The combination of colonial shipbuilding and carriage also helped British North America reduce the huge deficits it incurred in its commodities trade.[67] (By contrast, French regulation tended to discourage multilateralism in the Atlantic by chaining ships to metropolitan ports.[68]) Freight may have been the second most lucrative North American export after tobacco.[69] What Great Britain gained, of course, was imperial maritime strength – a large, inexpensively created pool of transport vessels and trained mariners.

On the whole, then, the pattern of British Atlantic trade and navigation prior to 1750 essentially reflected London's policy. To be sure, confusion of aims, unenforceability and neglect were part of the picture, but there were very strong positive reasons why certain 'mercantilist' principles were contravened.[70] In the corridors of power as well as in the press the claims of self-sufficiency and a favourable balance of trade were often heard, but other claims were heard as well: 'traffick', navigation, mariners, royal revenue, hard money for currency and preserving the mother country's main export markets from colonial competition. In practice, these held priority over the more generalized and sometimes mutually contradictory principles of 'mercantilism'.

Our concentration thus far has been on commerce, but one task remains to complete the analysis of the maritime-imperial system in its heyday. What roles did colonies and conquests play?

To discover the real priorities one needs to take a close look at why certain possessions were fought for and kept, and others not. The possessions most valued were those that (1) served to assist and protect 'nurseries of seamen'; (2) offered strategically located naval bases; (3) provided strategic materials for the navy; (4) were well situated for lucrative trading; and (5) offered commodities whose shipment could enhance navigation, royal revenues and re-exports. An example of each, in order, would be: Newfoundland, Antigua, New Hampshire, Jamaica and, for the last, all the plantation colonies. (No priority of importance is implied by the list's order.) Colonies, as Peggy Liss has written, were in this era looked upon as 'adjuncts of empire rather than integral parts of it'; 'Empire did not solely, or even primarily, mean territory'. Although England sometimes engaged in hostilities against the Spanish in the New World, the English wanted no territory from them. She quotes Defoe (1707): 'We want not the dominion of more countries than we have; we sufficiently possess a nation when we have an open and free trade to it'. Along with this went the view that possession, settlement, governance and territorial defence entailed needless and unwise costs, so long as trade could be carried on otherwise.[71] One may see here the conception of what a later age would call 'informal empire'.

Between the 1670s and the later 1740s this disposition of policy fended off the popular clamour for taking on new territories to be developed. Although at first glance it may look as though Great Britain waged war overseas to capture fountain-heads of commerce and especially of a rival's commerce – French sugar islands, for instance – the historical record shows that captured places of this sort were generally returned at the peace-table. Strategically, the capture of an island might be undertaken for a number of reasons: to obtain a prize easily acquired through superior seapower for exchange at the peace-table in recouping setbacks elsewhere; to deprive the enemy's treasury in wartime of revenues generated by the island's trade; to occupy a base used by enemy privateers or naval squadrons; to develop it as a British base; and to 'capture trade', that is, add the island's production to the empire's resources. Only the last two of these clearly pointed to permanent retention, and only the last was a commercial object. During the seventy-five years before 1750 there was in fact no instance where the government contemplated retention mainly for a commercial object. Even in the 1750s and 1760s non-commercial considerations dominated policy decisions.[72]

One factor was that statesmen shied away from political complications. British West Indian planters, who feared the competitive weight of added production within the system, generally opposed retention of foreign sugar islands.[73] However, the main factor was that statesmen avoided the costs and responsibilities of new territory unless there was a compelling strategic consideration. The captured places most likely to be retained after a successful war were those that facilitated and lowered the long-run expense of defending existing British resources, or else offered locations for bases that could monitor and inhibit an enemy's sea communications.

Of course, annexation for the purpose of bolstering defences or holding in check the growth of a rival's seaborne trade can be limitlessly rationalized, and thus the logic of maritime empire could readily lead to territorial aggrandizement. This may be labelled 'defensive annexation' – a seemingly inexorable process. Defensive annexation undeniably and decisively influenced the course of territorial expansion in the two decades after 1750, but the process was not much in evidence before 1750. The only instance of its occurring in the Atlantic sphere during the first half of the eighteenth century was the establishment of Georgia in 1733. In time of war, London had its eye on maritime defensive positions generally, and sometimes ordered attacks on Spanish trade centres, but did not promote a strategy of permanent conquest either in the Caribbean or on the North American continent.

To students of American colonial history this proposition may seem strange. Were there not numerous expeditions against French or Spanish settlements and against their Indian allies? There were, but before 1750 they were initiated in the colonies and relied very heavily upon colonial soldiers. The plans were not hatched in London. The low wartime priority given by Whitehall to North American defence was consistently evident, though on a number of occasions a small measure of naval assistance was supplied.[74] This minimalist policy persisted in time of peace. Colonial governors expressed their concerns, and the Board of Trade in 1721 urged that the defence of British North America, now managed with 'a very sparing hand', should be 'thought worthy of greater attention'. Yet, even though the board rested its case on the need to protect customs revenues, trade and navigation, almost nothing was done.[75]

Defensive annexation was not characteristic of the First British Empire until after 1750. Improving the defence of British North America, however great the French menace on the inland or northern perimeter might seem to colonists, was not considered in Whitehall to be worth the expense. The position in the Caribbean was considered in a different light. The primary aims were to protect British sugar plantations and prevent France from dominating trade with New Spain. Statesmen and public understood that if the commercial regulation of Spanish America were to fall under France's more efficient direction, British trade would be closed out. That was utterly unacceptable: it was worth fortifying bases and fighting wars to prevent it. Yet territorial annexation scarcely occurred. A number of Spanish peripheral positions could have been easily taken (perhaps not so easily held), but the British government by treaty in 1714 renounced any intention of annexing Spanish territory in the New World and adhered to that policy for a long time. Preservation of Caribbean traffic and suspicion of French manipulations at Madrid were more influential in the British government's decision to go to war against Spain in 1739 than is commonly recognized.

In sum, the controlling idea in Whitehall before 1750 was to hold the costs of imperial defence and administration to a minimum, to keep transoceanic military activity overseas confined, and to fight with and for maritime advantages.[76] Any policy that failed to do this was missing the point. In homespun terms, the Atlantic empire was a 'back-yard' in which sinews of war were generated for use in the 'front-yard', that is to say, in Europe and European seas.

THE SYSTEM SUBVERTED 1750–1775

All this changed during the next two decades. The Anglo-French Seven Years War, although its great naval contests still took place in and around Europe, was essentially a contest for empire, and impressive numbers of British regular troops campaigned in North America. By the peace terms of 1763 vast territories on that continent were acquired from France and Spain. The British government immediately decided to place a large peace-time force of regular troops in North America, announcing that it would be paid for by the colonists. The consequent need for a sizeable, visibly American revenue led to an immediate tightening of customs collection, which entailed significant restrictions on North American trading, an imposition of new duties and the passage of the Stamp Act.

Historical attention has focused chiefly on the Stamp Act (1765) and the enormous ire it aroused in the colonies; but the changes most relevant here are the measures of 1763–4 which overturned the tradition of minimal military expense in North America and deliberately constrained the multilateral flexibility by which British colonial trade in the Atlantic had blossomed. The standard textbook accounts have generally presumed that British statesmen in those immediate post-war years had no choice but to pursue such measures. Of course, the measures proved disastrous, but that has been dismissed as unforeseeable at the time. For our purposes the interesting point is that the new policies were egregiously inappropriate to the Atlantic empire anyway.

This last section begins by discussing the decision to place a large army of British regulars in America and then turns to the sweeping measures affecting American commerce which were introduced by 1764. The remainder of the section is devoted to the background of change – an exploratory tracing of the circumstances which gave rise to the new line of policy.

On 4 March 1763 the ministry of Lord Bute proposed to Parliament that the country should maintain the largest peacetime army in its history; 21 battalions of British regulars (10,000 soldiers) would be stationed across the Atlantic; 7,500 were slated for garrisoning North America. Presenting the estimates, the Secretary of State for War informed the House that in 1749 'you had only 4 battalions in America. Now you will have the foundations of a great army there'. No attempt was made to disguise what was being done and no one could doubt that this would mean a tremendous new expense.[77]

Probably because the expense was to be borne by the colonists, neither in Parliament nor, evidently, within the ministry was the necessity of this large force seriously debated, and it is therefore not easy to ascertain the rationale. George III himself upon learning that a Member of Parliament had questioned the need for so many soldiers responded: 'As to the ten thousand men in America, that is become necessary from our successes.'[78] Recently it has been argued that the King and his cohorts considered a large garrison in North America to be necessary for defence against a retaliatory attack by France or Spain, and there is some evidence to indicate that when the King first turned his attention to the matter this was uppermost in his mind. Evidently, Bute also became persuaded of the danger.[79] They may have sincerely believed this; William Pitt professed to believe it.[80]

If so, it is an interesting error. In 1763 France no longer had any strategic purchase on the North American continent. By the treaty terms Britain kept Canada and added East and West Florida, all the way to the Mississippi River. France had no bases or harbours except New Orleans. Moreover, Britain was now able to dominate, by means of three or four forts at well-chosen choke-points, all rivers that gave access to the American interior. Without river access the French (or Spanish) would be unable to give meaningful assistance or direction to Indian or French-settler insurgency. In 1749 this had not been the case. Then the cold war in North America had been intense; the allocation of effort and expense to resisting French encroachment in Nova Scotia, for instance, was at that time strategically unavoidable. But in the Seven Years War Britain's primary war-aim, once success was assured, was to simplify and reduce the burden of defending its American territories and commerce. That aim was achieved in 1763. From the standpoint of defending against powerful rivals the military requirements in North America should have been much less than those in 1749. Proposals to expel France from the North American continent had always rested on this very point, and the decision to keep Canada was clearly a prime instance of defensive annexation.

It is amazing that strategic considerations which had dominated practically all discussion before 1756 were so little remembered in 1763. As John Murrin has suggested, Englishmen were apparently unable to assimilate the fact that their nation had won the war and thereby rendered North America strategically secure: 'London by-passed the lessons of victory to embrace projects stimulated by fear of defeat.'[81] At least one person, however, did recognize realities. In the papers of Charles Jenkinson (Bute's secretary) there survives a memorandum dated 10 March 1763 which argued that there was minimal need for new forts and garrisons beyond those taken over from the French and Spanish: 'while we maintain our superiority at Sea', this writer argued, the continent stands safe from 'being invaded by a formidable enemy; & 'tis needless to erect forts to keep ye trees in subjection'. The argument continues:

> As our territories in North America are bounded every where by water, excepting towards ye north, where they are inaccessible, they may be looked upon entirely as an island; therefore as they have no internal enemy but Indians, who may be easily made friends, their proper defense is not land forts, but a naval force, which we ought to keep always ready to be exerted. In that case, tho' there were not a man in actual service in ye Colonies, they would have nothing now to fear from a European Enemy; for a formidable armament could not sail from Europe in secret.

'The French cannot now as formerly steal over one Regiment after another', he continued, except to New Orleans, and a fort at Natchez could prevent any further penetration.[82] No notice was taken of this memorandum by the administration then nor has it attracted any attention since. Benjamin Franklin mapped out an argument along similar lines three years later but never concluded or published it.[83]

Of course, the Indians could not be so 'easily made friends' as the writer supposed. Important tribes before and after the Pontiac uprising hoped for a French return and expressed this hope often enough to alarm British traders, army officers and civil officials. British authorities sincerely, though mistakenly, believed that the French had a hand in promoting such uprisings.[84] No doubt, this belief helped to sustain the idea that the British troops were there to defend against French and Spanish machinations. In any case, the government found it expedient to focus public attention on strategic defence against Bourbon power and influence.

British parliaments had traditionally opposed large budgets for the army in peacetime. Moreover, though the actual annual cost of the army in North America during the six years after 1763 became triple that of the period from 1749 to 1755, and no evidence materialized of any immediate threat from the Bourbon rivals, the expense was allowed to continue.[85] All this commitment to a new military expense without critical examination of the strategic arguments justifying it would, of course, have been inconceivable if the government had not promised that American colonists would be paying for it.

Although this crucial promise quenched controversy, it also meant that a substantial revenue had to be visibly collected in America. The task fell to George Grenville, who moved over from the Admiralty to the Treasury and became Prime Minister in April 1763. Heads of the Treasury in the eighteenth century, as now, were commonly disposed to question new or heavy expenditures. Although Grenville recognized straightaway that American revenues could not cover more than about one-third of the cost,[86] he never murmured about the large army in America. Tightening customs collection was something he wanted to do anyway, and the military plan gave him an urgent reason for pursuing this vigorously.

When Grenville was still at the Admiralty, legislation was passed which empowered warships in American waters to enforce trade restrictions. Royal Navy captains were deputized as customs officials, and officers and crew were allotted half the value of condemned cargoes and vessels as an incentive. Although the navy had traditionally assisted customs officials upon request, especially in wartime, this direct and interested role in peacetime was new. The service which had long protected British imperial trade in time of war was now authorized and encouraged in time of peace to prey upon British merchant vessels whose paperwork was not in proper order.[87]

The main statutory instrument for collecting duties and enforcing restrictions was the Sugar Act (4 Geo. III, c. 15). It is sometimes called the Revenue Act of 1764, and the connection between this statute and the need to support the expense of defending America is stated in its preamble.[88] The choice of new dutiable items, the character of most of the enforcement clauses and the discussions within the Treasury branch during the bill's formative period all point to a strong emphasis on revenue.[89]

Yet, although the act appears to have aimed primarily at revenue collection, the effects of the whole programme were so devastating to colonial commerce as to make one wonder. A New York merchant remarked in July 1764 that 'The floating Customs Houses ... Distress us in Our Trade ... and the Laws Latly [sic] made in London [the Sugar Act] will Compleat Our Ruin'.[90] Taken together, the sweeping powers and immunities given to enforcers by the Sugar Act, the exacting documentation required and the ferocity of naval enforcement caused severe disruption. The severity was not introduced just for the purpose of generating an 'American revenue'.

More than any other statute of the eighteenth century the Sugar Act opened up basic questions as to the uses of the Atlantic empire. Its preamble stated that, in addition to revenue, its purpose was to regulate trade, with a view toward 'extending and securing the navigation and commerce between Great Britain and your Majesty's dominions in America'. On the basis of evidence which there is not space to display here, it is certain that the Grenville ministry was intent on tightening and confining the trading system. The rationale was expounded in a pamphlet, *The Regulations Lately Made concerning the Colonies*, written by Thomas Whately in order to justify the ministry's American programme.[91]

The pamphlet's arguments are diffuse. Its commercial principles are ostentatiously derived from the authority of statutes passed a century earlier. Whately claimed to regard the original Act of Navigation as the fundamental repository of England's principles of trade and treated it as holy writ. The leading objective of the navigation acts, he believed, had been to proscribe all colonial foreign trade. The intention had been to bind the colonies more closely. The new trade regulations were thus designed to 'cement' the colonies to the mother country – to render 'their Communication with the Mother Country more frequent, and their Dependence upon it more secure'.[92] Whately's conceptual framework ruled out any attempt to understand the realities of the maritime-imperial system. It was blind to money-flows. It adhered to the simple dogma that colonial trade with foreigners was an 'evil'.[93]

Many historians have supposed that the regulatory programme of 1763–4 was a well-considered effort to restore continuity and redress problems and weaknesses that had developed in the Atlantic commercial system. In reality, the Grenville administration – full of confident rectitude but without attention to expert advice, even from its own customs department – instituted a deluded, reactionary overthrow of three-quarters of a century of successful development. While the statesmen who imposed these constraints professed to believe, and probably did believe, that they were bolstering and improving the commercial and maritime system, they understood neither the system nor the manner in which it served Great Britain's vital needs.

It was not until 1768 that anyone in England presented to the public a studied critique of these delusions. Thomas Pownall was a former Governor of Massachusetts who had been pondering the whole question since at least 1764. Finally, in the fourth edition of *The Administration of the Colonies* he came so near to describing the maritime-imperial system as it actually functioned that the passage is worth quoting at length:

> The laws of trade respecting America, were framed and enacted for the regulating of *mere plantations*. . . . But the spirit of commerce, operating on the nature and situation of these external dominions, beyond what the mother country or the Colonists themselves ever thought of, planned, or even hoped for, has *wrought up these plantations to become objects of trade*; has enlarged and combined the intercourse of the barter and exchange of their various produce, into a very complex and extensive commercial interest: The operation of this spirit, has, in every source of interest and power, raised and established the *British government on a grand commercial basis*; has by the same power to the true purposes of the same interest, extended the British dominions through every part of the Atlantic Ocean, to the actually forming A GRAND MARINE EMPIRE.

Pownall went on to warn:

> If . . . we are predetermined to carry into strict and literal execution,
> the navigation act, and other laws respecting the plantation trade –
> without reviewing and considering what the very different circum-
> stances of the Colonies now are, from what they were when they
> were first settled . . . we must determine to reduce our Colonies again
> to such mere plantations. . . . But if we would profit of them in those
> great commercial benefits, to those great political purposes, which
> they are capable to produce; which they lead to; which the whole
> strain of our politics have, for many years, taught us to value our-
> selves upon; and which have really been the source of all our wealth
> and power; we must examine thoroughly the state of this commercial
> interest.

It must be done, he continued, with the aim of remodelling the 'laws of
trade' under 'true and more enlarged principles', so as to sustain 'one great
commercial dominion'.[94] The only important point that Pownall seems not
to have realized is that the laws had not been strictly and literally enforced
even in the early days when the colonies were 'mere plantations'.

A year later Edmund Burke turned his powerful intellect to the question.
Burke had become involved with this subject when the Rockingham administration set about in spring 1766 to revise the Sugar Act (after it repealed
the Stamp Act). He evidently absorbed the views of merchants whom he
helped line up as expert witnesses.[95] In responding to a pamphlet written
by William Knox, which had taken a Grenvillite position on colonial trade
very similar to Whately's, Burke digested his thoughts. *Observations on a
Late Publication Entitled The Present State of the Nation* (1769) has a
terrible title, but for a student of the maritime-imperial system it is a
remarkable document – in its way as remarkable as Thomas Pownall's
fourth edition, which Burke read.[96] Its importance to this subject can only
be briefly suggested here, by reference to a couple of fragments:

> For instance, what does he mean by talking of an adherence to the
> old navigation laws? Does he mean that the particular law, 12 Car.
> II c. 19, commonly called 'The Act of Navigation', is to be adhered
> to and that the several subsequent additions, amendments, and excep-
> tions ought to be all repealed? If so, he will make a strange havoc in
> the whole system of our trade laws. . . . That 'the regulations for the
> colony trade would be few and simple if the old navigation laws
> were adhered to', I utterly deny as a fact. That they ought to be so
> sounds well enough, but . . . as that trade is in a great measure a
> system of art and restriction, they can neither be few nor simple.[97]

Burke tended to carry his arguments about commerce on to Whig political
ground (as he did right after the passage quoted at the top of this chapter);
but near the end he offered a statement of the commercial principles that

had guided the Rockingham administration's revision of 'the system of 1764'. Where issues of revenue and trade were entwined, he wrote, revenue should be subordinate; trade should not suffer. Where trade alone was concerned, the Rockingham administration's reforms in 1766 were founded on the fact that the colonies had

> very few means of traffic with this country. It became therefore our interest to let them into as much foreign trade as could be given them without interfering with our own, and to secure by every method the returns to the mother country. Without some such scheme of enlargement, it was obvious that any benefit we could expect from these colonies must be extremely limited. . . . As to the confining the returns to this country, administration saw the mischief and folly of a plan of indiscriminate restraint.

Even at this point Burke did not actually say that this principle captured the essence of colonial trade policy during the preceding half-century, though it is an observation he might have made in view of his earlier remarks about the original Act of Navigation.[98]

In the last year of his life, 1770, George Grenville said to the House of Commons: 'I have ever said, I wish to see a plan and a system. . . . I framed a plan. I framed a system'.[99] His commercial plan rested on long-repeated and widely accepted 'mercantilist' dogmas about trade and empire (which explains why Whately's appeal to the authority of the original navigation acts seemed so plausible to readers). Pitt, for all his apprehensions that the Atlantic power-system could be ruined by bad policy, was also captive of these dogmas. Even when experienced merchants started talking about 'principles of trade', they tended to fall back on the same well-worn mercantilist maxims. As we have just noted, these maxims had not, until 1768, been subjected to any studied criticism grounded in the actual context of affairs. In fact, it took Thomas Pownall four years to formulate a counter-paradigm derived in this way. Having done it, he told his readers: 'Would statesmen . . . doubt for a while, the predetermined modes which artificial systems prescribe; would they dare look for truth in the nature of things; they would soon adopt what is right, as founded upon fact'.[100] What chance had this demanding approach or Burke's explication – embedded in historical and geographical conditions, functionally opportunistic and implicitly evolutionary – have in public debate against the traditional maxims? As propaganda, Grenvillite principles on trade had the upper hand and would continue to have the upper hand until a monumental imperial disaster – the American Revolution – followed in the 1790s by dire geopolitical, commercial and financial necessities, forced British policy-makers to confront reality and reconsider. But in the 1760s and early 1770s the opposition lacked an easily understandable paradigm.

In fact, it is not clear that Grenville and his colleagues had much of a plan or system, in the sense of something well thought-out and well adapted. With respect to military defence, the question raised by John Shy remains eminently worth asking: 'Exactly what was the British government doing when it assigned 15 infantry battalions to North America in 1763?'[101] As Shy recognized, there is no obvious answer. One powerful motive seems to have been a desire to retain an enlarged peacetime army, but to do it in a popular, imperial way and at no apparent expense to the British taxpayer.

More central to this chapter's theme is the degree to which the measures were designed to execute an *imperial* mission. Granted, a military presence of some kind was necessary to claim the new territory and support British rule in Canada, yet the old method of trying to get the colonists to co-operate in military defence was abruptly and unilaterally put aside in favour of an imperial force. Trade regulation and revenue collection served to justify a larger naval force on the American seaboard. Many of the new commercial provisions were intended to focus patterns more inwardly on the empire and in a manner more specifically tailored to the mother country's commercial and fiscal needs. There is no doubt that Grenville and Whately sought firmer control of colonial trade: whatever the system's commercial success, it was in danger, they thought, of becoming an imperial failure.[102] In sum, the ministers of the early 1760s were strongly, not resignedly or reluctantly, disposed toward imperial intervention. Their policy inclined tentatively toward establishing a measure of territorial dominion. It definitely aimed at confining the system of Atlantic commerce. They evidently believed the costs were worth bearing.

It remains to explain how this new policy – expensive, administratively arduous, commercially disruptive and politically hazardous – came to the fore. What brought the change? The rest of this chapter will attempt an answer.

The central fact is that in the later 1740s North America suddenly came into the limelight and stayed there. As noted earlier, during the heyday of the maritime-imperial system Whitehall's level of anxiety concerning either the control or the defence of North America was quite low. The centre of attention in those years was the Caribbean, and strategic concerns were mainly focused on the question of trading access to the Spanish empire.

The occasioning cause of the shift of emphasis from the Caribbean to the northern colonies may be pin-pointed: Louisbourg, 1745. Although the war that Britain initiated against Spain in 1739 was fought in the West Indies, the focus of hostilities reverted to Europe in 1741 because of dangers posed there by French arms, and for Britain the contest in Europe went from bad to worse. However, in the summer of 1745, when a Jacobite army was marching in the north of England and a French army was mastering the Low Countries, news reached London that the great fortress at Louisbourg had surrendered and Cape Breton was in British hands. It came as a bolt from the blue, wholly unexpected because the expedition had been planned not in London but in Boston, and was accomplished by New England transport vessels and soldiers along with the naval squadron that happened to be on station. It proved to be a deliverance. By giving Cape Breton back to France in 1748, Great Britain was able to salvage a drawn peace. The government's willingness to part with Cape Breton might be interpreted as confirming its long-standing indifference to North America, but in fact the exchange was made for the compelling strategic reason of getting the French to pull back from the Low Countries, and was viewed by those who did it as a politically painful step. Moreover, many informed persons were aware, especially on the French side, that in 1747 British naval supremacy had finally reached a level where it could cut France's supply lines to her transatlantic possessions. Thus, a North American expeditionary coup and seapower in the Atlantic had salvaged the situation in Europe. No one in Britain doubted that France would work for every advantage across the Atlantic and rebuild her navy.

Successive administrations from 1746 to 1756 had to pay attention to North America because opposition politicians noisily exploited the Cape Breton issue as well as the French menace.[103] In North America the most dangerous rival was now being directly confronted, whereas formerly, when the Caribbean was the centre of attention, the primary danger posed by France (command of Spanish American trade) was indirect. Moreover, in the early 1750s the Duke of Newcastle, as Secretary of State, was busily proposing that the problem of overseas defence should be mainly solved by restraining France through British alliances and commitments in Europe. Since it was popular to deplore such commitments, this gave opposition politicians a spectacular opportunity. Pamphlets challenging Newcastle's approach to grand strategy proliferated.[104] At the same time, the realization dawned in London that the northern colonies, populous and thriving, were indispensable to Great Britain's survival and future prosperity, both as markets for British manufactured goods and as furnishers of maritime resources. Writings on trade and colonies strongly reflected this realization, yet, curiously, many of them also took on a gloomy, defensive tone, perhaps because of the menacing posture in North America which France had adopted. They argued that France's colonial trade, being better organized and controlled, would gain the upper hand unless British statesmen woke up.[105] Also, it was urged, the system of imperial defence had to be improved, and 'projects stimulated by fear of defeat' were urged forward; the miserable performance of British arms between 1754 and 1758 seemed to confirm the worst prognostications. In the great war fought from 1754 to 1763 Britain's main object was to ensure the preservation of what she now regarded as the primary locus of her maritime and financial strength, North America.

Thus, in the anxiety-ridden milieu of the 1750s a focus of discourse and

211

a tonality of argument were being developed that would serve a few years later to justify 'a policy of strict supervision and control'. The 'apparent breakdown of metropolitan control' in America, always insufferable to imperial officialdom, was now considered directly relevant to national security. The Seven Years War itself amplified these currents. The unprecedented commitment of British armed forces to the American theatre inclined the thoughts of policy-makers toward more authoritative instruments of control backed by Parliament.[106] It was easy for generals and governors to impress British statesmen and the public with the idea that all American merchants and shippers shamelessly assisted the enemy by trading with the French Caribbean for mere profit.[107] Toward the end of the war, when successes mounted, the big debate over whether Guadeloupe or Canada should be retained produced another barrage of pamphlets and parliamentary speeches on the relation of colonial trade to the interests of state. Most of the premises were by now familiar and maxims abounded, for the trade-versus-territory debate was hardly new. Undoubtedly, the decision to keep Canada raised new questions about the nature and governance of the empire. Simultaneous territorial acquisition in India may also have served to focus attention on such questions. Thus a climate of opinion inviting an active and more territorially inclined imperial policy was in place; but this is not to say that the public had swung entirely over to a revised conception of empire. The debate over the wisdom of keeping Canada continued into the post-war period.[108]

Notwithstanding the new terms of discussion, it may be doubted whether a set of measures so expensive, arduous and disruptive would have been undertaken in 1763, and persisted in thereafter, if the domestic political situation had not become fundamentally altered. 'A revolution in national politics had taken place', and it was a determined and vindictive one. The new, young King, who did not have his heart in Hanover, naturally encouraged a different set of ministers; his mentor, Bute, was fiercely determined to clear out the old Whig gang and build a new system of support around the throne.[109] The old Whigs were thus forced on to the unfamiliar ground of opposition. Furthermore, although Newcastle lived on for a while, the two men who served as the group's steadying influence, Hardwicke and Devonshire, died in 1764. Even while they lived they found it impossible to make common cause with Pitt, not just because of Pitt's bouts of illness, but because of his deep-seated mistrust of them, and because his ideas about American colonial policy in time of peace hunted recklessly among misconceptions. The coming into office of an old Whig remnant under Rockingham in 1765 was an unlikely political accident, and almost everyone (correctly) anticipated that Rockingham's tenure would be brief.

The consequence of this revolution in politics in the 1760s was that court favour exercised a powerful magnetism not only at the top but also at the second level of government – that is, at both the levels responsible for formulating policy. Enthusiasts for imperial reform whose proposals had received indifferent support from the Whig leaders of the 1750s now came into office in droves. Attitudes were transformed at the Treasury. The Board of Trade assumed a know-it-all stance:

> After 1764 the Board considered no petitions from Anglo-American lobbies, heard little testimony, and indeed sought none from traditional Anglo-American interests. Its reports rarely mentioned the opinions of such interests; it appears to have ignored them in its recommendations. In its reviews of colonial legislation the Board referred only to the opinions of the legal advisor as to the compatibility of the laws with relevant British legislation, never mentioning the views of affected interests as to their workability in America.[110]

Confident in their knowledge of the true path, most of these new men were disposed to remain resolutely uninformed about any unsettling commercial and financial complexities and to steer clear not just of colonial influences but of the claims of businessmen generally. The need for the Rockingham administration to bring merchants' testimony into the House of Commons – to counter, as it were, these government experts – may be seen against this background.

A revolution had also occurred in the external, or geopolitical, sphere. The new King was comparatively indifferent to Hanover's fate. More important, the situation in Europe was neither immediately dangerous to British interests nor capable of offering anything but scant returns on possible diplomatic investments.[111] In other words, the 'front-yard' was dormant. If this had not been the case – if ominous alignments favouring a preponderance of French power on the continent had developed in the 1760s and 1770s – the Grenvillite programme might have been postponed long enough and under such circumstances as to remind Whitehall of the multiplicity of ways in which the maritime-imperial system provided its benefits to the state. As matters stood in the 1760s and 1770s, however, British statesmen were afforded a window of opportunity to attempt, indeed to persist in, a bold and ultimately disastrous effort to reorder American commercial policy and governance.

One is driven to the conclusion that the imperial policies instituted in 1763–4 were counter-productive and would have proved so, even if those policies had not contributed so fatally to the permanent alienation of the thirteen colonies. The commercial and fiscal measures alone, if persisted in, would have diminished rather than enhanced Great Britain's maritime and financial strength.

It is important, however, to ask whether the basic motives and concerns of the Grenvillite programme might have been sound although its methods were faulty – in other words, whether Grenville was right, in the largest sense, to fear that an unreformed Atlantic empire, while continuing to generate ever more copious maritime and financial resources, might eventually cease to provide them on suitable terms to the British state. The ramifications of this line of speculation run beyond the scope of this chapter. It can, however, be briefly observed that the problem of impressing seamen for the Royal Navy on the North American coast was already serious in the 1740s and grew steadily worse. This was not simply a North American problem; the practice of impressing seamen for the navy in West Indian waters had been generally considered unwise, and in fact became illegal in the early years of the eighteenth century. It may also be observed, however, that other important benefits of the Atlantic empire – maritime, financial, strategic and even military assistance – would probably have remained available under the unreformed system for many decades, as in fact they did, though more awkwardly, in the residual Atlantic empire after 1783.[112]

If one looks farther forward into a time-period this chapter cannot explore, it is interesting to note that the policy of the post–1783 truncated Atlantic empire was forced by circumstances to adjust to the logical patterns of traffic. In the 1790s even the shipping restrictions of the navigation acts had to be eased to allow vessels of the United States to trade to the British West Indies. After 1815, as is well known, the whole system of British seaborne trade gradually became more open. There was a reversion to the pre–1750 mode. In other words, if the special case of territorial India is left out of the picture, the maritime-imperial policy of the British empire as it actually developed after 1783 resembles in many ways the policy of the Atlantic empire as it had actually developed in the century before 1750.[113] The policy that nurtured the impressive power and prosperity of the 'First British Empire' in the Atlantic basin was more comparable to that of the nineteenth-century 'Second British Empire' than to a dubious historical construct called the 'Old Colonial System'.

NOTES

I wish to thank Ian K. Steele and John M. Beattie for reading the present chapter in draft and offering valuable suggestions.

1 Edmund Burke, *Observations on a Late Publication Entitled The Present State of the Nation* (London, 1769), in *Selected Writings and Speeches on America*, ed. Thomas H. D. Mahoney (Indianapolis, 1964), 46.

2 See Daniel A. Baugh, 'Great Britain's "Blue-Water" Policy, 1689–1815', *International History Review*, 10 (1988), 33–58. See also Daniel A. Baugh, 'British Strategy during the First World War in the Context of Four Centuries: Blue-Water versus Continental Commitment' in Daniel M. Masterson (ed.), *Naval History: The Sixth Symposium of the U.S. Naval Academy* (Wilmington, 1987),

85–110. These articles emphasize the point that Britain fought and won most of her eighteenth-century wars on the basis of financial attrition.

3 On the 'fiscal-military state' see John Brewer, *The Sinews of Power: War, Money and the English State 1688–1783* (New York, 1989).

4 As Michael W. Doyle has pointed out in *Empires* (Ithaca, 1986), 11–47, 118–19. In fact, Doyle would appear to consider the English Atlantic empire as delineated in this chapter not to have been a true empire, because his definition accents bureaucratic control.

5 *Empire* (Cambridge, 1961), 68–93; quotations from 74, 80.

6 Quotation from *The Wealth of Nations* (London, 1776), Book IV, ch. 2. One remarkable instance is Smith's casual dismissal of the Portugal trade in Book IV, ch. 6, but the whole discussion of colonies and the mercantile system (Book IV, chs 7 and 8) is interesting for what it leaves out. Smith did recognize, however, the state's obligation to protect commerce (Book V, ch. 1, part 3, art. 1).

7 These may be read in Joan Thirsk and J. P. Cooper, *Seventeenth-Century Economic Documents* (Oxford, 1972), 502, 520.

8 A similar approach is explicitly set forth in Conyers Read, 'Mercantilism: The Old English Pattern of a Controlled Economy', in C. Read (ed.), *The Constitution Reconsidered* (New York, 1938), 64–5; James A. Williamson, 'The Beginnings of an Imperial Policy, 1649–1660', in J. H. Rose, A. P. Newton and E. A. Benians (eds), *The Cambridge History of the British Empire*, vol. I (Cambridge, 1929), 207; and Wesley Frank Craven, *The Colonies in Transition, 1660–1713* (New York, 1968), 47.

9 Ralph Davis, *The Rise of the English Shipping Industry in the Seventeenth and Eighteenth Centuries* (London, 1962), 1–11.

10 Gillian T. Cell, *English Enterprise in Newfoundland 1577–1660* (Toronto, 1969), 23.

11 See Carole Shammas, 'English Commercial Development and American Colonization, 1560–1620', in K. R. Andrews, N. P. Canny and P. E. H. Hair (eds), *The Westward Enterprise* (Liverpool, 1978), esp. 159. Shammas's chapter assesses motives on the basis of conduct and style rather than relying on promotional tracts written by Peckham, Hakluyt and others; it also distinguishes between the period before 1603 and afterwards.

12 John Parker, *Books to Build an Empire* (Amsterdam, 1965), 93, 95, 115–16.

13 Kenneth R. Andrews, *Trade, Plunder and Settlement: Maritime Enterprise and the Genesis of the British Empire* (Cambridge, 1984), 10.

14 George N. Clark, 'The Colonial Conferences between England and the Netherlands in 1613 and 1615, Part II', *Bibliotheca Visseriana*, 17 (1951), 107, 116.

15 Richard Pares observed, 'whereas the French transatlantic joint-stock companies were mainly interested in trade from the first', the English transatlantic companies were designed to take profits from both land and trade (*Merchants and Planters* [Economic History Review Supplement 4; Cambridge, 1960], 3): 'The lords proprietors were interested in land rather than in trade: to be more exact, they wished to receive dues from the colonists, something like the manorial dues which they were receiving at home' (2).

16 Summaries of modern authorities' views – which sometimes overreach in trying to find a channel for coherence – may be found as follows: Andrews, *Trade, Plunder and Settlement*, 1–40, and David B. Quinn and A. N. Ryan, *England's Sea Empire* (London, 1983), 155–62. Theodore K. Rabb's *Enterprise and Empire: Merchant and Gentry Investment in the Expansion of England,*

1575–1630 (Cambridge, Mass., 1967), usefully discriminates between the merchants' profit-orientated investments and the gentry's inclination toward higher-risk social or national goals (35–69).

17 Charles M. Andrews, *The Colonial Background of the American Revolution* (New Haven, 1924), 5.

18 In my view Brewer's *Sinews of Power* does not pay sufficient attention to the manner in which the English state developed between 1660 and 1688.

19 See generally Wayne Neil Hammond, 'The Administration of the English Navy, 1649–1660' (Ph.D. dissertation, University of British Columbia, 1974), 2–3; Hans-Christoph Junge, *Flottenpolitik und Revolution: Die Entstehung der englischen Seemacht während der Herrschaft Cromwells* (Stuttgart, 1980), 319–23; Bernard Capp, *Cromwell's Navy: The Fleet and the English Revolution, 1648–1660* (Oxford, 1989), 60–86. For the extension of commerce protection see Samuel R. Gardiner, *History of the Commonwealth and Protectorate* (4 vols; London, 1894), vol. I, 339–40, and also Hammond, 'Administration', 299–301. In October 1650 a surcharge was placed on the customs, to be allocated for convoy protection.

20 The act of 1651 was somewhat foreshadowed in 1650 by the 'Instructions to the Council of Trade' on which a bill of 1 August was founded; a navigation ordinance concerning the colonies was enacted two months later. See Thirsk and Cooper, *Seventeenth-Century Economic Documents*, 501–2.

21 Charles M. Andrews, *The Colonial Period of American History, IV, England's Commercial and Colonial Policy* (New Haven, 1938), 13–21, 35–8. This book, comprehensive and well-grounded, remains a very reliable guide to the development of policy during the second half of the seventeenth century. Another reliable guide is Wesley Frank Craven, *The Colonies in Transition*, esp. ch. 2. These two studies have helped me more than my notes hereafter will indicate. On the state of global shipping as background to the act of 1651, particularly Dutch competition, see Jonathan I. Israel, *Dutch Primacy in World Trade, 1585–1740* (Oxford, 1989), 198–209.

22 Williamson, 'Beginnings of an Imperial Policy', 218.

23 Hammond, 'Administration', 5–6; Capp, *Cromwell's Navy*, 86.

24 Hammond, 'Administration', 5–6, 77–8, 97–116.

25 Experts well know that the term 'New Model Navy' was not used then. So far as I know, Admiral Sir Herbert Richmond was the first to suggest it; see *The Navy as an Instrument of Policy, 1558–1727* (Cambridge, 1953), 97. Although the usage does not deserve currency, the historical point it makes is valid, and Lord Halifax's essay, 'A Rough Draft of a New Model at Sea', *c.* 1667, gives some warrant for it (the essay is printed in *Halifax: Complete Works*, ed. J. P. Kenyon [Harmondsworth and Baltimore, 1969], 151–63).

26 Lawrence A. Harper, *The English Navigation Laws* (New York, 1939; repr. 1973, 57–9.

27 For a succinct account see Craven, *Colonies in Transition*, 33–6, quotation from 36.

28 Bernard Bailyn, 'Communications and Trade: The Atlantic in the Seventeenth Century', *Journal of Economic History*, 13 (1953) 378–82; *The New England Merchants in the Seventeenth Century* (Cambridge, Mass., 1955), 86–7, 105, 113, 126–7.

29 Andrews, *Colonial Period*, vol. IV, 113–14.

30 Craven, *Colonies in Transition*, 59; Andrews, *Colonial Period*, vol. IV, 117.

31 Ian K. Steele, *The English Atlantic 1675–1740: An Exploration of Communication and Community* (New York and Oxford, 1986), 17.

32 See A. P. Thornton, *West-India Policy under the Restoration* (Oxford, 1956), 224–43.

33 That the Navigation laws were not incompatible with New England interests in the early years is pointed out in Bailyn, *New England Merchants*, 128–9.

34 The position was outlined in a way similar to this in the 1720s by Joshua Gee in *Trade and Navigation of Great Britain* (London, 1750 edn), 77–8.

35 The government's initial naval allocations for the tobacco trade did not begin to meet the need. Losses multiplied alarmingly. See Arthur P. Middleton, 'The Chesapeake Convoy System, 1662–1763', *William and Mary Quarterly*, third series [hereafter *WMQ*], 3 (1946), 186–7.

36 Robert C. Ritchie, *Captain Kidd and the War Against the Pirates*, (Cambridge, Mass., 1986), 135–227. See also Ian K. Steele, *The Politics of Colonial Policy: The Board of Trade in Colonial Administration, 1696–1720* (Oxford, 1968), ch. 3.

37 Richard Pares, *War and Trade in the West Indies, 1739–1763* (Oxford, 1936), 17. Experts in the field have inferred from strong clues that effective suppression did occur between 1715 and 1750, but there is no scholarly monograph on the topic, not even an article.

38 Daniel A. Baugh, *British Naval Administration in the Age of Walpole* (Princeton, 1965), 347–50.

39 Herbert W. Richmond, *The Navy in the War of 1739–48* (3 vols; Cambridge, 1920), vol. III, 52.

40 Frank W. Pitman, *The Development of the British West Indies, 1700–1763* (New Haven, 1917), 277, provides a table showing that 'there were but seventeen ships of the royal navy stationed in North America and the West Indies' in 1735. Given the circumstances, this may be considered as quite a lot. It was, as the book observes, too few to prevent smuggling, but that was a task to be executed by putting into commission numerous smaller vessels.

41 Malachy Postlethwayt, *The Universal Dictionary of Trade and Commerce* (second edn, 2 vols; London, 1757), vol. II, 307.

42 Thomas Lediard, *The Naval History of England* (London, 1735), Preface.

43 Peggy K. Liss, *Atlantic Empires: The Network of Trade and Revolution, 1713–1826* (Baltimore and London, 1983), 1.

44 Quoted in Steele, *Politics of Colonial Policy*, 13.

45 William J. Eccles, *France in America* (New York, 1972), 110–17.

46 Stephen S. Webb, *The Governors-General: The English Army and the Definition of the Empire, 1569–1681* (Chapel Hill, 1979), should be read against this background. Webb has avoided the word 'policy' and that leaves a large ambiguity as to the thrust of his claim.

47 In 1750 the premium for a one-way transatlantic voyage was about 2 per cent (Steele, *English Atlantic*, 224–7).

48 The important interpretive synthesis of recent work is John J. McCusker and Russell R. Menard, *The Economy of British America, 1607–1789* (Chapel Hill, 1985); they have judged the growth to be impressive in practically all respects and speak of 'one grand "Atlantic economy" ' (87). See also T. H. Breen, who has enlarged upon its social and cultural implications in 'An Empire of Goods: The Anglicization of Colonial America, 1690–1776', *Journal of British Studies*, 25/4 (1986).

49 Steele, *English Atlantic*, 62–3, 91, 224–8. See also David W. Galenson, *Traders, Planters and Slaves: Market Behaviour in Early English America* (Cambridge, 1986).

50 The 1700–70 figures come from Jacob M. Price, 'Colonial Trade and British

Economic Development, 1660–1775', in Claude Fohlen and Jacques Godechot (eds), *La Révolution Americaine et L'Europe* (Paris, 1979), 222–3.

51 Ralph Davis, 'Merchant Shipping in the Economy of the Late Seventeenth Century', *Economic History Review*, second series, 9 (1956) 70.

52 On the complexities of what was 'illicit' or 'illegal' see Pitman, *Development*, 189–92, 236–41; and Pares, *War and Trade*, ch. 9.

53 To save space it is necessary to exclude the question of colonial imports. These according to law had to come from English merchants, regardless of country of origin, though there were significant legal exceptions (Portuguese wines, for instance). No doubt there was some smuggling, but in view of the massive growth of English exports to North America in the eighteenth century, only a purist would regard such smuggling as a problem.

54 Steele, *English Atlantic*, 72; Andrews, *Colonial Period*, vol. IV, 95–7, 119. See also H. E. S. Fisher, 'Lisbon, its English Merchant Community and the Mediterranean in the Eighteenth Century' in P. L. Cottrell and D. H. Aldcroft (eds), *Shipping, Trade and Commerce: Essays in Memory of Ralph Davis* (Leicester, 1981), 27–33.

55 England's problem of wartime transfer payments is analysed in a pioneering book: D. W. Jones, *War and Economy in the Age of William III and Marlborough* (Oxford, 1988). Jones speaks of a 'huge "sterling" trade area' having been created, in which deficits east and west were in due course globally balanced (49–50, 221–2).

56 Former Governor Thomas Pownall later wrote about it: 'the fact is, and matters have been so managed, that the general currency of the Colonies used to be in Spanish and Portuguese coin. This supplied the internal circulation of their home business, and always finally came to England in payments for what the Colonists exported [i.e. imported] from thence. If the act of navigation should be carried into such rigorous execution as to cut off this supply of a silver currency to the Colonies, the thoughts of administration should be turned to the devising some means of supplying the Colonies with money of some sort or other' (*The Administration of the Colonies* [fourth edn; London, 1768], 177–8).

57 Nuala Zahedieh, 'Trade, Plunder, and Economic Development in Early English Jamaica, 1655–89', *Economic History Review*, second series, 39 (1986), 222.

58 See generally Pares, *War and Trade*, 1–64, and Jean O. McLachlan (Lindsay), *Trade and Peace with Old Spain, 1667–1750* (Cambridge, 1940).

59 Zahedieh, 'Trade', esp. 213–18. See also Nuala Zahedieh, 'The Merchants of Port Royal, Jamaica, and the Spanish Contraband Trade, 1655–1692', *WMQ*, 43 (1986), 570–93. She points out that the French islanders continued to be orientated more toward plundering raids than peaceful commerce until the late 1680s (593). The geographical situation of Jamaica, thanks to patterns of wind and current, gave it a great advantage in regular traffic over the French islands, and even over the Dutch islands.

60 Details of the story are laid out in Curtis P. Nettels, 'England and the Spanish-American Trade, 1680–1715', *Journal of Modern History*, 3 (1931), 1–32. (This article forms the first chapter of Nettels, *The Money Supply of the American Colonies before 1720* [Madison, 1934; repr. London and New York, 1964].)

61 McCusker and Menard, *Economy*, 162–4. Still the most penetrating account is Charles M. Andrews, 'Anglo-French Commercial Rivalry, 1700–1750: The Western Phase, II', *American Historical Review*, 20 (1914–15), 761–80, but there are additional details and a listing of pamphlet literature in Pitman, *Development*, ch. 11. On the point that the British West Indian interest took

the lead in trying to enforce the Molasses Act, see Pares, *War and Trade*, 396–402.

62 The trade was essentially speculative. Avoidance of an empty run and hitting upon some way 'to secure remittances more quickly' are primary objects for persons engaged in a carrying trade. See, for instance, Marc Egnal, 'The Changing Structure of Philadelphia's Trade with the British West Indies, 1750–1775', *Pennsylvania Magazine of History and Biography*, 99 (1975), esp. 162.

63 Neither Andrews nor Craven made this mistake. As Andrews asserted, 'The first object even [sic] of the navigation acts was navigation not trade; and the building of ships, the breeding and increase of seamen, and the preservation and defense of the kingdom preceded trade, just as trade preceded plantations in the general scheme of things' (*Colonial Period*, vol. IV, 357).

64 ibid., 77–84.

65 Price, 'Colonial Trade', 227–8.

66 One important reason was that in the period from 1650 to 1675 the English captured lots of merchant vessels: Davis, *Shipping Industry*, 51–2; Steele, *English Atlantic*, 17.

67 Although most of the points I have made about the maritime-imperial system were well known to experts at the time, it seems that the large role played by colonial shipbuilding and freighting in reducing the North American balance-of-payments deficit was not then appreciated because the statistics of the time focused on commodities, ignoring even vessels sold. See generally McCusker and Menard, *Economy*, 71–82, 111, which adopts the average annual value of colonial shipping services as worked out by James F. Shepherd and Gary M. Walton, and that of colony-built ships sold as worked out by Jacob M. Price. Together these were almost equal to the value of exported commodities from the thirteen colonies to the West Indies.

68 See Dorothy Burne Goebel, 'The "New England Trade" and the French West Indies, 1763–1774: A Study in Trade Policies', *WMQ*, 20 (1963), 332.

69 Liss, *Atlantic Empires*, 32.

70 A conception that mercantilist principles prevailed in policy-making, or ought to have prevailed, may be found throughout the historical literature. Walter L. Dorn's *Competition for Empire, 1740–1763* (New York, 1940), still an admirable survey in many respects, is a case in point: see 263–6. Evidently, Dorn was heavily influenced by J. F. Rees's chapter, 'Mercantilism and the Colonies', in the *Cambridge History of the British Empire*, vol. I, esp. 592. Even Andrews, in ch. 10 of *Colonial Period*, vol. IV, spoke of mercantilist ideas as 'ideas that actuated Englishmen of the period in shaping their commercial policy and in defining their relations with the plantations in America' (318), and there are passages, especially in ch. 10, that give an impression that London policy-makers would have pursued a 'mercantilist' commercial agenda if only they could have obtained colonial co-operation. The chapter, however, sets forth a large and varied menu of English 'mercantilist' ideas and stresses the great differences of opinion about them as well as the impossibility of harmonizing them all. The book sometimes refers to 'the strict mercantilist' or 'true mercantilist' – evidently someone desirous of a commercial system centred upon the mother country and focused on particular trade balances. Andrews's discussions of mercantilist ideas are in many respects difficult to reconcile with the thrust of his work as a whole.

71 Liss, *Atlantic Empires*, 4–5; also 13.

72 The instance of strategically located St Lucia is illustrative. Richard Pares

remarked that the British 'did not want to own the island themselves, so much as to prevent the French from doing so' (*War and Trade*, 179–86, quotation 199), which is true but may be put more precisely. What the British government really wanted was a fortified position in its bay – because St Lucia stood opposite the French naval base on Martinique – without having to rule or cultivate the island.

73 ibid., 179–84.

74 See Gerald S. Graham, *Empire of the North Atlantic* (Toronto, 1950), 66–8, 84–93, 119–125; also Eccles, *France in America*, 109. An exception occurred in 1692–3 when London envisioned an attack on Canada, after an attempt by New Englanders failed. Ships and some troops were sent, but the letter advising the governor to prepare a colonial force arrived too late and nothing useful could be done.

75 Memorandum of the Board of Trade, dated 8 September 1721, printed in Edmund B. O'Callaghan, *Documents relative to the Colonial History of the State of New York* (Albany, 1853–87), vol. V, 531–630, esp. 621–2.

76 See Sir Herbert W. Richmond, *Statesmen and Sea Power* (Oxford, 1946), 284.

77 John L. Bullion, in 'Security and Economy: The Bute Administration's Plans for the American Army and Revenue, 1762–1763', *WMQ*, 45 (1988), 499–509, has shown how conscious the ministry and especially George III himself were of the contrast with 1749 (quotation from 503).

78 Quoted by John L. Bullion, ' "The Ten Thousand in America": More Light on the Decision on the American Army, 1762–1763', *WMQ*, 43 (1986), 651.

79 See generally John L. Bullion, 'Securing the Peace: Lord Bute, the Plan for the Army, and the Origins of the American Revolution' in Karl W. Schweizer (ed.), *Lord Bute: Essays in Re-interpretation* (Leicester, 1988), 17–39, and Bullion, ' "The Ten Thousand" '. See also John W. Shy, *Toward Lexington: The Role of the British Army in the Coming of the American Revolution* (Princeton, 1965), 68–72.

80 Bullion, 'Security and Economy', 505–7.

81 John M. Murrin, 'The French and Indian War, the American Revolution, and the Counterfactual Hypothesis: Reflections on Lawrence Henry Gipson and John Shy', *Reviews in American History*, 1 (1973), 314, also 318.

82 'Some Thoughts on the Settlement & Government of our Colonies in North America', 10 March 1763, esp. 5–8: BL Add. MSS 38, 335, ff. 69–77 (in *American Material in the Liverpool Papers*, ed. Geoffrey Seed [Micro Methods, 1965], reel 1).

83 In a partially completed pamphlet probably sketched out in the winter of 1765–6, which is printed in *Benjamin Franklin's Letters to the Press, 1758–1775*, ed. Verner W. Crane (Chapel Hill, 1950); the relevant passage is on 66.

84 See Gregory Evans Dowd, 'The French King Wakes Up in Detroit: "Pontiac's War" in Rumor and History', *Ethnohistory*, 37/3, (1990), 254–78. I owe this reference to my colleague Daniel Usner.

85 Rough statistics may be derived from calculations for the army during the 1760s in Peter D. G. Thomas, 'The Cost of the British Army in North America, 1763–1775', *WMQ*, 45 (1988), 510–16, and the figures for 1749–55 in Julian Gwyn, 'British Government Spending and the North American Colonies, 1740–1775', *Journal of Imperial and Commonwealth History*, 8/2 (1980), 77.

86 Peter D. G. Thomas, *British Politics and the Stamp Act Crisis: The First Phase of the American Revolution, 1763–1767* (Oxford, 1975), 61. Grenville held this view from the outset. (Throughout the 1760s the directly attributable taxes

and duties in colonial America yielded scarcely one-tenth of the American army's cost.)

87 The authorizing legislation was 3 Geo. III, c. 22, which became law in April 1763. For details see John L. Bullion, *A Great and Necessary Measure: George Grenville and the Genesis of the Stamp Act, 1763–1765* (Columbia, 1982), 52–8, and Neil R. Stout, *The Royal Navy in America, 1760–1775: A Study of Enforcement of British Colonial Policy in the Era of the American Revolution* (Annapolis, 1973), 27–31. My indebtedness to these two books is more extensive than precise references can indicate.

88 The preamble observed that it was 'just and necessary that a revenue be raised in your Majesty's dominions in America for defraying the expenses of defending, protecting, and securing the same'.

89 The Sugar Act of 5 April 1764 is partly printed in *Prologue to Revolution: Sources and Documents on the Stamp Act Crisis, 1764–1766*, ed. Edmund S. Morgan (Chapel Hill, 1959), 4–8, and in *English Historical Documents*, vol. IX: *American Colonial Documents to 1776*, ed. Merrill Jensen (London, 1955), 643–8. The two abridgements are somewhat complementary. See also Bullion, *A Great and Necessary Measure*, chs 4–6.

90 Stout, *Royal Navy in America*, chs 3–5; see esp. 36, 41, 43, 88–9. See also Edmund S. and Helen M. Morgan, *The Stamp Act Crisis: Prologue to Revolution*, revised edn (New York, 1963), 46–8. Oliver M. Dickerson's *The Navigation Acts and the American Revolution* (Philadelphia, 1951) devotes a long chapter to the subject ('Era of Customs Racketeering', 208–65). Dickerson took too cynical a view of the government's motives. Thomas C. Barrow's treatment in *Trade and Empire: The British Customs Service in Colonial America, 1660–1775* (Cambridge, Mass., 1967), which exhibits the enforcers as struggling to do the right and necessary thing under difficult circumstances (182–212), amounts to an uncritical endorsement of the programme.

91 *The Regulations Lately Made concerning the Colonies, and the Taxes Imposed upon Them, Considered* (London, 1765).

92 Whately, *Regulations Lately Made*, 4, 20, 87.

93 There is not space in this chapter to provide particular citations to justify these general observations. I have substantially completed another (forthcoming) essay in which I examine the ideas of Grenville, Whately, William Knox, Thomas Pownall, Edmund Burke and Adam Smith in the light of my conception of the maritime-imperial system. I wish to take an early opportunity here to thank the Huntington Library for enabling me to accomplish this part of my research.

94 Pownall, *Administration of the Colonies*, 282–4 (italics etc. in the original). This fourth edition is the first in which this passage occurs, and pieces of it are reiterated in other parts of the book. The quoted passage occurs in substantially the same form in the fifth edition (1774), 251–3.

95 This historical episode is little known, and most of the historical attention it has received denigrates the achievement. Lucy Stuart Sutherland, 'Edmund Burke and the First Rockingham Ministry', *English Historical Review*, 47 (1932), was the pioneering study. Paul Langford's account in *The First Rockingham Administration, 1765–1766* (Oxford, 1973) is very valuable though the author's denigration is quite intense; see esp. 198–212, but also the important background in chs 4 and 5. A full and somewhat more generous treatment may be found in Thomas, *British Politics*, ch. 13. The brief word in Barrow, *Trade and Empire*, 214, is misleading.

96 Burke, *Observations on a Late Publication*, in *Select Writings*, 6–56, cited at

the start of this chapter. Burke believed that *The Present State of the Nation* had been written under Grenville's direction (22). He observed: 'It may be considered as a sort of digest of the avowed maxims of a certain political school, the effects of whose doctrines and practices this country will feel long and severely' (8). Burke's reference to Pownall is on p. 30. For evidence that Burke read Pownall's fourth edition, see John Shy, *A People Numerous and Armed* (New York, 1976), 64.

97 Burke, *Select Writings*, 31–2. Burke went on to point out that nobody departed more from 'the author's ideas of simplicity', by imposing on the American trade a 'multiplicity and intricacy of regulations and ordinances, than his boasted minister of 1764'.

98 ibid., 53–4.

99 Quoted by Bullion, *A Great and Necessary Measure*, 209–10.

100 Pownall, *Administration of the Colonies*, 163. It may be relevant to remember, when pondering why Thomas Pownall was slow to develop his liberal ideas on imperial trade, that his brother favoured a Grenville hard line; and John Pownall was the key permanent secretary in offices directly in touch with American affairs during the 1760s, first at the Board of Trade and then under the Secretary of State: see F. B. Wickwire, 'John Pownall and British Colonial Policy', *WMQ*, 20 (1963), 543–54.

101 Shy, *Toward Lexington*, 52.

102 The imperial purposes behind the Sugar and Stamp acts are strongly presented by Robert W. Tucker and David C. Hendrickson, *The Fall of the First British Empire: Origins of the War of American Independence* (Baltimore, 1982), esp. 191–4. My disagreement with this book's basic interpretation concerning the continuity of policy is profound, but I admire its scholarly and thought-provoking approach.

103 Arthur H. Buffington, 'The Canada Expedition of 1746: Its Relation to British Politics', *American Historical Review*, 45 (1940), esp. 562–73.

104 A list of titles may be found in the bibliography of Carl William Eldon, *England's Subsidy Policy towards the Continent during the Seven Years' War* (Philadelphia, 1938).

105 e.g. Malachy Postlethwayt, *A Short State of the Progress of French Trade and Navigation* (London, 1756); *Britain's Commercial Interest Explained and Improved* (2 vols; London, 1757). See especially the dedicatory prefaces.

106 The quotations are on pp. 30 and 39 of Jack P. Greene, ' "A Posture of Hostility": A Reconsideration of Some Aspects of the Origins of the American Revolution', *Proceedings of the American Antiquarian Society*, 87 (1978), where all this is beautifully laid out. Greene extended his argument into the war years in 'The Seven Years' War and the American Revolution', *Journal of Imperial and Commonwealth History*, 8/2, (1980).

107 On whether this impression was fair see Alan Rogers, *Empire and Liberty: American Resistance to British Authority, 1755–1763* (Berkeley and Los Angeles, 1974), ch. 8.

108 See Philip Lawson, ' "The Irishman's Prize": Views of Canada from the British Press, 1760–1774', *Historical Journal*, 28/3 (1985), esp. 575–86.

109 Lucy S. Sutherland, *The East India Company in Eighteenth-Century Politics* (Oxford, 1952), 91.

110 Alison G. Olson, 'The Board of Trade and London-American Interest Groups in the Eighteenth Century', *Journal of Imperial and Commonwealth History*, 8/2 (1980), 44.

111 H. M. Scott, *British Foreign Policy in the Age of the American Revolution* (Oxford, 1990), esp. 340–3.
112 On the role of these resources between 1793 and 1802, see Michael Duffy, *Soldiers, Sugar, and Seapower: The British Expeditions to the West Indies and the War against Revolutionary France* (Oxford, 1987), esp. 19–25 and his final chapter.
113 The starting-point of research on the post–1783 period would still have to be Gerald S. Graham, *Sea Power and British North America, 1783–1820: A Study in British Colonial Policy* (Cambridge, Mass., 1941); also important is John E. Crowley, 'Neo-Mercantilism and *The Wealth of Nations*: Commercial Policy after the American Revolution', *Historical Journal*, 33/2 (1990).

9

Union, State and Empire
The Britain of 1707 in its European setting
John Robertson

THE BRITISH EMPIRE AND THE BRITISH STATE

It is easy to speak of the British empire in the eighteenth century, but perhaps less easy, as John Brewer's book bears witness, to speak of the British state.[1] By the 'British empire' we mean Britain's possessions overseas, the colonies in North America and the settlements and trading posts in the West Indies and India. The composition of this empire changed, and by 1783 what is often referred to as the 'First British Empire' had been lost; but another empire remained, and the term 'the British empire' continued to have an obvious reference. Behind the British empire, it is not so difficult to add, lay the commitment of the British people and the power of the British state. It is well known that the Scots (and the Welsh) were as actively involved as the English – perhaps more so in proportion to their population – in settling, defending, administering and profiting from the empire. Their efforts, moreover, were supervised by one government in London, acting when necessary on legislation passed in a common parliament. In relation to the British empire, therefore, both the British people and the British state take on recognizable identities.

When the British state is considered on its own, however, its identity seems less clear. In the eighteenth century the Britain to which the term 'British state' refers is presumably the entity created by the Act of Union of 1707 between the two kingdoms of Scotland and England. Under this act there was declared to be 'one United Kingdom by the name of Great Britain', and one 'Parliament of Great Britain'.[2] (So defined, Britain in the eighteenth century would certainly not include Ireland, to which a comparable union was not extended until 1801.) Although Scotland and England had shared the same kings for a hundred years before 1707, neither the United Kingdom nor the Parliament of Great Britain had existed hitherto, except in so far as James VI and I had had himself proclaimed 'King of Great Britain', a style which his heirs had not continued. Yet, if the Act of 1707 established one kingdom and Parliament, it left much else distinct. The Scots preserved their legal system and the Presbyterian Church, and continued to enjoy considerable administrative autonomy. They also sustained their sense of national identity: for all their well-advertised desire to be known as North Britons, their Scottishness was ineradicable.[3]

The English, meanwhile, had especially good reasons to believe that the Act of Union hardly affected their political identity. For centuries, as they constantly reminded themselves, they had enjoyed one monarchy, possessed of an apparatus of government and the authority to dispense justice through the common law to the entire country. For centuries too (if just how many was disputed) there had been one parliament for the whole of England, untramelled by any regional assemblies: it might have contested the authority of the King, but never the unity of the realm. By contrast, the Scottish political community had lacked such institutional props, its famously ancient monarchy apart; and, having shared that monarchy in 1603, the Scots appeared to have contributed nothing to the unitary institutions created in 1707, but simply to have been incorporated in the Parliament at Westminster. Faced with this further evidence of the strength and continuity of English institutions, it is little wonder that so many historians have baulked at the term 'British state', and continue to refer to the 'English state', using the term 'British state' either as an occasional variation or specifically in relation to the British empire.

The historian's sense that Britain and the British state have owed the best part of their identity to the development of the British empire overseas was apparently reinforced by the process of imperial withdrawal in the twentieth century. As decolonization overseas drew to an end, demands for regional self-government within Britain moved up the political agenda. By the 1970s successive governments were prepared to accept that the end of empire required corresponding constitutional adjustment at home. Yet, when it came to it, the devolution bills failed, the government fell; and in the 1980s the British state resolutely refused to pass away with the British empire. On the contrary, a Conservative government in Westminster proved to command ample resources to exercise central authority over a Scotland which has repeatedly refused it a mandate. Faced with this impasse, the Scots themselves have turned to a new setting in which to press the case for self-government – a Europe in which the quickening consolidation of the western European Economic Community has been accompanied by the still more rapid disintegration of the eastern bloc, within as well as outwith the Soviet Union. In these new circumstances, it becomes less and less clear that the British state owes its rationale to the British empire alone. It is perhaps an opportune moment to take a fresh look at the union which brought Britain into being in 1707, and at the relation between state and empire which it established, in their European setting.

This requires, I shall argue, a fresh examination of the categories of 'state' and 'empire' themselves, as they were understood and as they existed in late-seventeenth-century Europe. As a first step, I shall outline the conceptual history of 'state' and 'empire' in the period, emphasizing the neglected but greater prominence of a particular concept of empire. Denoting territorial dominion within Europe, this concept identified empire specifically with monarchic rule over dependent provinces. In turn, I shall go on to argue, the prominence of this concept reflected its continuing political actuality. Seventeenth-century Europe was not composed of independent states so much as dominated by a small number of imperial monarchies ruling over far-flung, sometimes rebellious provinces. There were, however, exceptions to this pattern of imperial monarchy in the various federal and confederal unions which survived, and in one notable case flourished, in seventeenth-century Europe. These provided the obvious contemporary alternative to imperial monarchy. It is in such a European setting, I shall end by arguing, that the British Union of 1707 should be reassessed, for in that setting the union can be understood as a response to a critical combination of problems – dynastic, confessional, commercial – which were characteristic of imperial monarchies throughout Europe. Fearful that they were being reduced to a condition of provincial dependence upon England, the Scots in particular viewed their predicament in these European terms, and it was they who engaged in the fullest and sharpest discussion of the issues involved. It is on the Scottish debate in the years before 1707 that I shall accordingly concentrate, as the most revealing of the union's implications for the British state and empire.

What follows, therefore, is a contribution to discussion of the 'contexts' for the emergence of the British state.[4] Both the starting-point and the conclusions of the chapter differ from those of Brewer and the great majority of English historians. My perspective derives not from 'the centre of the core',[5] but from the periphery – from the provincial kingdom of Scotland, and hence from Europe. It is from the provincial viewpoint of Scotland that the European character of the British kingdoms' relationship becomes clear. From this viewpoint it is the similarities between the Scottish and English experiences and those found across the continent that stand out; the supposed distinctiveness of the English state is diminished. In part this is because the view from the provinces entails an altogether larger conception of the European context, one reaching from Sweden and its provinces in the north to the Mediterranean kingdoms of the Spanish monarchy in the south, while the view from the centre customarily looks no further than France for a comparison. A larger conception of Europe in turn directs attention to the territorial dimension of political authority. In early-modern Europe the exercise of power was first of all a matter of the co-ordination of authority over territories and their communities; the means of co-ordination, whether social, institutional or cultural, were as the superstructure to the territorial base. By contrast, the view from the centre too often takes territorial authority for granted, isolating the institutional apparatus of the state as the object of study. In the perspective adopted here, the securing of the territorial base is treated as integral to the process of building the British state. Ultimately, it is the argument of this chapter that without a grasp of the territorial basis of the British state, as it was created in 1707, there can be no understanding either of the British approach to empire in the eighteenth century, characterized as it was by an increasingly intransigent insistence on the territorial sovereignty of Crown and Parliament, or of the British state's capacity to survive the loss of that empire in the twentieth century.

CONCEPTS OF STATE, EMPIRE AND PROVINCE

The conceptual history of 'the state' in the early-modern period has been relatively well studied: by the end of the seventeenth century the term was increasingly in use, and the concept was, it is argued, understood in a sense approaching the modern. Two intellectual traditions made explicit use of the term itself: the Machiavellian tradition of 'reason' or 'interest of state' (in its various vernaculars); and the tradition of jurisprudence concerned with the *ius gentium*, in which by the late seventeenth century the terms *civitas* and *respublica* were being used in ways that best translated as 'state'.[6] Behind this increasing usage of the term lay an elaboration of its meaning: the state was now understood as distinct from and superior to both the person of the ruler and the members of society.[7] With this emerging sense of the state's impersonal authority over society went another development, so far less studied, the identification of the society over which the state ruled with a distinct people (*gens*) as well as a delimited territory. Though the concept of the 'nation state' may have been a later development, the identification of a state with a particular people and territory was at least latent in the principles of a *ius gentium*. A sense of territorial domination was certainly manifest in the jurists' adaptation of the term 'province' to designate peoples and territories subordinate to the state. In Samuel Pufendorf's phrase, provinces were but 'the appendages of other states, having no kind of sovereign authority in themselves'.[8]

The concept of the 'province', however, was rather more familiarly associated with a concept of 'empire'. The connection between the two went back to the Roman empire, when *imperium* had designated both the territory formed by the provinces and the authority exercised over them by the Republic and later the Emperor. Since the fall of Rome this simple association of empire with rule over dependent provinces had of course been enormously complicated by the rise of Christianity and the struggle between the heirs of Rome's barbarian conquerors to assume the imperial mantle. The concepts of *imperium* and *monarchia* had been entangled in the eschatological prophecies of the four great empires which were to

227

precede the fifth of Christ himself, and further caught up in the great controversies over the temporal authority of the papacy. On the part of secular rulers *imperium* was by the late middle ages increasingly associated with *regnum*, the kings of France, England and Scotland as well as the German emperor all claiming to be emperors in their own kingdoms. Although these developments had greatly complicated the concept of 'empire', the original, Roman meaning of territorial authority did not disappear. It was present, reinforcing the claim to regal independence, in the declaration of the realm of England's pretension to be an empire in the 1530s;[9] and its use was renewed and broadened by the Spanish and Portuguese conquest of vast new colonial possessions in the Americas.[10] By the end of the seventeenth century, moreover, both eschatology and the issue of papal authority were losing their force, while the Holy Roman Empire itself was increasingly treated by its jurists and publicists as a German entity, without an exclusive claim to the inheritance of Rome. Detached from these intervening associations, it seems that 'empire' was once again being understood predominantly in its original, territorial sense of the possession of and exercise of authority over dependent provinces.[11]

The use of 'empire' in a straightforwardly territorial sense was further strengthened by association with the concept of 'Universal Monarchy'.[12] This was not a new idea: until the mid-seventeenth century Universal Monarchy too was often set in an eschatological framework, a usage which culminated in the extraordinary treatise *De Monarchia Hispanica* (1641) by the Neapolitan Tommaso Campanella.[13] When not accorded this eschatological significance, moreover, the term was almost always used pejoratively, as an accusation to be laid at the throne of a rival prince. Taken literally, the accusation implied that the monarch was seeking to bring all the other kingdoms of Europe, and their overseas possessions, under his sole rule. The significance of the accusation was not that it referred to a foreseeable reality: its use was quite compatible with the hard-headed recognition that in any particular conflict the statesmen would be content with much lesser, more specific military and diplomatic objectives. Rather, the accusation characterized what was believed to be the expansionist, territorially aggressive tendency of any large monarchy: in this sense, it provided a common organizing principle for the explanation of the rivalry of Europe's kings.

In the second half of the seventeenth century, the natural target for the accusation was Louis XIV. It was a charge that he seems at first almost to have welcomed, though later his propagandists would strive hard to turn it against the Austrian Habsburgs.[14] The case against him was most famously made out by the Franc-Comtois Franz von Lisola in the *Bouclier d'estat et de justice contre le dessein manifestement decouvert de la monarchie universelle* (1667). On the Habsburg side it was echoed from Germany to Naples, Leibniz giving it particularly forceful expression in a series of attacks on the French king.[15] Long accustomed to hurling the accusation at the King of Spain, the English came late to this anti-French chorus; in the 1660s royalist English writers were busy accusing the Dutch of seeking the equivalent of a universal monarchy over the seas.[16] Once the revolution of 1688 had brought England into the field against France, however, the charge against Louis was taken up there too, notably by Daniel Defoe and Charles Davenant, both of whom used the terms 'Universal Monarchy' and 'Universal Empire' interchangeably.[17]

Two implications of this usage of Universal Monarchy should be underlined. First, the idea of a 'balance of power', invoked with increasing frequency in the late seventeenth century, was specifically related to the perceived threat of Universal Monarchy. A 'balance of power' thus did not yet denote a self-sustaining system of independent states in rough equilibrium; rather, it referred to an alliance to check one over-mighty monarchy in particular, or, as French and imperial writers could (in principle) agree, a balance between two great monarchies alone.[18] A second implication of Universal Monarchy was the specific association of territorial ambition with monarchies. Throughout the early-modern period republics were usually regarded as incapable of such expansionist tendencies. Although Machiavelli had held up Rome as the model of an aggressive, imperial republic, and Harrington and fellow English republicans had renewed this ideal in the 1650s, the model republic of early-modern Europe was Venice – in Machiavelli's and Harrington's (dismissive) phrase, a commonwealth for preservation, not increase.[19] It is true that the republican Dutch (who admired Venice) were accused of imperial ambition, but that was at sea, not on land. The pervasive assumption of republican indifference to territorial empire does not mean that republican principles were taken to offer a sufficient alternative to Universal Monarchy: as we shall see, such an alternative required the addition of other principles, hitherto marginal to city-state republicanism. What the assumption does underline, however, is the close conceptual association of monarchy with territorial acquisitiveness, the preconception that, as Defoe put it, 'every king in the world would be the Universal Monarch if he might'.[20]

It is this understanding of the concepts of Universal Monarchy, empire and province which, I believe, provides the best starting-point for an examination of the actual political structure of late seventeenth-century Europe. For this was indeed a Europe shaped by the rule of a few great imperial monarchies over numerous more or less dependent provinces.

EUROPE IN THE AGE OF THE SPANISH SUCCESSION CRISIS

The great monarchies of seventeenth-century Europe were those of the Spanish and Austrian Habsburgs, the Swedish Vasas and the French

Bourbons. (I omit two others, perhaps less comparable but certainly imperial – the monarchies of Russia and Turkey.) In these monarchies, one king or queen ruled over a plurality of more or less distinct territories. These territories might have been acquired by inheritance, marriage, treaty or conquest. A claim of dynastic right carried much the greatest legitimacy, but was all too often disputable. Force was accordingly essential to make good any claim and to retain territories which in almost all cases would have alternative possible allegiances. The territories of the monarchy might, but need not, be geographically contiguous: given the uncertainty and multiplicity of borders, contiguity was still relatively unimportant. The territories could come in various political forms – cities, duchies, principalities, kingdoms – and each would possess its own legal, fiscal and representative institutions. They might, but often did not, coincide with the extent of a population defining itself (if only through its leaders) as a people or nation. In short, these were what H. G. Koenigsberger and J. H. Elliott have called 'composite monarchies'.[21] These monarchies had a further, structural feature which leads me to want to go beyond that term, and to characterize them as 'imperial' and not simply 'composite' monarchies. Despite the formal equality which the various territories habitually claimed to enjoy under their monarchs (an equality registered in their monarchs' multiple titles – there was no King of Spain, but the King of Castile, of Leon, of Aragon, of Sicily, of Naples and so on), one of the territories can none the less be seen to have served as a core or metropolitan centre. The core territory contained the royal court and the administrative capital, and provided, at least initially, a disproportionate share of the monarchy's resources. In relation to this core the monarchy's other territories found themselves in the position of provinces.

The pattern was implicit in the break-up of the empire of Charles V in the mid-sixteenth century. Charles had been profoundly committed to the integrity of his monarchy and to the equality of its component parts. Yet as the pressures upon him mounted in the 1540s and early 1550s, and the parts had to be ever more intensively taxed to support the whole, there was an increasingly perceptible tendency to displace the burden on to the richest territories, the Netherlands and, ultimately, Castile, on the strength of its bullion imports. By 1555 neither Charles nor his son Philip could defy the logic of partition, long expected by other members of the family. The Spanish and German monarchies were separated, and their territories regrouped around new centres.[22]

Inherited by Philip II, the Spanish monarchy was to constitute the leading territorial power in Europe for the next hundred years. In Castile it possessed a core of strength whose resources, human and moral, flowed outwards by way of the *Reconquista* into both the Mediterranean and the newly discovered Atlantic worlds. As its authority spread, the monarchy deliberately equipped itself with imperial institutions – councils, viceroys and governors. Equally important for the smooth running of its empire, it learnt how to exploit its most valuable resource, the silver of the New World, to secure credit and finance its wars in the Old. In financing its wars, the bullion also enabled the monarchy to relax (for a time) its fiscal pressure on its Iberian and Italian provinces. Though clearly provinces, subject to Castilian viceroys and councils, these were permitted to retain many of their local liberties, along with the institutions, especially the Estates, which defended them.[23]

The monarchies of Sweden, the Austrian Habsburgs and France formed variations on this imperial pattern. Of the three, the Swedish monarchy perhaps most closely resembled the Spanish. Sweden was its own Castile: at least as underdeveloped economically, and short of manpower, but rich in minerals and strong in morale. The empire of the Swedish monarchy was purely one of conquest within Europe (a small, temporary colony in Delaware apart); the laws of war, not dynastic right, were the Vasas' title, and what they won they and their high nobility plundered with an opportunism and a flair that brooked no rival. To hold its gains the Swedish monarchy did not even attempt to construct an administrative structure like the Spanish; but it did learn to balance the exploitation of its German and Baltic provinces in war with relaxation of its demands and respect for their liberties in peace.[24] The Austrian Habsburg monarchy, by contrast, founded its rule on a dynastic legitimacy, including a virtually hereditary claim to election as Emperor, to which the parvenu Vasas could never aspire. Legitimacy had to compensate both for the relative weakness of the monarchy's core, the Austrian *Erblande* lacking the resources of either Castile or Sweden, and for the limitations, entrenched by the treaties of 1648, on its authority in the German lands of the empire. The monarchy successfully bypassed these obstacles by carrying out its own 'reconquest' in the east, recovering the kingdoms of Bohemia and Hungary from the Protestants and the Turk respectively. Again, the links that were forged to secure these provincial kingdoms to the core were less institutional than social and cultural, above all the creation of a single Habsburg imperial nobility which regarded the court at Vienna as its common centre.[25] The last of the early modern imperial monarchies, Bourbon France, possessed the strongest core but took longest to acquire an empire. The former provinces of the English kings, along with Burgundy and Brittany, had been integrated by the early sixteenth century; and the French kings had immediately enlarged their ambitions to encompass territory in the western empire, Italy and northern Spain – only to be distracted by the long period of civil wars and reconstruction that lasted until the 1630s. It was not until then that imperial ambitions were revived, in the aggressive propaganda of Richelieu's publicists.[26] Often regarded as a prototype of absolute monarchy, Bourbon France was at the time simply a latecomer to imperial monarchy.

So formed, these monarchies were far from exercising an absolute authority over their provinces. The rhetoric of absolute monarchy was indeed far removed from the practice of imperial monarchy. Whether the provinces were joined to or distant from the core made little difference; to the ruling elites the provincial relationship was often one of more or less mutual advantage. The highest provincial offices might be reserved for nobles from the core; but at every other level the provincial elites had to be confirmed, and often strengthened, in their hold on power over their own communities. In the Kingdom of Naples Castilian viceroys came and went; power remained in the hands of the rural nobility and the city's jurists. Provincial nobles could also avail themselves of the opportunities for service in the imperial monarch's armies. Despite its experience with Wallenstein, the Austrian Habsburg monarchy continued to be generous with such opportunities, while the Vasas elevated the Estonian Karl Gustav Wrangel, a competent general but a magnificent looter, to the highest ranks of the Swedish nobility. For all the mutual advantage, however, the relationship between a monarchy and its provincial elites was not a static one, and over the seventeenth century there were a number of pressures tending towards the consolidation of power and resources in the metropolitan core.

The first of these pressures was confessional: conscious of the churches' powers in education, the control and dissemination of ideas and, not least, impressive ceremonial display, dynasties regarded it as essential to identify their monarchy with one confession to the exclusion of others. This was as true of the Lutheran Vasas as of their Catholic Majesties in Spain, both of whose allegiances were firmly established by 1600; in the seventeenth century it was a policy pursued afresh, to new extremes of bigotry, by the Austrian and French dynasties. Wherever a monarchy's territories harboured adherents of a rival confession, kings and their clerical henchmen almost always felt justified in flouting provincial liberties and enforcing conversion.[27]

A second pressure was military, the growing scale and rising cost of warfare in early-modern Europe.[28] In some respects the looseness of these monarchies' structures was well adapted to allow them to take advantage of the variety of forms of military organization in this period, from territorial militias to large, semi-privatized mercenary armies. Yet the need to harness more and more resources, human, mineral and financial, also impelled the monarchies to concentrate authority at the centre, the better to exploit both their core and their provincial territories. The Spanish monarchy led the way, Olivares's Great Memorial of 1624 identifying the problem and proposing as a solution to make Philip IV de jure and de facto 'King of Spain' (so enlarging the monarchy's core to include the whole of Spain) and to create an imperial nobility, drawn from throughout the lands of the monarchy. From this followed the Union of Arms and the determined attempts to raise more men and money from the provincial

232

kingdoms of Aragon and Naples.[29] Ever uncomplicated in their methods, the Swedish monarchy preferred the policy of *Reduktion*, reclaiming for the Crown lands earlier granted to the nobility. First mooted in 1650, the policy was applied in Sweden itself in 1680, and extended to the Baltic provinces within the decade.[30] In the same decade the beginnings of the reconquest of Hungary enabled the Austrian monarchy to exert stronger military and fiscal control over that kingdom.[31] In France, where territorial integration had been formally achieved, concentration took the form of centralization through a combination of aggressive taxation and the multiplication of offices to facilitate the complicity of regional elites.[32]

Closely connected with the tendency to concentrate power for military ends was a third pressure, the new awareness of the significance of commerce as a source of wealth and hence power. In the 1620s the Spanish monarchy deliberately exerted itself to cripple Dutch commerce, and pursued the policy with a tenacity that may have done greater harm to the Spanish economy itself.[33] Initially committed to upholding freedom of commerce in the Baltic, the Swedish monarchy began in the 1650s seriously to claim a *dominium maris Baltici*. But it remained cautious in dealing with the Dutch, and did not follow through Oxenstierna's institution of a College of Commerce in 1651.[34] Land-locked Hungary saw the Austrian monarchy follow the reassertion of control with the rudiments of an economic policy. By far the most aggressive in the quest for commercial power was the French monarchy. French manufactures and overseas trading ventures were supported by regulation, charter and even conquest. When Colbert proposed in 1672 to absorb by conquest the commerce of the United Provinces of the Netherlands, he had moved well beyond the destructive aims of Olivares in the 1620s.[35] By then it was clear that a confessional, centralized, commercially aggressive France was setting a new and frightening standard of imperial monarchy.

Yet of all the manifestations of the concentration of power at the centre of these imperial monarchies, none was as striking as the growth of their capital cities. Against the secular trend of demographic decline, the populations of these grew spectacularly. Madrid's population of 50,000 in 1600 had tripled by 1650; Vienna's, likewise 50,000 at the start of the century, had more than doubled by 1700; even Stockholm's grew, in a country otherwise without cities, to just under 50,000 by 1700. Above all these towered Paris, rising from over 200,000 in 1600 to over 500,000 in 1700. Unlike the others, Paris was a port as well as a capital; and with it should be associated Versailles, whose population is estimated to have grown from 5,000 to 25,000 between 1650 and 1700.[36] To these capitals were drawn every kind of resource which the provinces had to offer; from them radiated the power and prestige of their imperial monarchies.

The provinces, of course, were by no means passively acquiescent in this process of imperial monarchic aggrandizement at their expense.

233

Repeatedly they flared up in revolt. The Spanish monarchy suffered first, revolts in Catalonia, Portugal, Naples and Palermo in the 1640s answering the centralizing measures begun in the 1620s. The Frondes of 1647–53 then allowed the French provincial elites a last, uncoordinated expression of their lingering resentment at the enhanced power of the Bourbon monarchy. In Sweden's Baltic provinces the imposition of the *Reduktion* in the 1680s provoked Johann von Patkul's attempt to organize the Livonian *Ritterschaft* in the 1690s. Greatest of all these revolts, however, was the last, when Ferenc Rakoczi led the numerous Hungarian nobility in an eight-year war (1703–11) against the Habsburgs' attempts to remove their constitutional liberties.[37] Common to all these far-flung revolts was the defence of provincial autonomy, the institutional liberties and fiscal immunities on which provincial nobilities had relied to protect themselves from outright dependence on distant monarchies. Yet few of these revolts involved a clear rejection of empire: as their leaders well knew, success depended on securing the intervention of a rival monarch.[38] Thus the Catalan, Portuguese, Neapolitan, Sicilian and Hungarian rebels appealed to France, the Hungarians also, following the Livonians, to Russia. With such intervention came the obvious danger that the revolt would simply result in a transfer of allegiance to another imperial monarchy. Such was most obviously the fate of Livonia, swallowed up by the Czar in the wake of the Great Northern War. It seemed that the best a provincial revolt could achieve, after the immediate period of repression, was a relaxing of imperial control and exploitation. Catalonia and Naples appear to have won such latitude from the – admittedly weakening – Spanish monarchy in the later seventeenth century.

Exceptionally, however, there were two provincial revolts which did succeed in winning independence, despite receiving foreign assistance. These were the revolts of the seven northern provinces of the Netherlands and of the Kingdom of Portugal against Spanish rule. Significantly, both had additional resources of their own, through commerce and colonies overseas. In the Dutch case, moreover, revolt led to the establishment of a political form quite different from that of imperial monarchy. As an equal union, the United Provinces of the Netherlands joined two other polities outside the pattern of imperial monarchies and their provinces: the Polish–Lithuanian Commonwealth created by the Union of Lublin in 1569, and the Helvetic League of the Swiss Cantons. With these the United Provinces had in common the deliberate decentralization of power to provincial estates, the commitment to consensus enshrined in the principle of unanimous voting in the Estates-General (as in the Sejm), effective religious toleration and an unwillingness to pursue territorial expansion.[39] It is true that one of the seven provinces, Holland, with its major city Amsterdam (whose population grew from 65,000 to 200,000 over the century), was much richer and more influential than any of the others, putting it in a position to act as a dominating 'core'; but the constitutional arrangements of the union carefully provided against Holland's acting unilaterally, while the mutual suspicion of Holland's oligarchs and the House of Orange served to check each other's independent political ambitions. Holland's priorities, indeed, were almost always defensive, the province more than once intervening to forestall the residual territorial aspirations of the Oranges.[40]

The resulting political form was something of a puzzle to contemporaries: as Sir William Temple remarked, 'nor will any man that understands the state of Poland, and the United Provinces, be well able to range them under any particular names of government that have yet been invented'.[41] Republicanism, Kossman has pointed out, had little to offer by way of explanation: although a few theorists in Holland cultivated the myth of Venice, this idealization of the city-state was hardly an adequate model for the United Provinces as a whole.[42] Leagues were not alien to republican thinking, Machiavelli and Harrington acknowledging that equal leagues of republics were ill-adapted for large-scale conquests.[43] Among the Dutch themselves, however, it was probably the jurists who made the best sense of the union, by interpreting it as a confederation. According to Grotius and later to Huber, the union was to be understood as a confederation of strictly sovereign provinces.[44] It was an interpretation that clearly precluded the subordination of any of the provinces to another; the connotation of dependence carried by the idea of a 'province' under a monarchy was effectively repudiated. In a quite literal sense, the United Provinces were a contradiction in imperial terms.

Not only were the Dutch much more thoroughgoing than the Poles or the Swiss in developing the principles and practice of confederation, they combined this political self-awareness with a devotion to commerce as an end in itself. Whatever their doubts and anxieties about the acquisition of wealth, the Dutch professed their commitment to commerce for enrichment, not for power. Since commerce flourished best in peace, the Dutch combined their renunciation of territorial ambitions with a conviction of the natural freedom of the seas (the doctrine of *mare liberum*).[45] This is not to say that the Dutch political authorities were indifferent to economic activity: on the contrary, they regulated industry and trade, and backed commercial shipping with naval force, to an extent and with an efficiency unmatched by any contemporary European government. Overseas, in particular, the Dutch used force at the expense of European as well as local rivals; but the territory that was acquired in the Indies was for trading stations, and was often made formally the property of the trading companies, not of the United Provinces.[46] Specious as the distinction might seem to rivals – Temple accused the East India Company of behaving 'like a commonwealth rather than a trade'[47] – the point had been made that the pursuit of commercial gain overseas was separable from the possession of territorial empire within Europe. By their devotion to commerce as by their commitment to confederation, the Dutch rendered the United Provinces the antithesis of imperial monarchy.

Even so, the Dutch could not stand alone in Europe. The aspiration to complete independence manifest under the leadership of de Witt in the 1650s and 1660s did not survive Louis XIV's ruthless invasion in 1672. Henceforth the security of the United Provinces depended, under William of Orange, upon a policy of alliances with their previous enemies, the English and the Habsburg monarchies. As the seventeenth century came to an end, moreover, the domination of Europe by the imperial monarchies was thrown into ever-sharper relief by anticipation of the crisis of the Spanish Succession. The issue was squarely dynastic, the inheritance of the multiple territories of the Spanish monarchy on the – long-expected – death of the last, childless Habsburg King, Charles II. Both the French Bourbons and the Austrian Habsburgs had claims on the succession; but for long both had appeared to accept that the best solution would be a partition of the monarchy's territories. In successive partition treaties in 1698 and 1700, Louis XIV conceded that the succession should pass to an Austrian Habsburg candidate, with France taking as compensation Spanish lands in Flanders and Italy. At the last, however, Charles II made a will of his own, leaving the monarchy entire to Louis' second grandson, Philip of Anjou; and once the will was known Louis accepted it rather than the Partition Treaty. Whatever the legitimacy of the will, this outcome was quite unacceptable to the Emperor, William III and the United Provinces. These allied to oppose Louis, and the crisis duly ended in the War of the Spanish Succession, which lasted from 1702 until 1713.[48]

It was, *par excellence*, a war of imperial monarchy. Louis XIV could rest his case on dynastic right, and argue that the two kingdoms would remain distinct; but to his opponents such a dynastic union was tantamount to the absorption of the Spanish monarchy by the French. A single enormous monarchy could come into being, with France at its centre, and Spain and all its territories, in Flanders, the Mediterranean and the New World, as its provinces. At a stroke the Bourbons would be put in a position to release the potential of France for territorial empire, and establish a predominance in Europe far exceeding that of the old Spanish monarchy. By the same stroke the French would also take over Spanish America, and thus obtain the base for a world-wide commercial empire. Never, it seemed, had the nemesis of Universal Monarchy come so close to realization.[49] To avert the threat, the allies fought for a 'balance of power' in Europe; but this did not imply an end to imperial monarchy as such. Among the allies the Austrian Habsburgs fought precisely because their pretensions to imperial leadership were as high as those of the Bourbons. The United Provinces might fight in self-defence and commercial interest; but they were well aware how much they now depended on their allies, and on the King of England in particular. In part, the English were engaged for reasons similar to those of the Dutch – for the security of Flanders as a barrier to French aggression, and for the maintenance of their dominant position in the Spanish colonial trade; but the English also fought to ensure the continued exclusion of the exiled Stuarts from their thrones – and here English participation in the war had a dynastic and territorial dimension of its own. The relationship of the English monarchy to the neighbouring kingdoms of Ireland and Scotland was necessarily involved. The repercussions of the revolution of 1688 had already required the forcible imposition of a settlement upon Ireland, but the relationship continued to be troublesome. In the case of Scotland, the relationship became critical during the war itself.

It is to the relations between the British kingdoms, and in particular to the Scots' discussion of their relation with England, that I now turn. For not only did the Spanish Succession Crisis provide the immediate political context for the Scots' attempts to reconstitute their union with England; it was in the European setting that they sought to understand their predicament and to identify the options available to them.

THE BRITISH UNION OF 1707

Scotland in the seventeenth century was one of three kingdoms joined by a dynastic 'Union of the Crowns' following the accession of its King, James VI, to the thrones of England and Ireland in 1603. From the union's inception, the Scots were aware that they faced an imperial future. Some, like Sir Thomas Craig, thought that the Scots would be treated equally with the English, and looked forward to a Britain matching the empire of the Spanish monarchy.[50] Others feared that dependent, provincial status might be imposed upon them. Anticipating such anxieties, James himself demanded of the English Parliament in 1607 whether it would want the Scots reduced to

> a naked Province, without Law or Libertie under this Kingdome. I hope you meane not I should set Garrisons over them, as the Spaniards doe over Sicily and Naples, or governe them by Commissioners.[51]

The Scottish Estates, meanwhile, made it quite clear to the King that they would have no viceroy imposed upon them.[52] James's own solution to the problems inherent in the new relationship was an imaginative, if rather vague, programme for fuller union, involving free trade and the eventual harmonization of churches and laws.[53] The Scottish response to this was cautious, the English downright hostile. With a long tradition of self-government in the absence or minority of their kings, the Scottish nobility were content to wait and see how the relationship developed. Fearful that any closer union would be a burden on them, and would compromise the status of their Parliament, the English simply pushed the problem aside.

Charles I thrust it at them regardless. Perhaps because he was so little involved in Europe, Charles and his English advisers wholly lacked James's sense of the problems inherent in composite monarchy. The Scots were promptly subjected to not one but two of the most provocative measures of centralization pursued by imperial monarchies: a *Reduktion*, the revocation of church lands in 1626, and the imposition of religious uniformity, in the new Prayer Book of 1636. Like other similarly affronted provinces, the Scots rose in revolt, with, initially, rather successful results. Another revolt broke out in Ireland, then civil war in England, so that the Scots were able to secure major concessions from the King. By renewing their attachment to the monarchy, however, the Scots' success in the 1640s had the unexpected consequence of exposing them to the more determined aggression of the English Commonwealth in the 1650s, military occupation being accompanied by an imposed parliamentary union. Restored to the status of a distinct kingdom in 1660, and left to self-government by their own nobility, the Scots nevertheless continued to feel the weight of English interests. There was renewed pressure for confessional uniformity with Anglicanism, followed by orders to tolerate Catholics. Though the Estates met in Edinburgh, the King's court was fixed in London; and while a small number of Scots noblemen had positions and influence at court, Englishmen had far more of both. (No serious attempt was made to integrate the Scottish nobility with the English peerage to create a single nobility for the monarchy as a whole.) London itself was by 1700 the largest city in Europe, with a population estimated at 575,000; with that of Edinburgh no more than 50,000, London's metropolitan pre-eminence was ever more visible.

Many of the Scottish elite accepted the deposition of James VII and II and the accession of William and Mary in 1689 with relief; a few did so with enthusiasm. Having escaped from the United Provinces, however, William himself had no intention of being distracted by his newly acquired provincial kingdom in the north. Like Ireland, Scotland was first and foremost a security problem, requiring a firm hand. Suppression of the resistance organized by Viscount Dundee in 1689, followed by the premeditated massacre in Glencoe in 1692, made William's point to would-be Jacobites. 'Loyal' Scotsmen, meanwhile, were heavily recruited for military service in Europe, and the magnates who led the factions in the Scottish Estates were, as far as possible, cajoled into following English ministerial wishes.[54] Most galling of all, however, was the Crown's repeated obstruction of the Estates' attempts to improve the economy, obstruction which culminated in the casual sabotage of the colony established by the Scottish African Company in 1698 on the isthmus of Darien in Panama.

As the expectations borne by the African Company had been high, so the reaction to its failure was fierce. It was now universally recognized that the relationship with England had become so unsatisfactory that it must be reconstructed. Constrained by the existence of a rival, Catholic claimant to the throne, non-Jacobite Scots, like the Protestant Irish, could no longer contemplate a provincial revolt to redress their grievances. However they were sufficiently provoked by the Darien fiasco to launch into a vigorous debate upon their predicament, while waiting to see what could be made of it politically. The lead in this debate was taken by Andrew Fletcher of Saltoun, an East Lothian laird. Twice exiled in the 1680s, and a veteran of the war against the Turk in Hungary, Fletcher had acquired in the camps of Europe an unusually cosmopolitan political culture; in this, as in his patriotism, he belongs in the company of men like the Livonian Johann von Patkul and the leaders of the dissident Hungarian nobility. In a series of pamphlets in 1698 and in his Speeches to the Scottish Parliament in 1703, Fletcher focused attention on three consequences of the existing union with England. There was Scotland's contribution to the creation of an English standing army, which drained the country of men, and gave the Crown a menacing new power.[55] There was the sabotage of the Darien Scheme and the persistent obstruction of Scottish trade. At the root of all, however, was the court in England, whose rewards had corrupted the – all-too-compliant – Scottish aristocracy, making of them venal tools of English interest. It was thus, as Fletcher urged the Parliament to recognize, that Scotland now 'appeared to the rest of the world more like a conquered province than a free independent people'.[56]

Fletcher's diagnosis was taken up by commentators of every political persuasion within Scotland. As the Jacobite Patrick Abercromby put it, 'we all own that we are unhappy ... because our Sovereigns reside in England'.[57] Those favourable to the ruling dynasty were as critical as those (like Abercromby) who were not. Both William Paterson, the Darien projector, and William Seton of Pitmedden, in Aberdeenshire, traced the collapse of Scottish trade back to 1603, and the loss of 'the imperial seat of government' to London, where the English naturally ensured that their interest was put first. Scotland, it was uniformly agreed, was poor, must be developed and could only achieve this through a new relationship with England.[58]

The Scots, however, were well aware that the relationship with England had a wider, European context. Again, it was Fletcher who dramatized the issue, in his extraordinary *Discorso delle cose di Spagna*, written in Italian and published in 1698 with the imprint 'Napoli'. The pamphlet was a transparently ironic demonstration of the opportunity afforded by a new Spanish succession to establish a Universal Monarchy. Previous Kings of Spain had failed in this endeavour because their religious intolerance had depopulated the peninsula and discouraged manufactures; but there were now several claimants to the throne who were not such bigots, and who could, by judicious exchanges of territory, endow the monarchy with a solid core of territory from which to extend its authority over the whole of Europe.[59] Through the irony Fletcher was seeking to expose the monstrosity of such dealing in peoples and territories. However, he was equally concerned with what the English King might make of the crisis. In a short tract of 1701, he accused William of seeking to consolidate the three kingdoms, the seven provinces of the Netherlands and the ten of Flanders into a single absolute monarchy, which would establish 'an empire of the sea, an entire monopoly of trade'. The power of France must be resisted, Fletcher agreed, but this was not the way.[60]

Though none expressed his fears quite so extravagantly, non-Jacobites were agreed that the threat of a French Universal Monarchy intensified the urgency of the need for a firmer relationship with England. Given that every King would like to be the Universal Monarch, George Ridpath observed (after Defoe), there must be 'leagues and confederacies' between 'little neighbours' in order to maintain 'the Ballance of Power in Europe'. It was thus in Scotland's interest, especially its commercial interest, to join with England against France.[61] Likewise preoccupied with the threat from the French monarchy were Paterson, Seton and the Earl of Cromarty, all of whom believed it underlined the need for closer union.[62] Jacobites naturally dissented, Abercromby suggested that the Scots would do better to renew their Old Alliance with the French monarchy, which, he argued, would protect Scotland without compromising its independence. Though Abercromby had ulterior motives, the distance between France and Scotland lent plausibility to the suggestion – the more so since (as he pointed out) England's proximity made an attempt by the English to settle the issue by conquest a distinct possibility.[63] It was a point whose force the advocates of a reconstructed union well understood, and which was to limit the freedom of manœuvre of those who opposed the specific form of union the English were prepared to offer.

Just how ruthless the English could be in asserting their interests over what they considered a conquered nation was being displayed even then in Ireland. Two issues in the 1690s had exposed the tensions in England's relation with Ireland (and specifically the Anglo-Irish): each had dangerous implications for the Scots. One, raised by William Molyneux in *The Case of Ireland Stated* (1698), concerned the extent of the English Crown and Parliament's authority over Ireland. According to Molyneux the English had no claim to such authority by right of conquest, and he indignantly rejected the suggestion that Ireland was England's colony. Ireland was 'an Ancient Separate and Distinct Kingdom from England', just like Scotland.[64] Molyneux was promptly answered by John Cary and William Atwood, with historical proofs of Ireland's conquest and subjection to the 'imperial crown of England'. The English writers were initially more cautious in their references to Scotland; but George Ridpath had already seen the danger, translating Sir Thomas Craig's hitherto unpublished refutation of English claims that Scots Kings owed homage to English. Ridpath knew his enemies. By 1704 Atwood was shamelessly asserting that Scotland too was subject to the English imperial crown.[65] Atwood was a Whig, and the leading contemporary exponent of English ancient constitutionalism: his position indicated how intransigent the English remained over modifying their historic institutions and pretensions in order to achieve a stable relationship with the other kingdoms in the monarchy. For the moment the point remained an ideological one; but if a negotiated settlement was not found, the English had justification to hand for Scotland's forcible subordination.

Of more immediate practical concern was the campaign by English cloth interests against Irish woollen exports. Beginning in 1695 and culminating in 1699 in an English Act of Parliament prohibiting the exports, the campaign was justified by Cary and Davenant on the grounds that the cheapness of Irish labour enabled them to undersell English producers, an advantage which must be cancelled in the interest of England. The danger was immediately apparent to several Scottish observers, and the larger implications of the English argument were brought out with particular cleverness by Fletcher, in his *Account of a Conversation concerning a Right Regulation of Governments for the Common Good of Mankind* (1704). Whether the conversation was actual or invented, its participants were well chosen: besides Fletcher and the Scottish Earl of Cromarty, the two Englishmen were Sir Christopher Musgrave and Sir Edward Seymour, who had both been active defenders of English interests against Irish.[66] Denying that England ruled Ireland by right of conquest (but accepting that it was a colony, of Scots as well as English), Fletcher pressed Davenant's economic argument, which Musgrave had repeated, on to its logical conclusion. If the Irish, by undercutting the English, were such a threat, it were better to cut Ireland off entirely, sink it in the sea and bring its population over to England. The same might then be done for the six northern counties and for Wales, until trade and people were concentrated around London. 'And do you not think – he concluded by asking – the same arguments would prove that all the considerable trade of the world might be brought into one city, and all mankind live within and about that place?'[67] If the Scots were to put their relationship with England on a new foundation, they could afford no illusions about the attitude of the English.

The opportunity for which the Scots had been waiting was provided by the Act of Settlement passed by the English Parliament in 1701. This provided that if Anne died without heirs (as was now expected), the succession to the English throne should pass to the Electress of Hanover and her heirs. The Scots were not consulted. English ministers attempted, but failed, to head off Scottish outrage by opening negotiations for an incorporating union that would create one Crown and Parliament for both kingdoms. Instead, the newly elected Scottish Estates voted an Act of Security (1703–4) which accepted the Hanoverian Succession for Scotland only on condition that the independence of the Scottish Parliament and church and free trade with England were guaranteed. Additionally, the Estates claimed that they would then decide Scotland's foreign policy. Furious in turn, the English Parliament passed the Alien Act (1705), threatening to seize Scottish property in England and bar all trade between the two countries unless the Scots accepted the Hanoverian succession; at the same time the Scots were again offered negotiations for a treaty of union. By implication, the Alien Act set aside the pretension to an imperial sovereignty over Scotland; but in treating the Scots as potentially hostile foreigners, it virtually made the conquest of Scotland under the laws of war the alternative to acceptance of incorporating union. There could be little doubt that the English government had the capacity to impose the Hanoverian succession on Scotland if it had to: the threat behind the Alien Act could not be ignored. However, it was also obvious that the English would much rather not be diverted from the Spanish to a British War of Succession. For the Scots, therefore, the situation was one of opportunity as well as menace: what form of settlement could be reached with an England likely to win but reluctant to try a recourse to arms?

The Scots canvassed three possibilities in a further round of sophisticated debate. One was obviously the Jacobite – a Stuart restoration, under French protection. The need for discretion made it difficult to spell out how this would be to Scotland's economic and social benefit, and how it would alter for the better Scotland's relation to England. It could be argued that a strong, even an absolute, monarchy was needed to secure the economic and social renovation which, Abercromby agreed with Fletcher, were so urgently required. If the Stuarts were restored in Scotland alone, then survival would depend on French support and the existence of an appropriate balance of power to restrain England.[68] If the Stuarts were to recover England and Ireland as well, there would presumably be a fresh Union of the Crowns, and a return to the pattern of imperial monarchy, though the Scots might now expect to enjoy 'most favoured province' status.

Those Scots who were hostile to France and a Stuart restoration accepted the need for a common succession in all three kingdoms, and hence also for a new form of union to replace the discredited Union of the Crowns; but there was a choice of possible forms of union. Either the Scots sought to secure a form of 'federal' or 'confederal' union (the two terms were used without a clear distinction between them) or they accepted and made the best of the incorporating form of union which was preferred by the English government.

The argument for a form of federal or confederal union was put by Fletcher, assisted by Ridpath and James Hodges. Fletcher offered it to the Parliament of 1703 in the form of Limitations to be appended to the Act of Security. These Limitations would guarantee the existence of a separate Scottish Parliament, militia and judiciary. What Fletcher was proposing resembled the legislation of the Covenanters in 1641; but Fletcher was careful to play down if not disown the comparison, as if to make the point that a new departure was needed.[69] Ridpath, by contrast, was keen to present the Limitations as an extension of the Whig–Presbyterian understanding of Scotland's ancient constitution.[70] Hodges set the case in a wider framework, carefully defining the forms that 'a confederate or federal union' might take, and discussing the examples of the Dutch, the Swiss, the Polish and the ancient Greek unions. It was unfortunate that having cleared the ground for a scheme specifically for Scotland, he failed to publish it.[71] All the advocates of this form of union assumed that by retaining its Parliament Scotland would have the power to secure its own interests, in particular its church and its trade. They supported the widely canvassed proposal for a Council of Trade, and more particularly John Law's scheme for a Land Bank to raise credit to stimulate Scotland's agriculture and commerce.[72]

The proponents of a federal union did not pretend that it would be easy to achieve. Fletcher's Limitations would have required radical institutional reform, and his avoidance of most of the shibboleths of patriotic rhetoric seems designed to suggest that a Scottish political community needed to be created, not simply restored. Meanwhile, critics highlighted other difficulties. Above all, it was asked how a federal union would prevent the English imposing their interest by virtue of their greater strength. The point was made, inadvertently, by an English writer who favoured this form of union, Peter Paxton. He envisaged Scotland and England as 'distinct and independent sovereignties', on the model of the United Provinces. This, he argued, was all the union England needed, since London would be able to attract to itself the wealth of both countries.[73] The argument that a federal union would actually be to England's advantage was driven home by Cromarty, who also made fun of its adherents' failure to understand the indivisibility of sovereignty.[74]

It was Cromarty, along with Seton, who best set out the alternative case for incorporating union. At the heart of their case lay a conviction of the benefits of creating a common, indivisible sovereignty for the two countries. The Scots, they argued, would not so much lose their sovereignty as constitute a new one under which there would be a full communication of rights between the two peoples. The consequent advantages would be political, religious and economic. The magnate factions which had so disrupted Scottish politics would disappear once deprived of the narrowly Scottish institutions that sustained them, leaving those below the magnates at liberty to administer the country under a distant parliament.[75] Likewise the establishment of the nations' churches by one common parliament would undermine the inclination of the religious to renew the animosities of the preceding century.[76] Finally, a single sovereign power would create the conditions for a single market throughout Britain. Turning Davenant's arguments to Scotland's advantage, Cromarty contended that the Scots would then be able to exploit their cheaper labour costs to undersell the English in England. At the same time, Scotland's overseas commerce would enjoy the protection of the navigation acts, and so be able to participate in the colonial trades from which it had hitherto been excluded.[77]

As put by Cromarty and Seton, the case for incorporating union was conceptually sophisticated and politically attractive. The insistence on the concept of unitary, indivisible sovereign power was clearly informed by an understanding of modern political jurisprudence, being supported by frequent reference to Grotius in particular. The Scots, indeed, were notably clearer about the implications of such a sovereignty than the leading English exponent of incorporating union, Daniel Defoe, who suggested that the supremacy of Parliament would be limited by the Treaty of Union.[78] To the Scots, the point of incorporating union was to set one sovereign parliament over Crown, churches, economies and peoples: thereby the succession would be secured in a Protestant line, the churches established on a civil basis, the economies merged in one market and the peoples formed into one set of subjects. So formulated, the Scottish case for incorporating union conveyed an appealing optimism. Recognizing the degree of England's need for union and preference for incorporation, Seton and Cromarty would show how this could be turned to Scotland's greater advantage. There was no need for the Scots to be cowed, still less conquered, by the English when incorporation offered so many benefits.

Yet this case too was open to the criticism that the benefits to England would be still greater. Defoe had seemed to suggest as much in his earlier pamphlets, when he addressed English readers and argued that an incorporating union would add land and people to one 'English empire'.[79] A parallel argument for incorporating union between Ireland and England showed still more clearly why doubts might arise. Recognizing that the English had no similarly compelling reason to accept such a union with Ireland, the Anglo-Irish Member of Parliament Henry Maxwell placed the emphasis of his *Essay towards an Union of England with Ireland* (1703) on persuading English opinion of its desirability. Describing Ireland as the 'province' and England as the 'superior state', he envisaged a union which would join the Irish to the English constitution, so that 'the subordination of Ireland to England would be the effect of its own choice'. Like the Scots, Maxwell had his eyes on the benefits of free trade under a union, believing that it would do most to develop the Irish economy; but he emphasized that this would not be at England's, or London's, expense, since the trade of Ireland, though increased, would come into the full and absolute possession of the English.[80] The same emphasis marked an anonymous pamphlet which hailed an incorporating union of all three kingdoms as making 'the Queen an Empress, and her Three Kingdoms one Empire'. To round off such a union, the Queen should simply create a new, imperial rank of the peerage, and set at its head a new ecclesiastical dignitary, the Patriarch of London.[81]

The possibility that England, and London in particular, stood to gain most by an incorporating union, to the point of rendering Britain an empire, was not missed by Andrew Fletcher. It was precisely this conclusion that he drew from considering the cases of Ireland and Scotland together in the *Account of a Conversation*. The creation of one market, he argued, would simply remove all obstacles to the concentration of resources in the richer kingdom. Pressing home his analysis of England's treatment of Ireland, Fletcher launched into a denunciation of capital cities. I am fully persuaded, he wrote,

> that all great governments, whether republics or monarchies, not only disturb the world in their rise and fall; but by bringing together such numbers of men and immense riches into one city, inevitably corrupt all good manners . . . Rome, the greatest of all, incessantly disturbed her neighbours for seven hundred years; and after the conquest of almost all the known world, was corrupted by excess of riches and power, and spread the infection over all the parts of that empire.[82]

When Sir Edward Seymour belatedly realized that the target of all this was London, 'the greatest and most glorious city of the world', and let out a furious protest, Fletcher threw it back: 'That London should draw the riches and government of the three Kingdoms to the south-east corner of this island is in some degree as unnatural as for one city to possess the riches and government of the world.'[83] An incorporating union with England, Fletcher was saying, would make London into a new Rome, the seat of an empire. It would be an empire, however, worse even than Rome's, for in combining the new urge for commercial monopoly with the old appetite for territorial domination, it would simply devour its provinces.

Fletcher not only criticized the incorporating unionist case; the *Account of a Conversation* also contained a new proposal. The idea of confederal leagues should be extended right across Europe. To the reported astonishment of his listeners, Fletcher explained that Europe could be divided into roughly equal geographic portions, each of which would be further divided between ten or twelve cities or kingdoms. These cities or kingdoms would be distinct sovereignties, but would be leagued together, under a council or a prince, for their common defence. Fletcher did not suppose that such leagues would prevent all wars, but they would ensure that wars were short-lived. What they would prevent was the formation of concentrations of power and riches around great cities. Instead, the existence of so many seats of government would encourage virtue and the cultivation of all the arts and sciences.[84]

Though Fletcher described his proposal as having almost no precedent, it was almost certainly inspired by the principles of federal or confederal union displayed in the Polish–Lithuanian Commonwealth, the Empire and the United Provinces.[85] Alert as he was to the renewed threat of Universal Monarchy arising from the Spanish Succession Crisis, Fletcher can be seen to have understood the choice facing Scotland as a variant of the European opposition between imperial monarchy and defensive confederation. In his view, an incorporating union would reduce Scotland to a yet more 'provincial' dependence upon England and its capital, a dependence both political and economic. For the sake of Scotland's freedom, independence and prosperity, therefore, it was essential that the two countries form a United Provinces rather than a United Kingdom of Great Britain, even if it took the reduction of London and the extension of confederations throughout Europe to achieve this.

AFTER 1707: THE BRITISH STATE AND THE BRITISH EMPIRE

However imaginative Fletcher's presentation of the confederal alternative, his arguments were to no avail. By the summer of 1706 commissioners from the two countries had agreed on a draft Treaty of Union; and once its articles had been individually approved by the Scottish Estates it was enacted by both Parliaments in March 1707. The incorporating unionists had 'won'. The triumph of one side rather than the other, however, does nothing to diminish the significance of the debate as a whole. The arguments themselves were never going to be decisive: though their contribution may have been undervalued, it was immediate, material economic and political pressures which swayed opinion and votes in the Estates.[86] The significance of the debate lies, rather, in the light it throws on the character of the union when understood, as both sides recognized it should be, in a European context. The arguments of the critics quite as much as of the proponents of incorporating union go far to clarify the nature of the British state and empire in the eighteenth century and beyond.

In their determination to reconstruct their relationship with the monarchy that dominated them, late-seventeenth and early-eighteenth-century Scots were by no means alone. Across the continent of Europe the same intention was being expressed, in response to similar pressures, from the Swedish province of Livonia to the Spanish viceroyalty of Naples. Between these can be found many resemblances as well as contrasts, the intellectual sophistication of the Neapolitan debate offering a particularly good comparison with the Scottish.[87] Nevertheless, the Scots' debate on their relation to England was distinctive, perhaps unique, in at least two respects. One is the freedom of expression and ease of publication which most of its participants enjoyed, encouraging both sophistication and breadth of perspective. Another is the striking optimism of many participants, their sense that Scotland ought now to be able to transcend the condition of provincial dependence.

The exponents of incorporating union exploited this sense to particular effect. The implication of their case was that a united Britain could distance itself conclusively from the pattern of imperial monarchy found on the continent. By uniting under a single, sovereign parliament, empowered to determine the succession and regulate the churches, the Scots and the English would be freed from the vagaries of dynastic inheritance and royal confessional allegiance to which all Europe's monarchies were characteristically exposed. A distinctively 'British' resolution of these problems would have been found: henceforth it would be clear that parliamentary and not dynastic or divine right was the foundation of both the monarchy and the two churches – in respect of the latter, as erastian a statement as could be made. The same sovereign parliament would also secure the access of all its subjects, Scots as well as English, to one British market and one overseas empire. Finally, that parliament would have full authority to tax the subject inhabitants of both countries, enabling a British government to harness their resources for war. Through the union, in short, the parliamentary monarchy of Britain would possess an institutionalized authority unmatched by any other European power, monarchy or confederation: it could bid defiance to any continental pretender to territorial empire, while pursuing commercial hegemony and colonial possessions overseas.

In effect, I suggest, what the Scottish incorporating unionists thus envisaged was the creation of the British state, both in its own right and as a precondition of empire. Though the term 'state' was not used regularly or precisely in their writings, these Scots had identified what were coming to be regarded by the most advanced political and jurisprudential thought of the time as the essential attributes of statehood: the concentration of authority in an impersonal sovereign body and, no less important, the consolidation of that authority over territories and their inhabitants.[88] To achieve the necessary concentration of authority required, the Scots accepted the adoption of the English model of a parliament as a sovereign representative, not an Estates. But the concentration of authority in Crown-in-Parliament must be accompanied by its territorial consolidation; for that purpose the sovereignty of the parliament must be British. It is possible that the existing English Parliament would otherwise have asserted a territorial sovereignty over Scotland by conquest – albeit at a cost that might have undermined its capacity for empire overseas. However, the union offered both England and Scotland a means to achieve territorial consolidation which was at once quicker, surer and, it seemed, mutually advantageous. Peacefully replacing a composite, imperial monarchy with a single sovereign state, it gave the exercise of political authority over Britain a legitimacy that an English state alone would have taken much longer to establish and might never have achieved.

The arguments of the Scots show why it is important, after all, to recognize the existence of a British state in the eighteenth century; but there were, of course, limits to what this entailed. It was not to be expected that the English would abandon their tenacious sense of superior peculiarity. The matchlessness of the English constitution and the 'Truth' of the Anglican Church remained the shibboleths of English public consciousness, and simple scotophobia remained potent. In the face of such particularism, reciprocated by many Scots, it is difficult to think of the British as a single 'nation' state; significantly, little of Scottish incorporating unionist argument pointed in that direction. Nevertheless, the creation of a British state on the terms agreed in 1707 altered the framework of English as well as Scottish public life. In important respects there no longer was an English state – and with it had gone any real (as opposed to imaginary) basis for the English dynastic *ancien régime* or the Anglican confessional state which some contemporaries and a few sympathetic historians would like to think still existed in the eighteenth century.[89] Instead, there was a state, as other contributors to this volume argue, that increasingly formulated its social and economic policies for Britain as a whole and had several ways of generating British patriotism in its support.[90] For all the surviving variety of administrative and legal forms, the territorial sovereignty of the eighteenth-century British state was not in doubt.

At the same time, this was a state ready and increasingly willing to impose its territorial sovereignty on possessions overseas. At an official level the territorial dimension of overseas empire might continue for some time to be subordinate to the concern with naval power, leading to a blue-water strategy in war and a reliance on colonists and merchants to look after themselves on land;[91] but the conviction that empire required the exercise of territorial sovereignty proved difficult to resist. It was not resisted at all in Ireland, over which a form of territorial dominion had long been asserted, and was soon rephrased in the terms of parliamentary sovereignty in the Declaratory Act of 1720.[92] In the case of North America, public attitudes in Britain were aggressively territorial from early in the century, and ministers felt obliged to follow suit after the Seven Years War. Henceforth the colonists were to be treated as subjects liable to parliamentary taxation and legislation no less than the British, a subordination duly confirmed in 1766 in another resounding Declaratory Act. When the colonists demurred, the intransigence of the British Crown and Parliament was such that they were happier to let the colonists go than to compromise over the principle of parliamentary sovereignty.[93] East, after all, lay another continent to dominate, as the mercantile East India Company was transformed into the instrument of British territorial sovereignty over India.[94] To an extent that it had never been for the Dutch, overseas empire had become for the eighteenth-century British state a territorial as well as a maritime enterprise.

The strongly territorial character of the British state and empire in the eighteenth century would hardly have surprised Andrew Fletcher and those who joined him in arguing for an alternative, confederal form of union. In their view, an incorporating union was no such decisive break from the continental pattern of imperial monarchy. On the contrary, incorporating union would simply renew and reinforce imperial authority of a sort all too familiar in Europe – the authority of the metropolitan centre over the outlying provinces. By substituting the absolute sovereignty of a single parliament for a dynastic monarchy and separate parliaments, the union would concentrate yet more power in the capital, rendering unassailable the pre-eminence of London within Britain, and ensuring that it would have first access to the wealth to be won from overseas empire. On this understanding of incorporating union, it is not difficult to see why the alternative, continental model of confederal union should have retained its appeal to Scots, however incomprehensible it might be to the English parliamentary mind. As Fletcher recognized, a confederal Britain was conceivable only in a European framework; but as the Dutch example demonstrated, confederation need not be incompatible with the pursuit of commercial, if not territorial, empire overseas. There was no cause, there-fore, to create a British state to enable the Scots to transcend their condition of provincial dependence: the 'British state' would prove to be but another name for empire within Britain, intensifying, not ending, that dependence. The Scots would do far better to stand by their fellows in Europe's provinces, resisting the lure of courts, capitals and states.

Alas for Fletcher, the lure proved irresistible to many of his countrymen. In the eighteenth century and for most of the next two, too many Scots stood to gain too much from participation in the British state and its empire. Yet neither Fletcher's analysis nor his alternative can thereby be discounted. His was an analysis of imperial power and provincial depen-dence as rooted in the actuality of seventeenth-century experience as that of his opponents, the incorporating unionists. His was an alternative, moreover, variant forms of which would be taken up afresh by those who offered resistance to the British empire later in the century. As the Anglo-Irish and the North American colonists both realized, Westminster's pas-sage of declaratory acts was a confession of an inability to impose in practice the sovereignty they asserted in principle.[95] Increasingly, the Irish Parliament recognized its scope for independent behaviour, and it was only after the Irish insurrection and the French intervention of 1798 that the British state imposed incorporating union in 1801. The North Americans, meanwhile, had already gone one better: finding themselves denied even a devolved authority to tax and legislate for provincial purposes, they declared and then successfully defended their independence as a confederation, subsequently a federation, of United States (not Provinces) of America.[96]

But it is with the abiding problem of the British state itself that this chapter should end. This is a state, I began by observing, whose identity has long seemed to historians and statesmen to be inseparable from the possession of empire overseas – yet which now shows every sign of outliving that empire. It is not the least of the contributions of the Scottish union debate, I wish finally to suggest, that it helps to explain why. For what the Scots understood was that the British state would have from its inception an identity of its own, as a territorial authority in its own right. It was an authority readily extendable to an overseas empire: the British state would certainly have no inhibitions about proclaiming its territorial sovereignty wherever it could feasibly be upheld. Yet the British state did not come into being in 1707 simply as a vehicle for empire elsewhere. It was created, first of all, to consolidate territorial authority within Britain. To its supporters, the incorporating unionists, such a consolidation of authority was essential if the two kingdoms were to put the conflicts inherent in an imperial monarchy behind them, and it promised to set Britain decisively apart from Europe. To their critics, however, the new state was but old empire reinforced, giving the metropolitan Parliament an authority over Scotland that it would always be loath to relinquish. It was therefore to Europe, as Andrew Fletcher foresaw, that the Scots would have to return, to seek an opportunity to develop the confederal alternative to imperial statehood. From the vantage-point of a Europe undergoing radical political reconstruction, Fletcher's is a point of view that can now be appreciated better, perhaps, than at any time since 1707; were they to find political will, it might even be possible for the Scots to act upon it and bring the British state to an end at last.

NOTES

I am grateful to participants in the Princeton Colloquium, to those who attended the meetings of the Formation of the English State Discussion Group at St Peter's College, Oxford, in 1989, and to the Oxford Seminar on the Fundamentals of Imperialism in 1990, and also to my colleague Colin Matthew for many helpful comments.

1 John Brewer, *The Sinews of Power: War, Money and the English State 1688–1783* (London: Unwin Hyman, 1989).

2 *A Source Book of Scottish History*, vol. III, *1567–1707*, ed. W. C. Dickinson and G. Donaldson (Edinburgh: Thomas Nelson, 1954), 480–1.

3 Despite its title, B. P. Levack, *The Formation of the British State: England, Scotland and the Union 1603–1707* (Oxford: Oxford University Press, 1987), emphasizes the limited extent of the union that was eventually agreed in 1707.

4 Brewer, *Sinews of Power*, ch. 1 ('Contexts').

5 ibid., xvi.

6 J. G. A. Pocock, 'States, Republics and Empires. The American Founding in Early Modern Perspective', *Social Science Quarterly*, 68 (1987), 4.

7 Q. R. D. Skinner, 'The State', in T. Ball, J. Farr and R. L. Hanson (eds), *Political Innovation and Conceptual Change* (Cambridge: Cambridge University Press, 1989).

8 Samuel Pufendorf, *Of the Law of Nature and Nations* (London, 1703), VII. v. 16, 185. Cf. Thomas Hobbes, *Leviathan* (London, 1651), ch. 22.

9 Graham Nicholson, 'The Act of Appeals and the English Reformation', in C. Cross, D. Loades and J. Scarisbrick (eds), *Law and Government under the Tudors* (Cambridge: Cambridge University Press, 1988), 23–4.

10 J. H. Elliott, 'Spain and its Empire in the Sixteenth and Seventeenth Centuries', in *Spain and Its World 1500–1700* (New Haven and London: Yale University Press, 1989), 7–10.

11 By contrast with that of 'the state', the conceptual history of 'empire' in this period has been neglected; but see Pocock, 'States, Republics and Empires', for observations in line with those above.

12 Franz Bosbach, *Monarchia Universalis. Ein politischer Leitbegriff der frühen Neuzeit* (Göttingen: Vandenhoeck & Ruprecht, 1988).

13 Composed in 1600–1, Campanella's tract was first published in German in 1620; English translations appeared in 1654 and 1659. For elucidation see now Anthony Pagden, *Spanish Imperialism and the Political Imagination* (New Haven and London: Yale University Press, 1990), ch. 2 ('Campanella and the Universal Monarchy of Spain').

14 Bosbach, *Monarchia Universalis*, ch. 6; Joseph Klaits, *Printed Propaganda under Louis XIV: Absolute Monarchy and Public Opinion* (Princeton: Princeton University Press, 1976).

15 G. W. Leibniz, *Mars Christianissimus* (1683); *Manifesto for the Defence of the Rights of Charles III* (1703), translated in *The Political Writings of Leibniz*, ed. Patrick Riley (Cambridge: Cambridge University Press, 1972). For a – much more cautious – Neapolitan discussion of Louis's pretensions see Francesco D'Andrea, *Risposta al trattato delle ragioni della Regina Cristianissima sopra il Ducato del Brabante et altri stati della Fiandra* (Naples, 1667, 1676); and the manuscript 'Discorso politico intorno alla futura successione della Monarchia di Spagna composto dal Regio Consigliero Francesco D'Andrea' (1697), printed as an appendix in Salvo Mastellone, *Francesco D'Andrea: Politico e giurista 1648–1698* (Florence: Olschki, 1969).

16 John Evelyn, *Navigation and Commerce, Their Original and Progress* (London, 1674), outlined the idea of a maritime Universal Monarchy. On the English debate see Steven Pincus, 'Protestantism and Patriotism: Ideology and the Making of English Foreign Policy 1650–1665' (Ph.D. thesis, Harvard University, 1990).

17 Daniel Defoe, *The Interests of the Several Princes and States of Europe Consider'd, with respect to the Succession of the Crown of Spain* (London, 1698); Charles Davenant, *An Essay upon Universal Monarchy* (London, 1701), repr. in *The Political and Commercial Works of Charles Davenant*, collected and revised by Sir Charles Whitworth (London, 1771).

18 Franz von Lisola, *Bouclier d'estat et de justice contre le dessein manifestement decouvert de la monarchie universelle, sous le vain pretexte des pretentions de la Reyne de France* (1667), 197–9.

19 Machiavelli, *Discorsi sopra la prima deca di Tita Livio* (Florence, 1531), modern edn by Sergio Bertelli (Milan: Feltrinelli, 1973), bk I, ch. v; James Harrington,

Oceana (London, 1656), in *The Political Works of James Harrington*, ed. J. G. A. Pocock (Cambridge: Cambridge University Press, 1977), 180.

20 [Daniel Defoe], *The Two Great Questions Consider'd. I What the French King will do, with respect to the Spanish Monarchy. II What Measures the English ought to take* (London, 1700), 15.

21 H. G. Koenigsberger, '*Dominium Regale* or *Dominium Politicum et Regale*: Monarchies and Parliaments in Early Modern Europe', in *Politicians and Virtuosi* (London: Hambledon, 1986); and 'Composite States, Representative Institutions and the American Revolution', *Historical Research*, 62 (1989), 148; J. H. Elliott, 'A Europe of Composite Monarchies', *Past and Present*, 137 (1992).

22 M. J. Rodriguez-Salgado, *The Changing Face of Empire: Charles V, Philip II and Habsburg Authority 1551–1559* (Cambridge: Cambridge University Press, 1988), 20–1, 33–40, 50–72, 118–32.

23 J. H. Elliott, *Imperial Spain 1469–1716*, (1963; repr. Harmondsworth: Penguin, 1970); H. G. Koenigsberger, *The Government of Sicily under Philip II of Spain* (London: Staple Press, 1951). Also J. H. Elliott, 'A Provincial Aristocracy: The Catalan Ruling Class in the Sixteenth and Seventeenth Centuries', in *Spain and Its World*, 72 n. 4 on the Catalans' relaxed understanding of their status as a 'province'.

24 Michael Roberts, *The Swedish Imperial Experience 1560–1720* (Cambridge: Cambridge University Press, 1979), chs 2–3, rather than G. Rystad, *Europe and Scandinavia: Aspects of the Process of Integration in the Seventeenth Century* (Lund: Lund Studies in International History, 1983).

The extent to which the Swedish and Spanish empires were acquired in spite (or, arguably, because) of the underdevelopment of their cores is missed in the synthetic sweep of Paul Kennedy's *Rise and Fall of Great Powers* (London: Fontana, 1988). Kennedy's broad argument for a long-run correlation between economic and political power misses precisely what is most interesting about these early-modern empires.

25 R. J. W. Evans, *The Making of the Habsburg Monarchy 1550–1700* (Oxford: Oxford University Press, 1979), Part II.

26 J. H. Elliott, *Richelieu and Olivares* (Cambridge: Cambridge University Press, 1984), 124.

27 In their own courts, financial necessity might make monarchs more flexible. On the toleration of Jewish financiers see J. I. Israel, *European Jewry in the Age of Mercantilism 1550–1750* (Oxford: Oxford University Press, 1985), chs V–VI.

28 Geoffrey Parker, *The Military Revolution: Military Innovation and the Rise of the West 1500–1800* (Cambridge: Cambridge University Press, 1988).

29 J. H. Elliott, *The Count-Duke of Olivares: The Statesman in an Age of Decline* (New Haven and London: Yale University Press, 1986), 179–202.

30 K. Agren, 'The *Reduktion*', in Michael Roberts (ed.), *Sweden's Age of Greatness* (London: Macmillan, 1973).

31 Orest Subtelny, *Domination of Eastern Europe: Native Nobilities and Foreign Absolutism 1500–1715* (Montreal and Gloucester: McGill-Queen's University Press and Alan Sutton, 1986), 79, 84–5.

32 William Beik, *Absolutism and Society in Seventeenth-Century France: State Power and Provincial Aristocracy in Languedoc* (Cambridge: Cambridge University Press, 1985).

33 J. I. Israel, 'A Conflict of Empires: Spain and the Netherlands 1618–1648', *Past and Present*, 76 (1977); but Israel suggests that there may have been benefits

for the Spanish economy in *The Dutch Republic and the Hispanic World 1606–1661* (Oxford: Oxford University Press, 1982), 153–4.

34 Roberts, *Swedish Imperial Experience*, 100–16.

35 On Colbert's ambitions at the expense of the Dutch see J. I. Israel, *Dutch Commercial Primacy in World Trade 1585–1740* (Oxford: Oxford University Press, 1989), 295–7. Such commercial calculations were not, of course, incompatible with Louis XIV's own greater concern with matters of status and sovereignty.

36 Jan de Vries, *European Urbanization 1500–1800* (London: Methuen, 1984). However approximate the estimates, the general pattern is telling. The estimates are given in Appendix I; there is comment on the growth of capital cities and ports between 1600 and 1750 on 141–2.

37 Subtelny, *Domination of Eastern Europe*, 113–20, 145–56, on the lesser-known Livonian and Hungarian Revolts.

38 J. H. Elliott, 'Revolution and Continuity in Early Modern Europe', now in *Spain and Its World*, 111; H. G. Koenigsberger, 'The Crisis of the Seventeenth Century: A Farewell?' in *Politicians and Virtuosi*, 166–7.

39 H. E. Dembkowski, *The Union of Lublin: Polish Federalism in the Golden Age* (Boulder and New York: Columbia University Press, 1982), explores the comparability of the Polish-Lithuanian Commonwealth with the Dutch and other unions, including the British Union of the Crowns.

40 J. G. Van Dillen, 'Amsterdam's Role in Seventeenth-Century Dutch Politics and its Economic Background', in J. S. Bromley and E. H. Kossman (eds), *Britain and the Netherlands in Europe and Asia*, vol. II (Groningen: J. B. Wolters, 1964); H. Wansink, 'Holland and Six Allies: The Republic of the Seven United Provinces', in J. S. Bromley and E. H. Kossman (eds), *Britain and the Netherlands in Europe and Asia*, vol. IV (The Hague: Martinus Nijhoff, 1971).

41 *An Essay upon the Original and Nature of Government, written in the Year 1672*, in *The Works of Sir William Temple, Bart.* (2 vols; London, 1720), vol. I, 96.

42 E. H. Kossman, 'The Development of Dutch Political Theory in the Seventeenth Century', in J. S. Bromley and E. H. Kossman, *Britain and the Netherlands in Europe and Asia*, vol. I (London: Chatto & Windus, 1960); and 'Dutch Republicanism', in R. Ajello, M. Firpo, L. Guerci and G. Ricuperati (eds), *L'età dei lumi: Studi storici sul settecento europeo in onore di Franco Venturi* (Naples: Jovene, 1985), vol. I, 453–86. E. O. G. Haitsma Mulier, *The Myth of Venice and Dutch Republican Thought in the Seventeenth Century* (Assen: Van Gorkum, 1980); but Mulier follows Kossman in regarding the main Dutch exponents of the myth, the de la Court brothers and Spinoza, as eccentric to Dutch political thought. Nicolette Mout suggests that the absence of a theory of the republic was made up by recourse to the historical example of the Batavians: 'Ideales Muster oder erfundene Eigenart. Republikanische Theorien während des niederländischen Aufstands', in H. G. Koenigsberger, *Republiken und Republikanismus im Europa der Frühen Neuzeit* (Munich: Oldenburg, 1988).

43 Machiavelli, *Discorsi*, II.iv; Harrington, *Oceana*, in *Political Works*, 323–4.

44 Hugo Grotius, *Liber de antiquitate reipublicae Batavicae* (Leiden, 1610); Ulrich Huber, *De jure civitatis libri tres* (third edition; Franeker, 1698), Lib. I, Sect. III, Cap. iii. Cf. Pufendorf, *Law of Nature and Nations*, VII.v.14–21. Both Huber and Pufendorf discussed the constitution of the German Empire in the same context, thus drawing attention to the similarities between it and that of

the United Provinces; Pufendorf, however, was strongly critical of the Empire's failure to evolve into a properly equal confederation.

45 J. W. Smit, 'The Netherlands and Europe in the seventeenth and eighteenth centuries', in J. S. Bromley and E. H. Kossman (eds), *Britain and the Netherlands in Europe and Asia*, vol. III (London: Macmillan, 1968); Simon Schama, *The Embarrassment of Riches: An Interpretation of Dutch Culture in the Golden Age* (London: Collins, 1987), 237–57.

46 Israel, *Dutch Commercial Primacy*, 411–15; on the Companies: M. A. P. Meilink-Roelofsz, 'Aspects of Dutch Colonial Development in Asia in the Seventeenth Century', in Bromley & Kossman (eds), *Britain and the Netherlands in Europe and Asia*, vol. III (London: Macmillan, 1968).

47 Sir William Temple, *Observations upon the United Provinces of the Netherlands* (1673), ed. G. N. Clark (Oxford: Oxford University Press, n.d.), 117.

48 William Roosen, 'The Origins of the War of the Spanish Succession', in Jeremy Black (ed.), *The Origins of War in Early Modern Europe* (Edinburgh: John Donald, 1987).

49 The danger of Universal Monarchy was the constant refrain of anti-French propaganda. For explicit comment that Spain would be reduced to a 'province' of the 'French empire' see Defoe, *The Interests of the Several Princes and States of Europe*, 31; Leibniz, *Manifesto for the Defence of the Rights of Charles III*, in *Political Writings*, 161.

50 Sir Thomas Craig, *De unione regnorum Britanniae Tractatus* (1605), ed. C. S. Terry (*Scottish History Society*, 60; Edinburgh, 1909), 41, 262.

51 James VI & I, 'A Speech to Both the Houses of Parliament . . . the Last Day of March 1607', in *The Political Works of James I*, ed. C. H. McIlwain (Cambridge, Mass.: Harvard University Press, 1918; repr. New York, 1965), 300–1.

52 Letter of August 1607, quoted by C. V. Wedgewood in 'Scots and English 1603–40', in *History and Hope: Collected Essays* (London: Collins, 1987), 145–6.

53 Bruce Galloway, *The Union of England and Scotland 1603–1608* (Edinburgh: John Donald, 1986), and Levack, *The Formation of the British State*, give James's proposals the attention they merit.

54 P. W. J. Riley, *King William and the Scottish Politicians* (Edinburgh: John Donald, 1979), and Bruce Lenman, 'The Scottish Nobility and the Revolution of 1688–90', in Robert Beddard (ed.), *The Revolutions of 1688* (Oxford: Oxford University Press, 1991), offer contrasting assessments of the Scottish nobility's response to William's rule.

55 Andrew Fletcher, *A Discourse of Government with Relation to Militias* (Edinburgh, 1698); *Two Discourses Concerning the Affairs of Scotland; Written in the Year 1698* (Edinburgh, 1698), both reprinted in *Andrew Fletcher of Saltoun: Selected Political Writings and Speeches*, ed. D. Daiches (Edinburgh: Edinburgh University Press, 1979).

56 Fletcher, *Two Discourses Concerning Scotland: Speeches by a Member of the Parliament which Began at Edinburgh the 6th of May, 1703* (Edinburgh, 1703), in *Selected Political Writings* (quotation on p. 70). The importance of Fletcher's contribution to the Scottish debate was first properly recognized by Nicholas Phillipson: see, *inter alia*, 'The Scottish Enlightenment', in R. Porter and M. Teich (eds), *The Enlightenment in National Context* (Cambridge: Cambridge University Press, 1981).

57 [Patrick Abercromby], *The Advantages of the Act of Security, Compar'd with these of the Intended Union* (n.p., 1706), 17.

58 [William Paterson], *Proposals and Reasons for constituting a Council of Trade*

(Edinburgh, 1701), Introduction and 29; [William Seton of Pitmedden], *The Interest of Scotland in Three Essays* (London, 1702), 97–101; [William Seton], *Some Thoughts, on Ways and Means for making this Nation a Gainer in Foreign Commerce; and for Supplying its present Scarcity of Money* (Edinburgh, 1705), 8–14.

59 Andrew Fletcher, *Discorso delle Cose di Spagna: Scritto nel mese di Luglio 1698* ('Napoli', 1698), not in *Selected Political Writings*, but in *The Political Works of Andrew Fletcher* (London, 1732) and translated in the third edition (Glasgow, 1749). The pamphlet was actually printed in Edinburgh: the conceit of the false imprint may have been a homage to Campanella or an invocation of Naples as the archetypal province of the Spanish monarchy. The evidence as to place of publication is considered by R. A. S. Macfie in 'A Bibliography of Andrew Fletcher of Saltoun', *Publications of the Edinburgh Bibliographical Society*, vol. IV (Edinburgh, 1901), 117–18, and John Robertson, 'Andrew Fletcher's Vision of Union', in R. A. Mason (ed.), *Scotland and England 1286–1815* (Edinburgh: John Donald, 1987), 224 n. 64.

60 Andrew Fletcher, *A Speech upon the State of the Nation; in April 1701*, in *The Political Works*, 262–3.

61 [George Ridpath], *The Great Reasons and Interests Consider'd Anent the Spanish Monarchy* (n.p., 1701), 20–1, 36–40.

62 [Paterson], *Proposals for a Council of Trade*, 107; [Seton], *Interest of Scotland*, 59–60; [George Mackenzie, Earl of Cromarty], *A Letter from E. C. to E. W. Concerning the Union* [Edinburgh, 1706], 3.

63 [Abercromby], *Advantages of the Act of Security*, 27–34.

64 William Molyneux, *The Case of Ireland's Being Bound by Acts of Parliament in England, Stated* (Dublin, 1698; repr., ed. J. G. Sims, Dublin, 1977), quotation on 75–6.

65 *Scotland's Sovereignty Asserted. Being a Dispute concerning Homage, against those who maintain that Scotland is a Feu, or Fee-Liege of England, and that therefore the King of Scots owes Homage to the King of England*, by Sir Thomas Craig, translated with a Preface by George Ridpath (London, 1695); on this debate, William Ferguson, 'Imperial Crowns: A Neglected Facet of the Bakcground to the Treaty of Union of 1707', *Scottish Historical Review*, 53 (1974).

66 For discussions of the *Account of a Conversation* see Robertson, 'Fletcher's Vision of Union'; Istvan Hont, 'Free Trade and the Economic Limits to National Politics: Neo-Machiavellian Political Economy Reconsidered', in John Dunn (ed.), *The Economic Limits to Modern Politics* (Cambridge: Cambridge University Press, 1990). I am indebted to this article for my understanding of the economic issues in the Irish–Scottish debates.

67 Andrew Fletcher, *An Account of a Conversation Concerning a Right Regulation of Governments for the common Good of Mankind. In a letter to the Marquiss of Montrose, the Earls of Rothes, Roxburg and Haddington. From London the first of December 1703* (Edinburgh, 1704); repr. in *Selected Political Writings*, 124–5.

68 [Abercromby], *Advantages of the Act of Security*, 28–34.

69 Fletcher, *Speeches*, in *Selected Political Writings*, 74–6 (the proposed Act of Security with Limitations), and the preceeding remarks on p. 73; also Robertson, 'Fletcher's Vision of Union', 206–7.

70 [George Ridpath], *A Discourse upon the Union of Scotland and England, Humbly submitted to the Parliament of Scotland, By a Lover of his Country* ([Edinburgh], 1702, 1706); *An Historical Account of the Ancient Rights and*

Power of the Parliament of Scotland ([Edinburgh], 1703); *Considerations upon the Union of the Two Kingdoms. With an Account of the Methods taken by Ancient and Modern Governments to effect an Union, without endangering the Fundamental Constitutions of the United Countries* ([Edinburgh], 1706).

71 [James Hodges], *The Rights and Interests of the Two British Monarchies . . . with a Special Respect to An United or Separate State, Treatise I* (London, 1703), *Treatise III* (London, 1706). Treatise II was to have contained Hodges's detailed scheme.

72 [John Law], *Money and Trade Considered, with a Proposal for Supplying the Nation with Money* (Edinburgh, 1705); James Hodges, *Considerations and Proposals, for Supplying the Present Scarcity of Money, and Advancing Trade* (Edinburgh, 1705).

73 P. Paxton, *A Scheme of Union Between England and Scotland, with Advantages to Both Kingdoms* (Edinburgh, 1705). Paxton was the author of *Civil Polity* (London, 1703), a work commended by Locke.

74 [George Mackenzie, Earl of Cromarty], *A Second Letter on the British Union* [Edinburgh, 1706]; *A Friendly Return to a Letter concerning Sir George Mackenzie's and Sir John Nisbet's Observation and Responce on the Matter of the Union* ([Edinburgh], 1706).

75 [George Mackenzie], *A Second Letter on the British Union*, 14–16; *A Letter to a Member of Parliament upon the 19th Article of the Treaty of Union between the Two Kingdoms of Scotland and England* ([Edinburgh], 1706), 4–8.

76 [William Seton of Pitmedden], *Scotland's Great Advantages by an Union with England: Showen in a Letter from the Country, to a Member of Parliament* (Edinburgh, 1706), 4. The extent of Seton's erastianism is made clear in the opening essay of his *Interest of Scotland*.

77 [Cromarty], *Parainesis Pacifica; or a perswasive to the Union of Britain* (Edinburgh, repr. London, 1702), 7–9, 13–15; *A Second Letter on the British Union*, 5–11; [Seton], *Ways and Means for Making the Nation a Gainer in Foreign Commerce*, 43–52; *Scotland's Great Advantages by an Union*, 5–12.

78 [Daniel Defoe], *An Essay at Removing National Prejudices against a Union with England*, Part III (London, 1706), 26.

79 [Daniel Defoe], *An Essay at Removing National Prejudices against a Union with Scotland*, Part II (London, 1706), 4–6. The claim was spotted by Scottish opponents, and Defoe had to cover his tracks in the subsequent *Essay at Removing National Prejudices against a Union with England*, Part III [Edinburgh], 3–6.

80 [Henry Maxwell], *An Essay towards an Union of England with Ireland* (London, 1703), 17–18, 52–6. Maxwell was Member of Parliament for Bangor, County Down, and a member of Molyneux's circle. On Irish unionism in this period see James Kelly, 'The Origins of the Act of Union; An Examination of Unionist Opinion in Britain and Ireland 1650–1800', *Irish Historical Studies*, 25 (1987).

81 *The Queen an Empress, and her Three Kingdoms One Empire: or, Brief Remarks upon the Present; and a Prospect of the Future state of England Scotland and Ireland, in a Happy Union. In a Letter to a Noble Peer* (London, 1706).

82 Fletcher, *Account of a Conversation*, in *Selected Political Writings*, 127.

83 ibid., 135.

84 ibid., 127–36.

85 For contrasting suggestions as to the specific sources of Fletcher's scheme see

Robertson, 'Fletcher's Vision of Union', 216–18; Hont, 'Free Trade and the Economic Limits to National Politics'.

86 William Ferguson, *Scotland's Relations with England: a Survey to 1707* (Edinburgh: John Donald, 1977), chs 13–14; P. W. J. Riley, *The Union of England and Scotland* (Manchester: University Press, 1978); and for the most up-to-date account of the economic issues, C. A. Whatley, 'Economic Causes and Consequences of the Union of 1707: A Survey', *Scottish Historical Review*, 58 (1989), 186.

87 I plan a separate comparison of the Scottish and Neapolitan debates.

88 See above, p. 227.

89 J. C. D. Clark, 'England's Ancien Regime as a Confessional State', *Albion*, 21 (1989).

90 See Joanna Innes, Chapter 5 above, and Linda Colley, Chapter 7 above.

91 See Daniel Baugh, Chapter 8 above.

92 On the novelty of this act, which superseded Poynings' Law, see Koenigsberger, 'Composite States and Representative Institutions', 144–5; more generally, Nicholas Canny, *Kingdom and Colony. Ireland in the Atlantic World 1560–1800* (Baltimore and London: Johns Hopkins University Press, 1988).

93 J. G. A. Pocock, *Virtue, Commerce and History* (Cambridge: Cambridge University Press, 1985) '1776: The Revolution against Parliament'; J. P. Greene, *Peripheries and Center: Constitutional Development in the Extended Polities of the British Empire and the United States 1607–1788* (Athens and London: University of Georgia Press, 1986); Koenigsberger, 'Composite States and Representative Institutions', 145–53; Kathleen Wilson, Chapter 6 above.

94 C. A. Bayly, Chapter 12 below.

95 Greene, *Peripheries and Center*, 61–2, 103–4; Nicholas Canny, Chapter 11 below.

96 Pocock, 'States, Republics and Empires'; on the Scottish contribution to American resistance, see Ned Landsman, Chapter 10 below.

10

The Provinces and the Empire
Scotland, the American colonies and the development of British provincial identity
Ned C. Landsman

There are few better places to begin a consideration of the development of provincial cultures in eighteenth-century Britain than with a sermon that some British observers came to regard as one of the more provocative proclamations of American resistance to imperial authority in 1776, 'The Dominion of Providence over the Passions of Men', preached in Princeton in May of that year by John Witherspoon, president of what was then the College of New Jersey. Witherspoon had come to America from the textile town of Paisley in Scotland only eight years before, but during that time he had managed to establish himself both as a prominent figure in the religious, political and cultural affairs of the colonies and as the principal spokesman for the Scottish and Presbyterian communities in America. It was in the latter role that he appended to his sermon a brief 'Address to the Natives of Scotland Residing in America', in which he defended Scottish-Americans against accusations of excessive loyalty to empire and antipathy to liberty and attempted to secure their support for the American cause. He began that endorsement of American independence with a strong declaration of the sense of patriotism and 'attachment to country' that he felt. Strikingly, the country to which he referred was not America but Scotland.[1]

The ability of Witherspoon to maintain such a dual allegiance in action as well as in expression requires elaboration at several levels. It suggests the development of a sense of identity that was sufficiently comprehensive to transcend established political boundaries, not only consecutively but even simultaneously, as Witherspoon apparently would do. Moreover, although he expressed his sentiments in consistently conciliatory language, Witherspoon's vision proved sufficiently unsettling to prominent British observers to attach considerable notoriety to both sermon and author for years to come.[2]

Witherspoon's involvement in the imperial crisis and with two provincial societies suggests as well a question raised by John Brewer's *Sinews of Power*: how the expansion of the apparatus of state and the bounds of

258

empire looked from the periphery. It would be foolhardy to attempt to provide a simple answer to a question involving the many and diverse cultures that existed on the periphery of the British empire. Nor would it be appropriate to the starting-point of this chapter, which involves not the periphery in general but the provinces – those remote sectors of the empire whose inhabitants lived far from the metropolis but who identified themselves nevertheless as imperial citizens, claiming the rights and privileges of Britons in general. Indeed, provincials probably identified themselves as Britons more consistently than anyone else in the empire, albeit Britons with a particular provincial point of view. In much of England, the term 'British' signified little more than a synonym for 'English', and 'North Briton' became a notorious term of abuse. Provincials, by contrast, insisted that the privileges of empire extended fully beyond the metropolis; it was British liberty that gave them their claim to citizenship.[3]

That Witherspoon identified with Scotland and America recalls still another argument. Nearly four decades ago, John Clive and Bernard Bailyn first pointed out the existence of significant cultural affinities between Scotland and America in the eighteenth century, which they attributed to their analogous positions as provincial backwaters, England's 'cultural provinces'. In the intervening years, scholars working in a wide variety of fields have expanded our knowledge of Scottish–American connections far beyond what those authors had anticipated. Yet there have been few attempts to reconsider the framework of that relationship or to move beyond the substantially static conception of provinciality offered by Bailyn and Clive.[4]

The extent of those connections is impressive; in a surprising variety of areas, Scotland and Scots managed to play important and disproportionate roles in American life. In commerce, Scottish merchants would assume prominent and even dominant places in many areas, not only in the tobacco trade, as is well known, but, increasingly, in the sugar trade, as powerful commercial cliques in several port-cities, and in the hinterland trade generally, extending to the far northern reaches of New York and into Canada. Scots would become firmly entrenched in the administrative structures of the empire also, as governors, provincial councillors and imperial officials connected with matters of war and trade.[5] In those areas they would attain a seemingly paradoxical position, including among their number both some of the most prominent proponents of imperial expansion and some of the more aggressive defenders of provincial liberty.

Scottish cultural influences were equally substantial. Scotsmen were especially prominent in colonial educational institutions, not only at Princeton under Witherspoon, but at the Colleges of Philadelphia and William and Mary, at the growing numbers of Presbyterian academies, both of the Old Side and the New, and as private tutors. More striking still was the pre-eminence of Edinburgh graduates in American medicine; almost everyone who mattered in the colonial medical profession was either a Scottish *émigré* or Scottish-trained. Scots influenced early American science generally, along with religion, politics, literature and philosophy; the vast academic enterprise that constituted Scottish moral philosophy would have ramifications in America as great or greater than it had at home.[6]

Such a list could be extended considerably. To date, our knowledge of those influences derives almost entirely from scholars pursuing their separate enquiries, most of which are limited to a single country and field; yet it is only when we view them together that their significance becomes apparent. It will be the argument of this chapter that, taken together, those varied transatlantic connections reflected a considerable shift in orientation within the provincial world during the eighteenth century, away from strictly local or national concerns and away from an exclusive focus upon relations between metropolis and province, towards the development of a marked transatlantic awareness, common identifications as British provincials and distinct provincial perspectives upon social life. The vast majority of treatments of relations between the provinces and the empire have employed the framework of centre and periphery. That perspective has tended to emphasize initiatives originating in the metropolis and to interpret provincial options as limited to those of submission or outright rebellion.[7] During the middle years of the eighteenth century, diverse groups of provincial citizens – not only lowland Scots and colonial Americans, but also some Protestant Irish, English dissenters and residents of provincial English towns and outports – came to identify with the interests of the provinces in opposition to those of the metropolis and to develop decidedly positive and optimistic views of provincial life. Those would have broad and important, albeit rather different, ramifications on both sides of the Atlantic, extending to such diverse areas as politics, religion, commerce and culture. They provided a basis both for Scotland's headlong plunge into the affairs of empire and for the eventual American challenge to imperial authority.[8]

THE IMPORTANCE OF AMERICA FOR SCOTLAND

That Scots involved themselves so extensively in early America was largely because, during the eighteenth century, America became increasingly important to Scotland. In the early 1770s, in the midst of a surge in emigration from Scotland to America, Witherspoon's former Scottish neighbour, the Reverend William Thom of Govan, penned a description of how well informed the common people of western Scotland had become about the American colonies. 'You would wonder', Thom wrote,

> to hear how exactly they know the geography of North America, how distinctly they can speak of its lakes, its rivers and the extent

and richness of the soil in the respective territories where British colonies are settled: for my part, did I not know the contrary, I would be tempted to think they had lived for some time in that country.[9]

That interest extended to many groups. It was manifest in the wild and speculative schemes for colonial settlement on the part of Scottish merchants and gentlemen that Bernard Bailyn has chronicled.[10] It would find equally spectacular expression among the common people in the 'emigration mania' of the 1760s and 1770s recorded by such observers as Johnson and Boswell. While visiting the remote port of Portree on Skye, they happened upon the emigrant ship *Nestor*, the 'largest in Clyde', loaded for departure, and that was not the only emigration vessel they encountered during their journey. Nearby they would also view the performance of a dance called 'America', in which the original dancers gradually drew in the entire company in a symbolic representation of the 'rage for emigration'.[11]

Of course, in the years just before the American Revolution, not only Scots but Britons in general were becoming increasingly cognizant of the significance of the colonial attachment, but for Scots that connection had special importance. Where English citizens considered the colonial relationship vital to the prosperity and security of the empire, for Scots it was as important to their nation's place within the empire. That perception was rooted in a century of Scottish experience. Scottish historians have by now well explained how, before the Union of Parliaments and as a necessary precursor to it, a substantial segment of Scotland's leadership had reached a consensus that their nation was threatened by an ever-increasing economic and political subordination to the interests of its wealthier and more powerful southern neighbour. Their solution was to narrow the gap by following the English and Dutch examples of economic growth based upon increased manufacturing coupled with expanded foreign trade.[12] It is less often noticed that from the beginning the American colonies played a pivotal role in that plan.

As early as the last two decades of the seventeenth century Scots began to follow that programme in earnest. About 1680 several closely linked groups of Scottish merchants and gentlemen embarked upon an unprecedented series of small manufacturing efforts, in such fields as mining and wool and linen manufactures. At the same time, those groups began to look to the American colonies to extend their trading sphere. A network of well over a hundred Scottish merchants and gentlemen, including most of those involved in the manufacturing schemes, established two colonies in America, one in Carolina and the other in East Jersey. A decade later, many of the same investors embarked upon the far more ambitious project of a Company of Scotland, which managed to assemble and then lose a considerable portion of Scotland's available capital in an attempt to turn

Scotland into a competitive trading power chiefly through the establishment of a Central American trading colony.[13] Only after that failed did some Scots begin to look instead towards a closer connection to England. The result was a full incorporating union, the principal attraction of which was the prospect of opening up the English and colonial markets to Scottish trade.

After the Union was completed, Scots paid particularly close attention to its effects. At first the economic benefits were disappointing, and for several decades they could do little more than lament that the sacrifice of national independence had produced so meagre a return. Implicitly, even opponents of union measured that loss against an essentially commercial standard. That led to a rather different reaction when the first signs of commercial advance began to appear towards mid-century. Those were celebrated and often exaggerated by Scotland's merchants and gentlemen, who embarked upon a campaign for the full-scale 'improvement' of Scotland's agriculture, manufactures and trade.[14]

After 1750 the growth of the economy became unmistakable, especially in Glasgow and the west, the areas most affected by the accelerating American trade. That was accompanied – although the exact relationship remains a matter of dispute – by improvements in agriculture and industry, as well as the various literary accomplishments that comprised the Scottish Enlightenment. While some recent historians have questioned how much of that growth was actually attributable to the Union and the colonial trade, their significance was simply assumed by eighteenth-century Scots, who would trace their advances in economy, technology and culture all to the watershed of the Union and the resulting American connections.[15]

Thus, from the beginning, Scotland's integration into a British state was predicated upon access to a larger commercial empire. Within a very few years, Scottish merchants began to turn up in force in almost all the colonial ports, where they quickly established a reputation for aggressiveness and clannishness. Their involvement extended beyond trading to imperial administration. Even before 1707 Andrew Hamilton had served as governor of both East and West Jersey, and James Blair was already established as the leading Anglican official in Virginia and in America. Scots appeared in far greater numbers after the Union, as governors, councillors and churchmen, including Robert Hunter, Alexander Spotswood, James Alexander and Cadwallader Colden. They became particularly identified with matters of revenue and trade, and the reports of such revenue officers as John Rutherfurd and Henry McCulloh of Carolina and Robert Dinwiddie of Virginia provided some of the best information available on the colonial trade. Their pervasive theme was the increasing importance of the colonies to Britain and to Scotland in particular.[16] In succeeding years, Scottish traders would labour diligently to develop that connection.

PROVINCIAL PERSPECTIVES UPON EMPIRE

Within that context Scots, and eventually provincials in general, paid considerable attention to imperial matters and developed some distinct perspectives upon the empire and the provincial world. In describing the provincial mentality, historians have usually emphasized its negative side, the sense of cultural inferiority among those living at the periphery and their desire to imitate more refined metropolitan styles – the very traits we usually associate with 'provincialism'. Yet there were positive aspects to provinciality that were at least as significant in the eighteenth century, as provincial Britons came to view themselves as inhabiting some of the most innovative and expansive segments of the empire. From diverse perspectives various groups of provincials came to articulate images of metropolitan life as reflecting the standards not only of culture and development, as was traditional, but also of stagnation and corruption, which, as they viewed it, often signified something not far removed from the extension of metropolitan authority. They would gradually develop a counter-image of provincial life as embodying piety, virtue (in several senses of that term) and Reformed religion, as well as liberty, innovation and growth. In their most optimistic moments, they would identify the provinces as both the moral centre and the most dynamic sector of the British empire.

In creating such images of metropolitan life, provincials drew upon several of the available political languages of early-modern Britain: the national, the Protestant, the civic and the jurisprudential. One of the striking aspects of provincial discussions during the eighteenth century is the extent to which, by tying their values so firmly to a particular concept of place, they were able to integrate elements of those diverse discourses around a common provincial ideal. Thus disgruntled Scots would characterize as corrupt a metropolitan authority that was lodged in a 'foreign kingdom', Presbyterians would complain of civil encroachments upon the independence of their church, and philosophers would apply natural-law concerns for equity and justice to the claims of the provinces within the empire. Although most provincial discussion was implicitly oppositionist in regard to imperial politics, provincials were unusually successful in incorporating the commercial perspectives of those who might be called 'Court' provincials, such as David Hume and the imperial expansionists in America.[17]

Historically, writers influenced by civic concerns had almost always maintained an uneasy attitude towards the prospect of commercial development. One of the distinctive features of much provincial discussion in the eighteenth century, as several have noted for Scotland, was the extent to which it was able to reconcile virtue with growth. As Scots observed the growth of their economy in conjunction with provincial trading, and as provincials in general perceived an acceleration of growth-rates throughout the provincial world, they began to develop a conception of development in which provincial trading – organized through private initiatives from the periphery rather than directed development from the centre – came to seem the very model for growth.[18]

A good illustration of the assumptions with which provincials perceived those developments appears in the writings of that most untypical Scot, Adam Smith, whose outlook was far more cosmopolitan than that of most of his countrymen but no less indebted to his provincial background. Contained within *The Wealth of Nations* is a suggestion Smith offered to remedy the then raging American crisis. Smith differed from most of his countrymen in that he actually preferred independence for America, but he offered the alternative of granting the colonies full incorporation into the empire, with parliamentary representation to be allocated upon the basis of revenues. When America's taxes and population surpassed that of Britain, as Smith assumed they would, the seat of government would also pass from England to America. That suggestion was rather extreme within the context of British opinion generally, but several of the assumptions upon which it was based were quite common both in Scottish discourse and in provincial discussions generally.[19]

One assumption reflected in Smith's proposal was the primacy of commercial and demographic factors in societal development, which led to an intensive interest in the analysis of population and trade. Of course, not only provincials but Britons in general evidenced a considerable interest in commercial enquiries during the eighteenth century, but those had particular implications for the provinces, where analysts had long debated whether 'poor' countries such as Scotland could ever catch up with their wealthier metropolitan neighbours. To the most optimistic, the burgeoning growth of trade in Scotland, the colonies and the English outports suggested that neither economic nor political relationships within the empire would remain forever fixed but would follow population and trade. It was no coincidence that political economy was largely born in Scotland. It would be difficult to overstate the ubiquity of commercial calculations in Scottish discourse; they were pervasive, among not only such political economists as Hume, Smith and James Steuart, but also a much larger group of merchants, landowners and even ministers. So widespread was the belief in the dynamic influence of commercial factors in social development that even orthodox and evangelical clergyman would publish sermons on such topics as 'Prayer for National Prosperity and for the Revival of Religion Inseparably Connected' and 'The Influence of Religion on National Prosperity'.[20]

There was considerable variety among those discussions. While a few, such as Hume and Smith, approached a pure free-trade position, most writers advocated something more nearly resembling structured trading, in which legislators would promote, but not direct, commercial development.

The latter position probably better reflected the realities of provincial trading, in which the Scots relied upon linen bounties to improve their manufactures and the competitive advantages of a regulated tobacco trade. Nevertheless, nearly all writers shared some basic sentiments, such as a pronounced antipathy to the metropolitan trading companies, which they viewed as contrary to both justice and efficiency. They preferred the private initiatives that developed away from the inherent corruptions they associated with metropolitan control, under conditions they defined as economic liberty. The key text here was Hume's essay, 'Of the Jealousy of Trade', widely cited on both sides of the Atlantic, which posited that free trading could benefit both commercial partners. That seemed to represent the very essence of provincial trading.[21]

Provincial writers also paid close attention to demographic analysis. As it became increasingly apparent that the increase of population in the provinces was exceeding that in England, provincial writers would emphasize the view, borrowed from Montesquieu, that demographic growth was among the surest indicators of social well-being. The population debates of mid-century produced an abundance of entries from provincials and dissenters. David Hume and Robert Wallace, responding to the pessimistic projections of the dissenting clergyman John Brown, debated general trends in British demography in essays they presented to the Philosophical Society of Edinburgh. Their ideas were further developed by such other Society members as Adam Smith and Benjamin Franklin. The Edinburgh clergyman Alexander Webster followed soon thereafter with Scotland's first attempt at a census, and he debated demographic methods with another prominent dissenter, Richard Price of Northampton.[22]

A second set of assumptions reflected in Smith's proposal was that, on the basis of their growing wealth and population and their increasing contributions to imperial revenues, the provinces were entitled to a larger voice in their own affairs and those of the empire. Provincials increasingly insisted upon their right to be treated as citizens rather than subordinates. That was manifest in the widespread demands of Scottish politicians after mid-century for a larger share of the benefits of empire, the increasingly vocal claims of colonial legislatures to the full-fledged prerogatives of local parliaments, and even the opposition groups that grew up in English provincial towns. What provincials came to identify as a 'liberal' point of view signified precisely a just regard for the interests of all parties, provincial as well as metropolitan, which they contrasted with 'confined' or 'narrow' metropolitan views.[23]

Provincials incorporated such perspectives into the theory as well as the practice of politics. As early as the 1730s Glasgow's Francis Hutcheson, influenced by a group of Irish provincial writers, applied the principles of natural law to provincial matters and asserted the rights of mature colonial communities to separate from imperial authorities that ceased to promote the welfare of their citizens. Just as important, his moral philosophy, which was highly influential throughout the provinces, was predicated upon similar assumptions; its general tendency was to shift the basis for ethical judgements away from the dictates of traditional authorities towards the collective sentiments of a reflective citizenry, provincial as well as metropolitan. David Hume's 'Idea of a Perfect Commonwealth', which would also be influential on both sides of the Atlantic, proposed strong provincial authorities as a counterweight to the natural and prejudicial power of the metropolis, creating something like a union of provincial communities. Hume explicitly criticized colonial policies that promoted exploitation rather than mutual development. Smith's proposal for an imperial parliament both anticipated and allowed for eventual provincial dominance as a matter both of natural development and of justice.[24]

If the specific points of Smith's proposal were unusual within the imperial debate, his assumptions about America – that the colonies were destined to become not only the demographic and commercial centre of the empire, but even its political capital – were already common predictions in the provinces, especially Scotland. Whether measured by commercial growth, population, resources or opportunity, all indicators suggested the eventual ascendancy of America within the empire. As early as the 1720s Scots in America and at home were already forecasting America's economic and demographic dominance. By the 1760s the prediction that it would also be the capital of the empire, if not an empire of its own, were increasingly common. A good example came in this letter written by Archibald Grant, Scottish landowner and improver, recommending investment in the farthest reaches of America:

> Since ever I could read on these subjects, I have been convinced, and am daily more and more confirmed in opinion, that America will at a period, I don't presume to say when, be the grand seat of Empire and all its Concomitants . . . Why should those who see, be blind and continue too far behind?[25]

Some of the most important considerations of provincial matters came not from political economists or philosophers such as Smith but rather those whose careers involved them directly with colonial affairs: the overseas merchants, the commercial writers and the growing legions of imperial officials, physicians, educators and clergymen who made their careers in America. By the second half of the eighteenth century, all those groups were expressing markedly optimistic hopes for America. Commercial writers began to develop increasingly ambitious and integral plans for the colonies, both as markets for Scottish products such as linen and as a source of raw materials for Scottish manufactures, such as flax and hemp. At the same time Scottish merchants and investors aggressively extended their colonial involvements into the back-country, the far north and the exotic south, from Florida and the West Indies to western Pennsylvania to Nova Scotia and Quebec. Increasingly, they looked to the most undeveloped regions as the likeliest opportunities for themselves and, as Archibald Grant suggested, for Scotland also. It was as though they had determined to put Hume's dictum about the mutually beneficial character of trade into practice; by developing the back-country they could benefit from its growing wealth.[26]

By the outbreak of the Seven Years War Scots both in the colonies and at home had become prominent advocates of territorial expansion in America. Thus Glasgow merchants played a leading role in the clamour for the annexation of Quebec. In spite of their own growing involvement in the sugar trade, they preferred the northern province even to the French West Indies, with commercial prospects greater, in their view, than 'Martinico or Guadeloupe, or even both put together'.[27] They were actively joined in that campaign by a prominent circle of Scottish-Americans, including John Mitchell and William Livingston.[28]

Scots were conspicuous for their efforts not only to expand the empire in America but to organize it. Scots and Scottish-Americans offered some highly detailed analyses of the imperial relationship and some of the most prominent plans for improving it. During the 1750s imperial officials such as James Abercromby and Henry McCulloh were pioneers in drafting plans to rationalize imperial relations and imperial revenues; so, in America, were Archibald Kennedy and William Livingston. Kennedy, Livingston, James Alexander and Cadwallader Colden, along with Benjamin Franklin, all played leading roles in instigating the Albany Conference in 1754, which tried and failed to implement a colonial union. John Murrin has recently observed that the very idea of a unified America was originally a British invention; to be precise, it was mostly the creation of a network of Scots and their colonial contacts who were predominantly Scottish-Americans.[29]

On occasion, Scottish statements about America could be as fanciful as the most exotic settlement schemes. One pamphlet, provocatively titled *North Briton Extraordinary*, argued that not only was Scotland's growth dependent upon America, but that a considerable portion of America's prosperity was similarly attributable to its connection to Scotland. Before the union, it contended, America had been nothing but a drain upon English finances. Not until Scottish merchants obtained access to the empire did the colonial economy grow to the point that it could add to, rather than subtract from, the imperial treasury. There was considerably more substance to a related and more common argument: that it was Scottish military prowess during the Seven Years War that had secured the colonies to Britain. Whatever the merits of the case, by the eve of the American Revolution, Scots had become particularly identified with the development, administration and security of the empire.[30]

PRESBYTERIANS AND PROVINCIAL LIBERTY

Strikingly, such optimistic predictions for America were not restricted to those whose concerns were primarily commercial in nature. That would become apparent in 1766, when the College of New Jersey, acting upon the advice of Scottish correspondents, offered its vacant presidency to Witherspoon. The pastor's wife was reluctant to emigrate, and Witherspoon initially declined the offer. It required the combined efforts of many Scottish and American Presbyterians to persuade them. The nature of those arguments was well illustrated in a letter to Witherspoon from a Scottish colleague, Thomas Randall, in words that sound surprisingly like those of Archibald Grant. As Randall wrote:

> I have long thought it the intention of Providence . . . to fix the great seat of truth and righteousness in America; and that N. Jersey seemed to promise fair for being the *nursery* of the most approved instruments, for carrying on that great design, in that wide continent.[31]

As Randall's words suggest, Scottish engagement with the American provinces involved not only merchants, landowners and literati, but a group that many among the literati considered their adversaries: the evangelical or 'Popular' wing of the Church of Scotland, the principal opponents of the reign of William Robertson and his circle of 'Moderate literati' in the Church. The Popular Party drew its strength from the trading classes of Glasgow and western Scotland. Beginning with the transatlantic religious awakenings of the 1730s and 1740s, they used their commercial connections to establish an extensive network of correspondence with both Presbyterian and Congregationalist ministers across the Atlantic.[32]

Few groups have been more poorly served by historians than have Scottish evangelicals. While their opponents have received abundant historical attention in recent years, there had been no adequate study of the Popular Party in this century. Most of them studied in the same newly reformed universities, in the same courses and under the same distinguished professors as the literati. Although they would disagree strongly with the Moderates over church polity, they shared a good many of their ideas and interests, including a substantially humanistic, Hutchesonian philosophy of morals and a decidedly commercial perspective upon social development. Most important, in the aftermath of the Jacobite Rebellion of 1745, they would develop an intense commitment to a particular concept of liberty that was British and Protestant rather than strictly national or sectarian.

Liberty, as evangelicals understood it, had both civil and ecclesiastical dimensions. It signified, in politics, freedom from absolute or arbitrary authority, and in religion, the independence of the church from civil control (although not from civil support). Thus the Jacobite Rebellion was doubly dangerous, in their view, threatening liberty in church and state. Their principal difference with the Moderates concerned the issue of lay patronage, in which patrons – usually wealthy landowners, but often the Crown – held the power of clerical appointment. That seemed a direct threat both to piety and to Presbyterian autonomy.

The evangelical concept of liberty implied a particular interpretation of the British past. Along with many others in the Whig tradition, those Presbyterians believed that their nation owed both its civil and its religious liberties to a century of struggle against the forces of arbitrary authority in church and state, culminating in what had indeed been a glorious revolution. What distinguished the evangelical understanding was their insistence that it had been a British rather than simply an English struggle, and that religious orthodoxy had led the effort, represented by convenanting Presbyterians in Scotland and English and New English Puritans. Liberty, in the words of one, had been 'purchased by religion', and civil and religious liberty would 'stand and fall with one another'.[33]

That had broad ramifications. As evangelicals surveyed the provincial world, those same centres of orthodoxy and Reformed religion – western Scotland and America's northern colonies – stood out also as regions of particularly marked commercial growth. From that they took away the lesson that liberty, piety and prosperity, even enlightenment – the 'spirit of enquiry', William Thom called it – were all connected. Within an environment of provincial liberty, commerce, rather than undermining liberty, was its product and its confirmation.[34]

Yet evangelicals were much less sanguine than many commercial writers about the prospects of Scotland itself. Along with other opposition writers, they worried about the growing power of the state which, as one wrote, seemed 'to be every day verging more and more towards absolute monarchy'. They worried even more about the effects of the Moderate reign in the church, which was threatening to turn its constitution 'from a truly Christian, British model into a despotic, French mould'. After recession struck the trading towns of western Scotland during the 1770s, they blamed metropolitan regulation for undermining the position of their mercantile and artisanal constituents. Increasingly, to evangelicals, America remained the sole refuge of liberty, the 'seat of liberty and true religion', as John Erskine called it.[35] That was the reason that Erskine and others urged Witherspoon to leave Scotland to head the growing Presbyterian college in New Jersey. For the same reason, Witherspoon and several others would undertake an extended campaign to promote Scottish emigration to America.

The emigration mania of the 1760s and 1770s was a vast movement, with multiple causes. During those years, as many as 40,000 Scots emigrated to the colonies, and the rate was still accelerating when it was abruptly cut off by the outbreak of war in 1775. Most interpreters have traced the movement to the disruption of Highland society that followed the '45, but that can explain only part of the migrations. There may have been as many Lowlanders as Highlanders among those emigrants, mostly from Glasgow and its environs. Most of those were probably tradesmen. Moreover, the Scottish emigrations were linked by their merchant promoters to the other large provincial migrations occurring at the same time from the north of Ireland and northern England.[36]

One aspect of those migrations that has drawn little attention is that all the lowland movements evidenced substantial evangelical connections. The most prominent Scottish promoters – the Buchanans of Glasgow and New York and merchant James Pagan of Glasgow – had long histories of evangelical involvement. The primary publicists of the movement were also evangelicals, including Witherspoon and his former Scottish neighbour, William Thom of Govan, and the rural and artisanal groups in western Scotland to whom they appealed were precisely those where evangelical Presbyterianism flourished. Emigration, for those groups, represented a particular fulfilment of the evangelical conception of liberty.[37]

No one argued more aggressively in favour of emigration than William Thom, the author of five extensive tracts on emigration. In many respects, Thom expressed a rather conventional civic view of Scottish society, reflected in the corruption of the body politic, the growth of arbitrary authority and a landed class that had abandoned its ancient virtue for present gains. Where Thom differed from other writers was in his espousal of a remedy, not in the renewal of virtue, but in emigration to America, where provincial liberty still flourished. If tenants and tradesmen in Scotland were improverished by oppressive landlords and artificially distorted markets, the economic liberty of America would allow them to raise their families in prosperity and independence. If piety and virtue were threatened by arbitrary power in the church and the state, in America they would experience complete liberty in matters civil and religious. Moreover, escape to America was no mere retreat from civility and culture. Rather, the colonies were 'daily growing in power, wealth, and science, and all the improvements that civilize and polish mankind'. In Thom's America, liberty, piety and prosperity went hand in hand.[38]

Not all those emigrants were responding to Thom or his ideas, of course – rent-hikes in the Highlands, the trade recession and a host of other factors played important roles – but among those emigrants whose motives were recorded by emigration officials, some offered explanations that paralleled those of Thom and other evangelicals and addressed recurrent provincial themes. The most frequent complaints voiced by emigrants were the high price of grain and inflated rents; several of those repeated Thom's argument that those resulted from the distorting influence of the metropolitan market, diverting grain to the production of luxury items such as spirits. Another frequent complaint was the oppressive conduct of the landed class; again, several blamed not simply greed, but greed inspired by the lure of the metropolis. Most of all, nearly all accounts implied that America retained the advantages of provincial societies: emigrants could settle in a land of religion, liberty, and prosperity while still remaining within the British empire and under its 'benign influence'. In America they could retain 'the true old British spirit before it be totally vitiated and extinguished'.[39]

AMERICAN PROVINCIALS

Americans responded to that extensive Scottish involvement in colonial affairs with considerable ambivalence. That the colonists developed decidedly negative images of Scots as clannish and aggressive and as tools of imperial authority is well known; yet Americans also became highly respectful of Scottish ideas, and they came to share much of their perspective upon province and empire. Nothing better illustrates that American ambivalence than Thomas Jefferson's draft of the Declaration of Independence, which derided 'Scotch and foreign mercenaries' in a document that owed a substantial debt to Scottish moral philosophy, in concept if not in language.[40]

Part of that responsiveness resulted from the substantial presence of Scots in positions of cultural influence. By the eve of the revolution, natives of Scotland held many of the most important positions in American cultural life everywhere south of New England. In the mid-Atlantic region, Witherspoon headed the College of New Jersey, where his lectures in rhetoric and moral philosophy closely resembled those of Hutcheson and his Scottish teachers. So did the lectures of the former Aberdonian William Smith and the Ulster-born Francis Alison, a former pupil of Hutcheson, at the College of Philadelphia. Both Scots and Scottish-trained clergymen from Northern Ireland supplied numerous pulpits in the region – Episcopalian as well as Presbyterian. The situation was not much different farther south. In Virginia, William Small, also from Aberdeen, taught moral philosophy at William and Mary, the only institution of higher education in the region until the rise of the Presbyterian academies, also dominated by Scots, near the end of the colonial period. A circle of Scottish doctors, including Alexander Garden and John Lining, helped set the tone for learning in Carolina. Even in New England most of the leading clergymen were involved in a network of correspondence with Scottish ministers.[41]

That Scotsmen held those positions was a reflection of more than just their availability; Americans increasingly sought them out. In America, as in Europe, the Scottish universities were highly respected as centres of learning and enlightenment. Equally important, they held reputations for Reformed religion and practical learning that seemed more suitable to a provincial and commercial citizenry than that offered at Anglican-dominated Oxford and Cambridge. Benjamin Franklin recruited William

271

Smith to head the College of Philadelphia after reading Smith's tract on education modelled upon the newly reformed curriculum of the Aberdeen colleges, emphasizing 'useful subjects' such as history, mathematics and natural and moral philosophy. The College of New Jersey chose Witherspoon as president largely because he seemed to balance the attributes of religiosity and learning in sufficient measure to heal the division between Old Side and New in the Presbyterian College. When his wife's reluctance initially induced him to decline the call, they continued to look to Scotland for a suitable replacement. Witherspoon soon demonstrated how well he understood those motives; in published advertisements for the college he listed among his strengths his own close acquaintance with eminent Professors at Glasgow University, and a college environment free from sectarian favour or governmental influence: in short, a place where students could imbibe the spirit of piety, liberty and enlightenment.[42]

Almost as important in establishing cultural links between Scotland and America were the physicians, more than 150 of whom enigrated to the colonies before the American Revolution. They comprised a remarkable group, incuding among their number such noted figures as Cadwallader Colden, William Douglass, John Mitchell, John Lining and Alexander Garden, who maintained intricate networks with provincial intellectuals in both provinces and helped to establish the reputation of Scottish medicine in America. After 1760 that process continued in reverse, and Edinburgh University became the medical school of choice for aspiring colonial doctors. The interests of those doctors were wide-ranging. They published highly detailed surveys of the social and geographic characteristics of the colonies. They wrote extensively on colonial political affairs. They studied the ways of the American Indians and provided ethnographic information for the anthropological speculations of William Robertson and Lord Kames. They transmitted New World seeds and plants to their countrymen at home and served as focal points of the transatlantic scientific community.[43]

One of their most frequent correspondents was Benjamin Franklin. Although Franklin has long been considered as perhaps the prototypical eighteenth-century American, many of his ideas were strongly indebted to common provincial discussions. Thus Franklin's famous *Observations concerning the Increase of Mankind*, which offered a highly original demographic interpretation of America's future that served as the basis for American political economy for years to come, was probably influenced by David Hume and Robert Wallace, who had debated contemporary demographic trends in the Philosophical Society of Edinburgh. Franklin became a member of that society. Like the Scots, Franklin moved from demography to politics, and his *Observations* became the basis for an increasingly assertive view of imperial politics. Soon thereafter, he began to promote both the political union of the colonies and further imperial expansion, views he shared with such Scottish-American colleagues as John Mitchell, William Livingston, Archibald Kennedy, Cadwallader Colden, and James Alexander. Eventually, Franklin would advocate a full incorporating union, but only after all prejudicial trade restrictions were removed from American commerce.[44]

Franklin was not the only prominent American thinker enmeshed in a network of Scottish contacts. Another was Jonathan Edwards, whose correspondence after 1740 was increasingly taken up with letters to and from his evangelical colleagues in Scotland. Historians have made much of the seemingly proto-national quality of Edwards's speculative statements at the time of the Great Awakening, when he suggested that the millennium might begin in the colonies; in fact, Edwards rather quickly broadened his outlook beyond America. With the passing of the colonial awakening, he began to look hopefully towards Scotland as the place where the true Reformed religion might be most secure. In 1745, in a letter to Scotland, Edwards applied the logic of the 'jeremiad' to the affairs of that province, suggesting that the Jacobite Rebellion might be considered as a providential test designed to effect a reformation of piety in a covenanted nation. A few years later Edwards joined with the Scots in promoting a 'Concert for Prayer' designed to revive religion through the joint action of Scots, Americans and the entire British Reformed community. In Edwards's treatment, the Puritan covenant had been extended beyond England and New England to the entire Reformed community in Britain and its provinces.[45]

Just as the concept of the covenant could be extended from a single region to the larger provincial world, so also could the conceptual link evangelicals assumed between piety and liberty, which became the common property of the principal Reformed denominations in Britain and America. Even New Englanders assimilated the theme of religious liberty into their version of their past, in the process adjusting the myth of the Puritan founding from an archetypal event to a single, particularly influential instance of a common Reformed striving for liberty in the provinces. That was a version of their history that New Englanders could share with other provincials.[46] Nathan Hatch has described the development of such a 'civil millennialist' rhetoric in New England during the wars against the Catholic and absolutist enemy in New France, in which the themes of Protestantism and liberty became inextricably linked. Similar themes appeared throughout the colonies. Presbyterians such as Samuel Davies and Samuel Finley employed much the same rhetoric in sermons on *Religion and Patriotism* and *The Danger of Neutrality in the Cause of God and Our Country*. Even the moderate Episcopalian William Smith would discuss the Seven Years War in similar terms, albeit from an Anglican but firmly Protestant point of view.[47]

That rhetoric could be applied to a variety of provincial issues. That was especially well illustrated during the 1760s, in the combined movement by colonial Presbyterians and Congregationalists to resist the effort by some American Anglicans to introduce an Anglican Bishop into the colonies. Since the episode took place shortly after the controversy over the Stamp Act, and the Bishop would derive his power from an act of Parliament, the causes of civil and ecclesiastical liberty were combined in the one issue. That was repeatedly noted by American opponents, who did their best to link the imperial claims of the Anglican Church to a legacy of religious intolerance and antipathy to liberty. Francis Alison, the leading Presbyterian spokesman, made the provincial implications of such charges quite explicit. Alison denied Anglican claims to represent a 'national religion', asking

> why is Episcopacy alone honoured with that name? Is it because it is established by Law in England? Is not Presbyterianism also established by Law ... in Scotland? But what is this to us in America? Because these Forms are established in Great Britain, must they also be established here?

Alison further maintained that 'All the Rejecters of Episcopacy have distinguished themselves in the Cause of Liberty ... their Principles of Church Government are Principles of Freedom'.[48]

As Hatch and others have shown, such a perspective would be utilized effectively by American Congregationalists and Presbyterians during the imperial crisis of the 1770s. It would be pointless, in view of the many and varied treatments of the origins of American revolutionary ideology that have appeared in recent years, to posit a single strand as the principal element in American thinking. Still, several general themes have emerged from that literature that suggest the importance of provincial viewpoints among revolutionary Americans. One of those is the argument by legal historians that the colonists did indeed play close attention to constitutional issues during the imperial crisis, maintaining throughout a consistent claim to their just rights as imperial citizens. For most Americans, that usually took the form of loyalty to the traditional privileges of their colonial assemblies rather than an appeal for more equitable representation in Parliament or an imperial union, as British provincials were more likely to envisage.[49]

Another theme that has emerged in the literature is that the colonists were persuaded to move beyond resistance to revolution not simply by Whiggish fears of British corruption, but also by far more optimistic views of America's potential as an empire of liberty, religion and trade. In religion, fears of possible Anglican impositions upon the colonial churches were superseded by occasionally millennial predictions of a dawning age of pure religion. During the trade recession of the 1760s and 1770s, complaints of the evil consequences of mercantile restrictions gave way to increasingly hopeful visions of an unvaryingly prosperous future outside the bounds of metropolitan restraint. That was the vision of America that appeared in Thomas Paine's *Common Sense*, the most influential document of the entire American revolutionary movement. Paine himself had close connections to Witherspoon's circle.[50]

No one was more effective in fusing the themes of liberty, piety and provinciality or in applying a provincial perspective to the situation of America during the imperial crisis than Witherspoon, in a series of sermons and tracts that he wrote on behalf of the American cause. His starting-point throughout was the growth of population and trade in America, a 'progress in improvement and population so rapid as no political calculations have been able to ascertain'. Like William Thom, he attributed that not to the land the colonists inhabited, but rather to the relative weakness of imperial authority and 'the degree of British liberty which they brought from home, and which pervaded more or less their several constitutions'. Indeed, the northern colonies, which were most notable for strictness in religion and 'the freest form of government', although 'greatly inferior in soil and climate, have yet outstripped the others in number of people and value of land', merely because the rest 'were under the influence of appointments and authority from home'.[51]

Witherspoon added several other distinctly provincial arguments. From the growth of the colonies, Witherspoon worked towards the position that they were now entitled to a larger voice in their own affairs. One of his principal goals was to persuade both sides that an equitable solution to the imperial problem did not require the permanent subjugation of the colonies. His target was what he called 'narrow, selfish views'. Following Hume, Witherspoon declared 'I cannot believe, that the misery and subjection of any country on earth, is necessary to the happiness of another'. Rather, the 'success and increase of one nation is, or may be, a benefit to every other'. A free government in America would lead to 'the peopling and enriching [of] this great continent'. The trade of America, once peace was concluded, would be as open and as beneficial to Britain as ever before.[52]

In *The Dominion of Providence over the Passions of Men* – the sermon with which we began this discussion – Witherspoon returned to the theme of empire in America, recalling Bishop Berkeley's prophecy of the westward course of empire; but Witherspoon's analysis went beyond simple conjecture. The past progress of religion from east to west, 'and in her train, dominion, riches, literature, and arts', did not by itself ensure the 'future glory of America'. Rather, that would come about from natural and determinable causes, the laws of commerce, demography and liberty. Conditions of liberty in America would revitalize its commerce and 'lay a foundation for the birth of millions, and the future improvement of a great part of the globe'.[53]

In the *Address to the Natives of Scotland*, Witherspoon applied that point directly to the concerns of Scottish-Americans, contending that American independence, by liberating American trade, would in the end benefit Scotland as well. Support for America, therefore, did not entail disloyalty to their native land. A few years earlier, Witherspoon had offered a similarly international conception of allegiance: 'What is it', he asked, 'for a man to be a friend to his country? Is it to wish well to the stones and the earth, or to the people that inhabit it?' He followed with a note that was distinctly Hutchesonian and provincial. Was it 'a liberal way of thinking', he asked, 'to say a man is an enemy to his country, while he promotes the happiness of the great body of the people, with a small diminution of the interest of an handful?'[54] It was just such a shift, from an identity rooted in historical boundaries to one based upon the welfare of the citizenry, that enabled Witherspoon to extend his patriotic loyalties from Scotland to America. Although he offered that conception in conciliatory language, by rooting resistance within a broadly based provincial ideology, Witherspoon raised the spectre of an oppositionist alliance among reformed Protestants in the provinces and reawakened metropolitan fears of renewed emigration – this time to a rebellious or even independent America – that would inevitably undermine metropolitan authority.[55]

Those fears were not without foundation. Although Scotland on the whole remained as supportive of empire as ever, much of the evangelical community, along with some prominent English dissenters, viewed the imperial crisis in a manner very similar to that of many colonials. Popular Party sermons and tracts linked Britain's suppression of American liberties to arbitrary authority at home, to encroachments upon the independence of the Scottish Church and plans to extend a dangerous and unwarranted toleration of Catholics to Quebec, and even to England and to Scotland. Such Popular Party spokesmen as John Erskine and Charles Nisbet became prominent defenders of the rights of the colonies. William Thom also expressed general agreement with colonial arguments. Strikingly, even those who opposed independence for America often did so not because they lacked sympathy for the American cause, but because they feared that a split between Britain and America would weaken both the Reformed interest and the cause of liberty within the empire as well as providing an opening for interference from Catholic powers abroad.[56]

As a teacher and a preacher, Witherspoon would attempt to convey those sentiments to his hearers. Both he and Francis Alison trained some of the most notable American patriots, including James Madison, Philip Freneau and Hugh Henry Brackenridge at the New Jersey College and Charles Thomson and Hugh Williamson, among many others, at Philadelphia. At the 1771 commencement at Princeton, Freneau and Brackenridge recited a poem they had written on 'The Rising Glory of America', which carried strong echoes of Bishop Berkeley and of Witherspoon himself. Moreover, Witherspoon surrounded himself with a substantial circle of Middle Colony patriots, most of them Presbyterians and immigrants, from the ministers John Rodgers and William Marshall to educators such as Samuel Stanhope Smith and the rest of the Princeton circle to the printer Robert Aitken. Collectively they preached, penned and published some of the most important endorsements of the American cause.[57]

Still, the main point is not that Witherspoon's students differed significantly from others in revolutionary America, but rather that they did not. As early as the 1750s New England's Nathaniel Ames was already predicting America's ascendancy. In 1768 Hugh Simm, another emigrant who accompanied Witherspoon from Paisley to America, described how he found 'the increasing power of America and her future empire' to be 'common subjects of conversation and the ordinary themes of theatrical declaration'. The Anglican missionary Andrew Burnaby, who travelled through the Middle Colonies during the 1750s, complained that everyone was repeating the 'strange and visionary idea' that empire was travelling westward. Those predictions, which helped prepare Americans to confront a final break with Britain, have often been cast as elaborations of specifically Puritan and New English conceptions of the covenant; in fact, they were founded upon shared provincial and British ideals.[58]

The American Revolution would have vastly different effects in the two sides of what had been the British provincial world. Once the war ended, Scots resumed their involvements with America almost without skipping a beat. Many Scottish merchants quickly resumed their ties to America, while even more looked northward, to the loyal provinces of British North America. During the 1780s Scottish emigrants streamed into the northern port of Halifax so rapidly that observers perceived a glut on the market. In subsequent years Scottish merchants worked so aggressively to open up Canadian frontiers that they came to resemble what one historian has termed a 'Scottish commercial preserve'.[59]

Nor were Scots slow to adapt their ideas to the loss of the American provinces. Even before the war had ended, various spokesmen began to offer what one called 'consolatory thoughts' to their countrymen on the implications of the loss of that part of the empire. One of the most interesting was that written by Thomas Tod, an Edinburgh merchant with both American and evangelical connections. Tod speculated that the American Revolution had been the work of a providential hand, which would result in the creation of a vast American empire. That, in turn, would open up the entire western hemisphere to British trade, to Scotland's benefit. In an almost millennial conclusion, Tod envisioned a new era for all of mankind, in which nations would beat their swords into ploughshares in a golden age of free trade.[60]

The effects of the revolution upon American ideas were considerably more ambiguous. During the 1780s Witherspoon and his students would continue to articulate a vision of American expansion and national unity on the principle of provincial equity that would aid in the formation of a national government. Witherspoon himself wrote popular essays on national culture and national capitals aimed at the 'illiberal' forces of local, 'provincial pride'. His former student, James Madison, and the Scottish *émigré* James Wilson worked actively to implement a national government, drawing upon the political essays of Hume and the moral philosophies of Hutcheson and Thomas Reid. Americans would long continue to rely upon those philosophies, which would form the basis for a national ethic well into the nineteenth century.[61]

The context of those ideals had changed markedly, however. Once Americans severed their connections with the empire and with her sister provinces, the liberal vision of boundless prosperity rooted in predictable social forces in an environment of provincial liberty could all too easily be transformed into declarations of a particular and providentially ordained national destiny. Out of a moral philosophy based upon the moral sense of a reflective citizenry Americans would select a particular 'Common Sense' variety that proved particularly adaptable to the needs of national elites, in Scotland as well as in America. It may be that the very nationalist interpretation of American origins so obliterated any recollection of its provincial beginnings that it has misled even some of our best historical interpreters. Thus that particular optimistic vision of unlimited American potential, which was, in origin, British, liberal and provincial, has often been reinterpreted as uniquely American, New English and exceptional.

NOTES

1 Printed in *Works of the Rev. John Witherspoon, D.D.L.L.D., Late President of the College at Princeton, New-Jersey* (second edn, 4 vols; Philadelphia: William W. Woodward, 1802), vol. III, 17–60. For a more extended discussion of Witherspoon, see my 'Witherspoon and the Problem of Provincial Identity in Scottish Evangelical Culture', in Richard B. Sher and Jefferey Smitten (eds), *Scotland and America in the Age of the Enlightenment* (Edinburgh: Edinburgh University Press, 1990), 29–45.

2 On Witherspoon's notoriety, see Richard B. Sher, 'Witherspoon's "Dominion of Providence" and the Scottish Jeremiad Tradition', in Sher and Smitten, *Scotland and America*, 46–64; also see the annotated, highly critical Glasgow edition of *Dominion of Providence* (Glasgow, 1777), and Hugo Arnot, *The XLV Chapter of the Prophecies of Thomas the Rhymer, in Verse: with Notes and Illustrations, Dedicated to Doctor Silverspoon, Preacher of Sedition in America* (Edinburgh: C. Elliot, 1776)

3 For a striking elaboration of the development of British imperial identities within London and the provincial towns of England itself, see Kathleen Wilson, Chapter 6 above.

4 *William and Mary Quarterly* (hereinafter *WMQ*), third series, 11 (1954) 200–13. The most extensive survey of Scottish-American connections, still far from complete, is W. R. Brock, *Scotus Americanus; A Survey of Sources for Links between Scotland and America in the Eighteenth Century* (Edinburgh: Edinburgh University Press, 1982); and see the introduction to Sher and Smitten,

Scotland and America, 1–27. See also Eric Richards's survey, 'Scotland and the Uses of the Atlantic Empire', in Bernard Bailyn and Philip D. Morgan (eds), *Strangers within the Realm: Cultural Margins of the First British Empire* (Chapel Hill: University of North Carolina Press, 1991), 67–114.

5 The literature here is considerable: see, especially, Jacob Price, 'The Rise of Glasgow in the Chesapeake Tobacco Trade', *WMQ*, third series, 11 (1954), 179–99; J. H. Soltow, 'Scottish Traders in Virginia 1750–1775', *Economic History Review*, second series, 12 (1959–60), 83–98; Ian C. C. Graham, *Colonists from Scotland; Emigration to North America, 1707–1783* (Ithaca: Cornell University Press, 1956); Thomas M. Devine, *The Tobacco Lords: A Study of the Tobacco Merchants of Glasgow and Their Trading Activities c. 1740–90* (Edinburgh: John Donald, 1975); Thomas M. Devine, 'An Eighteenth Century Business Elite: Glasgow's West India Merchants 1750–1815', *Scottish Historical Review*, 57 (1978), 40–63; Richard B. Sheridan, *Sugar and Slavery: An Economic History of the British West Indies 1623–1775* (Baltimore: Johns Hopkins University Press, 1973); David S. Macmillan, 'The "New Men" in Action: Scottish Mercantile and Shipping Operations in the North American Colonies, 1760–1825', in David S. Macmillan (ed.), *Canadian Business History: Selected Studies 1497–1971* (Toronto: McLelland and Stewart, 1972), 44–103; and W. Stanford Reid (ed.), *The Scottish Tradition in Canada* (Toronto: McLelland and Stewart, 1976).

6 The literature here is far too vast to list. On education, see especially Douglas Sloan, *The Scottish Enlightenment and the American College Ideal* (New York: Teachers College Press, 1971), and Howard Miller, *The Revolutionary College: American Presbyterian Higher Education 1707–1837* (New York: New York University Press, 1976); on science, Raymond Phineas Stearns, *Science in the British Colonies of North America* (Chicago: University of Illinois Press, 1970); on medicine, C. Helen Brock, 'Scotland and American Medicine', in Brock, *Scotus Americanus*, ch. 6; on literature, Terence Martin, *The Instructed Vision: Scottish Common Sense Philosophy and the Origins of American Fiction* (Bloomington: Indiana University Press, 1961); and Andrew Hook, *Scotland and America: A Study of Cultural Relations 1750–1835* (Glasgow: Blackie & Son, 1975); and, on philosophy, Henry May, *The Enlightenment in America* (New York: Oxford University Press, 1976), Donald Meyer, *The Democratic Enlightenment* (New York: G. P. Putnam's Sons, 1976), and Daniel Walker Howe, 'European Sources of Political Ideas in Jeffersonian America', *Reviews in American History*, 10 (1982), 28–44; and see the more specialized works cited below.

7 See especially Michael Hechter, *Internal Colonialism: The Celtic Fringe in British National Development, 1536–1966* (London: Routledge & Kegan Paul, 1975); also Jack P. Greene, *Peripheries and Center: Constitutional Development in the Extended Polities of the British Empire and the United States, 1607–1788* (Athens: University of Georgia Press, 1986). J. C. D. Clark, in 'England's Forgotten Context: Scotland, Ireland, Wales', *Historical Journal*, 32 (1989), 211–28, denied that the provinces possessed commonalities of any sort. See also J. G. A. Pocock, 'The Limits and Divisions of British History: In Search of an Unknown Subject', *American Historical Review*, 87 (1982), 311–36.

8 The most ambitious attempt to assess the impact of provincial status upon Scottish culture appears in the essays of Nicholas Phillipson; see especially 'Culture and Society in the 18th Century Province: The Case of Edinburgh and the Scottish Enlightenment', in Lawrence Stone (ed.), *The University and Society* (2 vols; Princeton: Princeton University Press, 1975), vol. II, 407–48; and 'Adam Smith as Civic Moralist', in Istvan Hont and Michael Ignatieff

(eds), *Wealth and Virtue: The Shaping of Political Economy in the Scottish Enlightenment* (New York: Cambridge University Press, 1983), 179–202. See also Jack P. Greene, 'Search for Identity: An Interpretation of the Meaning of Selected Patterns of Social Response in Eighteenth-Century America', *Journal of Social History*, 3 (1970), 189–220.

9 *A Candid Enquiry into The Causes of the Late and the Intended Migrations from Scotland* (Glasgow: P. Tait, [1771]), 50–1.

10 Bernard Bailyn, *Voyagers to the West: A Passage in the Peopling of America on the Eve of the Revolution* (New York: Alfred A. Knopf, 1986), chs 12–13.

11 James Boswell, *Journal of a Tour to the Hebrides with Samuel Johnson, LL. D.*, ed. R. W. Chapman (Oxford: Oxford University Press, 1924).

12 See especially T. C. Smout, *Scottish Trade on the Eve of the Union* (Edinburgh: Oliver & Boyd, 1963); and Phillipson 'Culture and Society'.

13 See especially Smout, *Scottish Trade*; Gordon Marshall, *Presbyteries and Profits: Calvinism and the Development of Capitalism in Scotland, 1560–1707* (Oxford: Clarendon Press, 1980); Ned C. Landsman, *Scotland and Its First American Colony 1683–1765* (Princeton: Princeton University Press, 1985); and two works by George Pratt Insh: *Scottish Colonial Schemes, 1620–1686* (Glasgow: Maclehose, Jackson and Company, 1922), and *The Company of Scotland Trading to Africa and the Indies* (New York: C. Scribner's Sons, 1932).

14 Smout, *Scottish Trade*; Phillipson, 'Culture and Society'; and see the essays in N. T. Phillipson and Rosalind Mitchison (eds), *Scotland in the Age of the Improvement* (Edinburgh: Edinburgh University Press, 1970).

15 See R. H. Campbell, *Scotland since 1707: The Rise of an Industrial Society* (Oxford: Blackwells, 1965), and 'The Enlightenment and the Economy', in R. H. Campbell and Andrew S. Skinner (eds), *The Origins and Nature of the Scottish Enlightenment* (Edinburgh: John Donald, 1982), 8–25; but see T. M. Devine, 'Colonial Commerce and the Scottish Economy, c. 1730–1815', in L. M. Cullen and T. C. Smout (eds), *Comparative Aspects of Scottish and Irish Economic and Social History* (Edinburgh: John Donald, 1976), 177–90; and T. C. Smout, 'Where Had the Scottish Economy Got to by the Third Quarter of the Eighteenth Century?', in Hont and Ignatieff, *Wealth and Virtue*, 45–72. A typical merchant view of the impact of the colonial trade is James Gibson, *History of Glasgow* (Glasgow: R. Chapman and A. Duncan, 1777).

16 See Louis Knott Koontz, *Robert Dinwiddie* (Glendale: Arthur H. Clark, 1941), 51–6; Henry McCulloh, *A Miscellaneous Essay concerning the Courses Pursued in the Affairs of the Colonies: With Some Observations on the Great Importance of Our Settlements in America, and the Trade thereof* (London: R. Baldwin, 1755); *Proposals for Uniting the English Colonies on the Continent of America* (London: J. Wilkie, 1757); and John Rutherfurd, *The Importance of the Colonies to Great Britain. With Some Hints towards Making Improvements to their Mutual Advantages: And upon Trade in General* (London: J. Millar, 1761), in William Boyd (ed.), 'Some North Carolina Tracts of the 18th Century', *North Carolina Historical Review*, 2 (1925), 351–76. The titles well indicate the positions of their authors.

17 On the diverse traditions present in Scottish discourse, see especially Istvan Hont and Michael Ignatieff, 'Needs and justice in the *Wealth of Nations*', in Hont and Ignatieff, *Wealth and Virtue*, 1–44; along with the essays by John Robertson, J. G. A. Pocock and Donald Winch in the same volume; also John Robertson, *The Scottish Enlightenment and the Militia Issue* (Edinburgh: John Donald, 1985), and Roger A. Mason (ed.), *Scotland and England 1286–1815* (Edinburgh: John Donald, 1987). Isaac Kramnick, 'The "Great National Dis-

cussion": The Discourse of Politics in 1787', *WMQ*, third series, 45 (1988), 3–32, discusses the integration of various political languages in America.

18 See especially J. G. A. Pocock, *The Machiavellian Moment: Florentine Political Thought and the Atlantic Republican Tradition* (Princeton: Princeton University Press, 1975), ch. 14.

19 Adam Smith, *An Inquiry into the Nature and Causes of the Wealth of Nations*, ed. R. H. Campbell and A. S. Skinner (2 vols; Oxford: Oxford University Press, 1976), book IV, ch. 7.

20 John Erskine, *Influence of Religion on National Prosperity* (Edinburgh, 1756); John Witherspoon, *Prayer for National Prosperity and the Revival of Religion Inseparably Connected* (London: Tho. Field, 1758). On the implications of that discourse, see especially Istvan Hont, 'The "Rich Country–Poor Country" Debate in Scottish Classical Political Economy', in Hont and Ignatieff, *Wealth and Virtue*, 271–316; and see Janet Ann Riesman, 'Origins of American Political Economy' (Ph.D. dissertation, Brown University, 1983), for the spread of commercial discourse to America.

21 An interesting commercial tract that advocates structured trade as a necessary antidote to the power of the English monopolies in David Loch, *Essay on the Trade, Commerce and Manufactures of Scotland* (Edinburgh, 1775). Also see Sir James Steuart, *Inquiry into the Principles of Political Oeconomy*, ed. Andrew S. Skinner (1766; 2 vols; Chicago: University of Chicago Press, 1967).

22 Robert Wallace, *A Dissertation on the Numbers of Mankind in Ancient and Modern Times* (1753; New York: Augustus M. Kelley, 1969); David Hume, 'Of the Populousness of Ancient Nations', in *David Hume: Writings on Economics*, ed. Eugene Rotwein (Madison: University of Wisconsin Press, 1970), 108–83; and Alexander Webster, 'An Account of the Numbers of People in Scotland in the Year One Thousand Seven Hundred and Fifty-five', in J. G. Kyd (ed.), *Scottish Population Statistics* (Edinburgh: Scottish Academic Press, 1952); Webster, *A Letter to the Reverend Doctor Price, of London, and Dr. Price's Answer, relative to the Establishment for a Provision to the Widows and Children of the Ministers and Professors in Scotland* (Edinburgh: Murray and Cochran, 1771); and see Hont, ' "Rich Country–Poor Country" '; Riesman, 'Origins'; and D. V. Glass, *Numbering the People: The Eighteenth-Century Population Controversy and the Development of Census and Vital Statistics in Britain* (Farnborough: D. C. Heath, 1973).

23 See especially Alexander Murdoch, *'The People Above': Politics and Administration in Mid-Eighteenth-Century Scotland* (Edinburgh: John Donald, 1980); John Dwyer and Alexander Murdoch, 'Paradigms and Politics: Manners, Morals and the Rise of Henry Dundas', in John Dwyer, Roger A. Mason and Alexander Murdoch (eds), *New Perspectives on the Politics and Culture of Early Modern Scotland* (Edinburgh: John Donald, 1982), 210–48; Greene, *Peripheries and Center*; and Kathleen Wilson, Chapter 6 above.

24 Smith, *Wealth of Nations*, Book V, ch. 3, followed Hume as well in viewing the spirit of 'party' as strongest near the metropolis. On Hutcheson, see especially Caroline Robbins, ' "When It Is That Colonies May Turn Independent": An Analysis of the Environment and Politics of Francis Hutcheson (1694–1746)', *WMQ*, third series, 11 (1954), 214–51, and T. D. Campbell, 'Francis Hutcheson: "Father" of the Scottish Enlightenment', in Campbell and Skinner, *Origins and Nature*, 167–85; and John Robertson, 'The Scottish Enlightenment at the Limits of the Civic Tradition', in Hont and Ignatieff, *Wealth and Virtue*, 137–78; and Corey Venning, 'Hume on Property,

Commerce, and Empire in the Good Society: The Role of Historical Necessity', *Journal of the History of Ideas*, 37 (1976), 79–92, on Hume.

25 Archibald Grant, letter, 7 March 1764, Grant of Monymusk MS, Scottish Records Office, Edinburgh; William Thom, *Seasonable Advice to the Landholders and Farmers in Scotland* (Edinburgh: J. Robertson, 1770), printed in the *The Works of the Reverend William Thom, Late Minister of Govan* (Glasgow: James Dymock, 1799), 159–229; William Thom, *The Present Conduct of the Chieftains and Proprietors of Lands in the Highlands of Scotland* (London, 1773), 6–7; see also John Lindsay, letter to his mother, 26 August 1729, Scottish Record Office; and the letter of Archibald Laidlie, 5 November 1773, Laidlie Papers, New York Historical Society.

26 See Rutherfurd, *Importance of the Colonies*; J. M. Bumsted, 'Sir James Montgomery and Prince Edward Island, 1767–1803', *Acadiensis*, 7 (1978), 76–102; Patrick Lindsay, *The Interest of Scotland Considered* (Edinburgh: R. Fleming and Company, 1733); Bernard Bailyn, *Voyagers to the West*, chs 11–13; and Macmillan, *Canadian Business History*.

27 *Glasgow Journal*, 26 January 1764, quoted in Macmillan, *Canadian Business History*, 56–7; and see Devine, 'Eighteenth Century Business Elite'.

28 See especially John Mitchell, *The Contest in America Between Great Britain and France* (London: A. Millar, 1757); William Livingston, *Review of the Military Operations in North-America* (London: J. Dodsley, 1757).

29 John Murrin, 'A Roof without Walls: The Dilemma of American National Identity', in Richard Beeman, Stephen Botein and Edward C. Carter II (eds), *Beyond Confederation: Origins of the Constitution and American National Identity* (Chapel Hill: University of North Carolina Press, 1987), 333–48. Murrin relies largely upon the discussion by J. M. Bumsted, ' "Things in the Womb of Time": Ideas of American Independence, 1633 to 1733', *WMQ*, third series, 31 (1974), 533–64; nearly all Bumsted's sources for this period were Scots or Scottish-Americans. See also Jack P. Greene, Charles F. Mullett and Edward C. Papenfuse, Jr. (eds), *Magna Charta For America: James Abercromby's An Examination of the Acts of Parliament relative To the Trade and the Government of Our American Colonies . . .* (Philadelphia: American Philosophical Society, 1986); McCulloh, *Miscellaneous Essays*; several tracts by Archibald Kennedy, including *Observations on the Importance of the Northern Colonies under Proper Regulations* (New York: James Parker, 1750), *An Essay on the Government of the Colonies* (New York: J. Parker, 1754), and *Serious Considerations on the Present State of Affairs of the Northern Colonies* (New York: 1754); and Max Savelle, *Seeds of Liberty: The Genesis of the American Mind* (New York: Alfred A. Knopf, 1948), ch. 6 *passim*.

30 *A North Briton Extraordinary: A Curious and Comprehensive Review of English and Scottish History*, (third edn; London: J. Knox, 1769), especially 41, 69, and see Thom, *Present Conduct*, 1.

31 Quoted by L. H. Butterfield (ed.), in *John Witherspoon Comes to America* (Princeton: Princeton University Library, 1953), 29–32. The letters in that collection demonstrate how extensive such hopes for America had become in both Scottish and American thinking.

32 Scottish–American religious connections can be traced in Susan O'Brien, 'A Transatlantic Community of Saints: The Great Awakening and the First Evangelical Network, 1735–1755', *American Historical Review*, 91 (1986), 811–32; G. D. Henderson, 'Jonathan Edwards and Scotland', *The Burning Bush: Studies in Scottish Church History* (Edinburgh: Saint Andrew Press, 1957), 151–62; and in the original transatlantic periodicals that O'Brien cites. Evidence of earlier

contacts can be found in Thomas Mcrie (ed.), *The Correspondence of the Reverend Robert Wodrow* (3 vols; Edinburgh: The Wodrow Society, 1842–3); The best study of the Moderates is Richard B. Sher, *Church and University in the Scottish Enlightenment: The Moderate Literati of Edinburgh* (Princeton: Princeton University Press, 1985).

33 David Grant, *The Living Manners of the Times, and Their Consequences: Together with the Motives to Reformation* (Edinburgh: David Paterson, 1779), 16; [William Thom], *A Short History of the Late General Assembly of the Church of Scotland, Shewing the Rise and Progress of the Schism Overture . . .* (Glasgow: James Duncan, 1766), 56; and see *An Essay on Civil and Religious Liberty* (Glasgow: John Gilmour, 1768) and the discussion below.

34 [William Thom], *A Letter to the Author of a Case of Patronage, Stated according to the Laws, Civil and Ecclesiastical, of the Realm of Scotland* (Glasgow: William Smith, 1783), 30; John Erskine, *Shall I Go to War with My American Brethren?* (London: G. Kearsley, 1769), 3; and see the works of John Witherspoon cited below, nn. 51–5.

35 Erskine, *Shall I Go to War?*, 3; Thom, *A Short History*, 46–7; and James Baine, *Memoirs of Modern Church Reformation; Or the History of the General Assembly 1766* (Edinburgh: William Gray, 1766).

36 Bailyn, *Voyagers to the West*, surpasses all previous works on those emigrations; see especially 108–9, 150–1, 162–3. Also see J. M. Bumsted, *The People's Clearance: Highland Emigration to British North America 1770–1815* (Edinburgh: Edinburgh University Press, 1982): Materials concerning the connections between merchant promoters in the various provincial migrations can be drawn from Bailyn, *Voyagers to the West*, 390–428; John Stevens to Campbell Stevens, 6 February 1751, Stevens Family Papers, New Jersey Historical Society; the notebook of an unnamed Glasgow linen merchant 1765–71, TD 111, Strathclyde Regional Archives; Gregg and Cunningham Letterbook 1756–7, New York Historical Society; and the advertisements in Scottish newspapers, especially *Glasgow Journal* (11 February 1773); and the sales of pamphlets such as William Thom's *Candid Enquiry into the Causes of the Late and the Intended Migrations* in Ireland as well as Scotland.

37 On the earlier evangelical activities of John Pagan, see *Extracts from the Records of the Burgh of Glasgow*, vol. VII, *1760–1780* (Glasgow: Scottish Burgh Record Society, 1912), 125–8, for John Pagan and the discussion thereafter of Glasgow patronage. The entire Glasgow merchant community had strong evangelical ties; see my 'Presbyterians and Provincial Society: Evangelical Enlightenment in the West of Scotland 1745–1775', in Richard B. Sher and John Dwyer (eds), *Eighteenth-Century Life*, n.s., vol. 15 (1991), 194–209. Evangelicalism among Yorkshire emigrants is discussed in Bailyn, *Voyagers to the West*, 420–6.

38 Thom, *Present Conduct*, 6–7. The other four pamphlets, all published without attribution, were *Candid Enquiry into the Causes of the Late and the Intended Migrations from Scotland; Seasonable Advice to the Landholders and Farmers in Scotland; Information concerning the Province of North Carolina, Addressed to Emigrants from the Highlands and Western Isles of Scotland* (Glasgow: James Knox, 1773); and *Information to Emigrants, Being the Copy of a Letter From a Gentleman in North-America* (Glasgow: Morrison & M'Allum, [1773]). Evidence of Thom's authorship is derived from William Thom, *The Revolt of the Ten Tribes* (Glasgow: Robert Chapman and Alexander Duncan, 1778), 46; and the volume of 'Thom of Govan Pamphlets', Colquhoun of Luss MS, National Library of Scotland.

39 Thom, *Information concerning the Province of North Carolina*, 11, 32: and

NED C. LANDSMAN

Viola Root Cameron (ed.), *Emigrants from Scotland to America 1774–1775: Copied from a Loose Bundle of Treasury Papers in the Public Record Office, London, England* (Baltimore: Genealogical Publishing Company, 1965).

40 Garry Wills, *Inventing America: Jefferson's Declaration of Independence* (Garden City: Doubleday, 1978). Wills has come under heavy criticism for homogenizing the ideas of a varied group of Scottish thinkers and exaggerating their influence upon the language of the Declaration: see especially Ronald Hamowy, 'Jefferson and the Scottish Enlightenment: A Critique of Garry Wills's *Inventing America: Jefferson's Declaration of Independence*', *WMQ*, third series, 36 (1979), 503–23. Hamowy's critique leaves much of Wills's conceptual argument intact.

There are numerous sources for American criticisms of the Scots; see especially Graham, *Colonists from Scotland*, ch. 7; and Hook, *Scotland and America*, ch. 3, which also develops the theme of American ambivalence towards Scotland.

41 See especially Sloan, *Scottish Enlightenment*; Miller, *Revolutionary College*; Jack Scott (ed.), *An Annotated Edition of Lectures on Moral Philosophy by John Witherspoon* (Newark: University of Delaware Press, 1982); also Robert Lawson-Peebles, 'The Problem of William Smith', in Jennifer Carter and Joan Pittock (eds), *Aberdeen and the Enlightenment* (Aberdeen: Aberdeen University Press, (1987), 51–60; Peter J. Diamond, 'Witherspoon, William Smith and the Scottish Philosophy in Revolutionary America', in Sher and Smitten, *Scotland and America*, 115–32; Stearns, *Science*, 593–619; and Provost R. Foskett, 'Some Scottish Episcopalians in the North American Colonies, 1675–1750', *Records of the Scottish Church History Society*, 14 (1963), 135–50.

42 The correspondence concerning Witherspoon's appointment is collected in Butterfield, *John Witherspoon*. Witherspoon's advertisements can be found in William Nelson (ed.), *Documents relating to the Colonial History of the State of New Jersey*, first series, *Extracts from American Newspapers, Relating to New Jersey*, vol. VII, (Paterson, NJ, 1904), 383–4, and vol. IX, (Paterson, NJ, 1916), 289–308; and see William Smith, *A General Idea of the College of Mirania; With a Sketch of the Method of Teaching Science and Religion, in the Several Classes* (New York: J. Parker and W. Weyman, 1753); and Peter Jones, 'The Scottish Professoriate and the Polite Academy', in Hont and Ignatieff, *Wealth and Virtue*, 89–118.

43 There is no adequate study of those doctors, but see Brock, *Scotus Americanus*, 174–91; Stearns, *Science, passim*; Savelle, *Seeds of Liberty*, 296–326; Roger L. Emerson, 'The Edinburgh Society for the Importation of Foreign Seeds and Plants, 1764–1773', *Eighteenth-Century Life*, 7 (1982), 73–95; and Roger L. Emerson, 'American Indians, Frenchmen, and Scots Philosophers', *Studies in Eighteenth-Century Culture*, 9 (1979), 21–36. Among their more important writings were William Douglass, *Summary, Historical and Political, of the British Settlements in North-America* (2 vols; Boston: Rogers and Fowle, 1747–52); Mitchell, *Contest*; and Cadwallader Colden, *The History of the Five Indian Nations Depending on the Province of New York in America*, (New York: William Bradford, 1727–44).

44 Franklin, *Observations Concerning the Increase of Mankind* and *The Interest of Great Britain Considered. With Regard to Her Colonies*, in *The Papers of Benjamin Franklin*, ed. Leonard Labaree et al., *The Papers of Benjamin Franklin* (New Haven: Yale University Press, 1959-), vol. IV, 22–34, and vol. IX, 53–8; and see Drew McCoy, 'Benjamin Franklin's Vision of a Republican Political Economy for America', *WMQ*, third series, 35 (1978), 605–28, and *The Elusive*

Republic: Political Economy in Jeffersonian America (Chapel Hill: University of North Carolina Press, 1980), 48–67; Riesman, 'Origins', 229 ff. Also see James Bennett Nolan, *Benjamin Franklin in Scotland and Ireland 1759 and 1771* (Philadelphia: University of Pennsylvania Press, 1935.)

45 Jonathan Edwards to James Robe, 12 May 1743; and to an unidentified Scottish correspondent, 20 November 1745, both in *The Christian Monthly History*, 5 (August 1743), 127–30; and 8 (November 1745), 234–54. The Concert for Prayer is discussed in John Gillies (ed.), *Historical Collections relating to Remarkable Periods of the Success of the Gospel* (2 vols; Glasgow: R. and A. Foulis, 1754), vol. II, 462–4; also in Henderson, 'Jonathan Edwards'. Much of Edwards's correspondence with Scotland can be found in S. E. Dwight, *The Life of President Edwards* (New York: G. & C. & H. Carvill, 1830). On the Puritan jeremiad, see Sacvan Bercovitch, *The American Jeremiad* (Madison: University of Wisconsin Press, 1970). That the jeremiad also was a Reformed rather than simply a New English or Puritan tradition is argued in Sher, 'Witherspoon's "Dominion of Providence"'.

46 A good example of the absorption of the New England myth into a larger British Reformed perspective by Presbyterians in Scotland and in America is Witherspoon, *Dominion of Providence*, 30–1 and note; see also Erskine, *Shall I Go to War?*.

47 William Smith, *Discourses on Several Public Occasions during the War in America. Preached Chiefly with a View to the Explaining the Protestant Cause, in the British Colonies* (London: A. Millar, 1759); Samuel Davies, *Religion and Patriotism the Constituents of a Good Soldier* (Philadelphia: James Chattin, 1755); Samuel Finley, *The Curse of Meroz, Or The Danger of Neutrality in the Cause of God and Our Country* (Philadelphia: James Chattin, 1757); and see Nathan Hatch, *The Sacred Cause of Liberty: Republican Thought and the Millennium in Revolutionary New England* (New Haven: Yale University Press, 1977).

48 See Elizabeth I. Nybakken (ed.), *The Centinel: Warnings of a Revolution* (Newark: University of Delaware Press, 1980), 87, 105; and Carl Bridenbaugh, *Mitre and Sceptre: Transatlantic Faiths, Ideas, Personalities, and Politics 1689–1775* (New York: Oxford University Press, 1962); and Patricia U. Bonomi, *Under the Cope of Heaven: Religion, Society and Politics in Colonial America* (New York: Oxford University Press, 1986).

49 Greene, *Peripheries and Center*, usefully summarizes much of that position; see especially 144–50.

50 The most explicit case for the optimistic, even imperial, basis for the ideology of revolution is Marc Egnal, *A Mighty Empire: The Origins of the American Revolution* (Ithaca: Cornell University Press, 1988), which exaggerates the difference between Whigs and Tories, but successfully highlights the appearance of increasingly optimistic predictions about American potential. Also see Hatch, *Sacred Cause*; John F. Berens, *Providence and Patriotism in Early America, 1640–1815* (Charlottesville: University of Virginia Press, 1978); Ruth H. Bloch, *Visionary Republic: Millennial Themes in American Thought, 1756–1800* (New York: Cambridge University Press, 1985); Bonomi, *Under the Cope of Heaven*; and Eric Foner, *Tom Paine and Revolutionary America* (New York: Oxford University Press, 1976). The role of economic discontents in pre-revolutionary America is amplified in Gary B. Nash, *Urban Crucible: Social Change, Political Consciousness, and the Origins of the American Revolution* (Cambridge, Mass.: Harvard University Press, 1979); and Marc Egnal and Joseph A. Ernst, 'An Economic Interpretation of the American Revolution', *WMQ*, third series, 29

(1972), 177–99. Paine worked for Witherspoon's friend and printer Robert Aitken in Philadelphia and was associated both with Witherspoon and Benjamin Rush.

51 Witherspoon, *Dominion of Providence, passim.* Witherspoon's many tracts on the crisis are scattered through volumes III and IV of his *Works.*

52 ibid.; see also [Joseph Blewer], *A Few Political Reflections Submitted to the Consideration of the British Colonies* (Philadelphia: John Dunlop, 1774), 16.

53 Witherspoon, *Dominion of Providence*, 36, 54.

54 'Letter Sent to Scotland for the *Scots Magazine*', in *Works*, vol. IV, 281–8.

55 Metropolitan fears of the consequences of emigration are discussed in Bailyn, *Voyagers to the West*, ch. 2. On Witherspoon's reputation, see especially George Paton to Thomas Percy, 20 June 1777, in A. F. Falconer (ed.), *The Percy Letters: The Correspondence of Thomas Percy and George Paton* (New Haven: Yale University Press, 1961), 144–6. I would like to thank Richard Sher for this reference.

56 Erskine, *Shall I Go to War?*; and *The Equity and Wisdom of Administration, in Measures that have Unhappily Occasioned the American Revolt* (Edinburgh: William Gray, 1776); Thom, *Revolt of the Ten Tribes*; and see Robert Kent Donovan, *No Popery and Radicalism: Opposition to Roman Catholic Relief in Scotland, 1778–1782* (New York: Garland Publishers, 1987). Exactly how extensive support for America in Scotland may have been is a matter of debate. It is certain that most of the literati opposed independence, some vociferously, although even they rarely disputed the American's claims to a more powerful and secure voice in political affairs. See Dalphy A. Fagerstrom, 'Scottish Opinion and the American Revolution', *WMQ* third series, 11 (1954), 252–75; Sher, *Church and University*, 262–76; and D. B. Swinfen, 'The American Revolution and the Scottish Press', in Owen Dudley Edwards and George Shepperson (eds), *Scotland, Europe, and the American Revolution* (Edinburgh: Edinburgh University Press, 1976), 66–74. For the positions of English radicals, see John Brewer, *Party Ideology and Popular Politics at the Accession of George III* (New York: Cambridge University Press, 1976), ch. 10; and Colin Bonwick, *English Radicals and the American Revolution* (Chapel Hill: University of North Carolina Press, 1977).

57 On Alison's influence, see David Fate Norton, 'Francis Hutcheson in America', *Studies on Voltaire and the Eighteenth Century*, 154 (1976), 1547–68. The printer Aitken, who, like Witherspoon, emigrated from Paisley, published many revolutionary works, including Witherspoon's *Dominion of Providence* and the *Pennsylvania Magazine*, on which he employed Thomas Paine as editor. Rodgers was an influential minister in New York; Marshall was probably the leading Scottish Seceder in America. A lucid treatment of Witherspoon's Princeton circle is Mark A. Noll, *Princeton and the Republic, 1768–1822: The Search for a Christian Enlightenment in the Era of Samuel Stanhope Smith* (Princeton: Princeton University Press, 1989).

58 Sam. Briggs (ed.), *The Essays, Humour, and Poems of Nathaniel Ames, Father and Son, of Dedham, Massachusetts, from their Almanacks 1726–1775* (Cleveland, 1891); Hugh Simm to Andrew Simm, 2 December 1768, Correspondence of Hugh Simm, Princeton University Library; Andrew Burnaby, *Travels through the Middle Settlements in North-America* (second edn; London: T. Payne, 1775), 110; and see Savelle, *Seeds of Liberty*, 581–3. On the New English origins of such conceptions, see especially, Bercovitch, *American Jeremiad*; and Berens, *Providence and Patriotism*.

59 Macmillan, *Canadian Business History*, 45; see also Bumsted, *People's Clear-*

ance; Bernard Aspinwall, 'The Scots in the United States', in R. A. Cage (ed.), *The Scot Abroad: Labour, Capital, Enterprise, 1750–1914* (Beckenham: Croom Helm Ltd, 1985), 80–111; and see Bernard Aspinwall, *Portable Utopia: Glasgow and the United States, 1820–1920* (Aberdeen: Aberdeen University Press, 1984).

60 Thomas Tod, *Consolatory Thoughts on American Independence; Shewing the Great Advantages that will Arise from it to the Manufactures, the Agriculture, and Commercial Interest of Britain and Ireland* (Edinburgh: James Donaldson, 1782); and see James Anderson, *The Interest of Great-Britain with Regard to the American Colonies Considered* (London: T. Cadell, 1782); and Loch, *Essay on Trade*.

61 For the effect of Scottish ideas on the Constitution of the United States, see Douglas Adair, ' "That Politics May Be Reduced to a Science": David Hume, James Madison and the 10th Federalist', *Huntingdon Library Quarterly*, 20 (1957), 343–60; Garry Wills, *Explaining America: The Federalist* (Garden City: Doubleday, 1981); Forrest McDonald, *Novus Ordo Seclorum: The Intellectual Origins of the Constitution* (Lawrence: University Press of Kansas, 1985); Stephen A. Conrad, 'Polite Foundation: Citizenship and Common Sense in James Wilson's Republican Theory', *Supreme Court Review* (1984), 359–88; and Shannon Stimson, ' "A Jury of the Country": Common Sense Philosophy and the Jurisprudence of James Wilson', in Sher and Smitten, *Scotland and America*, 193–208. See also John Witherspoon, 'A Few Reflections on the Federal City' and 'The Druid', both in *Works*, vol. IV, 403–12, 425–75. On the legacy of Common Sense, see especially May, *Enlightenment in America*; Donald Meyer, *The Instructed Conscience: The Shaping of the American National Ethic* (Philadelphia: University of Pennsylvania Press, 1971); Daniel Walker Howe, *The Unitarian Conscience: Harvard Moral Philosophy, 1805–1861* (Cambridge, Mass.: Harvard University Press, 1970); and Nicholas Phillipson, 'The Pursuit of Virtue in Scottish University Education: Dugald Stewart and Scottish Moral Philosophy', in Nicholas Phillipson (ed.), *Universities, Society and the Future* (Edinburgh: Edinburgh University Press, 1983), 82–101.

287

11

Irish Resistance to Empire?
1641, 1690 and 1798

Nicholas Canny

It is a commonplace in British historiography that Ireland was already in the seventeenth and eighteenth centuries, as it was to become in the nine-teenth and twentieth centuries, the 'restless dominion'.[1] Whenever evidence is cited in support of this assumption it is to the effect that Irish society was relatively poor and hence more violent than English society, or that the population of Ireland were innately rebellious because they had never become reconciled to the conquest of the country that had been effected at the outset of the seventeenth century. Some historians of England and Scotland attribute the disturbed history of modern Ireland to religious considerations, but all who make reference to Ireland's discontent are primarily concerned with the extent to which insurrection there precipi-tated challenges to authority within Britain itself. Thus several historians of the English civil war explain the outbreak of hostilities in England by reference to developments in Ireland which culminated in the 1641 rising.[2] Similarly, the conversion of King James II to Catholicism is often blamed upon Irish influence, and the rule of the agents of King James in Ireland, most notoriously that of Richard Talbot, Earl of Tyrconnell, is sometimes cited as one reason why the leaders of the English political nation had no option but to offer the British throne to Prince William of Orange and his English princess. To this extent the conflict, which culminated in the Glorious Revolution, is also attributed to Irish precipitants, and thus further authority is given to the assumption that British rule in Ireland has always been unstable even to the extent of threatening good order in Britain itself.[3]

For the eighteenth century, historians of English radicalism have further implied that Ireland was a hotbed of discontent by the frequency with which they make reference to radical thinkers who originated there.[4] More-over those historians who would like to believe that Britain, like France, came to the brink of revolution at the close of the eighteenth century draw special attention to the connections that were established between radicals in Britain and Ireland and especially between English Jacobins and United Irishmen.[5] In this way these too provide their tacit endorsement to the notion that the Irish were an essentially rebellious people watching for every opportunity to strike at the heart of British imperial power.

What has been assumed in relation to Ireland by a variety of historians of Britain has been asserted by those in the nationalist tradition of Irish historiography. These proceed from the premiss that, ever since the sixteenth century, Ireland has been seething with indignation because of the injustices then inflicted upon all elements of the Irish population by the English authorities, and they believe that historians have a special responsibility to detail the iniquities of British rule and to focus attention on those Irish leaders who mobilized opposition to British rule in Ireland and in the Empire. When evidence of opposition has failed these enthusiasts have not been deterred but have referred instead to the existence of a Hidden Ireland of Irish literary and spiritual leaders who cultivated the concept of an Irish independence on those occasions when it proved impossible to attain these objectives by political means.[6]

Historians in the Irish Unionist tradition have naturally displayed scant sympathy with the view that British rule in Ireland has been unjust or that Irish people enjoy some God-given right to political independence. However, they too have lent authority to the belief that Irish society has been continuously unstable, by their shrill insistence that Protestants in Ireland have been obliged, every half-century, to defend their own and the British interest in Ireland from treacherous assault.[7]

These various assumptions and assertions have been questioned by most recent academic historians of modern Ireland. This questioning can in part be explained as an academic reaction to the populist version of Ireland's past, enshrined in nineteenth-century songs and ballads, that came to enjoy official recognition and support from an independent Irish state during the first decades of its existence. To the extent that academic historians of Ireland have deliberately set out to explode the myths associated with this historiographical tradition they have been consciously revisionist.[8] However, questioning of the received version of Ireland's past has resulted also from the training and professional experience of recent historians of modern Ireland who, for the most part, have been as outward-looking and innovative as they have been an energetic group of scholars. Thus while there has been an undoubted concern on the part of some to present a sanitized version of Ireland's past by passing over the gory episodes that held such fascination for their nationalistic predecessors, others have set themselves the task of analysing those insurrections and revolts which, it was previously assumed, were consciously directed against British authority in Ireland.[9]

The result of this entire historical endeavour has been to provide us with more detailed information than we have previously had concerning those disturbances that did occur during the seventeenth and eighteenth centuries. A special effort has been made to ascertain the motives of those who can be identified as the leaders of these movements, and to establish the extent of the support that they enjoyed throughout Irish society. The principal conclusion advanced by these historians is that Ireland during the seventeenth and eighteenth centuries was, by the standards of contemporary Europe, an ordered and relatively harmonious community which enjoyed a modest prosperity as a generally contented partner within a broader British jurisdiction. This conclusion holds good even when account is taken of the major political disruptions that followed upon the rising of 1641 and the rebellion of 1798. Apart from these two conflagrations, good order in Ireland was interrupted only by the conflict between Kings James and William, which was principally external in origin; by some regionalized peasant revolt during the 1760s and 1770s; and by more widespread and more complex popular disturbances during the troubled 1790s. When this tally is placed beside that for disturbances in England and Scotland over the same two centuries, it appears that Ireland was no less orderly than either of these two kingdoms, and certainly not so if we disregard the 1798 rebellion which occurred at the very end of our period.[10]

Those historians who indulge in the construction of such comparative tables of disturbance do not, of course, ignore the tensions and divisions that characterized Irish society during the full course of the two centuries. However, their study of the motivation for revolt on the occasions when it did occur challenges the contention that this was always, or even frequently, directed against British control over Ireland. Instead, they suggest that friction was more frequently occasioned because people were excluded from privilege and patronage than because the Irish people were opposed to the source of that patronage, which ultimately was the British Crown. Those historians who have devoted attention to economic developments have also discredited the notion that Ireland suffered from grave, unrelieved poverty during the centuries when British power there seemed most secure, and they also point to the fact that whatever prosperity Ireland did enjoy was due principally to the trading opportunities that became available to it in the expanding British empire.[11]

1641

The extent of these revisions to the received version of Ireland's past has made it difficult for more traditional historians of Ireland to absorb them, regardless of whether their tradition is the nationalist or unionist one.[12] The new interpretation can be equally startling for those who have had but a passing acquaintance with developments in Ireland, and who have assumed that there, if anywhere, they would find plentiful examples of British opportunism sometimes legitimated by deliberate misrepresentations of native society and always countered by ferocious if inchoate opposition. This pattern, similar to what Christopher Bayly has discerned in eighteenth-century India, did develop in Ireland, but in the sixteenth rather than in the seventeenth and eighteenth centuries. Ireland then also produced the equivalent of Tipu Sultan in the person of Hugh O'Neill, Earl of Tyrone, whose military and organizational ability threatened the English presence in Ireland. As with Tipu Sultan, historians have not been able to agree on what precise objectives O'Neill had in mind when he entered upon his insurrection against the Crown, and those who would appropriate him to the nationalist cause can do so only by disregarding entire episodes in his career. One point on which all are agreed, however, is that O'Neill's defiance of the English Crown forced Queen Elizabeth to mobilize an army of 20,000 men which eventually brought O'Neill to submit, albeit some days after the queen had died. This fighting force was the largest brought together by any of the Tudor monarchs and its presence in Ireland during the years 1599–1603 effected lasting changes in the nature of Irish government and society.[13]

Besides the military defeat of Hugh O'Neill and his associates, the English army pinned down all those Irish lords who had defied the authority of the English Crown in arms and forced them to choose between offering their loyalty to the government and making careers for themselves as mercenary soldiers in the army of Spain. Where the Irish leaders chose the latter course the way was left open to the government to take possession of their estates and to assign them to 'servitors' – that is, Englishmen who had served the Crown in Ireland in a civil or military capacity. By this means a leaven of English proprietors was introduced into all parts of Ireland, and the military success of the Elizabethan government also created the environment whereby the extensive plantation which had been implemented in the province of Munster during the 1580s and which had subsequently collapsed could be resuscitated. This plantation in Munster developed to the point where it had absorbed about 20,000 English settlers by the late 1630s. The rapidly changing circumstances in Ireland also persuaded Hugh O'Neill and his erstwhile comrades in arms that they too would best seek their fortunes on the continent rather than persist in Ireland. Their sudden departure in September 1607, known to historians as the 'Flight of the Earls', opened the way for an extensive plantation in the province of Ulster. This plantation, which provided opportunities for Scottish as well as English proprietors had absorbed a settler community of at least 34,000 people by the 1630s.[14]

These plantations and other changes in landownership served to break down the localism that had previously characterized Irish society. Then also, as the government extended its authority even into the most remote areas, account was taken of all property that had previously belonged to the Catholic church, and this was now assigned to the use of the clergy of the Protestant Church of Ireland, which was established as the church of the state. The presence of landowners and clergy who owed their positions to state intervention meant that the government in Ireland could now set about the business of establishing judicial and administrative procedures in the provinces similar to those practised in England. This endeavour was facilitated by a series of judicial decisions, taken by the judges of the central courts in Dublin with the approval of their counterparts in London, which decreed that Gaelic legal codes would enjoy no further recognition from the Crown and that the only rights and titles which would enjoy recognition before the courts were those that might be proved good in common law.[15]

The judicial decisions became the capstone to a process of centralization which was pursued relentlessly by the government in Ireland in the aftermath of its military victory. The establishment of county divisions in place of the lordships which had previously prevailed, the appointment of sheriffs and Justices of the Peace, and the creation of circuits of assize all symbolized the new central authority that claimed a monopoly on people's loyalty; and if symbol was not enough, the authority of the government was asserted by the garrisons of soldiers who were retained on the official payroll and situated strategically throughout the country even after peace had been established.[16]

Even a brief summary such as this will suggest that the new administrative structures established in Ireland at the outset of the seventeenth century were alien to the bulk of the population. Their alien character at the local level was further accentuated by the presence of provosts marshal side by side with the Justices of the Peace in those counties which had but recently been brought under common-law jurisdiction. These provosts made liberal use of their powers of martial law to round up those within their jurisdictions who might represent a challenge to the civil order, and those who were not hanged were encouraged to leave the country to serve as soldiers in continental Europe. This scheme of ridding the country of 'masterless men' and would-be trouble-makers, which was given official sanction at the outset of the seventeenth century, was persisted with throughout that and much of the subsequent century. This is one reason why the previously Gaelic areas of the country which had been troubled by incessant warfare now suddenly gave way to more ordered conditions.[17]

The alien character of the regime at the central level of government was apparent because, due to the strict enforcement of the oath of supremacy – which no Catholic could take in good conscience – all administrative and judicial positions fell to English-born Protestants and in subsequent generations to the descendants of these settlers. The Gaelic and Scottish elements of the population who, at this point, fostered no ambitions to serve in central government would have had no occasion for complaint over this development, and those who felt deprived were the anglicized Old English in Ireland.

Those descendants of twelfth-century Anglo-Norman settlers had been the traditional upholders of the Crown interest in Ireland. It was they who had dominated all Irish parliamentary assemblies until the seventeenth century, and they also enjoyed a near-monopoly over appointments in the Dublin administration. They were settled most densely in the fertile river valleys of the east and south-east of the country and there they had upheld an economic and social order that was hardly distinguishable from that in England itself. Their leaders had continued to be active supporters of Crown policy in Ireland until the 1570s but thereafter their rigid attachment to the old religion jarred with the increasingly strident Protestantism of officials and soldiers appointed from England to service in Ireland. The Old English had argued consistently that their profession of Catholicism in no way compromised their loyalty to the Crown, but this argument lacked conviction during the decades following the Armada, and most especially so once Hugh O'Neill and his adherents had procured military assistance from King Philip III of Spain through the solicitation of Irish priests on the continent. At this point it made good sense to the English Crown that the ultimate test of political loyalty should be loyalty to the religion established by law in Ireland as well as in England. This explains the concern of the Crown to enforce the oath of supremacy with the result that people newly appointed from England had taken over control of the administration in Ireland by the first decade of the seventeenth century.[18]

These drastic changes in the government and administration of Ireland were proceeded with by proclamation and judicial decree rather than through consultative procedure. The leaders of the two principal elements of the indigenous population were in no position to oppose what was taking place because both had been compromised by the developments of the previous decades: the Old English because they were committed Catholics and had been lukewarm in their support of the government's military effort during the years of hostility, and the Gaelic provincial lords because many of them had actually been engaged in hostilities against the government forces at some stage of the previous war (1594–1603) or because they could not show good title to the estates which they occupied. As a consequence, those at the upper social levels of Irish society who wished to remain in the country in the aftermath of war sought to accommodate themselves to the new social and political order that was being promoted. They sought to function within that system rather than to bring about their own destruction by attempting to oppose it.[19]

What held true of the leaders of Irish society was more true of their subordinates. Historians who have studied the evolution of plantation communities, through the examination of estate records, have been so impressed by the ready willingness of all elements of the Irish population to become absorbed into the new social order that was being shaped that one writer has suggested that, from the perspective of Irish tenants, plantation involved little more than a substitution of 'new lords for old'. As

293

for those who chose to remain in Ireland rather than go as exiles to the continent, even members of the bardic families within the Gaelic order acquiesced in the changes that were enforced in the aftermath of defeat. Some Gaelic poets who provided assistance to government officials when surveying and apportioning plantation land were suitably rewarded with estates or tenancies; others played a key role in familiarizing the Irish population with English legal procedures; while three bardic poets employed their professional talents to welcome King James VI of Scotland as their monarch and to compose legitimations of his claim to be rightful king of Ireland. The allegiance thus pledged to the first of the Stuarts on the English throne was reiterated in Gaelic verse for future monarchs in that line, and Old English writers of political texts in the English language were equally enthusiastic for the Stuart cause.[20]

While historians have always paid due attention to the political advice that was provided by the moral leaders of both the Gaelic and the Old English communities, it is now also acknowledged that this advice was given heed, and that landowners and political leaders in Ireland focused their loyalty upon the persons of the Stuart monarchs over the full course of the seventeenth century. This loyalty was reflected in their willingness to provide financial and military support directly to the king whenever the occasion demanded it.[21] Irish landowners (including those of Gaelic ancestry) also provided evidence of their willingness to conform to English ways by dressing after the English manner on public occasions, by constructing or renovating residences after the English fashion, and by providing their heirs with an English-style education, including some time at the Inns of Court. This rapid anglicization of Irish society which proceeded during the early decades of the seventeenth century was most evident at the upper social level, and it was members of the Old English community, including Old English priests, who were the usual educators of the more Gaelicized elements of the population. Change was also evident among farmers in all parts of Ireland who became attracted by the market economy that was promoted principally by the recently arrived settler population. There is also evidence that the native farming population, especially those in the planted areas, acquired some knowledge of the English language from their dealings with their settler neighbours, while some of the settlers learned some of the Irish language from their daily contacts with Irish farmers and cottiers.[22]

This intermingling of the settler and natives was disapproved of, on the one hand, by Protestant clergy and the advocates of plantation and, on the other hand, by those Irish who had chosen to live in exile on the continent. These, whether Catholic clergy or dispossessed landowners, were implacable opponents of the British authorities who had become entrenched in Ireland, and they looked for every opportunity to solicit assistance from Britain's continental enemies so that they could overthrow the hated plantation system in Ireland and the regime that supported it. The Irish Catholic clergy on the continent also feared that contact between settler and native in Ireland would lead ultimately to the complete absorption of the natives into planter society and with it their abandonment of the Catholic faith.[23]

To this extent the success of English arms in Ireland at the end of the sixteenth century did create a new cohort of opponents to British rule in Ireland and in Britain itself. The vast majority of the Irish population who wished to survive at home evinced little sympathy with the propositions espoused from the continent and sought to work with or around the new regime. This attention to the extent to which the Irish population conformed to English ways during the decades of plantation serves to concentrate our minds on the one area in which they did not conform – in religion. Considerable efforts were made by the English Crown and its officials to induce or compel the leaders of the Irish political nation to become Protestant but their efforts met with but limited success. Instead, the majority of Irish landowners, again through the influence of Old English educators, became more attached to and better instructed in the doctrines of the Catholic church, as redefined at the Council of Trent. This attachment, as we saw, exposed Irish landowners to attack from English Protestant officials and settlers who insisted that no Catholic could be regarded as a true subject of a Protestant monarch. King James was in agreement with this view, and he supported his Protestant officials in Ireland in their contention that those who were but 'half-subjects' should not be permitted to hold office under the Crown.[24]

This royal endorsement provided the recently established Protestant officials with the assurance that they would continue to enjoy a monopoly of office for the foreseeable future. Once this was assured, they identified the use to which they wished to put this monopoly of power and they sought royal approval for the programme of government that was agreed upon by the officials in Dublin. Their essential proposition was that the Protestant, and hence the British, interest was insecure in Ireland because the majority of landowners, who held considerable influence over their subordinates, were firmly attached to Catholicism. The immediate resolution for this problem was to retain a standing army which would be an exclusively Protestant force, but the officials looked for a longer-term solution whereby landowners in the country would be exclusively Protestant. This, it was argued, could be achieved either by compelling the existing Catholic landowners to convert to Protestantism or by removing them from their estates to make room for Protestant servitors who would take over their properties. Both schemes, it was agreed, would involve the administration in using all the resources at its disposal to bring about the desired changes.[25]

The conversion stratagem that won favour with the officials was related to the financial exigencies of the government. The continued maintenance of an army meant that the government was run at a deficit, and it was now proposed that this financial problem could be solved by the systematic collection of recusancy fines which would either force Catholic proprietors into bankruptcy or bring about their conformity in religion. This was to be linked to a biased use of the Court of Wards, whereby responsibility for the education, upbringing and marriage of Catholic heirs who were left as orphans by their parents would be assigned to Protestant officials or landowners.[26]

Opportunity existed for the removal of Catholic proprietors from their property because many of these landowners in the previously Gaelic areas of the country could not produce title to their properties which might be defended in law. Such defects in title were inevitable when a system of kin-ownership of land, which had prevailed under the Gaelic system, gave way to individual ownership and succession by primogeniture which was required under common law. Many *de facto* owners of estates in the previously Gaelic areas could not, under these circumstances, establish why it was they rather than other members of their kinship groups who had gained possession of the property. Such situations were ones which Crown officials could turn to their own advantage because whenever defects in title were exposed the property reverted to the Crown and thus provided fresh opportunities for plantation. Other opportunities presented themselves where it could be established that occupiers of property had once been engaged in acts of rebellion for which they had not been pardoned, or where it could be proved that they were not the legitimate heirs to their fathers. This latter was again a frequent defect because no distinction had been drawn between the claims of legitimate and illegitimate children under the Gaelic legal code which had just been supplanted.

This undisguised onslaught against all Catholic proprietors in Ireland, which was launched during the reign of James I and persisted with during that of Charles I, was greatly resented by the Catholics. They had all the more reason for resentment when it became clear that some of the administration, both minor officials in the localities, and those who held positions in Dublin, were primarily concerned to advance their personal interests at the expense of the Catholic landowners, by extra-legal as well as by legal means, rather than to serve any grander purpose.[27] The Irish took advantage of this corruption to discredit the administration in the eyes of the king. Spokesmen for the Catholic proprietors also emphasized that they represented no challenge to the established religious order because they strove only for the right to attend Catholic worship in the privacy of their homes and for a more tolerant climate under which they would not be fined for their refusal to participate in the services provided by the state church. In this they were making it clear that they were but limited participants in the Counter-Reformation movement, and they sought further to provide evidence of their political loyalty, and thus to lay claim to an entitlement to hold office under the Crown, by offering to take a simple oath of allegiance to the British monarch instead of the oath of supremacy which they found offensive. An even more potent means of establishing proof of political loyalty was by offering, at their own expense, to raise regiments of soldiers to serve the cause of the Crown either at home or abroad. They had opportunities to do so during the reigns of both monarchs on the occasions when war with Spain threatened and when King Charles I experienced difficulty in dealing first with his Scottish subjects and then with the members of the lower house of the English Parliament. The financial difficulties of King Charles I also presented the Catholic leaders of Ireland with the opportunity to stave off the threat of further plantation by paying substantial sums directly to the king in exchange for his royal promise that he would process legislation through the Irish Parliament granting full legal title to all who had enjoyed undisputed occupancy of land in Ireland for sixty years.[28]

These overtures were addressed directly to the English monarch over the head of his administration in Dublin. For this reason they were all the more resented by that administration which was, in any event, opposed to everything being requested by the Catholics because it set out to cancel what little progress had been made by the officials towards the fulfilment of their ambitions. The negotiations between the king and his Irish subjects are of interest therefore because they reveal the essential differences that had developed between Catholic subjects and the Protestant administration in Ireland. The spokesmen for the Catholic landowners revealed these to be a cautious and conservative group in both political and social terms. They accepted the plantations that had been implemented and the Protestant domination of the Dublin administration as accomplished facts. Therefore they strove principally to conserve whatever property still remained in Catholic ownership, and to earn Catholics the right to hold some positions in the Dublin administration and on the bench. Catholic landowners, whether of Gaelic or Old English ancestry favoured the use of English common law in Ireland, raised no objection to an Anglican code of worship being designated as the state religion and sought only for the tacit toleration of Catholic worship.

As conservatives, these Catholics were opposed to change and especially opposed to any change that would effect a further erosion in their position. They consistently challenged the idea, fostered by Protestant officials in Ireland, that the instruments of the administration should be used to promote change, and they contended that the principal function of government should be to maintain the status quo. In this they showed themselves to be in the mainstream of European political thought and they showed also that their opponents in the Dublin administration were outside the mainstream by being conscious promoters of innovation. These

297

administrators were also precocious, at least within the British dominions, as we learn from John Brewer, in conceiving of the state as an organism that had a life of its own independent of the society that supported it. That they conceived of it as such emerges clearly in the writings of Sir John Davies, the most energetic and the most intelligent of the administrators who rose to power in Ireland during the reign of King James I. Writing in 1612, Davies made it clear that, in Ireland at least, he conceived of the 'state' as having an interest separate from society and as being an active agency with responsibility to reform and mould that society. Thus, for example in detailing the steps that had been taken to establish common-law procedures in Ireland, Davies gave full credit to 'the state [which] proceeded to establish the public justice in every part of the realm'. While acknowledging this commendable work of the state he identified further measures which it might take in the years ahead.[29]

The Old English were quick to recognize the novelty of the theory of state expounded by Davies and, from an early stage, they sought to discredit it by pointing to the corruption of the officials who occupied positions in the state machine.[30] Moreover, on those frequent occasions when spokesmen for the Catholic interest reiterated their loyalty to the British monarch they made it clear that such pledges did not include any obligation towards the Dublin administration. Indeed, as we saw, one of the principal purposes behind these overtures to the king was to persuade him to modify the administration so that it would include Catholics as well as Protestants, thus making it responsive to the needs of the broader community.

It appeared for a time during the reign of King Charles I, after the monarch had accepted money from the Catholic landowners in Ireland, that they would have their wish in this matter and that the active role of the state would be discontinued. These hopes were disappointed during the years when Thomas Wentworth, Earl of Strafford, served as the king's governor in Ireland, and Strafford further alarmed the Catholics by his insistence that he, as governor, was the ultimate authority from whom there was no appeal to the English Crown which he represented. This constituted a fundamental alteration to the customary relationship between Irish subjects and the English Crown, and it was particularly alarming because it occurred at a time when developments in both Scotland and England were creating a situation where the king might have to appoint a governor to Ireland who would be even more hostile to the Catholic interest than Strafford had been.[31]

It was in these circumstances that Irish Catholic leaders in 1641 entered upon an insurrection which they hoped would strengthen their negotiating position with the king, just as the Scottish Covenanters had consolidated their position by having resort to arms. By doing so, they hoped also to strengthen the position of the king against his adversaries in England and

Scotland, in the belief that when he was thus freed from extreme Protestant pressures he would live up to the promises he had previously made to his Catholic subjects in Ireland. To this extent the intention which lay behind the action taken by the leaders of the Irish insurrection of 1641 was conservative and certainly guided by no malevolence towards the king. The participants in the revolt were not, however, upholders of the status quo as it had existed in the several previous decades. One group of insurgents asserted that they had been driven to revolt by 'the state of Ireland' which had been consistently hostile towards them. They hoped, therefore, to gain control over the administration which would thereafter advance their interests together with those of the Crown.[32]

Thus, while not directed against British imperial authority, the Irish insurrection was very consciously pitched against the precocious state authority that had established itself in Ireland over the previous half-century. What was intended as a limited and specifically targeted action quickly adopted a broader dimension, and for two reasons. First, the leaders, while seeking to resolve their own grievances, took no account of those of their subordinates who took advantage of the break-down of political authority to advance a popular onslaught against all British settlers in Ireland. Second, once the planned limited action had become 'bloody' as a consequence of the peasant uprising, the leaders saw no escape from their predicament other than to achieve total military victory against their local opponents so that they could dictate terms to the king. To this end, they solicited support from their kinsmen who served as soldiers in the Spanish army in the Netherlands. Once these, and the clergy who accompanied them, had arrived in Ireland they would settle for no less than a cancellation of the plantations that had been implemented over the previous half-century, the recovery of all property that had been lost to the Catholic church since the Reformation and the establishment of Catholicism as the official religion of Ireland. Significantly, there was no mention of a return to the lost Gaelic social order, but even without this the programme was one that could only have been achieved in the aftermath of fundamental changes in Britain as well as in Ireland.[33]

What began in 1641 as a conservative uprising, aimed at curbing the power of the administration in Dublin, had by 1642 become a revolutionary movement intent on reversing every achievement of the state authorities in Ireland. The revolution failed initially because it never enjoyed the full support of those Catholic landowners who had remained in Ireland. The absence of a united Catholic front meant that the state authorities in Dublin, and some Protestant landowners in the provinces, managed to maintain a foothold in the country. Even if this had been lost it is unlikely that the Catholic dominance would have been sustained once the English Civil War had come to an end and once Oliver Cromwell was at liberty, in 1649, to devote his attention to Ireland. In the absence of unity among

Catholics the victory of the Cromwellian army was a foregone conclusion. Once victory was achieved, the Cromwellians set about the consolidation of the state authority in Ireland to the point where it became one of the most forceful instruments of government achieved anywhere in Europe up to this point.[34]

The most striking aspect of the Cromwellian government in Ireland, at least in its initial phase, was that it dispensed with all consultative institutions and ruled through military governors. These assumed responsibility for maintaining order, for directing a religious and educational programme aimed at making Ireland a Protestant society, and for implementing a comprehensive plantation of the country. To this end a survey of the land resources of the country was got underway and Ireland acquired the dubious distinction of being the best-mapped country in Europe. These maps provided the government with details both of the ownership of every acre of land in the country in 1641 and of the quality and potential of the land in every Irish parish. This formidable body of information was employed by the government to facilitate the transfer of property from Catholic to Protestant ownership in three of the four provinces of Ireland, and the assignment of smaller holdings of land in the fourth province, west of the river Shannon, to those Catholic proprietors who could demonstrate their 'constant good affection' towards the government ever since the outbreak of hostilities in 1641. The authorities also pondered the possibility of removing the entire Catholic population from the three provinces across the river Shannon, so that an entirely new Protestant population could be introduced in the three most fertile provinces of the country.[35]

This draconian measure was not proceeded with, but we can say with certainty that the Cromwellian state in Ireland had a more detailed knowledge of the resources and the people of the country over which it ruled than any other government of its time. The programme on which it launched was also more formidable than that undertaken by any other state authority in Europe with the possible exception of the Habsburg state in Bohemia, since it aimed at nothing less than the erection of a completely new society in place of the old which it set out to destroy.[36]

The achievements of the Cromwellian regime in Ireland fell far short of their objectives but they were nevertheless formidable. The institutions of a Catholic church which had been slowly put in place in the decades before 1641 were destroyed, and some success was attained in compelling the Irish Catholic population to attend at Protestant religious service. All tokens of opposition were broken down and Catholic proprietors were systematically dispossessed of their estates in the designated provinces even if not satisfactorily re-settled westwards of the line of the Shannon. Catholic merchant families were also dismissed from port-towns and Protestants appointed in their place, and Protestants, mostly officers in the Cromwellian army, were assigned the estates that had been declared confiscate. This plantation was to be the most enduring legacy of Cromwellian rule in Ireland, because where Catholics owned 59 per cent of the land of Ireland in 1641 this had been reduced to substantially less than 20 per cent by 1659.[37]

The land settlement of the Cromwellians was subjected to minor modifications after the restoration of Charles II to the British throne in 1660. These modifications were effected principally to allow compensation to those, whether Catholic or Protestant, who had been unfailing in their loyalty to the royalist cause during the interregnum and who had been deprived of their property by the Cromwellians. Apart from this, the Cromwellian confiscation was permitted to stand with but minor adjustments. This came as a disappointment to the Catholics who had been dispossessed, and the only real benefit that came to them with the restoration was a relaxation in the persecution of Catholic priests and some retraction in the power of the state. This retraction involved a restoration of authority to the central administration and the cancellation of the military jurisdictions which, in any event, were being wound down during the closing years of the Cromwellian era. This cut-back in the power of the army did not involve a demobilization of the army which was retained in garrison, sometimes with the old Cromwellian commanders, during the reign of Charles II. Similarly with the administration: many of the Cromwellian servants continued in office, side by side with officials nominated by the King, and Ireland continued to be governed through administrative decree rather than through the rule of Parliament, which only assembled on one occasion during the reign of Charles II. The improvement in the position of Catholics was due principally to the fact that for much of that reign the administration was headed by James, Duke of Ormond, who, although a firm Protestant, had many Catholic relatives and through them was open to overtures from Catholics.[38]

One might think that the limited nature of the concessions would have left Catholics in Ireland in a rebellious mood, watching for every opportunity to challenge the government that had disappointed them. This was not the case, and the only rumblings of resistance that occurred during the reign of Charles II came from Cromwellian officers or the more extreme Protestant landowners who asserted that the government was being excessively conciliatory towards Catholics.[39] The quiescence of the Catholics is explained in part by their recognition that the government was firmly in control and that any disturbance on their part was likely to result in an immediate cancellation of those few rights and privileges that they still enjoyed. It is also true that those Catholics who retained property in Ireland and who now emerged as leaders of the Catholic interest were those who had a proven record of loyalty to British government and institutions even during the turbulent years 1641–59. These were strict constitutionalists who contemplated an improvement in their position only through negotiation or through the purchase from Protestants of some of the property that had recently changed hands through confiscation.

These Catholic leaders, like their counterparts before 1641, argued that their attachment to Catholicism in no way compromised their loyalty to the British Crown. On the religious front, they negotiated for sufficient toleration so that the Catholic church structure that had been demolished by the Cromwellians could again be put in place. They also wished to be relieved from the religious persecution that had prevailed under Cromwellian rule, and they sought after official protection on those occasions when anti-Popery hysteria was whipped up in England during the reign of Charles II. On the political front the great issue was a persistent negotiation for some further dilution of the Cromwellian settlement. No longer did they plead, as did the pre-1641 leaders, for the appointment of Catholics to government office, and the most they sought was the appointment of a governor who would be neutral or even conciliatory towards Catholics.[40]

The Catholic leaders who established this agenda were accorded an undisputed social pre-eminence within their own community such as their pre-1641 predecessors had not enjoyed. Priests who crept back from exile on the continent in the years after 1660 recognized these as their only support; so also did the surviving Gaelic poets who, in their verses, recommended support for these last remnants of the old Catholic gentry. Such recommendations now came more easily than before 1641 because there was no longer an Irish regiment waiting on the continent to be called upon for succour in the hour of need. Britain's continental enemy was now the United Provinces from which no assistance might be expected to serve a Catholic cause.

Thus, secure within their own community, Catholic landowners worked vigorously, sometimes in co-operation with their Protestant counterparts, to promote the English appearance of the country. English management procedures were now generally applied on estates throughout the country; manorial courts were introduced to complement the assize procedures that had been in operation since the beginning of the seventeenth century; and towns and villages were established and supported by landowners everywhere in Ireland. The pinnacle of this achievement was the expansion of Dublin, which became a city of 50,000 people by 1685 – a commercial as well as an administrative capital to a flourishing kingdom.[41]

Catholics as well as Protestants in Ireland benefited from the prosperity of the restoration years. Some merchant families who had been expelled by the Cromwellians worked their way back into business in the port-towns, and many who profited from trade purchased land from some Cromwellians who wished to return to England. By this and other such devices the amount of land in Catholic ownership slowly moved upwards until it had reached 22 per cent of the total by 1688.[42]

It was assumed on the Catholic side that, short of some unforeseen development, any future improvement in their position would come only by such gradual increments. The unforeseen happened not due to any effort on their part but because the heir to the British throne, James, Duke of York, converted to the Catholic faith. This development, which nobody could have foreseen in 1660, naturally heightened the expectations of the Catholic elite that they would recover some of the power and property which they had believed lost for ever. King James, once he had succeeded to the throne, was quite circumspect over the question of Irish land, recognizing that any move on his part to disturb the existing plantations in Ireland would quickly arouse the antagonism of the Protestant interest in the three kingdoms. When it came to office, however, King James was prepared to be more generous towards Catholics, since appointing Catholics to positions in the administration and on the bench was consistent with what he hoped to do in England.[43]

This turn of events was identified by Irish Catholics as providential and their leaders seized at this God-given opportunity to accept every position that was offered them, including the office of Lord Deputy which was held 1687-9 by Richard Talbot, Earl of Tyrconnell. Once appointed, Tyrconnell forced the pace of change and was especially associated with the appointment of Catholic officers in the army in place of the Protestants who served there and the recruitment of Catholics into the ranks. Already by 1688 some 5,000 Catholics were armed in this way, and at the same time Tyrconnell recalled weapons from those Protestants who had previously served in the militia.[44] This role-reversal was welcomed by all Catholics, as is clear from the poetry of Dáibhí Ó Bruadair who composed a chronology in verse of this period.[45] The reversal was equally reviled by the Protestants of Ireland who recognized that the entire state machine which they had constructed to serve their purpose would now be used against themselves. Already it was apparent that the safeguards which they had introduced into the system were being rendered worthless because Tyrconnell was not requiring the oath of supremacy from those he was appointing to office and to commissions. Furthermore, it was clear to them that Tyrconnell was moving to dismantle the Cromwellian settlement through parliamentary means because his recently appointed officials were using their powers to change representation in the corporations from Protestant to Catholic. All that now stood between Irish Protestants and perdition was a Catholic monarch, because the royal consent was required before a parliament could be convened. Here surely was the final ironical proof of the extent to which roles had been reversed.[46]

As it happened, it was the establishment of a Catholic army in Ireland more than the threat to the Cromwellian settlement which weighed with political leaders in England when they decided to oust James II from the throne in favour of his Protestant daughter, Mary, and her husband, Prince William of Orange. To this extent, developments in Ireland during the 1680s did have a bearing on the Glorious Revolution, but the fact that Ireland entered at all as a factor was due to the recklessness of James II in appointing Tyrconnell as his representative in Ireland even against the advice of his Catholic advisers. Where Irish Catholic leaders were concerned they grasped at the opportunity provided them to improve upon their position but in the course of doing so they always acted within the law. Instead of rebelling against the state that had been instituted by British authority in Ireland they were in fact taking the instruments of the state into their own hands, and they sought to prove their responsibility in their new role in their efforts to prevent unlicensed assault upon the Protestant population of the country such as had occurred in 1641. They were so successful in this that when, after the outcome of the Glorious Revolution had been settled, the Protestants charged them with having re-enacted the events of 1641 they could only support this by stating that the Catholics had devoured them 'in their imagination'.[47]

One reason why, in the aftermath of the Jacobite/Williamite struggle, Irish Protestants thus saw the need to level the accusation of intended assault against the Catholic community was because it was they and not the Catholics who had been the first to resist established authority. This resistance took the form of Protestant towns in Ulster and elsewhere refusing to acknowledge the authority of King James once word had reached them that he was being challenged in England by the Prince of Orange. This Protestant action, which culminated in the celebrated siege of Derry, meant that a bridgehead existed for William's army to move into Ireland and to challenge the position that had been held there for King James by Tyrconnell and his supporters. From the moment that the two kings had arrived in Ireland the local breakdown of support was predictable, with most Catholics coming forward to support the legitimate monarch and most Protestants favouring Prince William. Although important, and even crucial at the outset, the local support dwindled in military significance as the struggle between the two monarchs became essentially a war between two armies brought into the country from outside.[48]

The result of this military struggle, with its set-piece at the battle of the Boyne, made it possible for William and Mary to make good their claim to the British throne. In a more narrow sense the struggle also determined that Protestants and not Catholics should control the Irish state, and it was expected also that the vexed question of which group, Protestants or Catholics, should own the landed resources of Ireland would be finally decided.

The issue of land was again on the agenda because the Catholics, in the Irish Parliament which had been convened reluctantly by King James in

1689, had sought to cancel the Cromwellian settlement and recover what had been lost to the Protestants at mid-century. Because the Catholics had thus revealed what they would have implemented if King James had been successful during the war, the Protestants were equally determined, once the victory of William was assured, to create a situation whereby Catholics would never again be in a position to challenge their ascendancy. This final blow was to be inflicted on Catholics not because they had challenged British authority or institutions but because they had committed themselves to a properly constituted authority that was overthrown by revolutionary action in Britain.

The Irish Protestants intended to make themselves secure for the future by one final plantation which would deprive all participants in the Irish army of James II of their association with the ownership of land. They were frustrated in this because the Irish Catholics decided, after the defeat at the Boyne, to persist with the fighting in the hope that further military support from Louis XIV of France would enable them to turn defeat into victory. Support of the kind that would have altered the outcome was not forthcoming but Catholic persistence was rewarded because William of Orange, in his anxiety to transfer his military resources from Ireland to the continent, offered generous terms to those Catholics who held out to the bitter end. This generosity was bitterly resented by Irish Protestants, and, despite their best efforts to overturn the terms conceded by William, the plantation which did follow upon the failure of the Jacobites-in-arms was altogether less comprehensive than the Protestants had hoped for. Its shortcoming as a plantation becomes immediately apparent when we recognize that the 22 per cent of land which was in Catholic ownership in 1688 had only been reduced to 14 per cent by 1703.[49]

When the settlement was inspected from a Protestant perspective they could foresee that this percentage of land would again drift upwards through lease or purchase from Protestants, as had happened after 1660. This possibility was all the more alarming because, under the terms conceded by William to the Catholics, those who were in arms were permitted to leave Ireland and serve in the continental army of their choice. A total of 15,000 chose to enlist in Irish Jacobite regiments in the army of Louis XIV and most were conveyed to France by King William's fleet. These, and others who enlisted in the armies of Spain and Austria, became known as the 'Wild Geese', and Irish Protestants were fearful that, given the appropriate circumstances, these would return to Ireland and engage in a renewed onslaught against the Protestant interest in association with those Catholic landowners who had escaped forfeiture of their property because of the leniency of King William.[50]

Because they considered themselves to have been betrayed by their new-found king, the Irish Protestants were from the outset the most truculent of King William's subjects. They moved immediately in 1692 to establish

305

three fundamental principles that they considered necessary to break what they saw to be the cycle of revolt that had repeatedly disturbed their security. The first of these held that a standing army, which would specifically exclude Catholics, together with a local Protestant militia, should always be maintained in Ireland to ward against invasion from without as well as insurrection from within. The second principle held that the state in Ireland should be strengthened and consolidated, that it should remain under Protestant control, and that it should be an active force to promote the interests of Protestants. The third principle favoured a regular convening of the Irish Parliament, which they envisaged as an exclusively Protestant body and which would identify a course of action to be followed by the government.[51]

The course of action which the Irish Protestants favoured in the short term was one that would compensate them for the opportunity that had been lost at the time of the Williamite settlement. To this end they came forward with a body of legislation – popularly known in Ireland as the penal laws – which was designed to weaken the position of Irish Catholic landowners and the Catholic church while creating the conditions under which Ireland would become a Protestant society. The government in Britain lacked enthusiasm for this legislation, both because of their fears that clearly anti-Catholic legislation would place a strain upon their relations with their Austrian allies and because they were suspicious of the constitutional autonomy claimed by the Protestants for the Irish Parliament. The Irish Protestants persisted and had their way through the device of tacking the required legislation on to money bills which were wanted urgently by the government. Both requirements were satisfied when the government in London imposed its veto on the more extreme anti-Catholic legislation while permitting sufficient bills through to satisfy the interest of the Irish Protestants.[52]

The result of this compromise was a series of acts which remained on the statute books until the late 1770s and which, if they did not make Ireland a Protestant country, did 'prevent the growth of Popery'.[53] Some directed specifically against Catholic clergy created a situation whereby only secular priests who had been approved by the state authorities could officiate in Ireland. Catholic bishops, members of religious orders and unregistered priests were subject, upon arrest, to death, expulsion or imprisonment. Legislation prohibiting the establishment of Catholic schools was also intended to curb the activity of priests. At the same time Catholics of property were depoliticized by being denied the right to be elected to Parliament and, ultimately, to vote in parliamentary or local elections. Related to this were ordinances denying Catholics the right to bear arms or to own a horse worth more than £5, both of which were designed to prevent Catholics being in a position to engage in armed insurrection. Finally, an elaborate series of acts was passed concerning the ownership of land by Catholics. They were not permitted to purchase or take long leases of land from Protestants; they were obliged to divide their property among all sons rather than leave it to a single heir; and any son who converted to Protestantism was granted immediate title to the entire inheritance.[54]

The enforcement of these acts required the further expansion of state authority which became more intrusive in Ireland than in any other dominion of the British Crown: not only did it concern itself with the raising of revenue but the presence of the state was also clearly visible with an establishment of 12,000 British troops scattered in 263 military barracks throughout the country.[55] The intrusive aspect of state authority was especially painful where wealthy Catholics were concerned. Vigilant observance by state authorities made it impossible for Catholic merchants to become full members of corporations, where they might defend their interests, and special agencies of government were established to monitor the enforcement of the penal statutes that concerned landed property. These agencies included the Registry of Deeds, which kept a detailed record of all land transactions and saw to it that the religious clauses were observed, and the Conversion Rolls, which kept a record of all Catholics who went through a formal procedure of converting to Protestantism to ensure that they would be allowed to enter the professions or to inherit property. Perhaps the most intrusive aspect of state activity where Catholics of substance were concerned was the opportunities which were now provided to informers who would appraise the authorities of any attempts by Catholics to circumvent the laws in relation to property. Intrusions by the state were also evident in matters of religious practice but here, once the initial formal registration of priests had taken place, the enthusiasm of Justices of the Peace, who might wish to enforce the law to the letter, was not always matched by the zeal of the central authorities who were generally agreeable to allowing Catholics to practise their religion without molestation. However, breaches of the law, in such matters as the maintenance of Catholic bishops, were usually checked by state authorities at moments of political tension or threatened invasion. Such checks reminded Catholics of their tolerated status within a Protestant state.[56]

Both the laws passed and the manner of their enforcement show that the primary purpose behind the penal laws was to ensure that Catholics would never again have the power over others that would make it possible for them to organize themselves militarily. Another purpose behind these, like previous penal laws, was to compel the remaining Catholic landowners to conform to the established church. They met with considerable success in this respect and the 14 per cent of Irish land owned by Catholics at the outset of the eighteenth century had been whittled down to about 5 per cent by the close of the 1770s.[57] The attempt to coerce landowners into conformity was not, however, combined with any evangelical drive to effect the conversion of the general population to Protestantism. This left Ireland in the unique position of having a landed elite who were not only mainly of a different ethnic origin from the population at large, but also of a different religion and who frequently spoke a language different from theirs.

It might appear at first sight that here, if anywhere, was a potentially explosive situation with a resentful Catholic peasantry watchful for every opportunity to remedy the wrongs that had been inflicted on their cause by a gentry who were in every way foreign to them. There is much evidence, particularly in Gaelic verse, that a collective sense of grievance was fostered within the Catholic community, and that the poets, at least, could imagine a different world where Catholics would be dominant over the hated Protestants.[58] Such conceptualizing of role-reversal was, however, common to all European societies in the eighteenth century and it was no more the source of political action in Ireland than in any other. Instead, what was notable about Ireland in the eighteenth century was the social calm which prevailed, at least down to the 1760s; and the peasant disturbances that occurred in that decade were essentially economic in character.

This calm was in some respects the product of the preceding war. The more militant of the Catholic leaders had departed for the continent once their bid for power had been defeated, and the discontented element in Irish rural society continued to make careers for themselves in Catholic continental armies to the end of the 1770s. Some who refused to recognize the established order still remained in Ireland to become 'rapparees' or 'tories' but these were summarily dealt with by the Protestant militia and toryism ceased to be a problem by the 1720s. The presence of a large standing army as well as an armed militia would have acted as a disincentive to any landowners who might have contemplated rebellion but the rate of conformity of Catholic landowners in religion makes it clear that social survival rather than rebellion was the ambition foremost in their minds. The docility of Catholics throughout the eighteenth century can thus be attributed to the absence within the country of political leaders who might have led the Catholic population in revolt, and any intervention by Irish Catholic leaders in continental armies could only have occurred in the event of France achieving victory over Britain in the continental wars.[59]

On the positive side it can be asserted that Ireland remained tranquil for most of the eighteenth century because social and political conditions remained tolerable for the majority of the population. The principal burden of the penal laws, as has been shown by Seán Connolly in his recent study of the subject, fell on landowners and merchants and the laws impinged little on the lives of the bulk of the rural population. Landlords also, although usually ill-disposed towards Catholicism were nevertheless paternalistic towards their tenants and cottiers. These latter welcomed the opportunity to establish a niche for themselves within the established order, and they supplemented their farming activities with an income from rural manufacturing, woollen as well as linen, which became widespread throughout the country as the eighteenth century progressed.[60] The more successful Catholic tenant farmers, like their Protestant counterparts, became heavily involved in commercial agriculture and those in the southern half of the country were especially active in meeting the requirements of the provisioning trade. Catholic merchants also quickly re-established themselves in business, even though they were denied the right to become full guild or corporation members. These too made their principal profit from trade with Britain and, after 1731, with British America, and they supplemented this with some trading involvement with France and southern Europe. Merchants were truly aggrieved over the operation of the penal laws, and their sense of grievance increased with the prosperity which they came to enjoy in the second half of the eighteenth century. When they then mobilized themselves to seek an improvement in their legal position they used constitutional arguments rather than the weapons of war, and their ambition was to become equals with their Protestant counterparts in the British imperial world rather than to overthrow that world.[61]

Those Catholics who endured, and even prospered, in eighteenth-century Ireland were therefore heavily reliant upon Britain and the imperial connection for their prosperity. To this extent they had no cause to challenge the established order, and whatever popular disturbances occurred were usually associated with perceived alterations in the status quo rather than with any desire to change the system. Thus, for example, the enclosure of previously common land, or the trespass of grazier tenants upon plots previously cultivated by cottiers led to the formation of secret oath-bound bands in the 1760s, as also did perceived inequities in the way in which taxes and fees were levied by the established church and the local authorities upon the poorer elements of the population. The formation of such organizations was immediately cited by the gentry as evidence of a Popish plot to assail the established order, and their suppression thus took on a decidedly sectarian tone. Those who have studied these rural disturbances, however, as also the disorder that occurred in towns, have concluded that they stemmed from particular grievances over procedures rather than because the aggrieved were attempting to challenge the sectarian foundation of power – much less power itself.[62] Even when they take these tumults of the 1760s and 1770s into account historians can argue that eighteenth-century Ireland was not especially disturbed even by English standards, and this argument is plausible if we disregard the especially violent decade of the 1790s. Seán Connolly has proceeded further to suggest that conditions in Ireland were so relaxed that the courts were deliberately lenient in their sentencing, but this suggestion is based on the experience of the decades before 1760 and does not take into account conditions under martial law.[63]

1798

The general good order of Irish society convinced the Protestants that they had finally defeated the sources of instability. This encouraged them to invest the profits from their rents in the development of the infrastructure, and Ireland quickly assumed the appearance of an anglicized Protestant society. This achievement is all the more remarkable when account is taken of the facts that Protestants never exceeded one-quarter of the total population (which ranged from about 1.5 million in 1660 to 3 million in 1760); that Protestants were heavily concentrated in the more fertile areas of Ulster and Munster and in the towns; and that they included a substantial number of Presbyterians who were of Scottish descent. Despite these obvious shortcomings a Protestant Anglican appearance was imposed everywhere on Irish society, first because the established church was plentifully endowed and could afford to maintain churches, clergy and cemeteries in every parish, and second because landlords tended to give preference to Protestants for the choice tenancies on the estates. The growth of towns that were encouraged by landlords also brought Protestant traders, professionals and artisans into areas that had few Protestant inhabitants. Frequently landlords promoted estate villages in regions that were poorly served by towns, and they invited Protestant artisans and school-teachers to settle in these villages which were usually situated at the entrance to their demesnes. Landlords also invested heavily in the construction and furnishing of houses after the English fashion; they devoted increasing attention to the development of ornamental grounds; and they linked their residences with the outside world through the making of toll-roads, which were constructed and maintained at public expense. The larger provincial towns and port-towns were dominated by Protestant commercial interests, and even more so the capital, Dublin, where the entirely Protestant Parliament and administration was seated, and where an increasing number of the gentry maintained secondary residences for social as well as political purposes.[64]

The Irish Parliament was a replica in miniature of that in London but it was altogether less representative than that body because only those who would take the sacramental test of the Church of Ireland could be elected members of the commons and only those willing to take the oath of supremacy, and who otherwise met the property qualification, enjoyed the vote. Because of these conditions, and because the Irish Parliament also included a disproportionate number of representatives from boroughs, the ability of powerful families to build up groups of members who would follow their directions in the house was even more pronounced than in

England. The administration in Dublin was narrowly confined in similar fashion for most of the eighteenth century with only those able to meet the requirements of the sacramental test of the established church being eligible for office.[65]

Looked at from a London perspective, the Irish Parliament was an irksome body because London had the responsibility to appoint the executive while it was considered good policy to have the agreement of the Irish Parliament to financial bills and important items relating to policy. The upper house, by virtue of the fact that it included the bench of bishops of the established church as also some great noblemen who held estates and titles in Britain as well as Ireland, was a generally compliant body. The commons, however, was made up of Irish Protestant gentlemen who were distrustful of the government in Britain and any executive which it appointed to Ireland, because they had learned from the outset of King William's reign that matters which were issues of principle to Irish Protestants were sometimes lightly regarded in London. Because of the accepted consensus that an Irish Member of Parliament had a special responsibility to uphold the principles that governed the survival of Protestants, the members were by definition all 'patriots' and watchful critics of government. Besides being concerned to uphold principle, members of the commons were also interested in gaining control over patronage. The patronage they had in mind was appointment to positions in the civil administration and in the Church of Ireland and some aspired also to influence appointments in the army. In this matter members exerted pressure to see first that appointments went to Irish Protestants rather than to Englishmen and then that the beneficiaries belonged to their own faction. This desire of the leaders of the Irish parliamentary factions to have their nominees appointed to office usually made it possible for the viceroy, through the judicious dispensation of patronage, to negotiate sufficient parliamentary support to get his legislation through the commons. However, whenever the government crossed the bounds of what appeared reasonable to the Protestant political nation the support that had been negotiated with the leaders of parliamentary factions could quickly evaporate, and a viceroy could find himself facing the ire of aroused patriots and unable to muster sufficient support in the commons to pass his legislative programme.[66]

The issues that gave rise to such confrontations, and the radical pronouncements associated with them, were predictable. Any threat to Irish Protestant control over property and political power, or any suggestion that penal legislation against Catholics or Presbyterians would be relaxed, was certain to bring a howl of protest from Irish parliamentarians. So also was the suggestion that the English Parliament was superior to its Irish counterpart and had the capacity to legislate for Ireland. Feeling over this issue was so strong that the English government sought to suppress it once and for all by the passage through the English Parliament of the

Declaratory Act of 1720, which decreed that the English Parliament enjoyed such power. This did not resolve the issue, however, and confrontation emerged on every occasion when the English Parliament exercised such power, as it sometimes did in matters relating to trade and manufacturing. Any move by the executive – including even the monarch – to act in an extra-parliamentary fashion also provoked opposition; whenever the executive acted even in a perfectly legal manner by nominating an English favourite to a senior position in the Irish church or state it was certain to meet with loud criticism in the Irish commons.[67]

This summary will make it clear that the concern of Irish parliamentarians, and the established-church Protestants whom they represented, was to win greater control over their own affairs. This did not extend to refusing to acknowledge the authority of the British Crown in Ireland or to questioning the existence of the state. On the contrary, Irish Protestants prided themselves over their loyalty to the Crown, and they had no objection to paying for a state apparatus, including a standing army, which they considered essential to their survival. Irish parliamentarians also acknowledged that Ireland's prosperity – which became considerable after 1740 – derived ultimately from their trade with Britain and its Atlantic empire, and they could never contemplate any severance of that connection. The truth of this was revealed during the 1770s, at the time of the crisis over the question of American independence, when Irish parliamentarians (and a wider Protestant nation) took advantage of that crisis to negotiate greater constitutional independence for themselves while ultimately remaining loyal to the British interest.[68]

Despite this somewhat cynical use of the American crisis by Protestant leaders, the decade of the American revolution did have important consequences for Ireland. The active mobilization of a broadly based public opinion behind the constitutional issue led naturally to a debate over the broader question of parliamentary reform. Those who introduced the subject, like their counterparts in Britain, were primarily concerned with eliminating influence and corruption from the political system. However, in an Irish context, the debate immediately raised the possibility of extending the franchise to propertied Catholics and permitting both Catholics and dissenting Protestants to be returned as Members of Parliament. The fact that this previously forbidden subject could be aired publicly by Irish parliamentarians, and was seen to enjoy the support of some senior politicians in Britain, raised the expectations of Irish Catholics and Presbyterians alike. Both groups, and especially the merchants among them, were impatient for reform because they had benefited from the steady expansion of the Irish economy during the second half of the eighteenth century and aspired to a legal status that was commensurate with their new-found wealth. These therefore took advantage of the opportunity offered to establish pressure groups which would negotiate their respective cases in

London as well as in Dublin. The most controversial of these was the Catholic Committee whose objective was the piecemeal dismantling of the penal laws. These were a cautious and conservative group but the formation of the Committee raised alarm in the Protestant ranks and their endeavours met with strident opposition from the more intransigent Protestant elements in both Britain and Ireland.[69]

Another consequence of the crisis associated with the American Revolutionary War was that it provided landed Protestants with the pretext to raise armed bands of volunteers to provide for the defence of the country while some of the standing army was released to serve in the war. This volunteering heightened the sense of self-sufficiency which was already manifest in the Irish Protestant community during the later part of the eighteenth century. The sympathy with the American cause which found frequent expression in Irish Protestant circles also suggests that they shared with Scots and Americans the notion, described in this collection by Ned Landsman, that 'the provinces' had become 'both the moral centre and the most dynamic sector of the British Empire'.[70]

The war in America also created the need for the recruitment of Irishmen, Catholic as well as Protestant, to serve as soldiers in the regular army. This arming of Irishmen on both sides of the religious divide was to have serious implications for rural disturbances in the decades ahead. By then rural disorder, especially in south Ulster and in parts of Leinster, had assumed a decided sectarian edge. This phenomenon derived ultimately from the scramble for limited resources that was triggered by a dramatic rise in population levels that had continued since the 1760s. Protestant armed bands in south Ulster sought to resolve their economic difficulties by forcing Catholics from the region but the Catholics retaliated by forming themselves into groups of Defenders. These soon became secret oath-bound cells and they adopted offensive as well as defensive objectives once they were radicalized by French revolutionary ideas. The Defender groups spread rapidly through Ulster and into Leinster and they stood opposed to parallel Protestant groups which, after 1795, were constituted as Orange lodges.[71]

The existence of men with military training in each of the opposing organizations exacerbated an already serious situation during the 1790s. The more conservative Protestants and the Dublin government thought it better to give their full backing to the Orangemen in the interests of preserving order, but reform-minded Protestants in Dublin and Presbyterian Ulster believed they could make use of the Defender organization to advance their demands for reform. The Defenders proved of even greater interest to those Protestant radicals who had despaired of reform through constitutional methods and who, in 1791, had constituted themselves into United Irish clubs, intent, after the mode of the French Jacobins, on the creation of a truly reformed and democratic Irish Republic which would establish its independence from Britain by force of arms. The initial force was to come from France but this was to be supplemented by a popular insurrection based on the organization of the Defenders as well as the United Irishmen.[72]

This grand scheme, if it had materialized, would indeed have constituted a threat to the security of the British Empire, and the scheme came close to becoming a reality when in 1796 only adverse winds prevented the landing of 15,000 French soldiers off the south-west coast.[73] What support they would have received if they had made a safe landing is something we shall never know. However, even localized rebellion in Ulster and Leinster, where revolutionary cells were most firmly based, added to a military challenge of that size, would have been more than the Irish state could have coped with, especially at a time when British military and naval strength was fully stretched.

Realizing that is had enjoyed a lucky reprieve, the government in Dublin immediately moved against all in the country who were suspected of dissent. Arrests, interrogations and executions of those suspected of being members of revolutionary organizations continued during the next two years, and those areas that manifested any evidence of disquiet, whether of a social or a revolutionary nature, were placed under the control of stridently Orange forces. These efforts of the government did succeed in breaking the back of the revolutionary organization where it was most firmly established in the Presbyterian areas of Ulster and in parts of Leinster. However, the threats and repressive measures of the militia, and the clear evidence that bigoted Protestants would enjoy a free rein in molesting Catholics, provoked a fresh sense of alarm and alienation among the Catholic rural population. Historians are now agreed that it was this development rather than any Catholic peasant aspiration for a republic that persuaded the Catholics of County Wexford and some neighbouring areas in South Leinster to make common cause with the revolutionaries when a small French force did make a landing in Ireland in 1798.[74]

This insurrection, and its brutal suppression, together occasioned the loss of about 20,000 lives in the single summer of 1798. Its occurrence did provide the government with the pretext to move against dissent in Britain as well as in Ireland but all informed opinion is now agreed that the '98 rebellion was far from being the glorious revolutionary cause that struck at the heart of British Imperial power. Not all historians would endorse Louis Cullen's judgement that the 1798 revolt was 'the last rural civil war in western Europe north of the Pyrenees'; they are in agreement, however, that the forces at work in 1798 were not sufficient to endanger the authority of the state in Ireland, much less in Britain itself, and they are also of one mind that the bloodiness of the affair was due more to the panic and incompetence of the government rather than to the wilfulness of the Catholics of Wexford.

Most especially, historians are agreed that the origins of the conflagration of 1798 should be sought in the complex configurations of that decade rather than attributed to some latent opposition of the Irish population to British rule.[75]

CONCLUSIONS

This narrative, and the secondary literature on which it is principally based, reveals that the topic assigned for investigation did not lead to the conclusion that might have been expected by people who have but a general understanding of Irish affairs. The overwhelming impression is that Ireland was not an unusually disturbed country during the seventeenth and eighteenth centuries, nor were the people especially opposed to recently established state power. Moreover, it appears that those major challenges to state authority that did occur were inspired by Irish dissidents in exile who had the opportunity to put their wild dreams into practice at moments of major international tension when support could be obtained from Britain's continental foes. That vast bulk of the Irish population who chose to remain at home were inevitably drawn into these tumults but usually reluctantly and sometimes half-heartedly and always with the purpose of defending their property and status which were placed in jeopardy because of the disturbances that had beset the country.

This reality serves as a reminder of the comprehensive nature of the conquest that was imposed on Ireland at the close of the sixteenth century and reinforced on two occasions during the course of the seventeenth. The general tranquillity that prevailed reveals much also of the adaptability of Irish Catholics even when they were confronted by a state authority that was avowedly hostile to their religion, if not to themselves. Their story is one of endurance under trying circumstance, but the significant aspect of this story for our present purpose is that when Irish Catholics went beyond mere endurance to work towards their social and political betterment their object was that of removing the Protestant sectarian character of the Irish and British states rather than that of destroying the state which had for long been their oppressor. This was clearly the objective of most Catholic leaders in Ireland during the seventeenth century; it was decidedly the objective of those who were involved in various Catholic associations in Ireland towards the end of the eighteenth century; and it continued to be the guiding principle of Irish Catholic leaders at least until the death of Daniel O'Connell in 1847.[76] Indeed, up to that point – the crucial watershed of the Great Famine – it is true to say that few Catholics in Ireland could imagine a political arrangement that did not involve the British Crown and a British state being supreme in Ireland.

There were, as we saw, sound economic reasons behind Catholic acceptance of state authority, but there were also sound economic reasons why senior politicians in Britain, if not their subordinates in Ireland, should seek to be more conciliatory towards Catholics and identify a position for them within the state establishment. One of those factors which would have influenced official thinking is that Ireland was an essential source of food for the population of Britain on those frequent occasions between 1756 and 1815 when Britain was cut off from its transatlantic sources of grain because of the exigencies of war.[77] Furthermore, British politicians during the later eighteenth century looked with longing eyes at the plentiful supplies of manpower available in Ireland for the war-effort, and looked for the opportunity to remove the statutory impediments which stood in the way of their enlisting.[78] In these circumstances, Catholics had every reason to place trust in constitutional methods, and it was a distinct minority of Catholics, together with some alienated Church of Ireland liberals and resentful Presbyterians, who were attracted to the revolutionary cause during the late eighteenth century. The weight of evidence therefore points to the conclusions that Ireland of the seventeenth and eighteenth centuries was not, as might be expected, a 'restless dominion'; that what restlessness existed was due principally to accident, or the excesses of the state, or foreign intervention; and that Catholics, while conscious that they had been treated unfairly, either had become reconciled to their lot or sought to improve it through reform rather than revolution.

NOTES

1 The phrase is that of David Harkness as used to describe the Irish Free State within the British Commonwealth: David Harkness, *The Restless Dominion 1921–31* (London, 1969).

2 For example, see Conrad Russell, 'The British Background to the Irish Rebellion of 1641', in *Historical Research*, 61 (1988), 166–82; Conrad Russell, 'The British Problem and the English Civil War', in *History*, 72 (1987), 395–415; Conrad Russell, *The Causes of the English Civil War* (Oxford, 1990); Conrad Russell, *The Fall of the British Monarchies, 1637–1642* (Oxford, 1991), 373–400. G. E. Aylmer, *Rebellion or Revolution?* (Oxford, 1986), 22–8.

3 John Kenyon, *The Popish Plot* (London, 1972), 38; John Kenyon, *Stuart England* (London, 1978), 232–5.

4 Caroline Robbins, *The Eighteenth Century Commonwealthman* (Cambridge, Mass., 1959); Isaac Kramnich, *Bolingbroke and His Circle: The Politics of Nostalgia in the Age of Walpole* (Cambridge, Mass., 1968); I. D. McCalman, *Radical Underworld: Prophets, Revolutionaries and Pornographers in London* (Cambridge, 1988); I. D. McCalman, ' "Erin go Bragh": The Irish in British Popular Radicalism, *c*.1790–1840', in Oliver MacDonagh and W. F. Mandle (eds), *Irish-Australian Studies: Papers Delivered at the Fifth Irish-Australian Conference* (Canberra, 1989), 168–84. The only interpretation by a recent historian which lends support to the idea that Ireland was a hotbed of discontent at the popular level is Jim Smyth, *The Men of No Property: Irish Radicals and Popular Politics in the Late Eighteenth Century* (London and Dublin, 1992). Although this is based on evidence from the 1790s, Smyth suggests that a popular radical tradition can be traced back at least as far as the 1760s.

5 E. P. Thompson, *The Making of the English Working Class* (New York, 1964), esp. 167–71.

6 Brendan Bradshaw, 'Nationalism and Historical Scholarship in Modern Ireland', in *Irish Historical Studies*, 26 (1989), 329–51; Daniel Corkery, *The Hidden Ireland* (Dublin, 1925); L. M. Cullen, 'The Hidden Ireland: Re-Assessment of a Concept', in *Studia Hibernica*, 9 (1969), 7–47. The political obligation of nationalist historians to pursue this teleological model was implied in the Proclamation of 1916, conveniently reprinted in R. F. Foster, *Modern Ireland 1600–1972* (London, 1988), 597–8. For a recent application of the model see Robert Kee, *The Green Flag: A History of Irish Nationalism* (London, 1972).

7 This notion which was absorbed into Protestant folk-memory was popularized in William King, *The State of the Protestants of Ireland under the Late King James's Government* (London, 1691); it was given scholarly respectability in J. A. Froude, *The English in Ireland in the Eighteenth Century* (3 vols; London, 1872–4). Examples of twentieth-century academic writing which give a sympathetic view of the Protestant perspective are J. C. Beckett, *Confrontations: Studies in Irish History* (London, 1972), and A. T. Q. Stewart, *The Narrow Ground: Aspects of Ulster, 1609–1969* (London, 1977). See also David W. Miller, *Queen's Rebels: Ulster Loyalism in Historical Perspective* (Dublin, 1978).

8 Bradshaw, 'Nationalism and Historical Scholarship'.

9 The sanitized version has been presented in *A New History of Ireland*, vol. III, *1534–1691*, ed. T. W. Moody, F. X. Martin and F. J. Byrne (Oxford, 1976); vol. IV, *1691–1800*, ed. T. W. Moody and W. E. Vaughan (Oxford, 1986). For a general critique see Nicholas Canny, 'The Power but not the Glory' in *Times Literary Supplement*, 4/368 (19 December 1986), 1432; Thomas Bartlett, 'Review Article: A New History of Ireland', *Past and Present*, 116 (1987), 206–19. For summaries of recent scholarship that confronts the unseemly aspects of Ireland's past, see L. M. Cullen, *An Economic History of Ireland since 1660* (London, 1972); Nicholas Canny, *From Reformation to Restoration, Ireland 1534–1660* (Dublin, 1987); David Dickson, *New Foundations: Ireland, 1660–1800* (Dublin, 1987). For detailed studies of particular episodes see Ciaran Brady and Raymond Gillespie (eds), *Natives and Newcomers: The Making of Irish Colonial Society, 1534–1641* (Dublin, 1986); Thomas Bartlett and D. W. Hayton (eds), *Penal Era and Golden Age: Essays in Irish History, 1690–1800* (Belfast, 1979); W. A. Maguire (ed.), *Kings in Conflict: The Revolutionary War in Ireland and its Aftermath, 1689–1750* (Belfast, 1990); Louis Bergeron and Louis Cullen (eds), *Culture et pratiques politiques en France et en Irlande XVIᵉ–XVIIIᵉ siècles* (Paris, 1990); L. M. Cullen, *The Emergence of Modern Ireland, 1600–1900* (London, 1981).

10 S. J. Connolly, 'The Houghers: Agrarian Protest in Early Eighteenth Century Ireland', in C. H. Philpin (ed.), *Nationalism and Popular Protest in Ireland* (Cambridge, 1987), 139–62; S. J. Connolly, 'Violence and Order in the Eighteenth Century', in P. O'Flanagan, P. Ferguson and K. Whelan (eds), *Rural Ireland: Modernisation and Change 1600–1900* (Cork, 1987), 42–62; S. J. Connolly, ' "Albion's Fatal Twigs": Justice and Law in the Eighteenth Century', in R. Mitchinson and P. Roebuck (eds), *Economy and Society in Ireland and Scotland, 1500–1939* (Edinburgh, 1988), 117–25; Samuel Clark and James S. Donnelly Jr (eds), *Irish Peasant: Violence and Political Unrest, 1780–1914* (Madison, 1983). See also the items listed in note 9 above.

11 See the items by Connolly, Cullen and Dickson in notes 9 and 10 above; also L. M. Cullen, 'Problems in the Interpretation and Revision of Eighteenth-Century Irish Economic History', in *Transactions of the Royal Historical*

Society, 17 (1967), 1–22; Thomas M. Truxes, *Irish-American Trade, 1660–1783* (Cambridge, 1988).

12 Bradshaw, 'Nationalism and Historical Scholarship'.

13 Hiram Morgan, 'The Outbreak of the Nine Years War: Ulster in Irish Politics, 1583–96' (Ph.D. thesis, University of Cambridge, 1986), now superseded by his *Tyrone's Rebellion: The Outbreak of the Nine Years War in Tudor Ireland* (London, 1993); Micheline Kerney Walsh, *'Destruction by Peace': Hugh O'Neill after Kinsale* (Armagh, 1986); Nicholas Canny, 'Hugh O'Neill, Earl of Tyrone and the Changing Face of Gaelic Ulster', in *Studia Hibernica*, 10 (1970), 7–35; Nicholas Canny, 'The Flight of the Earls, 1607', in *Irish Historical Studies*, 17 (1971), 380–99.

14 For a general survey of these developments see Canny, *From Reformation to Restoration*, 150–87; for more particular studies see Michael Mac Carthy Morrogh, *The Munster Plantation, 1580–1641* (Oxford, 1985); Philip Robinson, *The Plantation of Ulster: British Settlement in an Irish Landscape, 1600–1670* (Dublin, 1984); Raymond Gillespie, *Colonial Ulster: The Settlement of East Ulster, 1600–1641* (Cork, 1985); *A New History of Ireland*, vol. III, 187–232.

15 Hans Pawlisch, *Sir John Davies and the Conquest of Ireland: A Study in Legal Imperialism* (Cambridge, 1983).

16 Pawlisch, *Sir John Davies; A New History of Ireland*, vol. III, 187–232.

17 The use of martial law in the early seventeenth century is a subject that has not been investigated but the granting of extensive powers to provosts is detailed in *A Repertory of the Inrolments on the Patent Rolls . . . In Ireland . . . The Reign of James I*, ed. J. C. Erck, vol. I, pts 1, 2 (Dublin, 1846, 1852).

18 On the Old English see Nicholas Canny, 'The Formation of the Old English Elite in Ireland' (published lecture National University of Ireland, Dublin, 1975); Aidan Clarke, *The Old English in Ireland, 1625–41* (London, 1966).

19 Nicholas Canny, *Kingdom and Colony: Ireland in the Atlantic World, 1560–1800* (Baltimore, 1988), 31–68; for a particularly good example of acculturation, see Aidan Clarke, 'Sir Piers Crosby, 1590–1646: Wentworth's "Tawny Ribbon" ' in *Irish Historical Studies*, 26 (1988), 142–60.

20 Robinson, *The Plantation of Ulster*; Breandán Ó Buachalla, 'Na Stíobhartaigh agus an t-Aos Léinn: Cing Séamas' [The Stuarts and the Learned Classes: King James], in *Royal Irish Academy Proceedings*, 83C/4 (1983), 4–134; Breandán Ó Buachalla, 'An Mheisiasacht agus an Aisling' [Messianism and the Allegory], in *Folia Gadelica*, ed. P. de Brún (Cork, 1983), 72–88.

21 Clarke, *The Old English in Ireland*, 28–43.

22 Canny, *Kingdom and Colony*, 31–68.

23 Jerrold I. Casway, *Owen Roe O'Neill and the Struggle for Catholic Ireland* (Philadelphia, 1984), 37–54.

24 *A New History of Ireland*, vol. III, 216–17.

25 ibid., 219–32.

26 Terence O. Ranger, 'The Career to Richard Boyle, First Earl of Cork, in Ireland, 1588–1643' (D.Phil. thesis, University of Oxford, 1959); H. F. Kearney, 'The Court of Wards and Liveries in Ireland, 1622–1641', in *Royal Irish Academy Proceedings*, 57C/2 (1955), 29–68.

27 Kenneth Nicholls, *Gaelic and Gaelicised Ireland in the Middle Ages* (Dublin, 1972); Kenneth Nicholls, 'Land, Law and Society in Sixteenth Century Ireland' (published lecture, National University of Ireland, Dublin, 1976); Terence O. Ranger, 'Richard Boyle and the Making of an Irish Fortune', in *Irish Historical Studies*, 10 (1957), 257–97.

28 Clarke, *The Old English in Ireland*.

29 Sir John Davies, *A Discovery of the True Causes why Ireland was never Entirely Subdued* (London, 1612), 264–87.
30 *Advertisements for Ireland*, ed. George O'Brien (Dublin, 1923).
31 Aidan Clarke, 'Colonial Constitutional Attitudes in Ireland, 1640–1660', in *Proceedings of the Royal Irish Academy*, 90C/11 (1990), 357–75.
32 The Deposition of Job Ward of Kilmartin, Queen's County (TCD, MS 815, ff. 277–87).
33 Aidan Clarke, 'The Genesis of the Ulster Rising of 1641', in Peter Roebuck (ed.), *Plantation to Partition* (Belfast, 1981), 29–45; Raymond Gillespie, 'The End of an Era: Ulster and the Outbreak of the 1641 Rebellion', in Brady and Gillespie, *Natives and Newcomers*, 191–213; Conrad Russell, 'The British Background to the Irish Rebellion of 1641'; Nicholas Canny, 'In Defence of the Constitution? The Nature of Irish Revolt in the Seventeenth Century', in Bergeron and Cullen, *Culture et pratiques politiques*, 23–40; Philippe Loupes, 'Le jardin Irlandais des supplices: La grande rebellion de 1641 vue à travers les pamphlets Anglais', in Bergeron and Cullen, *Culture et pratiques politiques*, 41–60; David Stevenson, *Scottish Covenanters and Irish Confederates: Scottish-Irish Relations in the Mid-Seventeenth Century* (Belfast, 1981), esp. 43–102; Casway, *Owen Roe O'Neill*, 55–83. The Scottish dimension to the Irish rising has now received comprehensive coverage in Jane H. Ohlmeyer, *Civil War and Restoration in the Three Stuart Kingdoms: The Career of Randal MacDonnell, Marquis of Antrim, 1609–1683* (Cambridge, 1993).
34 *A New History of Ireland*, vol. III, 336–86; T. C. Barnard, 'Crises of Identity Among Irish Protestants, 1641–1685', *Past and Present*, 127 (1990), 39–83.
35 ibid.; Karl S. Bottigheimer, *English Money and Irish Land: The 'Adventurers' in the Cromwellian Settlement of Ireland* (Oxford, 1971); T. C. Barnard, *Cromwellian Ireland: English Government and Reform in Ireland, 1649–1660* (Oxford, 1975); T. C. Barnard, 'Planters and Policies in Cromwellian Ireland', in *Past and Present*, 61 (1973), 31–69.
36 Barnard, *Cromwellian Ireland*; Canny, *From Reformation to Restoration*, 218–23.
37 *A New History of Ireland*, vol. III, 353–86 and 428: the statistics of landownership have been worked out by J. G. Simms for 1641 and 1688, and he allows 22 per cent in Catholic ownership for the latter date. What belonged to Catholics in 1659 was clearly much smaller because the 1688 figure includes what was returned to Catholics under the Restoration settlement as well as purchases between 1659 and 1688.
38 *A New History of Ireland*, vol. III, 420–53.
39 ibid.
40 Patrick J. Corish, *The Catholic Community in the Seventeenth and Eighteenth Centuries* (Dublin, 1981), 53–72.
41 *Duanaire Dháibhidh Uí Bhruadair: The Poems of David O'Bruadair*, ed. J. C. McErlean (3 vols; London, 1910–17): see vol. II covering poems written 1667–1682, esp. 12–13, 42–9, 50–97, 106–7, 108–23, 142–5, 154–7, 204–5; *A New History of Ireland* vol. III, 387–407; 448–9.
42 *A New History of Ireland*, vol. III, 428.
43 J. G. Simms, *Jacobite Ireland, 1685–91* (London, 1969), 19–43.
44 James McGuire, 'James II and Ireland, 1685–90', in Maguire, *Kings in Conflict*, 45–57.
45 *Duanaire Dháibhidh Uí Bhruadair*, vol. III, esp. 12–29, 38–43, 76–93, 94–111, 112–13.
46 McGuire, 'James II and Ireland', pp. 45–57.

47 William King, *The State of the Protestants of Ireland*, 290. More generally see Raymond Gillespie, 'The Irish Protestants and James II, 1688–90', in *Irish Historical Studies*, 28 (1992), 124–33.

48 Harman Murtagh, 'The War in Ireland, 1689–91', in Maguire, *Kings in Conflict*, 61–92.

49 J. G. Simms, *The Williamite Confiscation in Ireland 1690–1703* (London, 1956); W. A. Maguire, 'The Land Settlement', in Maguire, *Kings in Conflict*, 139–56.

50 Murtagh, 'The War in Ireland'.

51 James I. McGuire, 'The Irish Parliament of 1692', in Bartlett and Hayton, *Penal Era and Golden Age*, 1–31; S. J. Connolly, 'The Penal Laws', in Maguire, *Kings in Conflict*, 157–72.

52 Connolly, 'The Penal Laws'; Maureen Wall, *The Penal Laws, 1691–1760* (Dundalk, 1961); S. J. Connolly, 'Religion and History', in *Irish Economic and Social History*, 10 (1983), 66–80. The subject has now received its fullest treatment in S. J. Connolly, *Religion, Law and Power: The Making of Protestant Ireland 1660–1760* (Oxford, 1992), esp. 263–313.

53 One statute passed in 1703 was described as 'An Act to Prevent the Further Growth of Popery'.

54 See the items in note 52 above and Corish, *The Catholic Community*, 73–81.

55 Thomas Bartlett, 'Army and Society in Eighteenth-Century Ireland', in Maguire, *Kings in Conflict*, 173–82.

56 See the items in note 52 above; Corish, *The Catholic Community*, 82–139.

57 Connolly, 'The Penal Laws'.

58 *Dánta Aodhagáin Uí Rathaille: The Poems of Egan O'Rahilly* (second edn; London, 1965); Breandán Ó Buachalla, 'An Mheisiacht agus an Aisling'.

59 *A New History of Ireland*, vol. IV, 1–83.

60 ibid., 123–93; Connolly, *Religion, Law and Power*, 263–313.

61 David Dickson, 'Large-Scale Developers and the Growth of Eighteenth-Century Irish Cities', in P. Butel and L. M. Cullen (eds), *Cities and Merchants: French and Irish Perspectives on Urban Development, 1500–1900* (Dublin, 1986), 109–23; L. M. Cullen, 'The Dublin Merchant Community in the Eighteenth Century', ibid., 195–209; L. M. Cullen, *Anglo-Irish Trade, 1660–1800* (Manchester, 1968); Truxes, *Irish American Trade*.

62 James S. Donnelly, Jr, 'The Whiteboy Movement, 1761–5', in *Irish Historical Studies*, 21 (1978–9), 20–54; Clark and Donnelly, *Irish Peasants*.

63 Connolly, 'The Houghers', 'Violence and Order' and 'Albion's Fatal Twigs'. The subject has been most comprehensively discussed in Connolly, *Religion, Law and Power*, esp. 198–262.

64 David Dickson, Cormac Ó Gráda and S. Daultrey, 'Hearth Tax, Household Size and Irish Population Change, 1672–1821', in *Royal Irish Academy Proceedings*, 82C (1982), 125–82; Cullen, *The Emergence of Modern Ireland*, 25–61; Dickson, *New Foundations*, 62–96.

65 J. C. Beckett, *Protestant Dissent in Ireland, 1687–1780* (London, 1948).

66 On political life see the essays in Bartlett and Hayton, *Penal Era and Golden Age*, and A. P. W. Malcomson, *John Foster: The Politics of the Anglo-Irish Ascendancy* (Oxford, 1978).

67 See the items in note 66 and *A New History of Ireland*, vol. IV, 105–21.

68 *A New History of Ireland*, vol. IV, 196–233. The true complexity of the impact of the American revolutionary struggle on Irish affairs has only recently been exposed in James Kelly, *Prelude to Union: Anglo–Irish Politics in the 1780s* (Cork, 1992).

69 ibid.; Dickson, *New Foundations*, 128–69; Kevin Whelan, 'Catholic Mobilis-

ation, 1750–1850', in Bergeron and Cullen, *Culture et pratiques politiques*, 235–58.

70 Ned. C. Landsman, Chapter 10 above, p. 263.

71 Tom Garvin, 'Defenders, Ribbonmen and Others: Underground Political Networks in Pre-Famine Ireland', in Philpin, *Nationalism and Popular Protest in Ireland*, 219–45; Thomas Bartlett, 'Defenders and Defenderism in 1795', in *Irish Historical Studies*, 24 (1985), 373–94; Thomas Bartlett, 'Militarization and Politicization in Ireland, 1780–1820', in Bergeron and Cullen, *Culture et pratiques politiques*, 125–36; Hereward Senior, *Orangeism in Ireland and Britain, 1795–1836* (London, 1966). The full plethora of factors that contributed to the increasingly sectarian character of social and political divisions in Ireland has been considered in Thomas Bartlett, *The Fall and Rise of the Irish Nation: the Catholic Question, 1690–1830* (Dublin, 1992), esp. 121–227. The interpretation presented here does not concede the popular dimension to Irish radicalism that is pleaded in Jim Smyth, *The Men of No Property*, esp. 33–51, 100–56.

72 Marianne Elliott, *Partners in Revolution: The United Irishmen and France* (New Haven, 1982); L. M. Cullen, 'Late Eighteenth Century Politicization in Ireland: Problems in its Study and its French Links', in Bergeron and Cullen, *Culture et pratiques politiques*, 137–56. The case for a masonic origin to the radicalism of Irish Protestants has been argued in A. T. Q. Stewart, *A Deeper Silence: The Hidden Roots of the United Irishmen* (London, 1993).

73 Marianne Elliott, *Wolfe Tone: Prophet of Irish Independence* (New Haven, 1989).

74 *New History of Ireland*, vol. IV, 339–74; Dickson, *New Foundations* pp. 170–97; Cullen, *The Emergence of Modern Ireland*, pp. 210–33.

75 L. M. Cullen, 'The 1798 Rebellion in its Eighteenth-Century Context', in Patrick J. Corish, *Radicals, Rebels and Establishments* (Belfast, 1985), 91–113 (quotation from p. 91); Kevin Whelan, 'Politicisation in County Wexford and the Origins of the 1798 Rebellion', in Hugh Gough and David Dickson (eds), *Ireland and the French Revolution* (Dublin, 1989), 156–78.

76 Thomas Bartlett, 'The Origins and Progess of the Catholic Question in Ireland, 1690–1800', in T. P. Power and Kevin Whelan (eds), *Endurance and Emergence: Catholics in Ireland in the Eighteenth Century* (Dublin, 1990), 1–19; Eamonn O'Flaherty, 'The Catholic Convention and Anglo-Irish Politics, 1791–3', in *Archivium Hibernicum*, 40 (1985), 14–34; Kevin Whelan, 'Catholic Mobilisation, 1750–1850'; Oliver MacDonagh, *The Emancipist: Daniel O'Connell, 1830–47* (London, 1989).

77 Brinley Thomas, 'Food Supply in the United Kingdom during the Industrial Revolution', in Jeol Mokyr (ed.), *The Economics of the Industrial Revolution* (London, 1985), esp. 140–3. I am grateful to Dr David Dickson for the reference.

78 Thomas Bartlett, 'An End to Moral Economy: The Irish Militia Disturbances of 1798', in *Past and Present*, 99 (1983), 40–64.

12

The British Military-Fiscal State and Indigenous Resistance

India 1750–1820

C. A. Bayly

This chapter considers two closely related issues: first, the nature of the East India Company's state as it evolved in India during the eighteenth century, and second, the form, incidence and timing of Indian resistance to that state. The resistance of indigenous and subject peoples to foreign rule has been a fashionable topic for Indian historians in recent years, but resistance cannot be explained outside its historical context, and underlying much of this work are assumptions about the nature of the colonial state in India. These need to be examined before the quality and form of the Indian response to British expansion can be properly understood.

When they come to consider the East India Company's regime, historians adopt two broad positions. These might be called the 'oriental' and the 'western' perspective. Keen to avoid the view that British conquest marked an abrupt break between tradition and modernity or between feudalism and capitalism in India, the 'orientals' have implied that up to 1830 or beyond, the East India Company operated essentially as an Indian state writ large.[1] According to them, the British were successful conquerors not so much because they represented the leading edge of a western technological power, but because they were able to build upon the machinery of territorial-revenue extraction and military traditions – the 'fiscal-military state', to use John Brewer's phrase[2] – which the Mughal rulers and their Hindu subjects had long been developing in India. It was quite appropriate that Company servants returning to Great Britain were given the Mughal title 'nabob', since they had amassed fortunes through partnership with Indian commercial interests, played the politics of factional alliance within Indian courts and camps, and patronized Hindu and Muslim shrines and deities. As Robert Frykenberg puts it, the British Indian Empire was 'Indian' in a very real sense.[3]

A corollary of this position is that Indian resistance to the East India Company can sometimes reasonably be described as anti-British, or even anti-foreign, but it would not be very meaningful to call it 'anti-colonial', since the Company at this time displayed none of the features of a mature colonial regime. The incidence of resistance to, or collaboration with, the white invader was determined not so much by the characteristics of the Company itself as by patterns of indigenous political or economic structure. Resistance was sometimes simply a continuation of the long crisis of succession to the Mughal empire; alternatively, it was a by-product of state-building or class-formation, but one also driven by Indian compulsions.[4] This present-day 'oriental' interpretation would, of course, have found support among the Company's eighteenth-century critics, such as Edmund Burke, who believed that it had become an oriental power corrupted by the legacy of 'Muhammadan tyranny' and riven by the venal private interests of the white nabobs.

Most Indian-born scholars and other radical historians reject all or part of this formulation, and might by contrast be called 'westerners'. On this issue they are unlikely bed-fellows with the few recent representatives of the imperial-history tradition which regarded empire as a 'good thing'. Many Indian scholars, for instance, tend to assert that the Company state was wholly external to Indian society and that throughout the British period it was little more than an exploitative western army of occupation. Other historians depict a deeper engagement between the British and indigenous social classes, but insist nevertheless that the Company, far from being Indian, worked in the interest of a foreign capitalist imperialism. For most of them British rule means the draining-away of the wealth of India in the form of tribute and major disruption to all levels of Indian life. For a few it means the establishment of peace and the beginning of state-led westernization and modernization. However, in all these interpretations, the Company is regarded as fundamentally different from all regimes that had preceded it.

According to the 'westerners', therefore, Indian resistance, whether it arose from organized states, from peasants, weavers or the tribal people of the forests and hills, is properly described as 'anti-colonial'. It was 'directed against the policy, systems and personnel of the colonial government'.[5] Eighteenth-century anti-British resistance was a lineal precursor of what is now called the 'subaltern' (that is, non-elite) anti-colonialism of the nineteenth and twentieth centuries. Under the fragmented surface of the multifarious outbreaks of the later eighteenth century there was a continuously developing core of protest against imperialism and capitalism (or against beneficent western modernization, if you will). This protest, according to one recent group of historians, reflected a coherent consciousness of opposition to the invading Other which was expressed in ballads, legends or oral histories and through the fashioning of symbols of revolt.[6]

To proceed further with this debate, it becomes necessary to examine again the ideology and interests of the expanding British state at a global level. It is not enough to argue, as some 'orientals' have done, that the

Company's rapid rise of territorial dominion over the subcontinent can be explained simply with reference to the age-old tendency of any successful Indian polity to construct a universal, over-arching empire in the subcontinent. The Company's regime was evidently something more than a white Mughal Empire. Nor, again, was the degree of disorder unleashed by the decline of the Mughals sufficient explanation for the Company's career of aggrandisement. On the other hand, a problem for those holding the 'western' position has been to find an explanation for the origins of British imperialism in India that relates it convincingly to the form of the domestic British state and economy. How can one reconcile the image we have of the bourgeois British constitutional and commercial state of the eighteenth century with its gaudy and aggressive Indian *alter ego*? The domestic Jekyll-state was supposed to have been weak, uncentralized and non-interventionist by comparison with its European contemporaries. It pursued a policy of 'blue-water' commercial expansion, not one of conquest and land-war. It was believed to have been rather ineffectual in fiscal and military matters, especially during the period when the oriental Hyde-state was conquering nearly one-quarter of the human race, albeit in a fit of 'absence of mind'. Over the last generation some attention has been given to the imperialism of private British trading interests; but it has not really proved possible to explain the main thrust of the Company's policies and conquests by reference to these or to any major change in Britain's trading interests in the east. The central question remains: if, as so many native-born Indian historians imply, the Company really was an extension of an expansive aggressive nation-state skilled in the practice of economic imperialism, why was so little of this apparatus of state power apparent in Britain itself?

One of the many merits of John Brewer's *Sinews of Power* is that it provides an opportunity to reconsider the relationship between the British state and its surrogate, the East India Company. For if, as he says, the British state was more powerful, flexible and effective than has been hitherto believed – if, indeed, it was a highly successful example of 'military-fiscalism' – then the Company Raj in India may not simply have been the luxuriant oriental aberration that is sometimes portrayed.

This chapter argues that, for all its indigenous penumbra, the East India Company's state enshrined at core two important features of the domestic state which, once set working in an Indian context, imbued it with much of its expansionist impetus. These were, first, a rigorous tradition of administrative accountancy and, second, an ideology of transcendent law and sovereignty. These features also provide a key with which to interpret the nature and timing of Indian resistance to the British empire. The chapter, then, sets out to transcend the distinction between 'oriental' and 'western' interpretations of the Company by analysing the interaction between its Indian and British components. In turn, it attempts to illustrate more precisely the extent to which Indian resistance to the Company differed from the ebb and flow of warfare and insurrection in the late Mughal polity.

THE 'SINEWS OF POWER' IN THE PERIPHERY

John Brewer's targets – the notion that metropolitan Britain was a weak state, that its military and political organization was attenuated and that England was, consequently, a little-governed society – has its parallels in the literature on India. Here the assumption that has guided many historians is that the Company as much as the British government was generally hostile to 'any military enterprise or expedition'[7] and that in India its agents in their official capacity wished only to trade without hindrance and had no desire for territorial conquest. Only the 'decline of the Mughals' and the rampant private interests of men-on-the-spot pulled the Company into schemes of dominion. However, Brewer's thesis might lead us to question some parts of this argument. From the mid-seventeenth century, the East India Company had the capacity, will and legal right to wage war and had an intermittent interest in territorial power and revenue. Its policies were often aggressive; and, in crises at least, it insisted on a rigid interpretation of its own rights and sovereignties in India. Powerful voices could always be heard in London and India arguing for caution; but a flexible structure for military conquest – and a set of arguments to support it – was already in place early in its history, even if the juggernaut was not loosed at full tilt until the mid-eighteenth century.

Events such as the war of the Company Chairman, Sir Josiah Child, with the Indian Emperor Aurangzeb (1688) or the conquest of Bengal (1756–65) have been seen as aberrations from a generally pacific policy or as unintended consequences of events in Indian politics. Yet during the key periods of the growth of the domestic British state (the late seventeenth century, 1740–63 and 1798–1820) a more militant discourse asserted itself in Company circles. Though there were never clearly defined 'war' and 'peace' parties, there were always voices arguing for the use of force if it could be effective. In 1676 Gerald Aungier, Governor of Madras, summarized it by saying that the 'general commerce' had to be driven 'with sword in hand'.[8] Child's basic premise was simply a logical extension of this. He differed from his contemporaries and successors more about means than about ends. He wrote in 1686:

> You see what a mighty charge we are at to advance the English interest and to make this Company a formidable martial government in India which formerly the Dutch despised as a parcel of mere trading merchants or pedlars ... [Without territorial revenue] it is impossible to make the English nation's station sure and firm in India

upon a sound political basis, and without which we shall always continue in the state of mere merchants subject to be turned out at the pleasure of the Dutch and abused at the discretion of the natives.[9]

Child's desire for unfettered sovereignty over Indian naval and commercial stations and his determination to reduce and if possible eliminate dues paid to Indian rulers were aborted by local confusion and the vigorous military response of the Mughal governors. However, quietly and without the same rhetorical flourishes, later governors in the main settlements took a similar line when it was prudent to do so. Thomas Pitt was arguing again in 1701 that the Nawab (Mughal viceroy) of the Carnatic (Madras) should be repulsed: 'we are in a good condition to bang him'.[10] The struggle between the 'old' and 'new' East India companies in the 1690s and 1700s also encouraged both bodies and their united successor to adopt an aggressive stance 'in the name of the English nation'.[11]

By the turn of the eighteenth century many of the institutions of domestic British governance had been translated in miniature form to Calcutta, Madras, Bombay and Surat. Armed shipping frequented the stations and bodies of troops guarded the factories. Courts of Admiralty had been set up to deal with interlopers – that is, free merchants or rivals who broke the Company's monopoly.[12] In 1688 a municipality was established at Madras with a mayor and twelve aldermen who had police powers and operated outside the authority of local rulers. In 1717 the British in Calcutta secured a charter from the Mughal Emperor which allowed them to trade free of all dues for an annual payment, to rent additional land and settle throughout eastern India, and also, as they took it, to fortify.[13]

Clearly the Company was already more than just another Indian trading community peacefully integrated into indigenous society during an age of Eurasian partnership; but more important than the intentions of the European actors was the Company's structure in India. It was beginning to resemble a fledgling version of John Brewer's domestic state. As in the case of its metropolitan sire, an important model and spur to aggressive management was the Dutch example. The continued success of the VOC (the Dutch East India Company) in the mid-seventeenth century had been one of the main reasons why the joint-stock organization was retained, despite the relatively poor results of the English Company before 1660.[14] After 1688 the weak financial position of the Treasury allowed the Company to fight off the various interests which were gathering against its privileges by making over its capital to the government. Once the United East India Company of 1708 had been fostered by the ministry,[15] state and Company moved into the same close relationship that had characterized the ties between the States General and the VOC. The British Government received direct payments from the Company and also benefited from the buoyancy of East India stock. In return, the Company received military aid from the Crown in its intensifying struggles with its European and Indian enemies.

K. N. Chaudhuri has demolished the assumption that the Company was a rather loosely controlled commercial organization which suffered continual financial haemorrhages. On the contrary, stock was scientifically controlled and Company accountancy was highly skilled.[16] As in the case of the Dutch Company, though unlike the Iberian powers, the cost of military action was built into the balance-sheet, so that a proper assessment of profit and loss could be arrived at. To adapt the words used by Niels Steensgaard in his study of the Dutch,[17] 'markets were transparent' for the English Company, and it had 'internalised protection costs'. Historians have sometimes been tempted to argue that by 1760 the English Company had become, like the Portuguese or Spanish overseas enterprises, decrepit predatory hulks harbouring hordes of individual parasites. After this date the English Company was indeed forced to borrow money from the Crown; but this was late in its career, and even then, the Company's financial position was quite clear and well accounted, enabling the funding of its debt on the London market.[18]

Next, we must address the issue of sovereignty, law and the state's perception of itself. Brewer attributes the British state's success to its refusal to countenance the persistence or emergence of a military or landholding *imperium in imperio*. It depended neither on overt military force nor on 'quasi-feudal forms of servitude, but on the rule of law'.[19] Consequently, as de Tocqueville argued, the English ruling class 'submitted that it might command'. The Company transplanted some of these ground-rules to India. Company servants were amenable to English law in all settlements. The Company tried to insist that their governors should be given cere-monial precedence over senior officers of the Royal Navy.[20] The superiority of civil over military power within India was maintained even after 1757, when the Company began to develop a powerful and well-trained infantry army.

British attitudes to Indian sovereignty were similarly robust from the outset,[21] despite the reverence that was apparently paid to the principles of social hierarchy embodied in Indian kingship. At various times the Company was content to rule in tandem with Indian princes, and even to share the symbols of sovereignty with them. After Plassey even Clive professed himself unwilling to trench on the authority still held by the Mughal governors of Bengal,[22] though at other times he appeared to be urging ministers to assume full sovereignty over Bengal. Hesitations of this sort arose from domestic political fears that were aroused by the prospect of the Crown's capture of the East India Company's patronage. Neverthe-less, there was an irreducible substratum of legal and political thinking in Britain as well as within the Company's Indian establishments that insisted that the Company directly embodied the authority of Crown in Parliament and was happy to conclude that Indian authority was nugatory or, at best, that it had been wholly and irrevocably granted to the 'English nation' in its Indian stations. Underlying the dealings of Company officials with Indian powers, even the Mughal emperors, was the prejudice that Muslims had no real rights in regard to Christian property and privileges. The presumption in the Laws of England that 'Turkes and other infidels were not only excluded from being witnesses against Christians, but are deemed also to be perpetual enemys and capable of no property'[23] was toned down but never entirely forgotten. Even compared with the Dutch, as Chaudhuri notes, the British were the most likely of European powers to insist on their privileged status in India, to brand Indian powers as aggressors and, above all, to resist paying forced levies to them.[24] For the English Company such exactions must be denied because payment implied not only fiscal dependence but also loss of sovereignty, for the two were closely allied in British political thought.

British insistence on their rights had several aspects. First, Government and Company usually tended to take a strong view of their sovereignty within India when dealing with the French, other Europeans and, later, Americans. From the earliest years Portuguese claims to Indian sovereignty were dismissed with an anglicized version of Grotius's doctrine that Asia was not 'terra nullius' to be expropriated by Portuguese armed with a papal grant.[25] By 1787 Eden (who was then negotiating a convention with the French) could speak flatly of British 'souveraineté possessoire et exclusive'[26] in eastern India, a status which the Company had generally asserted in dealings with European enemies since the Peace of Paris in 1763. Secondly, this 'hard' interpretation of British authority had already been adopted in the main Company settlements and in the territories immediately dependent on them. In Bombay from 1668 the Company conceived of itself as an absolute sovereign, ruling as surrogate of the British Crown.[27] It minted its coin not in the name of the Mughal Emperor but of the Crown;[28] it administered justice to Indian and European inhabitants through common courts of judicature. The establishment of a public gallows (which was abhorrent to both Hindus and Muslims) was a visible manifestation of the new supremacy of law. In Madras the Company's rights were theoretically derived from local Hindu princes and later acknowledged by the incoming Mughal conquerors. After 1752, however, the Company's ally Muhammad Ali (who was supposedly himself a representative of the Mughal Emperor) relinquished the quit-rent he had been paid by the English for the settlement, and thus effectively abolished 'the last fragment of dependence upon an Indian prince at Madras'.[29]

In Calcutta and north India the Company still formally acted in the name of the Mughal Emperor until the 1840s (the final tatters of Mughal overlordship being abolished after the Rebellion of 1857). Yet Company officials showed a strong tendency to invade and modify Mughal sovereignty. At the same time the British contrived to apply the rights devolved on them by the Mughal emperors with relentless rigour as far as they applied to petty kings and princes. In its dealings with the larger post-Mughal states the Company insisted on jurisdiction over its own subjects and over their dependents, thus turning the concept of 'extra-territoriality' into a powerful engine of subversion.[30]

Since 1694 the Company had been *zamindar* (landlord) in Calcutta, and its receivers of the revenues had exercised rights of life and death over Indian residents. However, the turning-point for the Company's construction of its authority in India was the grant of the decree by the Emperor Farrukhsiyar (1717) allowing it leave to trade freely within the whole of Bengal and its dependencies and giving it certain exemptions from taxation.[31] In Indian theory and practice this was simply the grant of a right or honour. It did not imply a perpetual sharing of imperial authority, nor did it necessarily rank the Company's officials above imperial officials or other royal officials within the provinces thereafter and forever. The practice of Mughal diplomacy or honour-giving was fluid; it did not seek to establish 'constitutional principles'. Nevertheless, from this time onward, Company officials interpreted the grant as conferring on them an all-encompassing devolved sovereignty: 'In all future disputes with the local governors, the point was repeatedly made that the company traded in India by right and not by any favour of the imperial officers.'[32]

In the light of the 1717 document, for instance, hostilities with the Bengal ruler in 1756–7 were justified on the ground that he was no more than an 'official' of the Mughal, intruding on the rights of a body (the Company) to which the Mughal Emperor had devolved authority in parallel.[33] From the perspective of the Bengal ruler (Siraj-ud Daulah), however, the Company's arming of its settlements and its brusque refusal to give him the customary presents upon his accession were open acts of rebellion against an overlord, for the Nawab was trying to reassert his dynasty's hold over the European companies and Indian commercial and landholding interests which had become far too powerful in his realm.[34] Moreover, he was insisting on his dynasty's legitimacy as the foremost sharer in Mughal authority in eastern India. Peter Marshall has convincingly argued that the Company never planned the 'revolution' which brought it to power in Bengal in 1757. As a judgement on the intentions and policies of the individual actors this is probably true. On the other hand, the Company's long-held desire to acquire a local fiscal base and its tendency to regard the Bengal rulers as mere officials rather than kings suggest that this 'revolution' was an outcome of basic organization and assumptions of its Indian establishments, as much as of the contingent struggles of Indian and European actors.[35]

The resolute nature of much of the Company's discourse about sovereignty and dominion was not only apparent in grand events such as the conquest of Bengal. It also informed the tenor of its relations with Indian princes and landowners from the point when Clive took on the revenue management of Bengal in 1765. The dominant official version was that there were no rights in India other than those derived from the Mughal Emperor. His sovereignty was indivisible but could be devolved. As Mark Wilks, along with Burke one of the dissenters from this view, observed, the British would dispossess proprietors under certain circumstances because 'they thought that the actual property of the soil is vested in government, who alone have the power of making an absolute sale of the land'.[36] This seems to have been based on misleading notions of oriental despotism which were common among European observers, but the British may also have had in mind early English land-law, where right was derived from the Conquest settlement. So the Company, which had inherited Mughal sovereignty and rights of conquest by virtue of the 1717 grant, and had later acquired the powers of Mughal governor and revenue manager, could dispose of all land-rights *de novo*. The British came to attribute great importance to the events which appeared to confirm this Indian 'constitution'. The 1717 document was repeatedly invoked. The grant of the revenue management of Bengal to the Company (1765) was similarly privileged. It became a founding document comparable to Magna Carta. Indeed, in Benjamin West's famous painting of the grant of the Diwani to Clive (*c.*1795) it was portrayed with appropriate grandeur.[37]

As we have suggested, the British interpretation ran contrary to Indian ideas of sovereignty and royal rights which suggested a corporate view of kingship and a symbiotic view of rights over men and land. Indian rulers, including the Mughals, garnered loyalty and support by giving honour through boons conferred in great assemblies (the *darbars*).[38] Such grants of office and honour could be redefined and rearranged according to changes in political circumstances. In the same way, titles to land as they had evolved in the later Mughal period represented a delicately balanced pyramid of rights to the usufruct of land and labour mediated by notions of social interdependence. There was no absolute dominion in the manner of Roman or English law, and the rights of landholders (*zamindars*) did not extinguish other inferior rights of occupancy and common use.[39] The right to collect land-revenue on the part of the state was quite independent of the *zamindari* right, so that the fiscal hierarchy could stand independently of the hierarchy of land rights.[40] The persistent revolts that the British encountered in the period of conquest were, in part, a consequence of their refusal to accept that Indians did not, in general, conceive rights in terms of simple proprietary dominion.

Among the British there was but little difference of emphasis between the men of the Enlightenment, such as Warren Hastings, and their more aggressive anglicizing successors, the generation of Cornwallis and Wellesley. Hastings's fundamental position, albeit modified and qualified at times was 'The sword which gave us the dominion of Bengal must be the instrument of its preservation; and if . . . it shall ever cease to be ours, the next proprietor will derive his rights and possession from the same natural charter.'[41] The velvet glove concealing this mailed fist was Mughal sovereignty, interpreted in an exclusive manner. Hastings's actions were entirely consistent with this doctrine. In 1775 the revenues of the territory of Benares collected by Raja Cheyt Singh had been transferred to the Company by his suzerain, the Nawab of Awadh (the Grand Vazir of the Mughals). The Governor-General chose to treat the Benares ruler as a mere landholder. He referred to him as the 'zemindar of Benares' and drew attention to his lowly origins as a revenue collector for the Nawab's father.[42] Hastings arrogated to the Company the right to increase the Benares revenue and dispossess the Raja at will. The attempt to seize and imprison the Raja badly misfired and put Hastings himself, and the British position in the mid-Ganges valley, in peril. Somewhat earlier, the Council in Madras, influenced by the avaricious creditors of the Nawab of Arcot, had conspired with him to occupy the rich, adjoining kingdom of Tanjore. A majority of the British in Madras enthusiastically supported the Nawab's claim on the ground that the Tanjore Raja was a 'mere landholder' who indirectly owed his position to Mughal grant,[43] though Mughal sovereignty was but a distant shimmer in this far southern land. Here again agricultural operations were brought to a temporary halt by the resistance of local farmers. Later the Court of Directors found it necessary to restore the Raja, but the dynasty's authority was already fatally undermined.

More than one European foreigner noted how absolute the Company's claims became in any crisis. A. H. Anquetil Duperron, a famous French orientalist and translator of Indian holy texts, was hot in his denunciation of the British. He dilated on 'their mercantile depredations . . . the spectacle of the overthrow of empires, of princes expelled from their estates, massacres, kings in irons; of fugitive peoples, of rich lands devastated'.[44] His particular target, however, was the monolithic interpretation of its sovereignty advanced by the Company, and theoretically justified by Robert Orme (the Company's historian) and others. If the Raja of Tanjore (whose territory had been usurped in 1773) was considered a mere revenue collector entitled to no share of sovereignty, 'by reasoning in this manner, one might say that the Grand Dukes of Muscovy were not sovereign and independent princes until Europe recognized them as emperors'.[45] Perhaps, again, as the British insisted, Maharaja Cheyt Singh of Benares was the son of a revenue collector, 'But in India the rajas, the nawabs, dependent on the Mughal are but the collectors of revenue for that monarch'.[46]

Anquetil Duperron implied that the British in particular had little time for shared sovereignties or hierarchies of royal rights. It is true that other European nations – notably the Dutch and the French themselves – were as violent in their commercial policies as the English Company had been.

Yet in theory and practice they appear to have left more space for indigenous sovereignty and rights during the period of the *ancien régime*. The Dutch, for instance, imposed heavy agrarian demands on their territories in north Java; but they left much of the structure of Javanese royal authority (the indigenous kings of *regenten*) undisturbed.[47] The Dutch governor-general was deemed to be the grandfather of the local princes and even acquired a symbolic pedigree linking him to the Goddess of the Southern Ocean, patron of the Javanese. It was not until the later Napoleonic regime of Marshall Herman Daendels and the despotism of Sir Stamford Raffles on the island (1811–16) that the religious and magical power of the indigenous kings was humbled and their ritual palace-centres desecrated.

We shall see that this powerful concept of paramount sovereignty was redoubled in force during the military empire-building of the Wellesley era. The insistence on 'public tranquillity' embodied in the Company's Regulations was to be manifested in the widespread use of the gallows and summary executions of minor princes and military leaders characterized as 'plunderers'. Devolved Mughal authority was used with exemplary vigour, and the Emperor himself was immobilized, becoming a static source of authority, rather than an active political agent.[48] Yet the question remains: from where did the British derive these muscular notions of law and sovereignty? One thing is clear: they were not particularly oriental. Indian rulers were, of course, arbitrary and brutal at times, but their justice remained personal, discretionary and specialized. Rebellion and recusancy in regard to the payment of revenues were part of the style of Indian political bargaining and were not generally met with extirpation or forfeit-ure of a family's underlying proprietary rights. It is difficult to avoid the conclusion that aspects of metropolitan political culture were important here. No challenge to the Crown in Parliament or to its surrogate, the Company, could be tolerated. Sovereignty could not be shared and royal rights such as those of the future 'native states' or landed proprietors could only subsist *after* the paramountcy (as it came to be called later) of the Crown in Parliament and the supremacy of the law had been established. The hierarchy of authority was to be clear and unilinear. When, for instance, the Nawab of Arcot, who was a subordinate ally of the Company, tried to make direct contact with the British Crown in 1773, he was brusquely rebuffed by the Company. However, to the British more than other Europeans, the clearest guarantee of 'public tranquillity' and political subordination was the easy collection of taxes and excise. In India the district collector (the persistence of this title to 1947 is significant), operat-ing an almost unlimited despotism in matters of taxation, was the local embodiment of the state. In practice, Cornwallis's separation of judicial and revenue power did little to impede the exercise of this despotism. At best, the British authorities wished the Indian nobility to 'acquire power by submission', as de Tocqueville might have observed. The office of district collector, in fact, reflected the merging together of two domestic traditions: the traditions of the permanent resident magistrate or Justice of the Peace ruling as a moral examplar and the powerful excise officer, highlighted by John Brewer.

In the last quarter of the eighteenth century, therefore, the East India Company's personnel already widely subscribed to an absolute notion of the rights of their state and of the 'rule of law'. This gave legitimacy to a flexible military and fiscal organization which displayed a remarkable capacity for territorial expansion. A new infantry army based on peasant recruits had been raised after Clive's victory at Plassey (1757). This army was supported by a more rigorously and regularly levied revenue, which a specialist body of collectors of revenue and customs attempted to administer uniformly, reducing a whole range of Mughal taxes, tributes and exemptions to more unified rates.

Much of this is reminiscent of John Brewer's picture of the British state as it had emerged a century before. However, there were three important differences. First, the East India Company embodied not only the 'British model', but also what might be called the 'Prussian model' of military-fiscalism: that is to say, through the system of subsidiary alliances, the Company also taxed the lands of its protected allies.[49] After 1763 the Company forced defeated enemies or cowed allies to support garrisons of its own troops on their territories. The pressures of these demands for military subsidy drove Indian states to resistance, but, ironically, also drew the Company into further territorial expansion and, ultimately, into spiralling indebtedness. Secondly, unlike the domestic state, the Company's Indian state remained highly venal until the end of the eighteenth century. Company officials, private traders and Indian financiers farmed Company revenues and lent it cash. The private interests of these groups and their desire for more revenue or access to new areas of trade also helped to propel the Company on its rise to power. Finally, as the next section will show, the financial networks that supported the Company also drew it into the world of Indian commerce and embroiled it in the internal conflicts of Indian society.

So was the English East India Company an oriental state writ large or the surrogate of western capitalist imperialism? At core, notions of transcendent law and the sophistication and rigour of its accountancy and its professional specialism certainly mark out the Company Raj as a version of the British state (as duly reassessed by Brewer); but this core was hedged around with institutions and ideologies of a different stamp. The Company operated systems of venality and predatory military taxation reminiscent of some of Great Britain's continental rivals. In the vast periphery of the Company's military and fiscal operations, its personnel did, indeed, assume the form of the Indian state, attracting the type of conflict and resistance that other Indian states encountered.

RESISTANCE TO THE STATE'S FISCAL ONSLAUGHT IN EIGHTEENTH-CENTURY INDIA

Indians resisted the growing power of the East India Company's tax-gatherers, its pretensions to regulate Indian kingship and also its commercial policies. In turn, this resistance limited and shaped the Company's 'state'. There were important respects in which the demands put on indigenous polities and populations were of a different order to their previous experience of political tribulation: to this extent we can talk about the origins of 'anti-colonial' or 'anti-British' resistance in the later eighteenth century. However, the Company was in other respects adapting the personnel, methods and strategies of indigenous polities during its rise to power. So there are ways in which this 'anti-colonial' resistance was a continuation of indigenous practices of opposition, evasion and bargaining with superior power and the disruptive forces of the 'world outside'.

What, then, was the nature of indigenous social and political conflicts into which the Company thrust itself after 1750? Three types of conflict stand out. First, there were the clashes resulting from the decline of the central authority of the Mughal Empire;[50] secondly, the consequences of the formation of states in the periphery; and finally, the heavy pressures resulting from the demand for cash-revenue and the attempt by rulers and commercial elites to control trade and production. All these pressures and the resistance provoked were independent of and prior to the rise of the East India Company; but all of them were quickly and inextricably enmeshed with the workings of the colonial state in its peripheries.

The so-called 'decline of the Mughal Empire' had seen a large part of the Indo-Muslim elite which had served the emperors move their base of operations from Delhi into the richer provinces. Here aspiring dynasts tried to establish regional kingdoms. Most of these state-builders continued to acknowledge the authority of the Emperor in Delhi, but they also established a closer hold on local resources and gradually diverted the profits of the land-revenue and trade into their own hands and that of their supporters. In the former imperial provinces of Bengal, Hyderabad and Awadh, the post-Mughal elites of soldiers and farmers of revenue repeatedly found themselves in conflict with the local (usually Hindu) landholders and warrior chieftains. Such notables (called *zamindars* throughout much of the north) often held general lordship rights over villages and their produce. Some of them also held more specific rights over markets, rivers, ponds and tanks within the villages, and were social leaders in their localities.

In many parts of India these rural notables and the communities they commanded put up stiff resistance to the incoming dynasts, who appeared to be intent on taking a closer hold on regional resources than Mughal governors had done before them. The most prolonged conflicts were generally in marginal areas where settled agriculture merged with the lands of nomadic 'tribal' people who kept cattle, the domains of forest-dwellers or areas of distinct culture and religion which the Mughals had kept on only a light rein. In the great northern state of Awadh, for instance, the new regional rulers at Lucknow waged long wars in the 1720s and 1730s against the Rajput Hindu chieftains and their clan levies. The founder of the regime (Burhan-ul Mulk), given the choice between collecting the revenue according to the 'coward's rent roll' or the 'real man's rent roll', engaged in countless marches and counter-marches against his over-mighty subjects, some of which are recounted in the family histories of the Rajputs.[51] As the British intervened in the politics of Awadh, their forces also became engaged with the Rajputs; the rebellions their revenue-collectors faced in southern Awadh in 1781,[52] and again in the Rebellion of 1857[53] were a continuation of the troubles of the Awadh regime.

Another example of the continuity of resistances can be found in Hyderabad. This large, sparsely populated tract of central Indian plateau was in the process of being transformed from a Mughal frontier-province into a kingdom by the family of a central Asian military leader who had once fought for the Mughal emperors. The Hyderabad rulers fought innumerable campaigns against the Telugu-speaking chieftains who controlled the land, allying first with one, then with another of these petty chieftains.[54] Villagers resisted the imposition of new demands by flight; the warrior leaders withdrew into the hills or jungles, emerging only to harrass the settled and destroy the deep-wells and irrigation systems from which the would-be dynasts of Hyderabad drew their resources. The resistance of local communities to the demands of the 'Turks' (Muslims) and other, local, enemies was lauded in numerous ballads recounting the forays and raids and valour of their chieftains. In some parts of the region, for instance, the warrior-god Khandoba appears to have been merged in the popular mind with the exploits of local rulers who protected them against the depredations of the Bhil tribal rajas. After 1802 when the British presence in Hyderabad was guaranteed by binding treaties, successive Residents used British troops to strengthen the Hyderabad state in its continued attempts to crush these rebellions in the periphery.

One of the most successful creations of all the eighteenth-century empire-builders was the Mysore state constructed by Haidar Ali and his son Tipu Sultan. The British saw Tipu as their most fearsome enemy and his destruction at the fall of Seringapatam in 1799 was to be celebrated in numerous pictures and books which attested to the new commercial demand for representations of the glories of colonial warfare. Mysore was itself a centralizing state.[55] It sought to conquer the Hindu Nayar communities on the west coast and the pepper-trade they controlled. Mysore also thrust westward into the forested 'tribal' zone of the Coorgis, whose loose raj-like political structure and inaccessible terrain formed a dangerous frontier for the sultanate. Haidar and Tipu both fought regular campaigns against the Coorgis, meeting their fierce resistance with the sack of population centres and the burning or clearing of forests in which the Coorgis took refuge. Several hundred thousand Coorgis, including members of their royal families, were seized and resettled in Mysore, while Muslim Sayyid soldier-colonists were settled in Coorg in their place.[56] The wars of the tribal people against Haidar and Tipu were glorified in their oral traditions and ballads. The burial spots of famous leaders who fell in the wars became reservoirs of sacred power and the 'coming of the Sultans' marked an abrupt caesura in the historical memory of the Coorgis[57] which was not effaced by later conflicts and accommodations with the British.

These wars of succession and conquest in eighteenth-century India were not simply, or even mainly, political struggles. The wars between rival successor states to the Mughals and the determination of the new power-centres to exact revenue from the peoples under their control or to gain control of artisan production were themselves consequences of the fragility of the economic resources on which these rulers based themselves. The cost of warfare was rising in a society which had long been used to transactions in cash.[58] However, cash revenues were volatile when trade-routes were abruptly redirected by political conflict and peasant farmers migrated to areas whose magnates offered them lower rates of rent and revenue. Empire-building was influenced by economic considerations long before the East India Company appeared on the scene, and India's economy was already linked by bullion imports to the wider world economy in which Europeans were now playing a growing part.

However, Indian states – even Tipu's Mysore – were not generally monolithic or hard-edged enough to forge either the tactical unity or the consciousness of opposition which might sustain such resistances over a long period or create persistent bonds between them. André Wink has argued that all pre-colonial states in India were created and sustained by revolt (*fitna* or *fitva*); they were shifting alliances of competing factions rather than structured administrative organizations.[59] For instance, the armed resistance of the western Indian Marathas to the Mughal Empire began as a social movement and incorporated elements of peasant rebellion; but the Maratha movement remained highly ambivalent, and its leaders aimed to associate themselves with aspects of Mughal legitimacy and siphon off imperial resources. Even in the 1740s and 1750s when Maratha power was at its height their aim was not, in any simple sense, to create a Maratha empire or to destroy the Mughal outsider, so much as to 'protect the domain of the Emperors of Delhi' against enemies from Afghanistan or central Asia.[60] Resistance could never become a unified form of social action or construct a coherent ideology when the nature of the state was so friable, sovereignty so extensively divisible and the market so labile.

War and resistance was therefore a tactic to secure a new symbiosis between ruler and ruled, between merchant and artisan. Figures of power from among the 'oppressors' became figures of power in the pantheon of the oppressed. Tactical alliances shifted and the local leaders, who had previously resisted fiercely, sought legitimation and incorporation from their erstwhile enemies. The method both of conquest and of resistance was the raid. Raiding and counter-raiding of villages took place until one or other of the parties was forced to an accommodation by the onset of the monsoon. The regional state would come to terms with a local magnate who would take a 'farm' of the revenue or tribute from the village population, and the contending armies would then march off for a season or two. Constant petty clashes ensued between the revenue farmer and villagers. Village leaders were in a strong position in the eighteenth century as they could control seed, credit and cattle and could often decamp with their whole following since labour was generally in short supply.

For the lieutenants of the regional states, the best method of dissipating resistance was not to extirpate but to try to recentre trade and agricultural production around fortified grain-markets which they themselves controlled. Such strong-points might develop into small towns. Nomads and migrant peasants might settle around them and become incorporated into the 'greater society' through brahminical temples or the missionary activities of Islamic Sufi teachers. However, these were changes which occurred only in the very long term. At times during the ebb and flow of state-building and resistance the local political power of the villagers, herders or tribals would reassert itself. The Indian state was never sure of a quick victory until it was cross-bred with the British fiscal-military state.

THE EMERGENCE OF RESISTANCE TO BRITISH DOMINION

Before 1765 the East India Company operated mainly as a powerful player in this great game of the end of the Mughal Empire. In its commercial capacity it was concerned to purchase cloth at the lowest possible price. It encountered resistance, therefore, from regional rulers, notably in Bengal and the south, and also from merchants and weavers seeking to impede European monopoly power. At this period, the Company's onslaughts were often made through proxies and the reactions to them were inchoate. During the first four decades of the century Mughal governors were often troubled by the audacity of the 'hatmen' (a reference to the distinctive headgear worn by the Europeans), but internal enemies were more important. Historians such as Khafi Khan and Ali Muhammad Khan denounced the pestiferousness of the 'farangs' (Franks).[61] Other chroniclers identified Europeans not so much as a political threat but as peoples remarkable for their easy resort to violence and their filthy personal habits. For the Muslim chroniclers, it was the 'Brahmins' (Marathas) who were the enemy (also,

of course, potential ally), at once wily and plebeian. For the Marathas, the
Muslims or 'Turks' were enemies of the 'Brahmin state', but also potential
founts of legitimacy; the British were scarcely noted until they had seized
power at Surat in 1759. Consequently, Indian powers hired European
military advisers, becoming dependent on European military technology
and trade with little thought for the future.

In south India the British did much of their early fighting through the
agency of the Muslim Nawab of Arcot, whom they had supported against
a French-backed rival in the 1750s. The Nawab certainly encountered fierce
resistance in his attempts to create a Mughal-type successor state in the
south; a jibe that was thrown at him was that he was a creature of the
British. One regional commander, Khan Sahib, a Hindu convert who drew
on levies from among military tribal people of the dry, inland territories
(people of Maravar and Kallar 'tribe'), denounced the Nawab as unclean
and a bad Muslim[62] for his consorting with the British. Khan Sahib was
hanged in 1764, and later passed into the ranks of the warrior-martyrs
who populated the local sacred landscape; but it was as an embodiment of
charismatic spiritual power, rather than as a victim of the British Empire,
that he was lauded in the 'Ballad of Khan Sahib'.

We have seen that in their dealings with Siraj-ud Daulah, ruler of Bengal,
the British were ultimately to insist that they embodied the absolute sovereignty of the Mughal; but Siraj's own 'resistance' appears to have been
unplanned. He was concerned to regain control over dangerous factions
in his realm, of which the English East India Company was only one. He
tried to keep the doors of negotiation open until the last possible moment,
and it is not clear that he was planning an exclusive alliance with the
French, as Clive feared. The myth of the implacable tyrant of the Black
Hole was given currency by the Company's personnel (notably the Governor, J. Z. Holwell) to justify their own enormous financial gains from the
'Bengal revolution'.[63] Siraj's successor, Mir Kasim (1760–4), was, perhaps,
more clearly aware of the ineluctable nature of the Company's advance.
He tried to build a new, more compact state in west Bengal and to exclude
from it private merchants and the private trade of the Company's officials.
It was Mir Kasim's acts of defiance in the face of the inroads of such trade
that led to the second Anglo-Bengal war and the beginning of direct British
territorial empire there in 1765.[64]

Up to 1765, then, the Company's dealings with the Indian states seemed
on the surface very much like those of any other state. It preserved some
features of the Mughal diplomatic system and often worked through Indian
surrogates. Equally, Indian 'resistance' was unformed; rulers tried to
entangle the Company's officials in their networks of power and honorific
exchange rather than to expel or destroy them. However, it becomes more
difficult to argue that the Company was simply 'another' Indian state in
regard to the period after 1765. Between 1765 and 1793 the land-revenue

settlement of British India was imposed, putting new burdens on landlord and peasant. At the same time the pressure of the subsidiary alliance system on the Company's allies precipitated a series of crises in the periphery of empire, modifying the form of Indian resistance. Finally, after 1793, the political language of the Company servants and of the British government began to take on an even more absolutist tone.

THE PRESSURES FOR REVENUE AND 'CONSTRUCTIVE IMPERIALISM'

After 1765 Indian resistance to the British became more general and more self-conscious as the Company's state itself changed form. It is true that British officials remained dependent on their Indian subordinates and often lacked the power, will and information to break with the existing methods of taxation. There was, nevertheless, a drift towards greater rigour. Historians are much divided on the question of how much the British revenue in Bengal after 1772 was in excess of that exacted by the last Nawab. When inflation and the disastrous loss of population during the great famine of 1769–70 is taken into account the answer is that the increase was probably significant but not massive.[65] Yet British methods of collection were stricter, embodying a notion of precise accountancy and meeting targets which was alien to the Indian system.[66] The Company had a growing and well-disciplined army of peasant soldiers to enforce its will, even in the fringes. While Mughal rulers had given significant amounts of aid to landlords and peasant farmers in cases where the seasons had been bad or where crops had been affected by war, the Company's Boards of Revenue discouraged officers from granting such aid. They also tried to reduce the enormous 'seepage' of resources back into the localities under the guise of costs of collection. This had been a regular feature of Mughal revenue administration, and it may have accounted for more than one-third of the sums apparently collected.[67] For reasons of financial security, the British also tried to weld together proprietors' rights (*zamindari*) and the right to collect revenue on the part of government and take a percentage (*mulguzari*). Failure to pay revenue therefore led to the forced sale of underlying proprietary rights for debt. The result was that large-scale auction sales of *zamindari* land took place, especially after Lord Cornwallis's Permanent Settlement of the Bengal land revenues in 1793. This settlement was made at a much higher level than many landholders could bear, at least initially.

It was less the financial squeeze itself than the political implications of an offensive against the rights of landholders and peasant leaders, signalled by the new revenue settlements, that explains the intensity of simultaneous peasant risings in Bengal in the later 1770s and the 1780s. Peasant leaders (*mandals*) in Birbhum, Rangpur and Dinajpur districts fought a fierce land-war against Company revenue agents between 1779 and 1781.[68] Large-scale resistance from tribal groups, which had hitherto avoided regular revenue payments, broke out during the same period on the fringes of Bengal and Bihar. These communities were variously identified by the British as Santals, Chuars, Pykes and Ghatwals. The ancestors of these people had fought Mughal governors in earlier days, but not at the same time, and they were not threatened with a comparable loss of autonomy.

It was not only peasant leaders, weavers and chieftains on the fringes of the old Bengal province who felt the pressure of the Company's intervention. In the later 1770s and early 1780s the external mechanism of accumulation represented in the subsidiary alliance system also went into higher gear. This was the period when the Company's Residents at Lucknow (notably Nathaniel Middleton) exerted themselves in trying to squeeze resources from the Nawab of Awadh, who was already paying a large percentage of his total revenue takings to the Company in rigidly fixed instalments. The Nawab of Arcot and the Nizam of Hyderabad in the south were also under pressure to cede valuable territories to the Company in lieu of 'balances' supposedly incurred under the terms of their own alliances. Private peculation also flourished. For instance, Sir Thomas Rumbold, one of the most famous of the 'Nabobs', was busy extracting presents from the landholders of the northern Circars (provinces) of the Madras Presidency, adding substantially to his private fortune. Such fortunes were regularly remitted to Britain through Canton and the Portuguese territory of Macao.[69]

The critical and novel feature of the Company's fiscal organization was its internal integration and its direct links to commercial power outside India. Administrative accountancy was now directly determined by patterns of European international trade and inter-continental warfare. Viewed from the Accountant General's office in Calcutta, commercial operations, military subsidies and revenue operations were all one. The Company had to pay its troops and also purchase the annual investment in Indian cloth for the home market.[70] Profitable sales alone would allow the Company to pay the annual dividend fixed by Parliament and so keep the prying eyes of ministers out of its increasingly embarrassed affairs.[71] The complex of official Company activities fronted a machine of private venality, with which it was deeply entangled.

The resistance of Indian rulers, landholders, weavers[72] and peasants became more intense in equal measure to the Company's demands. As European and American warfare was followed by renewed conflict in India, the attempts of Warren Hastings to protect and enhance his sources of revenue and tribute became more aggressive. The passive resistance of Tanjore farmers against the agents of the Nawab of Arcot and the Company (1776)[73] was followed by the revolt of the Raja of Benares and many of the landholders of southern Awadh.[74] In 1781 and 1782 at the height of the American War the Indian empire also seemed to be slipping to the edge of destruction. The Company was fighting the Marathas, Hyder and Tipu; it faced revolts in its northern territories and the loyalty of its great central Indian ally, the Nizam of Hyderabad, was dubious. The alliances between these rulers were tenuous, riven by old enmities and differences of interest at the local level. However, it was more than flaws in Hastings's diplomacy or the machinations of Company servants on the spot that had brought about this concatenation of dissidence. The logic of the revenue and subsidiary alliances systems with their rigid internal accounting, lack of responsiveness to local agrarian circumstances and complex links to the international economy, was causing deep stresses within the Indian polity. The British military-fiscal state which had emerged a hundred years earlier was now firmly entrenched in the subcontinent.

In the short run, the Company's seemingly limitless expansion was held in check by the triumph of the Pittite Whigs and the pressure for 'economical reform'. Cornwallis, who was sent to India in 1787 by the Younger Pitt and his Indian expert, Henry Dundas, made strenuous efforts to eliminate internal venality through his Permanent Settlement of the Bengal revenues (1793) and the creation of a salaried and disciplined cadre of district officers. Cornwallis's external adventures were restricted to a preemptive war against Mysore, but elsewhere, and especially in Awadh, he tried to curb the Company's tributary demands and the activities of private traders, both of which had intensified Indian resistance and the turbulence of the British-Indian frontier. However, circumstances had not modified the ingrained contempt for what Cornwallis himself regarded as the depraved principles of 'Asiatick government', and the financial requirements of the indebted Company were only temporarily satisfied. The French Revolutionary and Napoleonic wars were to set the fiscal juggernaut moving again, but this time its forward roll was justified by reference to a heightened sense of national mission and a new emphasis on the legitimacy of British authority in India.

CONSTRUCTIVE IMPERIALISM AND THE END TO THE INDIAN POLITY 1798–1818

Lord Cornwallis's lieutenants sought to infuse a new dignity into the Indian empire. Precedents of Roman civic virtue were emphasized and the painter, Robert Home, depicted the Governor-General receiving the hostage sons of Tipu Sultan of Mysore in an act of classical 'benevolence'.[75] It was Richard Wellesley, Lord Mornington, who imparted an uncompromisingly regal status to the office of Governor-General. He viewed Indian rulers in the same light as the 'territorial aristocracy' of Great Britain and Ireland and himself as a direct representative of the king and as embodiment (rather than agent) of Mughal sovereignty.[76] To further his battles with the

'Cheesemongers of Leadenhall Street' (the Directors of the East India Company), Wellesley created his own private office and a series of family circles of protégés in the military, civil and political services which were entirely dependent on him. He introduced new ceremonial and etiquette to the Governor-General's round and built a Palladian mansion with which to emphasize his new status.

A variety of themes justifying British power in India were voiced by Wellesley and his circle. The danger to the 'British nation' from French imperialism, both republican and Catholic, was invoked to justify a forward policy. The argument of the 'French threat' was used to some effect: it was employed to discipline recalcitrant newspaper editors in Calcutta and silence the free press. Now Parliament was also susceptible to appeals to the French danger and loathe to question the forward march of British arms. Pitt and Dundas themselves were complacent about additional conquests, the one viewing them as useful bargaining-counters at any later peace negotiations, the other glimpsing a long-term commercial advantage.[77] Advocates of the new consensus for imperial expansion in India stressed the virtues of loyalty to the Crown and of British racial separateness. Eurasians and Portuguese-Indian Catholics were regarded with suspicion; young British officials were to be trained in a new Fort William College, removed from hazards of continual contact with the 'depravity' of the people of India.

Sir Arthur Wellesley, the Governor-General's brother, could be heard arguing that British conquests were justified by the Laws of War and conquest which went back to the times of the 'ancients'. British India became a society infused with military values. Of course, there had always been conquistadores and freebooters at large, notably during Clive's conquest of Bengal, but such men had been fleet-footed commercial entrepreneurs as well, suspicious of authority and used to insisting on the rights of 'freeborn Englishmen' to justify their private interests. By 1800 the markers between merchants and patrician military class were now more firmly drawn, a change reflected in the abolition of the old titles of Merchant, Factor and Writer. As the military strength of the Company's armies swelled from about 90,000 to nearly 230,000 during the period 1793–1820, military officers occupied a larger percentage of posts as Resident to Indian courts.[78] In some ways the British imperial elite became more like the French; but there remained an important difference. Even Arthur Wellesley remarked on the importance of civilian supremacy. It was true that 'outside Bengal' the Company's authority had a 'predominantly military character', but it was a civilian despotism which the Company wished to create.[79] The rigorous use of military power against Indian rebels was always carried out in defence of the civil power and the supremacy of law.

At the same time Company officials appealed, with apparent inconsistency, to Mughal supremacy and the 'ancient Hindoo constitution' when enforcing political settlements to their own advantage. Mughal sovereignty had long been construed as a once-and-for-all grant to the British; it was no longer negotiable, fluid and constructive. Now the Company refused to accept bilateral relations betwen nawabs and other rulers who acknowledged this supremacy. They also restricted the Mughal ruler's access to Calcutta and intervened in matters of succession in Delhi.[80] The old practices of bargaining and of tempting one's enemies to alliance within the complicated hierarchies of Indian kingship were now to be regarded as 'treason' and grounds for deposition. This was the case of Umdat-ul Umara, Nawab of Arcot, who was accused of treasonable correspondence with Tipu Sultan.

The harder edge of British empire-building after 1798 was in part a reflection of commercial and financial pressures. The Company's debt soared upwards even as Wellesley tried to stabilize it, drawing more states into lucrative subsidiary alliances. The Indian and European wars also encouraged both the Company and private entrepreneurs to attempt to gain direct control of supplies of tropical produce and manufactures. The wars in the south, for instance, were in part struggles over control of the pepper-trade; but these were also conflicts about power and authority. The experience of international war with French republicanism, alongside the changing temper of Indian resistance, laid bare the absolutist concept of sovereignty that had always been implicit in British thinking and institutions.

Wellesley's assumption that Indian, like English, notions of sovereignty were absolute, and that lesser rulers were not sharers in sovereignty, but a kind of territorial aristocracy, was put to the test in the case of the Marathas, still regarded as a dangerous constellation of powers in western India. The Governor-General tempted the Peshwa Baji Rao II into a subsidiary alliance at Bassein in 1802. The Peshwa was indeed a sovereign, but he was not the only one, and certainly not the embodiment of Maratha kingship (the Raja of Satara, descendent of the Marathas' founding leader, Shivaji, approximated much more closely to this position). The Peshwa was, instead, descendant of the hereditary 'mayor of the Palace' of the leading Maratha royal family whose own dynasty had taken on a kingly status. Nevertheless, Wellesley regarded the Peshwa as 'head of the Maratha Confederacy', expecting him to draw the other chiefs into alliance, since he thought that they 'held places like that of himself and his fellow hereditary peers in the British Constitution'.[81] Rather than this stabilizing the politics of western India, profound misunderstandings of their status as sharers in sovereignty pushed the other Maratha rulers into a fatal war of resistance to the Company (1802–4).

Tipu Sultan, however, represented the clearest example of an Indian ruler who had forged new political and military weapons with which to fight off the Company's threat. Sir Thomas Munro remarked that Tipu's state was 'the most perfect despotism in the world'; the fact that 'almost every employment of trust or consequence being conferred on men raised from obscurity, gives to the government a vigour unexampled in India'.[82] It is true that Tipu had dispensed with the service of his flaccid Mughal-style army and nobility and had tried to build up new fighting force based on mercenary soldiers who owed him devoted loyalty.[83] Tipu had also tried to galvanize his revenue-collecting machinery, eliminating intermediary magnates in an effort to deal directly with the peasantry who controlled the villages. Yet Tipu was ultimately unsuccessful in building a despotism on the shifting sands of the Indian corporate state. Even his status as an Islamic zealot, much advertised by the British and his Muslim enemies, is somewhat overdrawn. He was careful, for instance, to show respect to and patronize the religious places of Hindus and Christians who were not his enemies. While he denounced the 'swine-eating infidel' to the Ottoman Sultan in an attempt to build a Muslim alliance,[84] he became a Citoyen of France and sought a marriage compact with one of the Hindu Rajput kings of Gujarat.

What made the British fear Tipu was not so much his 'perfect despotism' or his Muslim zealotry, but the fact that he was fighting, like the Company, with the weapons of trade, monopoly and boycott. He also refused to be drawn into the gossamer network of subsidiary alliances and military dependency that had eroded the complex polities of his Indian peers. Rightly judging his enemy's insistence on its superordinate sovereignty or its status as proxy of Mughal sovereignty to be a deadly threat, he declared himself emperor in his own right (*padishah*) and tacitly repudiated Mughal overlordship.[85] The resistance of Tipu was thus precisely calculated. It had the object of countering the two critical and novel features that we have attributed to the Company: the fiscal engine of the 'subsidiary alliance' and British claims to absolute sovereignty, whether in the name of Tamberlane's Mughal descendants or that of the Crown of King Edward.

DEBELLARE SUPERBOS . . .

The opposition of Mysore and the Marathas reached a crushing end when their main forces were defeated in battle between 1799 and 1818. The effort of conquest was costly. It greatly increased the East India debt and embarrassingly conjured up the hostile scrutiny of Parliament. As critical for the British, though less fully covered in the literature, was the suppression of local kingdoms and sovereignties. Some of these had never been firmly subjugated by the post-Mughal states because they lay on the fringes of the arable, in jungle or hill-land. Others represented complex parcels of shared sovereignty where rulers could count on the support of extended kin-groups or armies of rural 'citizen levies'. Whatever their status, Wellesley was determined to assert the Company's (at times, the

Mughals') status as transcendent sovereign: 'A more active and vigorous control is necessary, as well over the corruptions of our own servants . . . as over the refractory spirit of the native princes and landowners'.[86] Here at last, the mailed fist of the modern western state had worn through the velvet glove of oriental bargaining and sovereignty-sharing.

Two important episodes of resistance illustrate these themes: the 'rebellion' of Kattaboma Naik in the Tirunelvelli District of Madras (1798–9) and of the Palassi (Pychee) Raja in Wynad on the west coast (1793–1806). Kattaboma was typical of the Poligar rulers of the dry southern tip of eastern India. Descendants of former Telugu settlers in this Tamil-speaking area, these local chieftains claimed a 'share' in the former sovereignty of the Vijayanagara overlords of south India who had flourished in the fifteenth century.[87] Their assumption of the trappings of kingship, however, was relatively recent, expressed through the patronage of the south's great temples and numerous local festivals; but to the official mind of the Madras Presidency, suffused with the new intransigence exemplified by Wellesley, Poligars such as Kattaboma were no more than 'auxiliary chieftains'. In an elaborate historical fiction, which strengthened previous Mughal claims, the chieftains were said to have 'rented villages' and derived 'police powers' from the Nawab of Arcot. The British considered themselves to rank above the Nawab, since they themselves had secured recognition of his authority from the Mughal Emperor in 1763. Consequently, the British deemed themselves overlords of these small kingdoms. This fiction legitimated the military campaign against Kattaboma mounted by Stephen Lushington, Collector of the Poligar Peshcush (that is, tribute). Kattaboma's lands were not particularly fertile, the trade he controlled a mere trickle. Though the Dutch allies of the French had put out some feelers to the southern chieftains, the strategic importance of the area was minimal. It is difficult to avoid the impression that Lushington and his military aids forced a confrontation with the Poligar in order to challenge his authority. When a British officer was killed in a mêlée, they had all the cause they needed to uproot his authority utterly in the interests of the newly invigorated imperial principle.

Kattaboma's fort-palace was stormed after a long siege and several thousand of his supporters were put to the sword.[88] Kattaboma and his younger brother, who was credited with supernatural powers by the local population, were publicly hanged. The public execution of a ruler, even a petty ruler, was new to Indian judicial practice. It announced the supremacy of English law and criminal justice. Soon after, the Arcot state was abruptly swept away, following the discovery of 'treasonable' letters in Tipu's palace and the refusal of a junior member of its royal house to accept the terms for accession to the throne which the British offered. British authority was now displayed as absolute and unchallengeable. Lushington was to write, with Livian sonority, that

By the energy and justice of Government, the rebellions have been subdued; the oppressed have been upheld and exalted; the obedient have been liberally rewarded; and the extinction of divided authority [between the British and the Nawab] has restored the fairest province of the Carnatic from an acknowledged state of anarchy to a state of subordination and prosperity.[89]

The social context of the second revolt considered here, that of the Palassi Raja, was more complex. The eighteenth-century wars of trade on the Malabar Coast had increased tension between different communities. Coorg tribals had fought on the British side because of their treatment at the hands of Mysore. Nayar Hindus on the coast had hit back at Muslim Mappila (Moplah) merchants, who had been favoured by the Muslim Mysore rulers when British supremacy was established after 1792. The British, for their part, tended to favour the Nayars, eliminating many of the subordinate land-tenures on which the Muslims subsisted; but they also recognized that the Mappilas were 'a useful merchant community', for at this time British policy on the west coast was powerfully influenced by the interests of Bombay pepper-traders.[90] Company policy toward the rajas and indigenous rights in general was often contradictory and riven with doubt. But faced with clashes between what they took to be 'two irreconcilable races of people', and the ever-present likelihood of war with nearby Mysore, their military and political response became firmer. The Company's Public Regulations, a virtual Code Napoléon for some officers, treated local kings as hereditary landowners. The Regulations effectively stripped them of their judicial authority, especially in matters of capital punishment, at the very time when demands for revenue were enhanced. Revolts broke out all over Malabar as kings and the powerful matri-local lineage groups (*tharavads*) rallied against the outsiders.

This combination of concerns fiscal and royal lay behind the resistance of Kerala Varma, the Palassi Raja of Kottayam, and his ultimate destruction by the British. The Company had passed over Kerala Varma's claim as 'renter' of a certain territory for that of his more malleable uncle, the Kurumbranad Raja. Tension with the Company rapidly escalated when the Palassi Raja tried to demolish a mosque belonging to the Mappila Muslims 'according to custom' which attached to his royal power.[91] Later, the Company infuriated the Raja by publicly flogging his servants 'in front of his face'.[92] The ultimate cause of war was the Raja's particularly cruel execution (by impalement) of some Mappila bandits who had pillaged the house of a Hindu Chetti. This merchant was a member of a community with which the Raja was close, and which acted as intermediary in the pepper-trade. The Company ordered the seizure of the Raja on a charge of murder and declared implacable hostility to him and his supporters, publicly advertising the statement that 'Not a sepoy shall rest in this province, until you and your adherents are utterly extirpated'.[93]

The pepper war and the patronage of the merchant intermediaries, the Nayars and Mappilas, was obviously an important issue here. More central was the clash of authority. The Raja, even though he was no longer 'renter', still saw himself as a residual sharer in the ancient sovereignty of the Keralan king Pirumal Cherumal. As such, he was entitled to adjudge on the height and nature of religious buildings and to hand out the cruel punishments reserved to great kings. His servants were ambassadors to the British, not menials to be flogged at will. The Company, in contrast, saw itself as representative of the Mughal and also as surrogate of the British Crown by right of conquest. The Keralan kings were simply 'chieftains' or 'landlords'; they must submit unconditionally to the rule of law, and they and their servants were amenable to process in public courts.

There followed a long civil war during which the Raja and his followers escaped to the hill region of Wynad and levied a remarkably successful guerrilla war against the Company for eight years. Kerala Varma supported himself on contraband pepper sales while, in the hallowed local tradition, he destroyed the Company's own crop with fire. This was a popular revolt, though one still mediated by ideas of corporate kingship. A large part of the rural population appear to have supported him, entertaining for him 'a regard and respect bordering on veneration'.[94] Proclamations ordering people to impede the foreigner were issued on behalf of the ancient deities of Wynad; but this local patriotism was considerably strengthened by the firm adherence to the Raja's cause of two groups. Hill-men and tribal peoples such as the Kurumba and Kurichiyar formed the heart of resistance to the probing British scout columns. These people saw a novel threat from the outside to their ancient status as lords of the forest; not unnaturally, they were labouring under the impression that 'it was the intention of our Government to extirpate the whole race'.[95] The strong cultural bond, which exists over much of India, between Hindu king and tribal people was reconstituted in this alliance of resistance. A second key group in Kerala Varma's long resistance were the Chetti merchants who supported him with arms and money long after it was in their economic interest to do so. Undoubtedly, the Raja had been their loyal patron during the long pepper wars with Mysore and the British; but here again strong traditional links of ritual and service also bound the Chettis to the royal house. Resistance mirrored the Keralan ideal of the martial king and his dependents. Even when in 1806 the British marksmen closed in on Kerala Varma, the Raja shouted to the closing rifleman that he should not come any closer to him because this would pollute his royal body.[96]

OUTCOMES

Many of the petty rulers who resisted British expansion in the eighteenth and early-nineteenth centuries passed quickly into popular culture as semi-divine warrior heroes. Kattaboma's execution-place attracted veneration, and the trees around it were still festooned with offerings when the *Tinnevelly Gazeteer* was being written in 1909. The Palassi Raja was assimilated into Malayali folk-ballads, already well populated by Robin Hood-like figures who sustained the poor. Even the Muslim Khan Sahib, who had been chastiser of the warrior-people of the south, passed into their pantheon as a figure of divine force. Parts of his dismembered body became objects of cultic worship for their respective tribal subdivisions.[97] All this happened a century or more before the appearance of articulate anti-British nationalism in south India. These leaders had died in warfare which in timing and in cause, if not in method, might properly be seen by historians as anti-colonial. Yet one has to be careful in building these and similar figures into a coherent, or evolving, tradition of anti-colonial resistance. The most important aspect of their heroic status remained the fact that they had died a martyr's death against great odds. No doubt the foreign intrusion was resented, but it was of a lesser order of importance to the participants that they were 'anti-British' or 'anti-colonial'. When the *Kampani, Sahibs* or *Angrezi Sarkar* (Company, 'white masters' or 'English government') are mentioned, little seems to be made of the fact, except when stories have been reworked under the influence of later, nationalist traditions. Figures who died in battle with Indian powers, or even notorious 'social bandits', attract equal respect, even veneration. In Rajasthan the death-monument (*samadhi*) of the horse of the heroic Raja of Mewar who fought against the Mughals was honoured in this way.

The great figures of anti-British resistance have also been the object of popular veneration, but, here again, it has proved difficult to assimilate them wholeheartedly into a nationalist pedigree. Tipu Sultan was revered as a martyr very soon after his death. Various outbreaks of millenarian revolt were associated with his name, and Muslim preachers invoked his spirit at the time of an outbreak of mutiny at the military station of Vellore in 1806.[98] The myth of Tipu the 'Muslim fanatic' sedulously cultivated by the British had also taken root so that up to the present day there has been an argument between those who see him as a 'secular' (that is, confessionally dispassionate) ruler and the Hindu right which sees him as a Muslim 'communalist'. Even amongst Muslims Tipu is a controversial figure, being claimed by some as a kind of early Islamic fundamentalist, by others as a broad-church 'secularist'.

One reason why a clear tradition of resistance did not emerge from the colonial wars of the late-eighteenth and early-nineteenth centuries was that the policy of the Company itself was ambivalent. Its officials were quite ruthless in the imposition of the 'rule of law', the assertion of British paramountcy and the sanctity of regular payments of revenue. Yet once these imperatives had been acted on successfully, ideology and practical reason conspired to hold them back from further intervention. The British needed magnate intermediaries to collect the revenue and keep the peace, especially now that the Company's finances were irredeemably in debt. Again, their own political culture, and what they believed they saw in India, predisposed them to leave in place a neutered form of Indian kingship once Company paramountcy was firmly established. Out of this ambivalence the British fashioned their policy towards princely states and rural magnates. Any of the magnate compères of the Palassi Raja or Kattaboma who would co-operate and were financially strong enough to stand the pace were in due course reinvested with many of their privileges and local powers.[99] Lushington and his like, no less than Wellesley, wanted India to possess a dignified territorial aristocracy rather than a volatile hierarchy of kingship. As in de Tocqueville's formulation quoted by John Brewer, the Anglo-Indian as much as the English aristocracy must 'submit in order to rule'. The official mind of British India came to favour the disarmed descendants of the rajas and village magnates who had offered the strongest resistance to the Company in the eighteenth century. When for a brief period between 1830 and 1857 a more interventionist and anti-magnate policy was pursued, the result, officials claimed later, was the Rebellion of 1857.[100]

Indian resistance was in part 'anti-colonial' rather than a continuation of the eighteenth-century Indian wars of succession in that it was directed against a state that was, at core, an accountant's and lawyer's state. On the other hand, it is difficult to detect a tradition of insurrectionary consciousness, let alone a pattern of social organization, connecting the magnate and peasant resisters of the later eighteenth century with the agitations of townsmen and middling peasants which inaugurated the nationalist era after 1880. Resistance was not a thing in itself, standing outside history and society; it closely reflected the form and social interventions of the colonial state. Indian aristocracy and village leaders fought British impositions in the later eighteenth century because they were novel, harsh and intrusive. Yet many later came to terms with the British military-fiscal state in the east because that state's aims were limited. The emerging alliance of lord and peasant against the Company during the years 1780–1820 was fragmented and dissipated in the next generation. For the Company sought a 'rule of law', paramount sovereignty and regular revenue. Its pretensions to civilize, to centralize or to construct a cultural order were quite weak by comparison with its French or Iberian predecessors and contemporaries, or even its Mughal predecessors. In this respect, too, the British Indian state mirrored its metropolitan model. While Great Britain may have supported a strong fiscal-military state, that state had little desire to mould and fashion the bodies and minds of its subjects, or to make windows into their souls.

NOTES

1 See, e.g., Burton Stein, 'State Formation Reconsidered. I', *Modern Asian Studies*, 19/3 (1985); F. Perlin, 'State Formation Reconsidered. II', ibid; R. Frykenberg, *Guntur District, 1788–1848* (Oxford, 1965); this is also the implication of André Wink, *Land and Sovereignty in India: Agrarian Society and Politics under the Eighteenth-Century Maratha Swarajya* (Cambridge, 1986).

2 John Brewer, *The Sinews of Power: War, Money and the English State 1688–1783* (London, 1989).

3 R. Frykenberg, 'Company Circari in the Carnatic, c.1799–1859; The Inner Logic of Political Systems in India', in R. G. Fox (ed.), *Realm and Region in Traditional India* (Durham, NC, 1977).

4 D. Washbrook, 'Progress and Problems. South Asian History, c.1780–1850', *MAS*, 22/1 (1988); S. Subrahmanyam and C. A. Bayly, 'Portfolio capitalists and the Economy of Early Modern India', in S. Subrahmanyam (ed.), *Merchants, Markets and the State in Early Modern India* (Delhi, 1990), 242–65.

5 K. S. Singh, *Tribal Society in India* (New Delhi, 1985), 117.

6 R. Guha, *Subaltern Studies*, III (New Delhi, 1984), and other volumes in this series; also R. Guha, *Elementary Aspects of Peasant Insurgency in Colonial India* (New Delhi, 1983). The 'proto-nationalist' position is better worked out in studies of the rebellion of 1857; see, e.g., R. Mukherjee, *Awadh in Revolt 1857–8: A Study of Popular Resistance* (Delhi, 1984), and 'Satan Let Loose upon Earth. The Kanpur Massacres in India in the Revolt of 1857', *Past and Present*, 128 (1990).

7 Directors to Fort William, 1764, cited in P. J. Marshall, *Problems of Empire: Britain and India 1757–1813* (London, 1968), 63.

8 Cited in Ian Bruce Watson, *Foundations for Empire: English Private Trade in India, 1659–1760* (Delhi, 1980), 290.

9 Despatch Book 9 June 1686, vol. 91, pp. 142, 145, India Office Library and Records, London [hereafter, IOL], cited in K. N. Chaudhuri, *The Trading World of Asia and the English East India Company, 1660–1760* (Cambridge, 1978), 454; see also, J. Child, *A New Discourse of Trade* (London, 1665).

10 Cited by Watson, *Foundations*, 306.

11 ibid., 297.

12 H. H. Dodwell, *The Cambridge History of India*, V (Cambridge, 1929), 101–3.

13 ibid., 112–13; the original entry for the *firman* is found in the diary of John Surman's embassy, Home Misc. 69, ff. 130–1, IOL.

14 Lucy Sutherland, *The East India Company in Eighteenth Century Politics* (Oxford, 1962), 3–5.

15 Dodwell, *History*, 98–9.

16 Chaudhuri, *Trading World*, 29–39, but also *passim*.

17 Niels Steensgaard, *Carracks, Caravans and Companies: The Structural Crisis in the European Asian Trade in the Early 17th Century* (Copenhagen, 1972).

18 Sutherland, *East India Company*, 173–5; Marshall, *Problems of Empire*, 83–6.

19 *Sinews of Power*, 62–3.

20 Chaudhuri, *Trading World*, 129.

21 For an extended, if opaque, discussion of this issue, see Dodwell, *History*, 589–608.

22 Robert Clive to William Pitt, 7 January 1759, in Sir G. Forrest, *Life of Lord Clive* (2 vols; London, 1918), vol. II, 412–14.

23 Chaudhuri, *Trading World*, 112.

24 ibid., 121.

25 ibid., 112.

26 'The French in India', MSS vol. III, IOL, cited by Dodwell, *History*, 596.

27 Sir C. Fawcett, *The First Century of British Justice in India* (Oxford, 1934), xvi, 2, 6; for interventions in the proceedings of Indian caste councils, 155.

28 See, e.g., Bombay Rupee 1678, 'By authority of Charles II', British Museum, Department of Coins and Medals, OR 5198.

29 Dodwell, *History*, 591.

30 See Michael H. Fisher, 'Extraterritoriality: The Concept and Its Application in Princely India', *Indo-British Review*, 15/2 (1988).

31 Dodwell, *History*, 111–12.

32 Chaudhuri, *Trading World*, 112.

33 Clive to Government, 14 July 1757, in H. N. Sinha, *Fort William House Correspondence. Public*, II (Delhi, 1957), 226–8.

34 P. J. Marshall, *Cambridge History of India*, II, 2, *Bengal. The British Bridgehead* (Cambridge, 1988).

35 Barun De, *The Colonialist Premise in the British Occupation of Bengal: Contributions by Clive and Pitt the Elder during 1757–9* (Calcutta, 1978); see also Watson's attempt to resolve the paradox: he says the aim of the Company was 'not to grasp at Indian sovereignty as such, though this was the logical extension of the military administration established by the English in Bengal at this time', *Foundations*, 296.

36 Mark Wilks, *Historical Sketches of the South of India* (written in 1799; 3 vols, London, 1810–17; repr., 2 vols, Madras, 1930), vol. II, 185; for the wider debate see R. Guha, *A Rule of Property for Bengal* (The Hague, 1963); Marshall, *Bengal*, 118–28.

37 See B. Allen's entry for item no. 112 in C. A. Bayly (ed.), *The Raj: India and the British, 1600–1947* (London: National Portrait Gallery, 1990), 102–3.

38 For an early discussion of India attitudes to sovereignty, see F. W. Buckler, 'The Political Theory of the Indian Mutiny of 1857', *Transactions of the Royal Historical Society*, fourth series, 5 (1922); also Wink, *Land and Sovereignty*.

39 B. R. Grover, 'Nature of Land Rights in Mughal India', *Indian Economic and Social History Review*, 1/i (1963).

40 E. T. Stokes, 'Agrarian Relations in North and Central India', in D. Kumar (ed.), *Cambridge Economic History of India*, vol. II (London, 1983), 41–3.

41 Hastings's minute to Bengal Select Committee, 12 October 1772, cited in Dodwell, *History*, 597.

42 C. C. Davies (ed.), 'The Benares Diary of Warren Hastings', *The Camden Miscellany*, 18 (London, 1948); see also his *Warren Hastings and Oudh* (Oxford, 1939).

43 [Directors of the East India Company], *Copies of Papers Relative to the Restoration of the Raja of Tanjour* (2 vols; London, 1787); for British intervention in the succession of supposedly subordinate princes, see Home Misc. Series, vol. 605, 121–5, 'Amir Singh', and vol. 605/11, 618–20, 'Tanjore', IOL.

44 A. H. Anquetil Duperron, *Recherches historiques et géographiques sur l'Inde par Anquetil Duperron*, ed. J. Bernouilli (Paris, 1886), 145.

45 ibid.

46 ibid., 10, cf. 256; cf. A. H. Anquetil Duperron, *Dissertation sur la propriété individuelle et foncière dans l'Inde et en Égypte* (Paris, 1787).

47 L. W. Nachetgaal, 'The Dutch East India Company and the Relations between Kartasura and the Javanese north coast, c.1600–1870', in J. van Goor (ed.), *Trading Companies in Asia, 1600–1830* (Utrecht, 1986).

48 For British relations with the Mughals see Home Misc. vol. 336, IOL.

49 For a study of the subsidiary alliance system at work, see Richard B. Barnett, *North India between Empires. Awadh. the Mughals and the British, 1720–1801* (Berkeley, 1980); also Michael Fisher, *A Clash of Cultures: Awadh, the British and the Mughals* (Delhi, 1987).

50 For the decline of the Mughals, see Satish Chandra, *Parties and Politics at the Mughal Court, 1700–40* (Aligarh, 1959); Noman Ahmed Siddiqi, *Land Revenue System under the Mughals, 1700–50* (Delhi, 1970); Stewart Gordon; 'The Slow Conquest: Administrative Integration of Malwa into the Maratha Empire', *Modern Asian Studies*, 11/1 (1977).

51 Muzaffar Alam, *The Crisis of Empire in Mughal North India: Awadh and the Punjab, 1707–48* (New Delhi, 1986), 21–3, n. 28.

52 Barnett, *North India*, 198–205.

53 R. Mukherjee, *Awadh in Revolt, 1857–8* (New Delhi, 1985); T. R. Metcalf, *Land, Landlords and the British Raj* (Berkeley, 1979), chs 5–6.

54 Sunil Chander, 'From a Pre-Colonial Order to a Princely State. Hyderabad in Transition', c.1748–1865 (Ph.D. thesis, University of Cambridge, 1987), 50–71.

55 Mohibbul Hasan, *A History of Tipu Sultan* (Calcutta, 1971); A. Sen, 'A Pre-British Economic Formation in India of the Late-Eighteenth Century', in B. De (ed.), *Perspectives in Social Sciences*, I, *Historical Dimensions* (Calcutta, 1977), 46–52.

56 'From the whole of the Sultan's servants six or seven thousand men of the Shaikh and Syud tribes were selected and despatched to Koorg to repeople that district', cited in *Mir Hussein Ali Kirmani's 'Neshan-i-Hyduri': A History of the Reign of Tippoo Sultaun*, trans. and ed. W. Miles (London, 1844), 83.

57 M. N. Srinivas, *Religion and Society among the Coorgs of South India* (Oxford, 1952), 14.

58 For the price-rise, see e.g. Chaudhuri, *Trading World*, fig. 8, 101.

59 Wink, *Land and Sovereignty*.

60 Raghoba's letter from Lahore cited by T. S. Shejwalkar, *Panipat, 1761* (Poona, 1946), 124.

61 Khafi Khan, *Muntakhabul Lubab*, trans. in H. M. Elliot and J. Dowson, *The History of India as Told by Its Own Historians* (8 vols; London 1867–77), vol. VII, 344–5, 354, cited in Chaudhuri, *Trading World*, 112; Ali Muhammad Khan, *Mirat-i-Ahmadi*, trans. M. F. Lokhandwala (Baroda, 1965), 883, 888, 899–900, for Marathas, 'tribals' and English respectively.

62 Susan Bayly, *Saints, Goddesses and Kings: Muslims and Christians in South Indian Society, c.1700–1900* (Cambridge, 1989), 215.

63 J. Z. Holwell, *A Genuine Narrative of the Deplorable Deaths of the English Gentlemen and Others who were Suffocated in the Black Hole* (London, 1758); see P. J. Marshall's entry on this work, item no. 98, in Bayly, *The Raj*, 94–5.

64 Marshall, *Bengal*, 84–8.

65 ibid., 123–5.

66 In the Mughal system the *jumma* was the assessed revenue and *hasil* what was actually collected; historians are discovering great divergences between the two, the *jumma* being often no more than an 'optimal statement'. The British, however, tried to base actual collections on the *jumma*.

67 See e.g., Barnett, *North India*, 186–7.

68 S. B. Chaudhuri, *Civil Disturbances during the British Rule in India (1765–1857)*

(Calcutta, 1955), 54–74; A. N. Chowdhury-Zilly, *The Vagrant Peasant* (Wiesbaden, 1982), 64–93; N. Kaviraj, *A Peasant Uprising in Bengal* (Delhi, 1982).

69 For Rumbold, see P. J. Marshall, *East Indian Fortunes: The British in Bengal in the Eighteenth Century* (London, 1976), 198, 238, 245; for commercial links outside India, ibid., 198–9; *Third Report of the Select Committee on the Affairs of the East India Company* (London, 1773), 100.

70 This point is made clearly in W. J. Wilson, *History of the Madras Army* (5 vols; London, 1882), vol. II, 141–2.

71 Sutherland, *East India Company*, 226–7.

72 Hameeda Hossein, *The Company Weavers of Bengal* (New Delhi, 1984).

73 'Dobbeer's Memorandum', in *Copies of Papers relative to ... Tanjour*, vol. I, 118.

74 Warren Hastings, *A Narrative of the Insurrection which Happened in the Zemeenday of Banaris in the Month of August 1781* (Calcutta, 1782), 1–16; Barnett, *North India*, 198–205.

75 See P. J. Marshall, 'Empire and Authority in the Later Eighteenth Century', *Journal of Imperial and Commonwealth History*, 15/2 (1987); ' "A Free though Conquering People": Britain and Asia in the Eighteenth Century' (published lecture, King's College, London, 1981); C. A. Bayly, *Indian Society and the Making of the British Empire* (Cambridge, 1988), 81–9; the picture by Robert Home is in the National Army Museum, London.

76 Edward J. Thompson, *The Making of the Indian Princes* (London, 1943), 8.

77 E. Ingram (ed.), *Two Views of British India* (Bath, 1970), 1–14.

78 Michael M. Fisher, *Indirect Rule in India: Residents and the Residency System 1764–1857* (New Delhi, 1991).

79 Arthur Wellesley to General Stuart, 3 July 1804, in S. J. Owen (ed.), *A Selection from the Despatches relating to India of Field Marshall the Duke of Wellington, K.G.* (Oxford, 1880), 439–49.

80 Home Misc. vol. 336, IOL.

81 Thompson, *Indian Princes*, 7–10.

82 Thomas Munro to his father, 17 January 1790, in G. R. Gleig, *The Life and Correspondence of Major-General Sir Thomas Munro* (3 vols; London, 1830), vol. I, 79 (I owe this reference to Professor Burton Stein).

83 Hasan, *Tipu*, 128–36.

84 Tipu to the 'Grand Seigneur' (Ottoman Sultan), 10 February 1799, in J. Kirkpatrick (ed.), *Letters of Tippoo Sultan to Various Public Functionaries* (London, 1811); for Tipu's alliances, see Home Misc., vol. 605, 'Zeman Shah', IOL.

85 Tipu sought recognition from the Ottoman Caliph (as spiritual leader of the Muslims) for his status as an independent prince; Hasan, *Tipu*, 128–36.

86 Wellesley to Dundas, 18 February 1789, cited in Ingram, *Two Views*, 39.

87 Nicholas Dirks, *The Hollow Crown: The Ethnohistory of a Little Kingdom in South India* (Cambridge, 1986), 19–55.

88 H. R. Pate, *Gazeteer of the Tinnevelly District*, vol. I (Madras, 1917), 78–83, 388; see also K. Rajayyan, *A History of Madurai* (Madurai, 1978).

89 Pate, *Gazeteer*, vol. I, 85.

90 P. Nightingale, *Trade and Empire in Western India* (Cambridge, 1970), 118.

91 W. Logan, *Malabar* (3 vols; Madras, 1887–91; repr. Madras, 1951), vol. I, 497; Home Misc. vol. 607, 193–7, 289 ff., 'Pychee Raja', IOL (I thank Dr R. Grove and Dr D. Menon for information about this uprising).

92 George, Viscount Valentia, *Voyages and Travels in India, Ceylon, the Red Sea, Abyssinia and Egypt* (written 1802–6; 3 vols; London, 1809), vol. I, 453.

93 Logan, *Malabar*, vol. I, 214.

94 T. H. Baber, Sub-Collector, Cannanore, to Collector, Malabar, 31 December 1805, Logan, *Malabar*, vol. I, 540.

95 ibid., vol. I, 545; P. C. Mathur, 'Political Awakening among the Tribes of Wynad', in K. S. Singh (ed.), *Tribal Movements in India*, II (Delhi, 1982), 339–53.

96 Logan, *Malabar*, vol. I, 545, cf. vol. III, 268.

97 S. Bayly, *Saints, Goddesses*, 200–2.

98 P. Chinnian, *The Vellore Mutiny, 1806* (Madras, 1982).

99 D. Ludden, *Peasant History in South India* (Princeton, 1986), 260–80; C. J. Baker, 'Tamilnad Estates in the Twentieth Century', *Indian Economic and Social History Review*, 13/I (1975).

100 E. Stokes, *The Peasant and the Raj* (Cambridge, 1978), ch. 2. My attention has been drawn to D. H. A. Kolff, 'The end of an *ancien régime*: colonial war in India 1798–1818', in J. A. de Moor and H. L. Wesseling, *Imperialism and War* (Leiden, 1989), which parallels several of the arguments here.

INDEX